Understanding Torture

Understanding Torture

Law, Violence, and Political Identity

John T. Parry

THE UNIVERSITY OF MICHIGAN PRESS
Ann Arbor

2013   2012   2011   2010   4   3   2   1

A CIP catalog record for this book is available from the British Library.

Library of Congress Cataloging-in-Publication Data

Parry, John T., 1964–
Understanding torture : law, violence, and political identity /
John T. Parry.
p.   cm.
Includes bibliographical references and index.
ISBN 978-0-472-07077-0 (cloth : alk. paper) —
ISBN 978-0-472-05077-2 (pbk. : alk. paper)
—ISBN 978-0-472-02178-9 (e-book)
1. Torture.   2. Torture—United States.   I. Title.

K5304.P37   2010
341.6'7—dc22   2009047779

Torture, properly understood, is prohibited absolutely, and states are obliged, *inter alia,* to prosecute those responsible.

—Helen Duffy,
The "War on Terror" and the Framework of International Law

Each State Party shall take effective legislative, administrative, judicial or other measures to prevent acts of torture in any territory under its jurisdiction.

No exceptional circumstances whatsoever, whether a state of war or a threat of war, internal political instability or any other public emergency, may be invoked as a justification of torture. . . .

Each State Party shall undertake to prevent in any territory under its jurisdiction other acts of cruel, inhuman or degrading treatment or punishment which do not amount to torture.

—Articles 2 and 16 of the U.N. Convention
against Torture and Other Cruel, Inhuman, or Degrading
Treatment or Punishment

[N]or shall any person . . . be deprived of life, liberty, or property, without due process of law.

—Fifth Amendment to the U.S. Constitution

The fact is, regardless of the terminology used, the precise content of most of the Constitution's civil-liberties guarantees rests upon an assessment of what accommodation between governmental need and individual freedom is reasonable.

—*Anderson v. Creighton,* 483 U.S. 635 (1987)

No more torture, but . . . go on torturing just the same.

—Colonel Marcel Bigeard, quoted in Rita Maran,
Torture: The Role of Ideology in the French-Algerian War

It was just for fun.

—Private Lynndie England, quoted in James Polk,
"Testimony: Abu Ghraib Photos 'Just for Fun,'" *CNN.com*

Contents

Preface and Acknowledgments

The impetus for this book was the use of coercive interrogation and detention tactics by U.S. personnel in the months and years after the September 11, 2001 attacks, and I completed the manuscript in the last days of George W. Bush's presidency. I was able to take account of some more recent events or disclosures during the editing process. But *Understanding Torture* is not a book about the Bush administration or the war on terror. It is neither a comprehensive account or chronology of events during those years nor an argument that a change of U.S. presidential administrations will moot the problem of torture. Rather, this is a book about the ongoing relationship of torture and state violence to contemporary liberal democracies and, even more, about the legal and political discourse of torture and the consequences and implications of that discourse. I spend significant time on the United States, but neither it nor the war on terror is my sole focus.

I received an enormous amount of substantive assistance while working on this book and its predecessor articles. People who commented on drafts or assisted me with issues related to this book include Elena Baylis, Harold Bruff, Bobby Chesney, John Grant, Oren Gross, Lisa Hajjar, Andrea Hibbard, Duncan Hollis, Sandy Levinson, Clark Lombardi, Ruth Miller, Sam Pillsbury, Darius Rejali, Alice Ristroph, Brad Roth, Juliet Stumpf, Doug Sylvester, Steve Vladeck, Elliot Young, and two anonymous reviewers for the University of Michigan Press. I also learned a great deal from participants at numerous talks and conferences, as well as members of the "Law of Torture" discussion list organized by Marty Lederman and Kim Scheppele. Andrea Hibbard's careful review of the manuscript helped me clarify my arguments and avoid embarrassing errors.

I particularly want to acknowledge my debt to my friend and mentor Welsh White. I regret that he will never see this book; his advice and guidance made it possible.

Summer grants from Lewis & Clark Law School and, before that, the University of Pittsburgh School of Law helped me write this book and its predecessor articles. I am especially grateful to Lewis & Clark Law School, where I developed the idea for this book, and to my colleagues there for providing me with a warm, supportive, and stunningly beautiful environment in which to write about these issues. Lynn Williams at Lewis & Clark's Boley Law Library helped me track down sources, and Lisa Frenz and Andy Marion helped me assemble the manuscript. Kate Mertes prepared the index.

The support of Melody Herr and Jim Reische at the University of Michigan Press has also been essential.

INTRODUCTION

~

Law, Language, and Difference

In 1987, a short review in *Contemporary Sociology* offered mild criticism of a book about the complicity of health professionals in torture: "The evidence and arguments presented are compelling, although one needs little persuasion to condemn such practices; thus the inclusion of photographs of torture rack[s] and exhumed bones of victims seem unnecessarily lurid." Torture is so obviously wrong that there was no need to shock readers into agreeing with that proposition. Seven years later, in the same journal, Daniel Chirot took issue with Darius Rejali's claim that the use of torture in twentieth-century Iran reflects that country's modernity. In what may have been intended as the clinching argument, Chirot asked, "If the growth of torture in twentieth-century Iran and its changing forms are caused by efforts to modernize, why do we not torture in the modern United States or Western Europe?" Modern liberal democracies simply do not torture, and it was important to stress that fact.[1]

Today, torture is a central legal and political issue in the United States. U.S. forces have abused prisoners at a variety of locations, including Guantánamo Bay Naval Base, Bagram Air Base in Afghanistan, Abu Ghraib prison in Iraq, and various CIA "black sites." Suspected terrorists have also been abused by U.S. allies, sometimes at the behest of U.S. officials. Newspapers, magazines, and Web sites published stories and reproduced pictures of the abuse to widespread interest and (it was assumed) revulsion. Remonstrating editorials accompanied each revelation. Members of Congress demanded information, held hearings, and decried the abuse (but sometimes defended coercive tactics). Human rights advocates researched, documented and condemned the abuse, while international lawyers called for more restrictions on interrogators and better enforcement.

Little emerged from this flurry of publicity and discussion. Accusations of torture were met by either denials or the assertion that the worst conduct was an aberration, a deviation from the norm of humane treatment. Arguments for respecting human or individual rights ran up against claims that it was time for the "gloves to come off" after the attacks of September 11,

2001. As one official said, "If you don't violate someone's human rights some of the time [during an interrogation] you probably aren't doing your job."[2] Criticisms of abuse thus occasioned a two-part response: the United States did not torture, but it might have to do some bad things to win what had become the "war on terror."

Efforts to understand Abu Ghraib, Bagram, and Guantánamo—place-names that have become metonymic for arbitrary detention, state violence, and coercive interrogation—also split. On the one hand, concern over abuse became lost in legal debates and political finger-pointing. Torture became simultaneously a technical legal question that required parsing of the kind usually reserved for the Internal Revenue Code, a partisan political issue, and a test of patriotism. On the other hand, the media repeatedly presented "both sides" of the issue of coercive treatment, leaving many observers to wonder how they could assess events that happened far away under conditions about which they knew little.[3] Better to shrug one's shoulders, hope for the best, and move on.

Although participants frequently invoke legal rules, the role of law in the torture debate is far from clear. Most lawyers assume torture is illegal. They may also believe that the creation of legal prohibitions against torture during the twentieth century is one of the great achievements of domestic and international human rights. It is more difficult to support that conclusion through rigorous legal analysis, however, than nearly anyone, in the United States at least, would have thought even just a few years ago. In fact, lawyers for the Bush administration worked hard to portray the legal category "torture" as a narrow term of art. They argued that conduct that might appear to be torture could actually be legal interrogation. In many quarters, these arguments were dismissed as partisan, slipshod, or repugnant. But despite its many flaws, some of the analysis advances defensible interpretations of U.S. and international law. The law of torture, in other words, is less categorical and less constraining than it first appears. Moreover, as I will argue throughout this book, law and legal rights provide no certain bulwark against state torture.

This book seeks to advance the discussion of torture and related forms of abuse by considering more deeply what law has to say about it. In this context, when I use the term *law,* I mean primarily the idea of rules that seek to constrain the behavior of a state or of state actors, not social norms in general or legal ideals in the abstract. My initial focus on formal law will highlight not only the malleability of carefully written rules but also their tenuous status. Ultimately, though, my effort to untangle this issue of formal legal interpretation will require a broader consideration of legal discourse, state practice, the importance of emergencies and states of exception, and examination of the nature and role of rights in modern states and societies.

This book, in short, moves from considering the law of torture to assessing its role in shaping legal and political identity.

The path of my analysis roughly tracks the quotations that serve as the epigraphs to this book. I move, first, from general statements about understanding torture to specific prohibitions. I then study the way in which those prohibitions dissolve into "reasonableness," as well as the impact of that dissolution on the political identity of rights-bearers. Finally, I examine the decisions of specific individuals to engage in torture for a variety of reasons, often with full knowledge that a ban on torture exists. In so doing, I seek to combine traditional legal analysis with history and something that might best be described as a cultural studies approach.

Along the way, I will stress that modern states pervasively regulate and control their populations and that their interactions with their citizens are regularly marked by violence that sometimes includes torture. Law's interaction with this violence is complex. It constrains state violence, but it also creates personal vulnerabilities alongside protections. Further, one characteristic of torture in contemporary law is the effort to define it rationally, with precision, and to conceptualize it against a background of individual rights. Thus, nearly every definition of torture treats it as conduct so harmful that everyone has an absolute right not to be subjected to it. But law rarely works in absolutes. Most lawyers subscribe to the idea that there is an exception to every legal rule, and states will use the standard tools of legal argument to seek exceptions for torture. The easy response of prohibiting exceptions does not resolve the issue; it simply creates enormous pressure to narrow the definition of torture.

All of this is simply to say that language is critically important to the debate over torture. The rest of this introduction will consider some of the language of the U.S. debate over torture in the war on terror. In so doing, it will indicate just how difficult it can be to talk about torture.

Choosing Words Carefully
∾

When allegations of abuse by U.S. forces in Afghanistan began to surface in late 2002 and early 2003, human rights groups quickly claimed that the United States was engaged in torture, although at least some of the practices probably were not torture under international law. The administration denied the claims and maintained that its actions were "humane and ... follow all international laws and accords," although that was almost certainly not the case for some of the reported conduct. Meanwhile, officials suggested that interrogation rules might need to be relaxed for the war on terror.[4]

In the spring of 2004, pictures of abuse at Abu Ghraib became public, and criticism reached a higher level. Once again, human rights advocates, joined more visibly now by editorialists and politicians, charged that U.S. forces had violated legal prohibitions against torture. Administration officials condemned the specific practices that had been made public, but they insisted that these were isolated actions that had nothing to do with government policy, let alone with American values. Thus, President George W. Bush asserted that the abuse at Abu Ghraib was the conduct of a few and "does not represent the America that I know."[5]

Accusations of rough or degrading treatment continued to surface, including numerous claims of cruelty or torture by CIA operatives or at Guantánamo.[6] Without the visual confirmation available for Abu Ghraib, however, these claims could be denied, recharacterized, or diverted into investigations. Further, unlike the thousands of people held at Abu Ghraib, the prisoners at Guantánamo—despite undoubted errors in many cases—were more likely to be connected with terrorist activity. Similarly, people held by the CIA were generally assumed to be "high-value" prisoners. Sympathy for their plight was more muted, and the official response was less contrite. Responding to an Amnesty International report that asserted ongoing abuse at Guantánamo, Bush asserted that the allegations were "absurd" and had been made by "people who hate America." As for people in CIA custody, he unapologetically declared that "the CIA used an alternative set of procedures" that were "tough, and . . . safe, and lawful, and necessary."[7]

The administration thus framed the debate in this way: torture is wrong, and we do not do it, but we use "tough" tactics that are both lawful and justified under the circumstances. Every official tactic is not-torture by definition, while tactics that qualify as torture are aberrations. Defenders of the administration could therefore argue that coercive measures short of "torture" are sometimes necessary against an enemy who operates in secret, across borders, and in violation of the laws of war. The debate over coercive interrogation, in short, seems to turn on whether the label *torture* can be attached to the conduct at issue.

Critics of the Bush administration thus had an incentive to use the term broadly. A 2005 report by Amnesty International, for example, used the word *torture* repeatedly—sometimes in conjunction with such terms as *abuse, ill-treatment,* or *cruel, inhuman, or degrading treatment*—to describe U.S. detention and interrogation practices. Yet the report does not provide any analysis of which practices actually rise to the level of torture. The report also described Guantánamo Bay as "the gulag of our times," and the organization called on other countries to investigate U.S. officials for criminal violations of international law and to arrest them if they traveled abroad.[8] Describing Guantánamo as a gulag and calling for prosecution of U.S. officials tended to play as extremist in the context of public debate within the United States—just as similar claims likely would in any liberal democracy. My point is not that these claims were extremist but, rather, that they clashed with the felt truth that democracies do not do such things. As a result, President Bush's statement that the report was "absurd" likely generated greater domestic agreement than Amnesty International's characterizations of U.S. detention sites and conduct.

Just as critics had an incentive to define torture broadly, administration officials had an incentive to define it narrowly, to preserve a larger potential field of action. Government documents reveal that some officials succumbed to this incentive. Most famously, the Justice Department's Office of Legal Counsel concluded in August 2002 that the phrase "severe pain" in the U.S. torture statute meant a level of pain "that would ordinarily be associated with a sufficiently serious physical condition or injury such as death, organ failure, or serious impairment of body functions."[9] As the writers of the memorandum must have known, this wording is significantly narrower than the definitions of severe pain in relevant international and U.S. legal sources. A Department of Defense working group advanced a broader definition of the pain associated with torture—"the adjective severe conveys that the pain or suffering must be of such a high level of intensity that the pain is difficult for the subject to endure"[10]—but most commentators likely would conclude it remains too narrow relative to international law.

The carefully negotiated U.N. Convention against Torture creates three categories of conduct with respect to interrogation and punishment: torture (which is illegal); other cruel, inhuman, or degrading treatment (which should be "prevented"); and conduct not covered by the convention and thus permissible unless subject to other international or domestic law constraints. The term *torture* is reserved for "any act by which severe pain or suffering, whether physical or mental, is intentionally inflicted on a person" by or with the consent or acquiescence of state actors. All other bad conduct is relegated to the category of "other cruel, inhuman, or degrading treatment," which is apparently so capacious relative to torture that the drafters of the convention made no effort to define it.[11] The most one can say from reading the text is that this second category applies to any conduct that should be prohibited but falls short of torture.

The convention also suggests another consequence of splitting illegal conduct into two categories. Torture is banned absolutely: "No exceptional circumstances whatsoever, whether a state of war or threat of war, internal political instability or any other public emergency, may be invoked as a justification of torture."[12] But this language does not explicitly apply to cruel, inhuman, or degrading treatment. The convention thus suggests the possibility of justifying violent interrogation or punishment that is illegal but does not rise to the level of "torture."

Within this framework, a state accused of mistreating prisoners can flatly deny that it acted illegally, but it can also argue that whatever it may have done, it has not tortured. If the state can put forward a sufficient justification for the conduct that it claims is not torture, it has not violated the convention. The focus of the debate easily becomes a definition game: Is the conduct torture as defined by law? If not, is there a sufficient legal justification? This game is exactly the strategy that the Bush administration employed. That is to say, the administration's public statements did not ignore international law; they followed its structure precisely.

Defining and Exploiting Difference

The language of torture also defines the victims of torture. One might say, for example, that people from different backgrounds or cultures expect or accept a certain level of violence from the authorities, so that a few slaps or blows are illegal when directed at some people but ordinary and permissible treatment when directed at others. The European Commission of Human Rights observed in the famous Greek Case of 1969 that some prisoners "tolerate . . . and even take for granted . . . a certain roughness of treatment . . . by both police and military authorities. . . . Such roughness may take the form of slaps and blows of the hand on the head or face." According to the commission, this conduct was not inhuman or degrading treatment within the meaning of the European Convention on Human Rights, because "the point up to which prisoners and the public may accept physical violence as being neither cruel nor excessive, varies between different societies and even between different sections of them."[13] Put differently, people detained for political reasons by the Athens Security Police in the 1960s would have expected some rough treatment, and they—or at least some significant proportion of the public as a whole—would have found rough treatment acceptable in the context of Greek society. By contrast, in other parts of Europe, this conduct might have been flatly illegal during the same period, even if police sometimes engaged in it.

One could also argue in the other direction and contend that certain forms of treatment are particularly distressing to victims from certain backgrounds. Thus, Nigel Rodley suggests that "forcing a devout Muslim to fall to his knees and kiss the cross might well fall within the prohibition [against cruel, inhuman, and degrading treatment], whereas similar behaviour towards prisoners who have no profound philosophical or religious aversion to the procedure would have no comparable significance."[14]

Both ways of thinking about torture strive for sensitivity to cultural differences. The critical question is what to do with this sensitivity. Should legal rules respond to subjective experiences, so that a particular practice will be ruled torture for some but not for others, even if that means calling something torture in cases when most people would not experience it that way? Or should law classify conduct on an objective scale, so certain things simply are torture, even if that means ruling that some conduct is not abusive—despite the pain it causes in individual cases—because most people (perhaps even "reasonable" people) would not find it distressing.

These choices reflect familiar debates about the best ways to address individual perceptions and harm within a framework of rules meant to have general applicability and to provide notice and guidance to people in varying circumstances. But that is not all. Anyone seeking to draw on cultural difference to craft an appropriate legal rule might want to consider how difference has become a practice in the war on terror, both for U.S. officials seeking to gain an edge in interrogation and for journalists and human rights advocates seeking to explain why the abusive behavior of U.S. forces is particularly harmful.

On September 14, 2003, Lieutenant General Ricardo Sanchez approved several interrogation techniques for use on prisoners in Iraq, including the "presence of military working dogs." According to Sanchez, this tactic was useful because it "exploits Arab fear of dogs while maintaining security during interrogations."[15] The source of this idea remains obscure, but it indicates that officials made an effort to learn about what they might have described as "Arab culture"—if only for the purpose of better controlling people from that culture. Importantly, accounts that discuss and deplore this use of dogs and its effect on prisoners also treat this understanding as correct.[16]

In the same way, U.S. officials at Guantánamo developed fairly strict rules on respect for what they understood to be Muslim religious practices. They took the trouble to think about the ways in which Muslim prisoners might be different from prisoners of other religious traditions. We find proof that Muslims require sensitive treatment in the fact that people rioted (and several were killed) in Afghanistan and other countries after *Newsweek* magazine reported that guards at Guantánamo intentionally desecrated copies of the Koran.[17] The fact that the religious attitudes of Guantánamo prisoners and the causes of the riots are more complex does not detract from the fact that U.S. officials sought to understand their detainees and to deploy those understandings.

Consider, too, the flurry of news reports about sexual aspects of the mistreatment of prisoners at Abu Ghraib and Guantánamo. Among other things, U.S. soldiers put women's underwear on the heads of male prisoners (sometimes while they were handcuffed), and male prisoners were forced to appear naked in front of women (and men) and were sometimes put on leashes. Women interrogated men, and female interrogators employed such tactics as making sexually explicit remarks, "rubb[ing] their bodies against the men," "sexual touching, wearing a miniskirt and thong underwear," and "numerous instances in which female interrogators, using dye, pretended to spread menstrual blood on Muslim men."[18] Many of the reports take care to point out that these tactics are particularly distressing to male Muslims. The writers quote experts who stress the "tribal" and "religious" aspects of Iraqi, Muslim, or Arab culture and suggest that physical contact with most women is a taboo to Muslim or Arab men: "To Muslim Arabs it would have been inconceivable to be placed in that degree of vulnerability before a woman"; "Having a woman conducting torture was grossly insulting to Muslims."[19] The logic, in other words, is that these practices may be more or less distressing to people in general—and some of these practices might not be objectively distressing at all—but when it comes to Muslim men, these practices are egregious because the victims are sensitive to and likely to be disturbed by women in positions of power and by open or aggressive displays of female sexuality.

The actions of U.S. forces and the reports and charges of journalists, experts, and advocates draw from an identical set of attitudes toward the victims of U.S. abuse. Concerns about Arab or Muslim cultural sensitivities are equivalent to the culturally sensitive mistreatment inflicted by U.S. forces in the specific way that both practices define, position, and control the victims of torture and the people who inflict, witness, or write about it. More broadly, this common element reveals the significant risks in using perceived cultural differences as a way of framing discussions about torture.

Either version of the cultural difference approach to torture—that people in some cultures can endure more pain or that people in some cultures are particularly sensitive to certain practices—exoticizes the victims of torture. This exoticization takes place regardless of whether the overarching goal is to harm or to rescue. Either way, the objects of this approach are from "traditional" or "tribal" societies in which rights do not exist, justice is rough, religious practices are more "profound," and people hold extreme views on issues of sexuality and gender, ideas that cause them to act or react in irrational ways.

Thinking about the victims of torture in this way works only if paired with a way of thinking about "us"—by which I mean not only the torturers but also those who condemn it or who seek to explain it away. Unlike the victims, we are from modern, progressive societies in which human rights are taken for granted. Either we should know better than to treat people this way, or we have a special responsibility to expose and try to stop it. Either way, we are in a superior position, and we have access to greater, perhaps universal knowledge. We are able to know and understand the victims— perhaps better than they understand themselves—and to take concrete steps to exploit or improve their circumstances.

Although these attitudes about torture are not new, they have become pervasive in the United States during the war on terror.[20] Supporters of U.S. military action in the Middle East have argued that the use of military force is part of a broader cultural struggle. For Bush, it was part of a "crusade," while British prime minister Tony Blair distinguished "between the civilized world and fanaticism." Norman Podhoretz made the point more explicitly when he urged "a benevolent transformation of the Middle East" by the United States that would include "the reform and modernization of Islam." Others who are less sure of military action nonetheless agree that something is wrong with Muslims and that they must be changed. *Time* magazine summed up the consensus view when it declared, "The war that began three years ago in lower Manhattan . . . is a fight for the hearts and minds and souls of millions of Muslims . . . whose life choices may have a greater impact on the long-term security of the U.S., its citizens and its allies than battlefield victories or intelligence reforms."[21]

In short, U.S. forces used abusive or humiliating tactics against Muslim detainees and suspected terrorists at the same time that the problem of terrorism became equated with the Muslim world. Meanwhile, government officials and commentators defined this world as exotic, uncivilized, and in need of guidance. These conclusions became "facts" as they were enforced by violence, asserted as true by powerful officials, and reported on by media representatives who already believed or were ready to believe such claims. In the current war on terror, accounts and practices of torture or other abuse draw on what is in effect a nonpartisan cultural and political discourse. This discourse is "Orientalist" in the sense intended by Edward Said. It conceives of the Orient, particularly the Muslim world, as "in need of corrective study by the West," and it draws on unreflective generalizations about people or cultures seen as different, backward, quaint, and exotic, but also as threatening. Importantly, these ideas about the Muslim world also help "to define . . . the West . . . as its contrasting image, idea, personality, experience."[22]

The talk and practice of difference in the context of torture and related forms of abuse goes further, however. Former Los Angeles chief of police Daryl Gates once claimed that "some blacks might be more susceptible than 'normal' people to injury when officers applied a choke hold."[23] Choke holds, which involve briefly cutting off the flow of blood to the brain, are an extremely dangerous but also extremely effective way to subdue a person who is or may be (or whom one is prepared to assume is) violent. Gates seems to have been asserting that when a choke hold caused harm, the victim was probably at fault, at least if the victim was black and therefore not "normal." In short, reliance on difference as a way of talking about abuse does not require thorough exoticization; any colonized or subordinated "other" will suffice. It may be that modern countries tend not to torture their own. Yet once separate groups are identified, whether internally or externally, and particularly if they are classified as inferior, the prohibition no longer holds as firmly. The exoticization or othering of the victims of abuse could thus be, as Michel Foucault put it, "the precondition that makes killing [or torture] acceptable" in a modern state.[24]

By stressing the supposed differences that define victims, the cultural difference approach to torture deflects the discussion away from the perpetrators and from the reasons for their actions. It ensures that discussion centers on the victims. Although it might seem appropriate to focus on the victims—they are, of course, the ones in pain—the cultural difference perspective does so by distancing them, turning them into spectacle, and rendering them mute. Instead of focusing on the infliction of mental or physical suffering, which reflects a relationship of perpetrator and victim within a context of state power, crude ideas of cultural relativism (i.e., claims that some kinds of people suffer more or less than the norm that "we" represent) create distance from a common denominator of pain.

This distance facilitates the effort to minimize abuse. Consider the post–Abu Ghraib statement by Senator James Inhofe of Oklahoma that he was "more outraged by the outrage than . . . by the treatment." He went on to assert that the Abu Ghraib detainees were not "there for traffic violations"; he declared, "they're murderers, they're terrorists, they're insurgents."[25] With respect to the vast majority of Abu Ghraib detainees, this characterization was flatly false, and it is unlikely that Inhofe really meant to say that murderers or even insurgents deserved rough treatment. But his statement conveyed a different truth about official attitudes toward the people supposedly liberated by U.S. forces. When Inhofe referred to the prisoners broadly as murderers, terrorists, and insurgents, his audience knew he meant they were Arab or Muslim murderers, terrorists, and insurgents, and that made all the difference.[26]

Others have taken care to point out that the war on terror is a tough business and that with respect to Iraq, Saddam Hussein's conduct was worse than anything U.S. forces have done. President Bush adopted this rhetorical strategy soon after the Abu Ghraib revelations, when he condemned the abuses but also took care to assert, "We're a society that is willing to investigate, fully investigate in this case, what took place in that prison. . . . That stands in stark contrast to life under Saddam Hussein. His trained torturers were never brought to justice under his regime. There were no investigations about the mistreatment of people." Likewise, writing in the *New York Times Book Review,* Michael Massing asked with palpable anguish, "How could Americans, imbued with all the right values, have committed such acts?" Rather than identify the right values or explain how they would have prevented torture, he offered a partial excuse: "Needless to say, the happenings at Abu Ghraib are a long way . . . from the murderous activities of Saddam Hussein."[27]

Consider, too, Mark Bowden's response to the claim of one Abu Ghraib prisoner that he expected to be killed by U.S. forces: "Of course he did. That's what happens to men thrown in jail in his part of the world."[28] Bowden generalized from Iraq to a suggestively unspecified "part of the world" and vaguely, yet forcefully, asserted that death in this region's prisons generally "happens." He neglected the fact that the prisoner was held by occupying military forces who were abusing prisoners, which suggests that the prisoner's fear was reasonable. Similarly, Bowden's unstated assumption about a relative lack of prison violence in the United States—when, as I discuss in chapter 6, violence in U.S. prisons is frequent enough to be a serious issue—recalls Daniel Chirot's denial of torture by the "modern United States or Western Europe." None of this was relevant to Bowden's claims, however, because his argument was ideological, not empirical. For him, the pain and anguish of those abused at Abu Ghraib was an opportunity not for recognizing shared humanity but, rather, for emphasizing difference.

The broad claim that the United States and its allies are different from or better than the people they are fighting or trying to save is less my target here than is the effort to define the cultural and political identity of the individuals over whom U.S. forces exercise power. Among other things, commentators should consider spending less time seeking to define the victims of U.S. abuse in terms of their difference, with more time devoted to thinking about the full experience and relationship of abuse. Some people, whatever their backgrounds and beliefs, would be better able to absorb or would be less distressed by slaps or blows than others would be, while others would be less able to bear the pain. Commentators might also consider how they would respond if any of them—again, regardless of their backgrounds or beliefs—were seized and held prisoner by an occupying army; were taken out of their cell at night, stripped, and escorted by people with guns into a room full of more people with guns and trained military dogs; and were then abused. In these circumstances, they might find the addition of underwear on their heads or the presence of people of the opposite sex to be among the least disturbing aspects of that experience—even if those particular things would be disturbing in other contexts.[29] For that matter, it is also possible that in an environment of sustained abuse while in military custody, these things would be particularly distressing even if they would be of little consequence in other contexts. Similarly, some people are more or less susceptible to religious and sexual taunting, but the decision to use such tactics may say more about the interrogators than about their victims.

Is Torture Special?

❧

Another way not to talk about torture—one that circles back more directly to law and legal categories—is to say that it is particularly horrible, must never happen, and could be eradicated if only we had better laws and better enforcement. This kind of argument treats torture as a separate, universally prohibited, egregious form of conduct that is categorically different from other forms of state violence. It also tends to treat torture as something that belongs to the history but not the current reality of liberal democracies, so that its occurrence there is by definition an aberration, in contrast with occurrences in other countries that have not progressed so far. My claim here is not that other countries do not torture or do not have policies of using torture. My point is that torture sits on a continuum of violent state practices, where the use of these forms of violence by modern states as a way of regulating populations is far more significant than whether "torture" is the particular form of violence used. Indeed, one could say that violence or the threat of violence against any political subject is a basic aspect of governance. Law's primary function is to channel and regulate that violence.

Instead of treating torture as a separate, universally prohibited, egregious form of conduct, I argue that it fits easily into a larger mosaic of state power and violence, imperialism, racism, and international law and relations. This larger context requires considering torture as it relates to interrogation, detention and confinement, war, and the broader question of how much control governments have or should have over our bodies. This effort, in turn, helps expose the ways in which law fails to confront torture, and it allows better exploration of other ways to understand and address torture. Just as important, thinking about torture in context forces us to confront the ways in which modern liberal states use violence to control and dominate their subjects—often to achieve ends that many of those subjects desire.

Admittedly, efforts to contextualize torture and to link it to such things as detention and state power in general risk normalizing torture. But my argument is precisely that torture—understood colloquially and broadly instead of as a strictly defined term of art—is already part of the modern state's coercive apparatus. Creating a separate category for an intentionally narrow set of practices labeled and banned as "torture" will thus inevitably normalize and legitimate—even if only in a relative sense—the remaining practices that are "not-torture." The implications of forcing torture back into the "normal" continuum of state violence explain why officials try, instead, to cabin it with narrow definitions. *Torture,* after all, is not a neutral word (as opposed to the terms *questioning* or *interrogation,* which may have ominous overtones but usually do not provoke viscerally negative reactions). To call something torture is almost always to condemn it, with the result that the term *torture* must be kept apart from normal government conduct, lest it call into question the legitimacy of other coercive practices or lead to acceptance of coercion as a routine aspect of personal, social, and political arrangements.

Plan of the Book

∾

Throughout this book, I spend considerable time exposing the weaknesses of international and domestic laws on torture and other forms of state violence. Although I propose reforms, I ultimately demonstrate that law will likely fail when it seeks to regulate state violence, of which torture is a central, but hardly singular, example. One of my core arguments is that to understand torture, we must recognize that law plays only a small part in the effort to contain, regulate, or prohibit it. I am suspicious, in other words, of the hope that law can play an important role in pervasively and effectively limiting modern state violence. Indeed, I doubt that law provides a meaningful language for talking about it at all.[30]

In keeping with that theme, chapters 1, 2, and 3 analyze international, European, and U.S. law on torture and state violence, with the primary goal of demonstrating that the absolute ban on torture is doctrinally porous. Chapter 5 highlights some of the ways in which Israel and many European countries have used torture even as they recognize its supposed illegality. Chapter 6 considers the persistence of torture in U.S. foreign and domestic affairs throughout the twentieth century, while chapter 7 addresses the role of torture in the war on terror. Taken together, these chapters illustrate the familiar conclusion that theory and practice diverge—that modern states fail to live up to their moral and legal commitments to reject torture and other forms of state violence.

Chapter 4 suggests a different set of conclusions. It builds on the legal analysis of the first three chapters but also looks ahead to my discussion of specific conduct by liberal democracies in the second half of the book. I use this middle chapter to argue that torture is consistent with liberal government. The relationships between torture and modern states and between torture and rights discourse are marked not by failure or inconsistency but by success. Thus, the placement of chapter 4 between the chapters on law and the ones on conduct is a deliberate disruption in the ordinary analysis, with the intention of casting a shadow on what has come before and altering the flow of what follows. The book's conclusion returns to these themes, with a specific focus on the political identities associated with torture.

CHAPTER ONE

Torture and International Law

"Torture" is forbidden by international humanitarian law (the law governing armed conflicts), international human rights law, and the laws of most countries. In the language of customary international law, the ban on torture is *jus cogens*, a peremptory norm from which no derogation is permitted and that overrides contrary treaty obligations.[1] In other words, international law and the laws of many countries appear to establish a general, universal human right not to be tortured. Or so we would like to think.

In this chapter and the two that follow, I describe the international, European, and U.S. law of torture both as it is commonly understood and as it appears from a more skeptical perspective. Subsequent chapters describe modern states' use of torture despite their apparent compliance with an absolute ban. One of the ways in which states attempt to explain or justify their conduct is by exploiting the ambiguities of international law. Whether or not these ambiguities are intentional, states use them in an effort to legitimate or at least avoid censure for torture. All of this casts doubt on the strength of the legal prohibitions.

Customary International Law and Torture

The Ban on Torture

Traditionally, customary international law reflects the "general and consistent practice of states followed by them from a sense of legal obligation." Both components—practice and a sense of obligation to a rule—are essential.[2] More recently, international lawyers have shifted from reliance on practice toward reliance on statements of obligation.[3] This contemporary version of customary international law seems to assume that the expression of norms leads to the practice or implementation of those norms. This assumption is problematic because the emphasis on expression often results in statements becoming substitutes for practice. Indeed, when formal statements overshadow practice, conduct that deviates from these statements can easily be dismissed as aberrant. States can portray themselves as committed to the norms of human rights and international law even as they engage selectively in conduct that violates those norms. Nonetheless, some commentators see this dynamic in positive terms because it allows an expansive concept of human rights: no matter what happens—that is, whether the state complies with the norm or violates it—the abstract norm is reinforced.[4]

This dynamic clearly plays out in the context of torture. A wealth of sources declares that official torture is prohibited by customary international law and that this prohibition is a peremptory norm. The U.S. Court of Appeals for the Second Circuit said in *Filartiga v. Pena-Irala,*

> The international consensus surrounding torture has found expression in numerous international treaties and accords. The substance of these international agreements is reflected in modern municipal—*i.e.* national—law as well. . . . The prohibition is clear and unambiguous, and admits of no distinction between treatment of aliens and citizens.[5]

Since that decision in 1980, the number of sources stating that the ban on torture is a peremptory norm of customary international law has continued to grow.[6] But the *Filartiga* court also recognized that the practice of nations does not live up to their rhetoric. The court minimized the discrepancy between statements and practice in a footnote, making the assertion that the former supersedes the latter and that violations thus were aberrational by definition.[7]

Any meaningful consideration of practice requires more than a footnote. As Paul Kahn observes, "despite the international law making effort of the twentieth century, it was the most violently destructive period of human history." More specifically, from 1997 to mid-2000, Amnesty International received reports of torture by state agents in 150 countries, with at least 80 deaths, and it concluded that torture was "widespread or persistent" in more than 70 countries. The U.N. special rapporteur on torture recently decried "continuing occurrences of the practice of corporal punishment, such as amputation, stoning, flogging, and beating."[8] The countries that use torture are not easily marginalized as minor actors on the international scene. The United States, China, India, Israel, and many European countries have employed torture in recent decades or have sent people to other countries for coercive interrogation. Thus, if the existence of a customary norm in international law depends on actual practice and not on substitutes for practice, proving the existence of a customary international law ban on torture becomes more difficult.[9]

Yet states rarely practice torture openly and do not publicly affirm its use. The transparency typically associated with democracy or "open" societies limits the use of torture, forces it underground, or requires it to take forms that such societies do not easily recognize as abusive.[10] Concerns about reciprocity and reputation create incentives for the deeds of states to match their words. When torture becomes public, states usually claim that it did not happen, that reports were overblown, or that it was committed by rogue officials. Many states also condemn the use of torture by other countries, albeit selectively and sometimes for reasons having little to do with human rights norms. The persistent practice of torture, therefore, is not a deliberate effort to change international law, even assuming that would be possible in light of the ban's classification as a peremptory norm.

In sum, many states observe the ban on torture only fitfully. They profess allegiance to it and are rarely willing to torture openly, but it is clear that they do not always intend to be bound by it.[11] Under the contemporary approach to customary international law, in which practice is less important than expressions of commitment, this degree of compliance with the anti-torture rule is sufficient to establish it as a peremptory norm of customary international law. Similar analysis supports the conclusion that customary international law also bans a lesser category of "cruel, inhuman, or degrading treatment"—although whether or not this prohibition is a peremptory norm is far less clear.[12]

Even more complicated is the practice of rendition—sending people from one country to another with little or no legal process and outside the context of deportation or extradition, often for the purpose of interrogation. Standing alone, rendition does not raise significant concerns in customary international law. But in the war on terror, officials in the United States and other states have sent people to countries that they know or suspect will use coercive interrogation tactics. The U.N. Convention against Torture bans the transfer of people from one country to another where torture could result, but it says nothing about the risk of cruel, inhuman, or degrading treatment. The International Covenant on Civil and Political Rights is entirely silent on rendition. Nonetheless, a U.N. committee declared that "the transfer of a person to a State where that person faces a real risk of being subjected to torture, cruel, inhuman or degrading treatment or extrajudicial killing would be a breach of customary international law."[13] The effort to address a distressing situation may be commendable, but the committee's inclusion of cruel, inhuman, or degrading treatment within the ban would make customary international law by fiat and in disregard of practice.[14]

The Scope and Limits of Customary International Law

Under any approach, customary international law is shifting and ambiguous. Broad outlines, however, still emerge. A relentlessly practice-based approach, for example, does not provide conclusive support for a sweeping ban on torture, but it does provide significant support for some kind of ban. First, if the amount and degree of coercive treatment—such as beatings during interrogation—has diminished over time and if one assumes that some acts of torture really are aberrations, this shift in practice would support a prohibition of some kind. Second, it is a marker of "real" sovereignty both to sign multilateral human rights and humanitarian law conventions and to profess adherence to related norms of customary international law. These professions of adherence require some level of backing in actual practice and also inform the terms of political discourse in many countries. States have little express interest in engaging in torture openly, because a pledge not to use arbitrary violence—that is, violence imposed outside of legal processes—is one of the hallmarks of a state committed to the rule of law, which, in turn, is a sign of full membership in the international community (of which customary international law attempts to be partly constitutive).[15]

The problem with all of this is the generality and lack of structure in customary international law. Torture may be banned absolutely, and that ban may have the status of a peremptory norm, but the definition of torture remains unclear, even as conduct that most people would call torture remains widespread. The same is true for the related category of cruel, inhuman, and degrading treatment. These absent definitions are critical, first, to determining exactly what is prohibited by a norm that depends so much on practice and, second, because not all of the prohibitions on cruel, inhuman, and degrading treatment can be peremptory norms under any account that takes state practice seriously. Further, to the extent practice remains important, it is difficult to conclude that all of the conduct commonly claimed to be illegal as cruel, inhuman, or degrading treatment really is. Finally, if the definitions are unclear, drawing the lines between the two categories of conduct, between the peremptory and nonperemptory categories, and between illegal and permitted conduct will be at best an inexact process.

The dynamic quality of customary international law also creates problems. Customary international law changes as state practice changes, and states often aspire to change it.[16] With the exception of peremptory norms, the customary international law of human rights need not develop in only one direction. States may properly seek to change customary international law on detention and interrogation. If the lines between the peremptory ban on torture, the possibly peremptory ban on some inhuman conduct, and other, nonperemptory bans on "rough" treatment are vague, the legitimate (if not necessarily desirable) efforts of states to change the nonperemptory norms of treatment may also weaken the ban on torture, despite its formally peremptory status.

The final problem is interpretation. Not only do the vague standards of customary international law make interpretation difficult, but the identity of the interpreter is crucial. The shape of customary international law differs depending on whether it emanates from executive officials in particular countries, domestic legislative bodies, judges on domestic courts, judges on international courts, or officials of nonjudicial international organizations. The lack of a single entity with a "last word" on its content ensures conflict and ambiguity.[17] The result is that customary norms of international law will resolve themselves as questions of politics and diplomacy as much or more than as questions of law decided by courts.

This ambiguity and lack of structure mean that violations of customary international law easily dissolve into disputes over definitions and classifications. These disputes make room for governments to argue that their abusive conduct is exceptional or justified by an emergency situation. To the extent states are able to explain and isolate torture and related forms of abuse, they can make plausible claims that they are complying with the vague standards of customary international law while still reserving the ability to pursue their interests. All of this has the effect, whether perverse or intended, of reinforcing the customary international prohibition even as it is being broken.

The obvious response to these concerns is that customary international law incorporates the definitions of torture contained in treaties and other international agreements.[18] But customary international law's reliance on treaties to obtain precision simply confirms its vagueness. Once we turn to the text of a treaty or other agreement, we have, for most practical purposes, left customary international law behind and moved to a different category of and way of thinking about international law.

From Customary International Law to Treaties

∾

The rest of this chapter examines international law as codified in multilateral conventions. In general, the move from customary international law to treaties frequently fails to produce clarity: either treaties often fail to define critical terms, or they address similar topics with different language. The Vienna Convention on the Law of Treaties provides that a treaty "shall be interpreted in good faith in accordance with the ordinary meaning to be given to the terms of the treaty in their context and in the light of its object and purpose." The convention notes that preparatory work, subsequent agreements about the meaning of a treaty, "relevant rules of international law," and "subsequent practice" are also important.[19] The combination of these approaches will often lead to tension or conflict, and their combined presence in the Vienna Convention indicates that treaty interpretation will be no more determinate than other forms of legal interpretation.

Even greater complexity arises when multiple treaties apply to the same topic in conflicting ways. The problem of conflicting treaties is not a new one in international law, and various competing rules have evolved to address it.[20] The lack of clear doctrine, however, confirms that the proliferation of overlapping international agreements cannot solve the problem of ambiguity.

Further, treaties often require implementing legislation in the countries that sign them,[21] but the resulting legislation may dilute a treaty's force. Countries often also sign a treaty with various reservations, understandings, or declarations (RUDs) that can modify its meaning or undermine its effect. The Vienna Convention insists that RUDs cannot be "incompatible with the object and purpose of the treaty," and controversies have arisen over the efforts of countries, including the United States, to limit the scope of human rights treaties.[22] Controversy notwithstanding, the persistence of RUDs ensures further ambiguity and conflict and suggests that the negotiated text of a treaty is merely a starting point.

Last, as with any statute or constitutional provision, treaty provisions are only a suggestion of the law. Law as people experience it consists far more of what gets enforced, not simply of what is written, and the distance between the aspirations of written law and the protections that emerge in practice is usually much greater for international law than for domestic law. A treaty that creates a specific, universal human right and requires prosecution of those who trample on it may be important on several levels, but if state officials do not investigate or prosecute claims of violations, such a treaty may be worth little to individuals at the level of personal safety and security.

Codified Humanitarian Law

⌒

The Geneva Conventions

The Geneva Conventions of 1949, consisting of four treaties that set important standards of international humanitarian law, provide broad protections to specific categories of people involved in "all cases of declared war or of any other armed conflict which may arise" between parties to the conventions, as well as in "all cases of partial or total occupation of the territory" of a party to the conventions.[23] Initially, then, rights under the Geneva Conventions are situational and categorical. People caught up in an international armed conflict can only claim the broadest rights under the conventions, and their rights will depend on their relationship to the conflict.[24]

For example, the Third Geneva Convention, "relative to treatment of prisoners of war" (hereinafter referred to as the "Prisoners Convention"), defines the categories of people who qualify as prisoners of war and insists that they "must at all times be humanely treated" and "protected, particularly against acts of violence and intimidation": "No physical or mental torture, nor any other form of coercion, may be inflicted on prisoners of war to secure from them information of any kind whatsoever. Prisoners of war who refuse to answer may not be threatened, insulted, or exposed to unpleasant or disadvantageous treatment of any kind." The Prisoners Convention also limits the ability of a state to transfer prisoners to other countries—a provision that has clear implications for the practice of rendition that has become an important part of the war on terror.[25] The Fourth Geneva Convention, "relative to the protection of civilian persons" (hereinafter referred to as the "Civilians Convention"), adds similar protections for people who "find themselves . . . in the hands of a Party to the conflict or Occupying Power of which they are not nationals." But the rights of people "definitely suspected of or engaged in activities hostile to the security of the State" may be limited if the exercise of those rights would be "prejudicial to the security of such State."[26]

In short, both categories of "protected persons" have a right to be free of torture and other forms of coercive treatment beyond those that inhere in being a prisoner of war or a civilian in a war zone. That right, moreover, is meant to be enforced. Parties to the Geneva Conventions must criminalize "grave breaches," which include "willful killing, torture or inhuman treatment [and] willfully causing great suffering or serious injury to body or health." In the Civilians Convention, "unlawful deportation or transfer or unlawful confinement of a protected person" comes under the category of grave breaches.[27]

The initial problem with the Geneva Conventions is not the scope of protection but the possibility that not everyone will qualify as a protected person. The negotiators had trouble writing clear classification rules, and the conventions' definitions of "protected persons" are "dense" and "riddled with ambiguities and obscure terms of art." These ambiguities have left states with "substantial interpretive wiggle room on a question made central in the protective schemes—the question of who is protected."[28] In part because of these ambiguities, some commentators claim that a group variously described as "unprivileged belligerents" or "illegal" or "unlawful" combatants is not protected by the Prisoners Convention or the Civilians Convention, and states are tempted to declare categorically that certain classes of combatants are illegal.[29]

But the ambiguities of the Geneva Conventions also support a different approach. The Civilians Convention can be read to include anyone who is not a prisoner of war and is "in the hands of a Party to the conflict or Occupying Power of which they are not nationals." The commentary maintains that the Civilians Convention covers "partisans" who fall outside the Prisoners Convention, and terms such as *partisan* and *illegal combatants* easily overlap.[30] Under this approach, illegal combatants are entitled to be treated with "humanity," which—despite that term's ambiguity[31]—presumably includes protection from torture and other forms of coercion.

In addition, for armed conflicts "not of an international character," Common Article 3, which appears in all four conventions, provides that "[p]ersons taking no active part in hostilities, including members of the armed forces who have laid down their arms . . . , shall in all circumstances be treated humanely." This right includes protections against "violence to life and person [including] mutilation, cruel treatment, and torture," as well as "outrages upon personal dignity, in particular humiliating and degrading treatment." The phrase "in all circumstances" strongly suggests that there can be no derogations from these protections.

Textually, Common Article 3 applies to "conflicts not of an international character"—although that category is undefined. No provision of the conventions clearly applies to international conflicts that are not between states, such as the kinds of conflict loosely described by the phrase "war on terror." This limitation raises the possibility that an illegal combatant (including almost all "terrorists") would not be a protected person under the Prisoners Convention, might not be covered by the Civilians Convention, and would receive residual protection under Common Article 3 only if engaged in a "noninternational" armed conflict. In other words, a gap in coverage could exist, and people in that gap would have no right to humane treatment.[32]

Several responses to this possibility suggest themselves. The first is that no gap exists because the people supposedly left unprotected are simply outside the purview of the laws of war. Such people may be criminals, but they are not warriors, combatants, rebels, or insurrectionists. As a result, their rights and protection derive from domestic law and international human rights law, not humanitarian law. Second, international lawyers have developed a broader interpretation of Common Article 3 as stating the minimum acceptable conditions of treatment for people covered in any way by the Geneva Conventions, whether or not the conflict is international, with the remaining provisions of the conventions providing more extensive rights or privileges to people who fit into the various "protected persons" categories.[33]

The 1977 additional protocols to the Geneva Conventions provide a third response by expanding protections for people "fighting against colonial domination and alien occupation and against racist regimes in the exercise of their right of self-determination," as well as for members of "dissident armed forces or other organized armed groups." Article 44 of the First Protocol expands the category of persons who qualify as prisoners of war and provides that people who do not qualify must still be treated as if they were prisoners of war: "civilians and combatants" not covered by its provisions or those of any other international agreement remain "under the protection and authority of the principles of international law derived from established custom, from the principles of humanity and from the dictates of public conscience."[34]

Article 75 of the First Protocol provides that "persons who are in the power of a Party to the conflict and who do not benefit from more favourable treatment under the Conventions or under this Protocol shall be treated humanely in all circumstances." It also prohibits "torture of all kinds, whether physical or mental," "corporal punishment," and "humiliating and degrading treatment." Article 4 of the Second Protocol extends similar protections to "[a]ll persons who do not take a direct part or who have ceased to take part in hostilities."[35] These broad provisions seem adequate to resolve any ambiguity over the coverage of Common Article 3. Although their protections fall short of those provided elsewhere in the conventions and protocols, they do ban "torture" and "degrading treatment." Many international lawyers and at least some governments, including the United States, also interpret Common Article 3 and Article 75 as codifying—and arguably creating—peremptory norms of customary international law.[36]

Nonetheless, problems remain. First, Common Article 3 provides fewer procedural rights than other parts of the conventions. Second, neither it nor the additional protocols say anything about renditions, with the result that any protection in that context for illegal combatants must be implied, if at all, from protections that say nothing on their face about movement of persons.[37] Third, enforcement of the conventions is uncertain. States must "provide effective penal sanctions" for grave breaches, but a grave breach can only be committed against a person "protected" by one of the conventions. People whose protections derive only from Common Article 3—including illegal combatants—appear not to fall into that category, which means that violations of their rights are not grave breaches.[38] The additional protocols contain no enforcement provisions, with the result that violations are not grave breaches that states must prosecute. Also open to question is how diligently states enforce the penal sanctions required by the conventions.

The most significant problem is that the conventions and protocols fail to define key terms, such as *torture, humane, degrading,* and *outrage.*[39] Their meaning must emerge from judicial proceedings—to the extent such proceedings are available—or from political decisions by states, as influenced by the assertions of the Red Cross and other entities. Despite this uncertainty, some commentators contend that certain specific forms of conduct are "plainly disallowed" by the Geneva Conventions.[40] Claims of this sort must be correct with respect to something like severe electrocution if the conventions are to have any meaning as humanitarian documents. But other forms of conduct, such as hooding, sustained interrogation, or sleep deprivation, do not "plainly" violate the conventions in all circumstances. The resulting ambiguities create space for states to make reasonable claims that their conduct may not be desirable but is also not prohibited.

Finally, the conventions and protocols do not cover all forms of armed or military action by state actors. According to Article 1 of the Second Protocol, "internal disturbances and tensions, such as riots, isolated and sporadic acts of violence and other acts of a similar nature," are not armed conflicts. The Rome Statute of the International Criminal Court draws the same distinction and suggests that "armed conflicts . . . in the territory of a state" do not implicate the full range of international law unless the armed conflict is "protracted" and involves "organized armed groups."[41]

To summarize, international humanitarian law attempts to draw a reasonable distinction between domestic violence and armed conflict, and that distinction is critical to maintaining a conceptually separate category of humanitarian law. But that distinction relies on terms that remain unclear, such as *internal, isolated, sporadic,* and *protracted.* If these terms are to have any specific meaning, the conventions and protocols cannot apply to "ordinary" or traditional enforcement of domestic criminal law, including the police and prison violence often associated with it—even though the term *armed conflict* applies without too much exaggeration to the relationship in some communities between the often militarized police and the populations they patrol. Similarly, the mere involvement of military forces in an "internal disturbance" cannot trigger the laws of war.

For the same reasons, the conventions and protocols do not apply to all actions against individual "terrorists," members of terrorist organizations, or terrorist groups. The laws of war apply to aspects of the U.S.-led war on terror, such as the invasions of Afghanistan and Iraq, but they do not apply to all of it under traditional analyses.[42] Still, terrorism does not fit neatly into the dichotomy of armed conflict and internal disturbance. How many attacks are required for terrorism to be "protracted"? If a terrorist act is committed by a lawfully admitted resident of a country, is it an "internal disturbance"? What if the perpetrators are from other countries? Clear answers to these questions will often be elusive, as with the U.S. Supreme Court's decision in *Hamdan v. Rumsfeld.* In that decision, the Court applied Common Article 3 to what it concluded was an armed conflict with al Qaeda, but it provided no definition of "al Qaeda" and no analysis of al Qaeda's or Common Article 3's relationship to a larger war on terror.[43]

In addition, the claim that a state's responses to terrorism fall within international humanitarian law broadens the idea of war in ways that will not enhance human rights. As Helen Duffy notes, war rhetoric emphasizes "the security imperative" and sometimes suggests that security "trumps observance of the law" or requires "different, and lower, standards of protection" than those of international human rights law.[44] Applying the Geneva Conventions to terrorism in general would thus entrench the idea that armed conflict is normal and routine. Indeed, if efforts to combat terrorism in general always involve an armed conflict, then—as Duffy and others have suggested—it is a conflict with no boundaries in time or space. It takes place everywhere, has no logical culmination, and irrevocably blurs the distinctions between civilian and combatant that are so important to the Geneva Conventions.[45] The resulting permanent state of emergency would undermine efforts to define and preserve a generous conception of rights (and here I am bracketing the problematic nature of rights in general). Those efforts would remain in a subordinate social and political position until the achievement of total victory or defeat. Indeed, if responses to terrorism necessarily invoke the law of war, human rights would become part of the conflict. They would be bound ever more closely to state power, and the amorphous distinction between individual liberty and state interests would further erode—or be revealed as eroded—along the lines I will discuss in chapter 4.

Finally, an armed conflict requires parties. A war against something as amorphous as "terror" might require defining social organization itself as a war for survival, so that war again becomes or is exposed as the normal condition.[46] If the conflict is a war on "terrorism," the enemy becomes a tactic but remains nameless and shifting, so that all forms of violence that threaten the state or the ideal of law and order potentially qualify.[47] Although al Qaeda is the most concrete enemy on the other side of the war on terror, the idea of an armed conflict with al Qaeda remains fraught with problems and ambiguities. Governments often identify other groups as "associated" or "linked" with al Qaeda, in part to bring themselves into what they anticipate is the less legally or politically constrained field of action represented by a global war on terror.

Taken as a whole, the Geneva Conventions and the additional protocols to the conventions provide a framework for the assertion of broad rights to humane treatment during war and other conflicts. The problem is that so many ambiguities riddle their classifications and protections that states easily can make reasonable arguments to interpret them in ways that enhance their power over the bodies of their prisoners. Resolution of these ambiguities is more likely to be political than strictly juridical, which means that a state's interests will sometimes outweigh the demands of international law.

The ICTY and the ICC

This section briefly discusses the effort to enforce humanitarian law and related human rights norms through the creation of the International Criminal Tribunal for the Former Yugoslavia (ICTY) and the International Criminal Court (ICC).[48]

The ICTY's role in articulating international law norms has been significant. Its jurisdiction extends only to events relating to the breakup of Yugoslavia, but it plainly has sought to expand the reach of international humanitarian law.[49] With respect to customary international law, for example, the ICTY has deemphasized "state practice." In the *Tadić* jurisdictional decision, the ICTY observed that "it is difficult, if not impossible, to pinpoint the actual behaviour of the troops in the field." It claimed that to solve this problem, "reliance must be *primarily* placed on such elements as official pronouncements of States, military manuals and judicial decisions."[50] Statements of policy thus substitute for proof of actual practice.

The ICTY has also expanded the definition of an "armed conflict" for purposes of the Geneva Conventions. *Tadić* declared that "an armed conflict exists whenever there is resort to armed force between States or protracted armed violence between governmental authorities and organized armed groups or between such groups within a State."[51] Not only has the ICTY insisted that Common Article 3 of the Geneva Conventions always applies as a minimum baseline of protection, but it has also insisted that all of the conventions are customary international law. Further, according to the ICTY, the Civilians Convention should be interpreted expansively in light of "the object and purpose of humanitarian law, which 'is directed to the protection of civilians to the maximum extent possible.'"[52]

The ICTY has been similarly active on the issue of torture. It has confirmed the ban on torture's status as a peremptory norm and has used the definition in the U.N. Convention against Torture to supplement the Geneva Conventions and customary international law. Notably, however, the ICTY has held that the U.N. convention's requirement of official involvement "is not a requirement under customary international law in relation to the criminal responsibility of an individual for torture."[53] This holding departs from the prevailing view that "torture and summary execution—when not perpetrated in the course of genocide and war crimes—are proscribed by international law only when committed by state officials or under color of law."[54] The ICTY has also declared that the requirement of severe suffering is not as intense as "extreme pain or suffering" and need not be accompanied by serious injury.[55] Further, the prosecution will not always have to present specific proof of severe pain, because "some acts [in this case, rape] establish *per se* the suffering of those upon whom they were inflicted."[56] In the context of torture as a war crime, the ICTY has held that the armed conflict "need not have been causal to the commission of the crime." A war crime exists if the conflict "played a substantial part in the perpetrator's ability to commit [torture], his decision to commit it, the manner in which it was committed or the purpose for which it was committed."[57]

The ICTY's interpretations of international law will undoubtedly play a role in the jurisprudence of the ICC. The Rome Statute of the International Criminal Court identifies and creates a process for codifying international criminal law in areas that overlap with humanitarian and human rights law. It seeks to make this codified law enforceable against any individual within its jurisdiction. To that end, the statute limits the court's jurisdiction to "the most serious crimes of concern to the international community as a whole," which it categorizes as genocide, crimes against humanity, war crimes, and the "crime of aggression."[58]

The Rome Statute then lists specific crimes within these categories. For example, "crimes against humanity" include "torture," "enforced disappearance of persons," and "other inhumane acts of a similar character intentionally causing great suffering, or serious injury to body or to mental or physical health." The statute borrows from the Convention against Torture to define torture as "the intentional infliction of severe pain or suffering, whether physical or mental, upon a person in the custody or under the control of the accused,"[59] although it omits the convention's requirement that the acts be taken with a specific purpose, such as obtaining a confession.[60]

According to the statute, all of these acts qualify as crimes against humanity "when committed as part of a widespread or systematic attack directed against any civilian population, with knowledge of the attack." This language prevents the category of crimes against humanity from applying to all forms of state violence or all acts of terrorism, even if the conduct at issue is horrific. The document is silent, however, on the issue of "state action." Nothing in the general provisions of the section on crimes against humanity—or in the general provisions of the other crime-defining articles—explicitly limits criminal liability to individuals employed by or acting on behalf of a government entity.[61]

The category of "war crimes" has four subcategories. The first is "grave breaches of the Geneva Conventions," which specifically includes "torture or inhuman treatment," "willfully causing great suffering, or serious injury to body or health," and "unlawful deportation or transfer or unlawful confinement." The second category—"other serious violations of the laws and customs applicable in international armed conflict"—includes "subjecting persons who are in the power of an adverse party to physical mutilation" and "committing outrages upon personal dignity, in particular humiliating or degrading treatment." The third category applies to "an armed conflict not of an international character" and includes "serious violations of article 3 common to the four Geneva Conventions," such as "cruel treatment or torture" and "outrages upon personal dignity, in particular humiliating and degrading treatment." The final category includes "other serious violations of the laws and customs applicable in armed conflicts not of an international character." As I discussed already, the Rome Statute takes care to distinguish these last two categories from "internal disturbances and tensions."[62]

The ICC Assembly of States Parties has adopted elements for all of these crimes.[63] Although the elements confirm that torture requires the infliction of severe mental or physical pain or suffering, they do not provide clear guidance on how to interpret these terms. The Rome Statute declares that "the definition of a crime shall be strictly construed and shall not be extended by analogy" and that "the definition shall be interpreted in favour of the [defendant]," but another provision allows the ICC to look at "applicable treaties and principles and rules of international law" when making its decisions.[64] The introduction to the elements suggests that such terms as *inhumane* and *severe* are "elements involving value judgement."[65]

The Rome Statute recognizes defenses to crimes, including defense of self or others, a broad idea of duress, and mistake of fact or law, including a limited "superior orders" defense. The ICC may consider other defenses derived from international law, but it is unlikely to recognize a separate general defense of necessity for these crimes in light of the broad definition of duress as "resulting from a threat of imminent death or of continuing or imminent serious bodily harm against that person or another person," where "the person acts necessarily and reasonably to avoid this threat, provided that the person does not intend to cause a greater harm than the one sought to be avoided."[66] The potential scope of this defense is quite broad, but only decisions in specific cases will determine its force.

In short, the Rome Statute adopts broad definitions of torture to be enforced in individual criminal proceedings against individual defendants. Nonetheless, the precise definitions of torture and possible defenses remain elusive. Theodore Meron notes that the statute operates at a "high level of generality," such that the court "will inevitably have to resort to customary international law to construe and apply the crimes that the statute enumerates."[67] Whatever interpretive method it adopts, the ICC will also require ongoing and consistent cooperation from the states that have agreed to its jurisdiction, and that level of cooperation will be difficult to achieve and maintain. If the ICC succeeds and becomes a forum for developing and extending international law norms, the ambiguities in the international law definitions of torture may become more like the ambiguities that are common to any legal system, which would be a significant accomplishment.

The rest of this chapter examines codified international human rights law. Importantly, the substantive provisions of humanitarian and human rights law cover similar conduct. In response, some commentators contend that human rights law does not apply at all to armed conflicts, while others claim that it overrides humanitarian law. A third view—the most plausible to my mind—suggests that the various provisions should be harmonized as much as possible, primarily by applying the more specific provisions of one document to explain the more general provisions of another. More important than any of these approaches is the fact that inconsistency or conflict between the laws of war and human rights law creates space for states to argue that human rights law has limited application in times of conflict.[68]

International Human Rights Law
∽

The Universal Declaration of Human Rights

The Universal Declaration of Human Rights of 1948 is the fundamental document of international human rights law and the precursor to both the International Covenant on Civil and Political Rights (ICCPR) and the U.N. Convention against Torture. It sets forth "a common standard of achievement for all peoples and all nations," and the thrust of this standard is that every human being should be defined as a bearer of "equal and inalienable rights." The rights include "the right to a nationality" and—perhaps related—"the right to marry and to found a family." All persons have the right to an "adequate" standard of living and to "social security" and even "the right to rest and leisure." Also, all people have the right to a "compulsory" education that will "promote understanding, tolerance and friendship among all nations, racial or religious groups, and shall further the activities of the United Nations for the maintenance of peace," as well as "the right to take part in the government of [one's] country," where the government is based in "[t]he will of the people." In return, citizens have "duties to the community in which alone the free and full development of [their] personality is possible." No methods of enforcement are specified beyond each nation's pledge "to achieve . . . the promotion of universal respect for and observance of human rights and fundamental freedoms."[69]

In short, the Universal Declaration is a document of almost boundless aspiration and of equally boundless ambiguity. Against the conduct of modern states and the brutality of war, it seeks to redefine the ways in which people and governments interact and to enshrine ideas of decency, respect, and liberty. Still, except that it purports to declare rights, the declaration is not law in any positive sense, nor was it intended to be—although some effort has been made to elevate its status, with the result that the legal weight of its aspirations is open to debate.[70] In a fundamental sense, it creates an ideal that will always be unrealizable and not even fully definable.

I want to suggest as well—in a preview of chapter 4's discussion of rights and state power—that these aspirations translate into an equally boundless conception of state power. If states must achieve rights that are by definition unachievable, their power must always be exercised, with greater and greater urgency, to attain these rights and create better rights-holders— more secure, better educated, and better employed people who are better participants in public life and better, too, at reproduction and leisure. This intense governmental interest in and management of all aspects of a person's daily life may not finally achieve those rights, but it risks tying citizens more closely to and making them more dependent on state power for the enforcement of rights that are themselves constraining (e.g., the "right" to marry and found a family, as opposed to and arguably exclusive of other ways of forming interpersonal bonds and expressing sexuality).

Other rights announced in the Universal Declaration presumably operate in the same way. The declaration states, "Everyone has the right to life, liberty and security of person." To that end, "[n]o one shall be subjected to torture or to cruel, inhuman or degrading treatment of punishment," and no one shall "be subjected to arbitrary arrest, detention or exile."[71] These sweeping statements, unattached to any enforcement provisions, would achieve more specific and ostensibly binding form in later agreements. Often, as we will see, the words of the declaration were repeated in follow-on agreements. Whether they are meaningful constraints on state power at a formal level or at the level of practice is a far different and more complicated issue.[72]

The International Covenant on Civil and Political Rights

Article 7 of the ICCPR, which went into force in 1976, echoes the language of the Universal Declaration: "No one shall be subject to torture or to cruel, inhuman or degrading treatment or punishment." Article 4 permits limited derogations "in time of public emergency which threatens the life of the nation," but it prohibits any derogation from the ban on torture and other cruel, inhuman, or degrading treatment. The ban is absolute.[73] The ICCPR also declares that "[a]ll persons deprived of their liberty shall be treated with humanity and with respect for the inherent dignity of the human person," but this right can be overridden "in time of public emergency," except to the extent that the nonderogable ban on torture and other cruel, inhuman, or degrading treatment provides a minimum content to treating people "with humanity and with respect."[74]

While the rights articulated in the ICCPR are significant, their ability to protect the bodies of individual people is less clear. Each state party "undertakes . . . to adopt such laws or other measures as may be necessary to give effect to the rights recognized in the present Covenant," and they also pledge "to ensure that any persons whose rights or freedoms as herein recognized are violated shall have an effective remedy."[75] These requirements go beyond the Universal Declaration, but "giving effect" to rights through "effective remedies" could take a variety of forms. Some remedies might impose strong limits on state violence, some might do little to prevent or compensate for harms, and others might control state violence at the cost of also controlling and managing large numbers of individual lives.

Article 28 establishes an additional enforcement mechanism: the Human Rights Committee. This committee evaluates reports from state parties on how they implemented the ICCPR and has a limited authority to investigate possible violations. It has also promulgated a series of "general comments" that provide nonbinding interpretations of the ICCPR. But the committee's direct powers of enforcement are weak, and commentators have concluded that the ICCPR's enforcement provisions are flawed—although those flaws could be a deliberate attempt to protect state sovereignty.[76]

Importantly, nothing in the ICCPR limits its application to peacetime or prevents it from applying to armed conflicts. The fact that Article 4 allows derogations from some rights "in time of public emergency" suggests that it was intended to apply broadly, including during war.[77] But how it applies at such times remains unclear, and this confusion is linked to uncertainty over the geographic scope of its protections. Article 2 declares that each state party "undertakes to respect and to ensure to all individuals within its territory and subject to its jurisdiction the rights recognized in the present Covenant." The phrase "within its territory" began as a way of ensuring that states would not have to extend rights to people in occupied territory, although it is not clear whether that was a goal of the majority of participants by the time the document was finally completed. Still, many states adhere to the earlier understanding. Similarly, the phrase "subject to its jurisdiction" could have an implicit territorial connotation, or it could apply more broadly to any person under the control of a state, wherever that person may be. Notably, by using *and* instead of *or* to link these phrases, Article 2 indicates that both conditions must be satisfied before any rights attach. This reading would impose significant geographic limits on the scope of the obligations that the ICCPR places on individual states.[78]

The Human Rights Committee and the International Court of Justice understandably have advanced a broader interpretation. The committee described Article 2 as requiring states "to respect and ensure the Covenant rights to all persons who may be within their territory and to all persons subject to their jurisdiction." In their construction, *and* remained important, but its grammatical function changed. The committee then substituted *or* for *and* when it asserted that "the enjoyment of Covenant rights . . . must be available to all individuals . . . who may find themselves in the territory or subject to the jurisdiction of the State Party." In case any doubts remained, the committee went on to declare, "This principle also applies to those within the power or effective control of the forces of a State Party acting outside its territory."[79]

The International Court of Justice relied on the committee's interpretation, but it also advanced an independent rationale. The court insisted that the text of the ICCPR could be read either to protect people within the territory of and subject to the jurisdiction of a state or to cover "both individuals present within a State's territory and those outside that territory but subject to that State's jurisdiction." To determine which interpretation was better, the court stressed the object and purpose of the ICCPR: "[W]hile the jurisdiction of states is primarily territorial, it may sometimes be exercised outside the national territory. Considering the object and purpose of the [ICCPR], it would seem natural that, even when such is the case, States parties to the Covenant should be bound to comply with its provisions."[80] In short, the court relied on abstract and undefined principle to override a straightforward textual reading of Article 2.

In its general comments, the Human Rights Committee has also advanced broad readings of the ICCPR on the issue of torture and cruel, inhuman, or degrading treatment. First, although the ICCPR provides no definition of torture or cruel, inhuman, or degrading treatment, the committee has resisted developing its own definition. In particular, it has refused to narrow the meaning of those terms by "draw[ing] up a list of prohibited acts or . . . establish[ing] sharp distinctions between the different kinds of punishment or treatment." Instead, the committee contends, perfectly reasonably, but also in a way that enhances its discretion to find violations of the ICCPR, that "the distinctions depend on the nature, purpose and severity of the treatment applied."[81]

Second, the committee has concluded that torture includes such things as electric shocks, near suffocation, anal penetration, other physical violence, threats, fake executions, or combinations of these and other practices. In reaching these results, the committee "does not follow a clear line in respect of the definition of torture or the difference between torture and other cruel, inhuman or degrading treatment or punishment."[82] Worth noting, however, is that the ICCPR's nonderogable ban on both categories takes away the incentive to develop a "clear line."

Third, the committee has interpreted the ICCPR to impose a duty on states to ban private acts of torture and "to take positive measures to ensure that private persons or entities do not inflict torture or cruel, inhuman or degrading treatment or punishment on others within their power"—an interpretation that, as we have seen, the ICTY found useful. The committee, in other words, has attempted not only to entrench a negative right against torture but also to establish a positive right to state protection from the acts of third parties.[83]

Finally, the committee has interpreted the ICCPR to include a ban on "expos[ing] individuals to the danger of torture or cruel, inhuman or degrading treatment or punishment upon return to another country by way of their extradition, expulsion or refoulement."[84] (The term *refoulement* typically refers to treatment of refugees.) Thus, although the ICCPR itself says nothing about these issues, the committee extended it beyond its text. Yet the scope of the ban remains unclear—including whether it applies specifically to renditions in addition to extradition, immigration, and/or refugee proceedings. Presumably, the committee meant to include the movement of people without process as well, and there is no territorial limitation.

The committee subsequently took a more precise and limited view when it wrote in General Comment No. 31,

> [T]he article 2 obligation requiring that States Parties respect and ensure the Covenant rights for all persons in their territory and all persons under their control entails an obligation not to extradite, deport, expel *or otherwise remove* a person *from their territory,* where there are substantial grounds for believing that there is a real risk of irreparable harm.[85]

On the one hand, the phrase "or otherwise remove" seems clearly to include renditions. On the other hand, the phrase "from their territory" seems to limit the scope of the ban. This limit is all the more significant in light of the committee's conclusion in the same document that Article 2 applies to actions outside a state's territory, particularly when the earlier comment arguably had already applied that view to rendition.[86]

In 2006, the committee advanced yet another view in response to the

U.S. practice of extraordinary rendition. It clearly included "rendition" in the list of practices covered by its extension of Article 2, and it insisted that the protection against torture and cruel, inhuman, or degrading treatment in this context encompasses actions "outside [a state's] own territory."[87] The different language in the committee's general comments provides arguments for human rights advocates seeking a broader restriction, as well as arguments for states seeking a narrower interpretation. The third interpretation—which did not appear in a general comment—strengthens the hand of human rights advocates but does so at the expense of consistency and predictability.

Under any interpretation, the ICCPR provides important protections against torture and cruel, inhuman, or degrading treatment. It fails, however, to define key terms, and it does not explicitly address the problem of rendition. The Human Rights Committee's general comments interpret the ICCPR expansively, but although many commentators tend to accept these broader interpretations, narrower views remain available to state officials. In the end, the ICCPR provides protections that are as ambiguous as they are important, and ample room remains for states to exploit those ambiguities. Without meaningful enforcement mechanisms, the ICCPR and the Human Rights Committee can do little more than articulate norms and shame states that transgress them.

The U.N. Convention against Torture

The U.N. Convention against Torture and Other Forms of Cruel, Inhuman, or Degrading Treatment or Punishment, adopted in 1984, is the most specific and significant international law document on torture. Unlike the Geneva Conventions and the ICCPR, the Convention against Torture provides a carefully negotiated definition. Torture is

> any act by which severe pain or suffering, whether physical or mental, is intentionally inflicted on a person for such purposes as obtaining from him or a third person information or a confession, punishing him for an act he or a third person has committed or is suspected of having committed, or intimidating or coercing him or a third person, or for any reason based on discrimination of any kind, when such pain or suffering is inflicted by or at the instigation of or with the consent or acquiescence of a public official or other person acting in an official capacity.

According to the convention, torture "does not include pain or suffering arising only from, inherent in or incidental to lawful sanctions."

Torture, so defined, is banned absolutely by the convention: "No exceptional circumstances whatsoever, whether a state of war or threat of war, internal political instability or any other public emergency, may be invoked as a justification of torture." Nor may states take advantage of information obtained by torture: "[A]ny statement which is established to have been made as a result of torture shall not be invoked as evidence in any proceedings, except against a person accused of torture as evidence that the statement was made." The convention also insists, "No State Party shall expel, return ('Refouler') or extradite a person to another State where there are substantial grounds for believing that he would be in danger of being subjected to torture."[88]

Each party to the convention must "take effective legislative, administrative, judicial or other measures to prevent acts of torture in any territory under its jurisdiction," a command that includes criminalizing torture. Other provisions of the convention created the Committee against Torture, which receives regular reports from states that have ratified the convention, prepares general comments on its meaning, and has limited powers to investigate claims that a state has violated the convention—although commentators have concluded that it "lacks the teeth necessary for real enforcement of the Convention." An optional protocol establishes a subcommittee on prevention of torture and other cruel, inhuman, or degrading treatment or punishment, which may visit "places where people are deprived of their liberty" in any state that has agreed to the protocol.[89]

So far, the Convention against Torture appears to take an absolutist approach to the problem of torture. Indeed, the convention's nonderogation clause, which applies to "war" as well as "public emergencies," is clearer than the ICCPR's version. Similarly, the convention is more expansive in geographic scope than the ICCPR. Article 2 of the convention imposes obligations in "any territory under [a state party's] jurisdiction." Read alone, this phrase arguably limits the convention's operation to within a country's borders—the "territory under its jurisdiction." But that reading is less plausible when compared to the phrase "within its territory and subject to its jurisdiction" in Article 2 of the ICCPR. Assuming that a strictly textual approach would limit the ICCPR to operating within the territorial boundaries of a party—because "within its territory" restrains the more ambiguous "subject to its jurisdiction"—the language of the Convention against Torture is comparatively more open-ended. The drafting history reveals that Article 2 of the convention was intended to "expand the scope of the Convention" to include "ships or aircraft registered in the State" and "occupied territories to which a State did not have legal title." International tribunals often declare that states must observe human rights law in territory outside their boundaries but under their control, as well as over the conduct of their agents acting outside their borders.[90] Not surprisingly, the Committee against Torture has taken the same view in its interpretation of the convention.[91]

Critically, however, the convention departs from the ICCPR in two important ways. First, the convention's definition of torture excludes "pain or suffering arising from, inherent in or incidental to lawful sanctions." Would a country whose statutes authorize beatings as a punishment for certain crimes fit within the exception, even though beating often rises to the level of torture? The "lawful sanctions" exception threatens an enormous loophole, especially if "lawful" includes common-law rules and particularly if it includes customs or practices that are the functional equivalent of law. Two participants in the negotiations put a hopeful spin on this ambiguity, while also admitting the potential power of the exception.

> [Article 1] does not make clear whether, in order to be lawful, a sanction must also be consistent with international law under which cruel, inhuman or degrading treatment or punishment is prohibited. It may therefore be argued that various forms of corporal punishment ... are not covered by the exception . . . , but this is undoubtedly a view that is not shared by everyone.[92]

The special rapporteur has declared that the exception must be interpreted along the lines originally proposed during negotiations: "[T]he 'lawful sanctions' exclusion must necessarily refer to those sanctions that constitute practices widely accepted as legitimate by the international community." More recently, the rapporteur plausibly suggested that the lawfulness of force should depend not simply on legal authorization but also on "the proportionality of the force applied in a particular situation" and on whether the victim is powerless and unable to resist.[93]

Second and more important, the convention takes account—as does the ICCPR—of a different category of state violence: "other cruel, inhuman, or degrading treatment or punishment." But the two documents treat this category of conduct in different ways. Instead of simply grouping this conduct with torture as absolutely forbidden and criminal, Article 16 of the convention provides, "Each State Party shall undertake to prevent in any territory under its jurisdiction other acts of cruel, inhuman or degrading treatment or punishment which do not amount to torture as defined in article 1." This language is not a clear ban on cruel, inhuman, or degrading treatment or punishment. Many human rights lawyers—not to mention the Committee against Torture—might disagree, but Article 16 reads more easily as the assumption of a commitment by state parties "to prevent" such conduct through domestic law. Further, the convention does not define this category of conduct, apparently because there was no agreement on what the definition ought to be. It simply refers to presumptively illegal conduct that is "not torture." The difference between Article 16 and the provisions that expressly deal with torture suggest that the convention articulates a right to be free from state torture but does not recognize a right to be free from cruel, inhuman, or degrading treatment inflicted by state officials.[94]

Significantly—and here the convention also differs from the ICCPR—the "no justification" clause does not apply to Article 16's discussion of cruel, inhuman, or degrading treatment.[95] This exclusion must mean that the convention treats cruel, inhuman, or degrading treatment as less serious than torture, which explains, in turn, why it is not subject to the same absolute and nonderogable ban. The possibility of derogation must also include the possibility that violent treatment of prisoners or others short of torture can be justifiable under some circumstances. Further, rendition of a person to face only cruel, inhuman, or degrading treatment does not violate the convention, and statements obtained through cruel, inhuman, or degrading treatment are admissible as evidence. This series of consequences makes the distinction between torture and the lesser category of cruel, inhuman, or degrading treatment into a fundamental aspect of the convention.

The convention's different treatment of these two categories also puts international human rights law at odds with itself. Whereas the ICCPR purports to ban torture and cruel, inhuman, or degrading treatment absolutely, the convention only bans torture and distinguishes it from "lawful sanctions." As a result of this divergence, the convention holds out the possibility that "exceptional circumstances," such as necessity, might justify cruel, inhuman, or degrading treatment or punishment. Finally, because the convention is the more specific and recent document, its prohibitions and silences arguably trump those of the ICCPR. In short, the most significant international law document to address state torture and other abuse appears deliberately crafted to leave room for states to engage in coercive treatment in compelling circumstances, so long as the conduct is not "torture."

Of course, this interpretation is controversial. Article 1 of the convention provides, "This article is without prejudice to any international instrument or national legislation which does or may contain provisions of wider application." Article 16, the same article that creates lesser protections against cruel, inhuman, or degrading treatment, states that it is "without prejudice to the provisions of any other international instrument or national law which prohibits cruel, inhuman or degrading treatment or punishment or which relates to extradition of expulsion." These provisions suggest that the convention does not supersede more expansive protections in other documents. One might even argue that the convention's provisions on cruel, inhuman, or degrading treatment derive from the ICCPR and thus must incorporate the ICCPR's nonderogable ban.[96] The Committee against Torture has made use of the fact that "the definitional threshold between ill-treatment and torture is not clear," to argue that "[t]he obligations to prevent torture and other cruel, inhuman or degrading treatment . . . are interdependent, indivisible and interrelated." It follows, for the committee, that regardless of the convention's text, "the measures to prevent torture must be applied to prevent ill-treatment," and the committee has accordingly "considered the prohibition of ill-treatment to be likewise non-derogable."[97]

These arguments draw strength from the idea that the convention essentially reemphasizes and makes more concrete the prohibitions of the ICCPR and the Universal Declaration of Human Rights. But the process of turning a small part of the largely aspirational ICCPR into the more concrete and sovereignty-infringing Convention against Torture required compromises. This process is apparent in light of an intermediate document, the Declaration against Torture. The declaration reiterates the ICCPR's ban on cruel, inhuman, or degrading treatment as well as torture and rejects any derogation from either ban. It also forbids admission into evidence of statements obtained by torture or cruel, inhuman, or degrading treatment.[98] To the extent that the declaration is a rough draft of the convention, the dilution or omission of these protections from the later document speaks volumes.

One could also argue that the Human Rights Committee's interpretation of the ICCPR to ban at least some transfers of people at risk of torture or cruel, inhuman, or degrading treatment should control interpretation of the Convention against Torture. Yet the Committee against Torture has refused to take a broad view of the prohibition on rendition. In General Comment No. 1, the committee insisted that the prohibition "is confined in its application to cases where there are substantial grounds for believing that the author would be in danger of being subjected to torture." With respect to the "consistent pattern of gross, flagrant or mass violations of human rights" that suffices to establish substantial grounds for believing that torture might take place, the committee declared that the only relevant violations are those committed "by or at the instigation of or with the consent or acquiescence of a public official or other person acting in an official capacity." Finally, the committee also specified that the person making a complaint about rendition bears the burden of proving that a state has violated the convention.[99] Nothing in this general comment suggests that rendition to face cruel, inhuman, or degrading treatment raises significant issues under the convention. The committee's General Comment No. 2 does not reverse the earlier comment, and the committee's 2006 discussion of U.S. rendition practices refers only to risks of torture, not to risks of cruel, inhuman or degrading treatment.[100]

The line between torture and other cruel, inhuman, or degrading treatment is thus a critical border, but the standards for distinguishing between them are unclear. Burgers and Danelius suggest that the "severe pain" characterizing torture includes "only acts of a certain gravity." They also suggest that the conduct need not be systematic; a single act can constitute torture. As for mental suffering, they propose it "can be of very different kinds," and they highlight threats that create fear and being forced to witness mistreatment of others.[101] These comments advance the definitional issue, but they are unlikely to lead to a clear jurisprudence of torture.

For its part, the Committee against Torture's jurisprudence is not expansive, except that it treats as a prohibition Article 16's language on "undertak[ing] to prevent" cruel, inhuman, or degrading treatment.[102] Nor does it advance a particularly precise analysis. When the committee makes a finding of torture, it usually notes that the conduct "can be characterized as severe pain or suffering intentionally inflicted by public officials." It then usually concludes with a statement along the following lines: "In the circumstances the Committee concludes that due weight must be given to the complainant's allegations and that the facts, as submitted, constitute torture within the meaning of Article 1 of the Convention."[103] In keeping with General Comment No. 1, the committee has not extended the definition of torture in this context to cover conduct that would normally be considered cruel, inhuman, or degrading treatment. The committee also denies the overwhelming majority of expulsion claims that it hears, sometimes even when the applicant has documented past incidents of torture.[104]

To summarize, the Convention against Torture is a puzzle. It creates two different levels of protection against certain kinds of abusive treatment but suggests that those different levels are irrelevant in light of "other international instrument[s]." While one could read the convention and ICCPR together to maximize protection of human rights, an equally legitimate reading could stress that the convention is later in time than the ICCPR, is more specific, and departs from the levels of protection in the earlier document. The ambiguous relationship between the documents allows governments to claim more room for state action and less need to protect people under their control.

Narrower interpretations of the convention also dovetail with a rhetorical approach to torture, which I discussed in the introduction. If the convention is the controlling document, a state will simply claim that its violent conduct is not torture. If that claim is correct under the convention, that state has at worst engaged in cruel, inhuman, or degrading treatment. If the state can come up with a sufficient justification for its conduct, it has not violated the convention at all. At this point, the discussion gets bogged down in definitions, which distract attention from the conduct, its consequences, and its victims.

The definitional game established by the convention has the potential to carry over into discussions of other international agreements that use the same or similar language, even though the consequences of distinguishing between torture and other illegal forms of coercion has little doctrinal value under these agreements. Indeed, the European Court of Human Rights, not the Committee against Torture, has developed the most extensive jurisprudence on the difference between torture and cruel, inhuman, or degrading treatment—as I will discuss in the next chapter. In this sense, the legal dispute over definitions serves state interests because the legal issues are refracted by and dissolve into political arguments. The goal is less to win a legal argument and more to win a social, cultural, and political debate in which the most important thing is to be in the "not-torture" category that international law creates. From there, political leaders can distance themselves and their governments from the aberrational conduct of rogue officials or justify their conduct based on whatever emergency happens to exist.

Conclusion

This chapter has detailed the ways in which international law attempts to create an international right to be free from torture and related abuse. These prohibitions overlap sufficiently enough that few instances exist in which a state can plausibly claim to be outside the coverage of customary international law, international humanitarian law, or international human rights law. Read together, these sources of law constitute an overlapping and encompassing protection against the wide array of violence, cruelty, and deliberate neglect deployed by modern states.

Despite this broad coverage, important exclusions and ambiguities remain. Chief among them is the frequent failure to define key terms. Refusal to cabin protections within explicit definitions leaves room for broad interpretations, but it also creates space for states to advance restrictive interpretations and reject the expansive decisions of international entities as nonbinding, activist, and illegitimate. Also significant is the distinction between torture and other cruel, inhuman, or degrading treatment, which achieves fundamental importance in the Convention against Torture. The vagueness of international human rights and humanitarian law can only be settled (and possibly unsettled) through ongoing interpretation rather than through textual analysis. Those interpretations inevitably will come from political actors as much as or more than from judicial actors, in domestic as well as international arenas.

From all of this, international law skeptics might describe the regime of international human rights—including the prohibition on torture—as a shell game, in which statements, membership in international bodies, and signing of international agreements helps states to divert attention away from their more or less hidden practices of abuse. This description, while telling, ultimately misses the mark. International human rights are part of the structure and discourse of international and domestic law that shapes the ways in which states exercise power and in which people are defined as citizens. In this context, international human rights are not impotent. Because modern citizenship is partly defined in terms of rights, international human rights represent one way in which people obtain a form of international and domestic citizenship.

Perhaps for that reason, human rights also function as a canary in a coal mine. Their presence indicates the accumulation of governmental, bureaucratic, and institutional structures that are channeling and constraining human activity in new or more encompassing ways. Whenever rights create security and define spaces of freedom, they also ensure that people are tied more closely to the structures to which their rights are related and from which those rights derive—and in so doing, rights increase the scope and power of those structures. Even more, rights help to enable some forms of state violence, particularly against people who have no rights or whose rights consist precisely of a right to be controlled.

My discussion in chapter 4 will expand on this criticism of rights and rights discourse, but this analysis does not change the fact that liberal or human rights represent one of the foundational ways in which modern states organize the relationship between individuals and governments. Further, rights and the structures within which they reside have the potential to provide or support important benefits amid their flaws, such as making people more secure from certain forms of state violence and defining spaces in which they may exercise a variety of freedoms. Thus, even from a critical perspective, one could conclude that to the extent that rights are fundamental to modern politics, they should work for the benefit of individuals as often as possible.[105] The problem, in short, is not that rights are ineffectual but, rather, that they are effective in a multitude of ways, not all of them desirable in every context.

Legal reform is not my goal in this book. I seek instead to straddle the gap between conventional legal analysis, with its penchant for doctrinal and policy prescriptions, and the approaches of critical or cultural studies of law. Recognizing, however, that some readers will be interested in the prospects for reform and the development of reform proposals, I close this chapter with a few suggestions.

In light of the number of international agreements that already address torture, reformers should be cautious about adding another document. A new agreement could close some gaps, but it might increase ambiguity and complexity. Reformers should work instead to amend the Convention against Torture or create a protocol to it, for the purposes of erasing or minimizing the consequences that flow from the distinction between torture and cruel, inhuman, or degrading treatment, as well as making clear that the document applies to all the actions of a signatory state and its agents, inside or outside territorial borders and whether or not the state is engaged in an armed conflict. The effect would be a broader definition of torture and the elimination of tiers of conduct that create space for undesirable legal and political arguments. Perhaps, too, a protocol to the convention could include a nonexclusive list of conduct that constitutes torture—particularly "stealth" methods that leave no marks but cause mental or physical pain.

Reformers should also focus on institution building. One way to accomplish this goal is to use the ICC. Clear, well-reasoned ICC decisions in high-profile or otherwise appropriate cases that pick up where the ICTY leaves off would serve the same purpose as some of the reforms to the convention that I just suggested. Judicial action by international bodies is often controversial, however, and increased pressure on individual states to prosecute their own offenders, possibly combined with the risk of prosecution by other countries under theories of universal jurisdiction, may be more effective than increased use of international tribunals.

Perhaps, too, reformers might encourage the Committee against Torture to take a more proactive role in the interpretation of the convention. For example, the committee could issue additional general comments and take on the effort to explain the convention's interaction with the ICCPR, the Geneva Conventions, and other documents. None of this would eliminate ambiguity, but it would reduce the space in which ambiguity operates.

Whatever the course of legal reform, readers should not delude themselves that international legal activity will translate into less torture and other abuse. Law is not always the enemy of torture and state violence. Indeed, even as the United Nations encourages compliance with human rights norms, the U.N. Security Council has declared "the need to combat" terrorism "by all means" and has required states to expand their counterterrorism activities by criminalizing more conduct, enhancing domestic security and law enforcement agencies, and increasing efforts to monitor the movements of people across borders. Although these efforts come with exhortations to respect human rights and due process, they also underscore that the role of international law is not simply to protect individual rights but also to safeguard the necessity or emergency-based "inherent right of individual or collective self defense."[106]

Efforts to achieve greater "transparency" in government operations, including greater access to places of detention, as well as advocacy and intervention on behalf of victims or people at risk, are likely to be at least as effective as strictly legal approaches. The same is true of protests, refusals to participate in or condone state violence, efforts to publicize it, and collective action against its use. These actions carry personal risks, however. To the extent that serious changes in the international practice of torture require such risks, the prospects for changing the ways that people's bodies are treated by the agents of state power will remain uncertain. Reformers must also remember that the moment at which they appear to have achieved the goal of real change is likely also to be the moment at which they should be most vigilant against its erosion. They should not lose sight of the fact that their own vigilance almost certainly will mask new forms of coercion.

CHAPTER TWO

The European Law of Torture

I consider the European law of torture in this chapter in order to follow the analysis of international law in chapter 1 with a discussion of a multilateral body of human rights law that is arguably more influential and certainly more operational than the ICCPR or the Convention against Torture. In the course of describing doctrines that have developed in European case law, I hope also to continue showing the ways in which—despite its rhetoric of an absolute ban—law continues to accommodate and make room for state violence and abusive treatment. I leave issues involving the twentieth-century practices of specific European countries for chapter 5.

Every state in Europe is a party to the European Convention for the Protection of Human Rights and Fundamental Freedoms, known as the European Convention on Human Rights, of 1950. Among the "protections" provided by the convention is Article 3, which declares, "No one shall be subjected to torture or to inhuman or degrading treatment or punishment"—although the convention offers no definition of the terms *torture, inhuman,* or *degrading.* Article 5 buttresses these protections by adding, "Everyone has the right to liberty and security of person. No one shall be deprived of his liberty [except pursuant to a lawful arrest or detention]."[1]

The convention allows derogations "[i]n time of war or other public emergency threatening the life of the nation," but the power to derogate does not encompass Article 3. In other words, the ban on torture and inhuman or degrading treatment—and the interpretation of that ban as applying to extradition and deportation cases—is absolute and nonderogable. The convention also requires member states to provide effective remedies for violations of its provisions, and it created the European Commission of Human Rights and the European Court of Human Rights to buttress this remedial structure. In 1998, the commission was abolished, and individuals can now bring claims directly to the court. Decisions of the court are not binding in the sense that, for example, countries must release people from jail in compliance with its judgments, but the court does have the power to award monetary compensation.[2]

The Council of Europe has also adopted the European Convention for the Prevention of Torture and Inhuman or Degrading Treatment or Punishment, which every European state has signed. This convention strengthens enforcement of Article 3 of the European Convention on Human Rights by creating the Committee for the Prevention of Torture and Inhuman or Degrading Treatment or Punishment. The committee has the authority to conduct "visits ... to any place within its jurisdiction where persons are deprived of their liberty by a public authority." The committee produces reports of its visits, which are designed to publicize instances of ill-treatment and thereby aid those suffering from abuse and also deter future harm, but the Convention for the Prevention of Torture does not create substantive, enforceable individual rights.[3]

The General Jurisprudence of the European Court of Human Rights

∽

The European Convention on Human Rights is a treaty, not a constitution, but the existence of enforcement mechanisms, including the Court of Human Rights, gives it a meaningful presence in the law of European countries. More pointedly, there is a general sense among commentators that the convention "articulates ... an 'abstract constitutional identity' prescribing limits, in terms of human rights, to the exercise of public power in European liberal democracies committed to the rule of law," which suggests that the convention's status is constitutive, even if not formally constitutional.[4]

The Court of Human Rights seems to share that view, despite its insistence on being "sensitive to the subsidiary nature of its role and ... cautious in taking on the role of a first-instance tribunal of fact." It also emphasizes that "the machinery of protection established by the Convention" requires "the national systems themselves [to] provide redress for breaches of its provisions," with the court taking a "supervisory role subject to the principle of subsidiarity." Nonetheless, the court has no difficulty characterizing its judgments in terms of foundational law for a post–World War II democratic Europe. In the Article 3 context, for example, the court has insisted that the ban on torture and inhuman or degrading treatment "enshrines one of the most fundamental values of a democratic society."[5]

The constitutive aspect of the court's role creates tension with the goal of ensuring basic human rights for people living in Europe. Some of this tension derives from problems of scale. With fewer than 50 judges, the court faces more than 20,000 new cases every year and is able to render judgments in only a small fraction: "[O]ver 90 per cent of individuals who feel they suffer a violation of their human rights and complain at Strasbourg are turned away."[6] To the extent that the court holds out—or is perceived as holding out—the promise of individual relief from state violence and other human rights violations, in other words, it falls short. In response to this problem, the former president of the court, Luzius Wildhaber, argued that the convention's discretionary scheme of "just satisfaction" "hardly supports the individual relief theory" of the court's role. He maintained that "the place of individual relief . . . is secondary to the primary aim of raising the general standard of human rights jurisprudence throughout the community of Convention States."[7]

Yet the goal of "raising the general standard of human rights jurisprudence" coexists with doctrines that hamper the development of standards that would realize the frequently broad statements of the convention. Textually, for example, some provisions have "accommodation clauses" that temper its impact. The convention allows states to derogate from many of its provisions, and in general, the court does not second-guess derogation decisions, because national authorities are better placed to make such judgments.[8]

In addition, the court has developed a "margin of appreciation" doctrine. According to Wildhaber, this doctrine embraces "an element of deference to decisions taken by democratic institutions." Wildhaber explains,

> [The court's role] is to exercise an international supervision in specific cases to ensure that the solutions found do not impose an excessive or intolerable burden on one sector of society or another. . . . The balancing exercise between such competing interests is most appropriately carried out by the national authorities. . . . The margin of appreciation recognizes that where appropriate procedures are in place a range of solutions compatible with human rights may be available to the national authorities. The Convention does not purport to impose uniform approaches to the myriad different interests which arise in the broad field of fundamental rights protection; it seeks to establish common minimum standards to provide a Europe-wide framework for domestic human rights protections.[9]

Seen in this way, the margin of appreciation emerges not simply as a doctrine of deference to reasonable legislative actions but, more important, as a central aspect of the court's mission and jurisprudence.

Even where the margin of appreciation does not play a specific role or where no derogation is allowed—such as with Article 3's prohibition on torture or inhuman or degrading treatment—the court's jurisprudence retains flexibility. As the court stated recently in an Article 3 case, "inherent in the whole of the Convention is a search for a fair balance between the demands of the general interest of the community and the requirements of the protection of the individual's fundamental rights."[10] Steven Greer explains that "while the principles in question are unqualified, and apparently absolute, the rights they suggest need not be because 'torture,' 'slavery' etc., may be defined in ways which exclude certain conduct in certain circumstances." Indeed, he suggests, "it is not uncommon . . . to find assertions in the Strasbourg case law that the rights in question are 'absolute,' followed in the next sentence or paragraph, by claims that subjective factors and the wider public interest may also have to be considered."[11]

I do not mean to deny that the court's decisions in specific areas have often been expansive in favor of individual rights. The court treats the convention as a "living document," and some of its doctrines protect unenumerated rights that are closely related to specific textual rights. For example, the court has imposed "the duty on states to undertake specific affirmative tasks" to ensure that the convention is effective or to safeguard specific rights, including Article 3 rights.[12] Still, the overall picture is mixed. Marie-Bénédicte Dembour suggests the following conclusions about the court's jurisprudence:

> [F]irst, state interests play a major role in the development of human rights law, though the Court can also come down hard on the state; second, the Court endlessly engages in trade-offs and compromise, gauging the potential consequences of its position even while creating the impression that human rights prevail over all other considerations; third, a privileged applicant has far greater chances to be heard by the Court than an underprivileged one, though even the latter can be heard; fourth, the prima facie objective of establishing common standards while acknowledging the need to respect social diversity, means that the Court cannot but pursue a controversial path; fifth, the Convention system remains biased towards men in many respects even if it is, on the face of it, gender-neutral and open to women.[13]

Placed in the context of national courts in Europe and elsewhere, these conclusions are hardly surprising. To the extent that the court aspires to something more, however—to the nurturing and expansion, for example, of "shared European values" and of a constitutional identity based on democracy, rights, and the rule of law[14]—Dembour's conclusions provide an important counterperspective.

Interpreting Article 3 of the European Convention on Human Rights

∾

The European Commission of Human Rights and now the European Court of Human Rights have interpreted Article 3 to outlaw three kinds of mistreatment, of increasing seriousness based primarily on the severity of the conduct and the intensity of the resulting pain or suffering: degrading treatment, inhuman treatment, and torture. The lines among these categories are not easy to draw, however. In the 1969 Greek Case, the commission explained that degrading treatment is conduct that "grossly humiliates [a person] before others or drives him to act against his will or conscience." Inhuman treatment is conduct that "deliberately causes severe suffering, mental or physical, which, in the particular situation, is unjustifiable." Finally, torture consists of "inhuman treatment, which has a purpose, such as the obtaining of information of confessions, or the infliction of punishment, and it is generally an aggravated form of inhuman treatment."[15]

Based on that taxonomy, the commission determined that "slaps and blows of the hand on the head or face" inflicted by police were neither inhuman nor degrading within the meaning of the Convention on Human Rights, but it also found that "severe beatings" with a stick or bar that leave no permanent marks and break no bones are "a method of torture known for centuries."[16] In other cases, the commission ruled that beatings and one or more of the methods of electric shock, mock execution, or refusal of food or water were either torture or cruel, inhuman, and degrading treatment, but because both are barred under the convention, it did not have to make a more precise finding.[17]

Regardless of these distinctions, the court requires applicants to prove their Article 3 claims beyond a reasonable doubt, even as it has made clear that "[w]here a person, when taken into custody, is in good health, but is found to be injured at the time of release . . . , it is incumbent on the State to provide a plausible explanation how these injuries were caused."[18] The court has also expanded the obligations of states under Article 3. Thus, states must "take measures designed to ensure that individuals within their jurisdiction are not subjected to torture or inhuman or degrading treatment or punishment, including such ill-treatment administered by private individuals."[19]

Further, the court has limited the authority to extradite or deport a person to another country. In *Soering v. United Kingdom*, the court explained,

> It would hardly be compatible with the underlying values of the Convention . . . were a Contracting State knowingly to surrender a fugitive to another State where there were substantial grounds for believing that he would be in danger of being subjected to torture, however heinous the crime allegedly committed. Extradition in such circumstances, while not explicitly referred to in the brief and general wording of Article 3 (art. 3), would plainly be contrary to the spirit and intendment of the Article, and in the Court's view this inherent obligation not to extradite also extends to cases in which the fugitive would be faced in the receiving State by a

real risk of exposure to inhuman or degrading treatment or punishment proscribed by that Article.

Since *Soering*, the court has faced a steady stream of cases in which applicants claim there are substantial grounds for believing that they face a real risk of torture or inhuman or degrading treatment in the country to which they will be sent.[20]

The court also indicated in *Soering* that deciding what conduct is inhuman or degrading might turn in part on a balancing test, at least in the context of extradition.

> What amounts to "inhuman or degrading treatment or punishment" depends on all the circumstances of the case. . . . Furthermore, inherent in the whole of the Convention is a search for a fair balance between the demands of the general interest of the community and the requirements of the protection of the individual's fundamental rights. As movement about the world becomes easier and crime takes on a larger international dimension, it is increasingly in the interest of all nations that suspected offenders who flee abroad should be brought to justice. Conversely, the establishment of safe havens for fugitives would not only result in danger for the State obliged to harbour the protected person but also tend to undermine the foundations of extradition. These considerations must also be included among the factors to be taken into account in the interpretation and application of the notions of inhuman and degrading treatment or punishment in extradition cases.

More recently, the court seems to have rejected the idea that inhuman treatment can be justified "in [a] particular situation."[21] Similarly, it declared in *Selmouni v. France* that "in respect of a person deprived of his liberty, recourse to physical force which has not been made strictly necessary by his own conduct diminishes human dignity and is in principle an infringement of the right set forth in Article 3." The court repeated that statement in the context of "the fight against terrorist crime" and stressed that "the nature of the alleged offense" does not dilute Article 3's protections.[22]

At the same time, however, the court continues to employ flexible approaches on the edges of Article 3. In recent cases, it has stressed that applicants who claim a violation of Article 3 must satisfy a "high threshold" of proof. Further, the court's assessment of whether the claimed ill-treatment violates Article 3 "is relative; it depends on all the circumstances of the case, such as the duration of the treatment, its physical and mental effects and, in some cases, the sex, age and state of health of the victim."[23] That is to say, Article 3 jurisprudence depends on a shifting mix of subjective and objective factors that allow careful and tailored decisions—but which also give the court flexibility to manipulate an always ambiguous doctrine.

This dynamic plays out in other Article 3 cases. In a recent deportation case, for example, the court repeated its description of the Convention on Human Rights as a balance of community interests and individual rights. With respect to force-feeding prisoners on hunger strikes, the court balances Article 3 rights against the state's Article 2 obligation to protect life. The result is that force-feeding someone who is at risk of death—the court speaks of "medical necessity"—does not violate Article 3, but force-feeding in other circumstances will violate Article 3 and will sometimes amount to torture. Finally, the court has distinguished between evidence produced as a "direct" result of ill-treatment in violation of Article 3 (e.g., drugs regurgitated as the result of an emetic) and "indirect" evidence (e.g., items obtained because the suspect disclosed their existence and location under coercive interrogation). Use of evidence in the former category makes a proceeding automatically unfair in violation of the convention, while a proceeding tainted by the use of evidence in the latter category will receive a more open-ended review that may include balancing.[24]

Returning to the core of Article 3, the distinction between torture and inhuman conduct has been particularly significant in the case law, despite the fact that both are barred and despite the court's general reluctance to draw firm lines between them. In *Ireland v. United Kingdom*—which I discuss in greater detail in chapter 5—the court held that the "five techniques" of wall-standing for hours, hooding, continuous loud and hissing noise, sleep deprivation, and restricted food and water were inhuman and degrading but did not rise to the level of torture. Roughly following the commission's approach in the Greek Case, the court explained that torture is an "aggravated" form of inhuman treatment that carries "a special stigma" and that it should be reserved for labeling practices that exhibit a "particular intensity and cruelty."[25]

The court adhered to that view in *Aksoy v. Turkey,* the first case in which it actually made a finding of torture. According to *Aksoy,* "torture" is "deliberate inhuman treatment causing very serious and cruel suffering." More recent cases continue to stress the distinctiveness of torture compared to inhuman or degrading treatment. The court has even suggested that several incidents that may not alone amount to torture could be torture when considered together.[26]

The court repeated the *Aksoy* definition in *Selmouni* but also quoted the definition in the U.N. Convention against Torture and asked whether the conduct could "be defined as 'severe' within the meaning of Article 1 of the United Nations Convention." Other recent cases forge links between the U.N. and European conventions—often by reference to "the purposive element" in the Convention against Torture—which suggests that the court may be seeking to resolve definitional questions by reference to the comparatively more precise terms of the U.N. convention.[27] For some of the reasons discussed in chapter 1, including the lesser status of cruel, inhuman, and degrading treatment under the U.N. convention, that task might prove to be difficult and ultimately frustrating.

In *Selmouni*, the court also declared its willingness to revisit earlier findings about the proper categorization of specific forms of conduct, based on "the increasingly high standard being required in the area of the protection of human rights and fundamental liberties." The British House of Lords recently cited and endorsed this view as well.[28] The holdings of the Greek Case and *Ireland v. United Kingdom*, in other words, may no longer be good precedents with respect to specific forms of conduct.

The Elusive State Amid the Persistence of Torture

∾

The Court of Human Rights has developed its doctrines on torture and other abuse through a steady docket of cases brought by individuals claiming that officials of European governments have subjected them to various forms of mistreatment. The allegations in these cases are often far from frivolous and are sometimes not very different from accounts of the conduct of U.S. forces at Abu Ghraib and other places. In *Selmouni*, for example, the court found that "a large number of blows were inflicted on Mr Selmouni" and also

> that [he] was dragged along by his hair; that he was made to run along a corridor with police officers positioned on either side to trip him up; that he was made to kneel down in front of a young woman to whom someone said "Look, you're going to hear somebody sing"; that one police officer then showed him his penis, saying "Here, suck this," before urinating over him; and that he was threatened with a blowlamp and then a syringe.

Selmouni was not suspected of terrorism; instead, he was arrested as part of an investigation into drug trafficking, which is a fairly routine subject of police work in Europe and the United States. More recently, the applicant in *Mikheyev v. Russia* was a police officer suspected in the disappearance of a teenage girl who later turned out not to have disappeared at all. He was handcuffed and electrocuted, slapped, and threatened with rape and more electrocution, leading him to a suicide attempt that caused permanent disability. The court found that this treatment "amounted to torture."[29]

Not only do cases like *Selmouni* and *Mikheyev* present serious allegations of abuse, but these allegations are not isolated. As Fionnuala Ní Aoláin observed in her overview of the jurisprudence of the Court of Human Rights on torture, "torture and other forms of degrading treatment are by and large not sporadic occurrences within institutional settings; rather they are evidence of systemic problems indicating widespread resort to such measures by officials of the state." Ní Aoláin further highlighted the court's reluctance to conclude that systematic violations of the European Convention on Human Rights, which bans torture and other inhuman or degrading treatment within a state, are attributable to the state itself: "The Court has played a game with states, treating each violation as if it were the sole violation ever to appear before it, even if the same state is appearing before it again and again in respect of the same types of violation." Ní Aoláin argued, for example, that *Akkoç v. Turkey,* where the applicant relied on "other cases concerning events in south-east Turkey in which . . . the Court had also found breaches" of Articles 2, 3, and 13, "revealed a pattern of denial by the authorities of allegations of serious human rights violations as well as a denial of remedies." The court responded tersely that it did "not find it necessary to determine whether the failings identified in this case are part of a practice adopted by the authorities."[30]

Ní Aoláin suggested that the reason for the court's reluctance to make systematic findings is not just a concern about political repercussions. Equally important is the sense that finding torture or inhumane treatment to be an "administrative practice" in a particular country would "undermine a central feature of the European self-definition of its rights identity," particularly when the country under review is seen as wholly democratic and not as flawed in some way. The court's recognition of state sovereign immunity against torture claims in civil cases underscores that conclusion.[31]

Any finding that a European state had a policy of abusing prisoners would fly in the face of what it means to be European. By definition, Europe is a part of the world that has moved beyond torture. Torture in Europe is always an aberration, no matter how systematic it may be. Systematic state torture in Europe is therefore hidden, in the sense that the Court of Human Rights does not acknowledge it even when it hands out remedies in individual cases. Of course, this careful approach, directed toward nudging countries into compliance with the Convention on Human Rights through decisions in individual cases, risks undermining the court's self-described role of guiding the constitutional development of Europe, because the results in each case confirm at a rhetorical level that the defendant state already meets the requisite standards in the aggregate, even if it sometimes falls short in individual cases.

The idea that torture is aberrational in modern civilized societies also follows from the choice of language used to describe specific forms of torture, as in the Greek Case, where the method of beating was said to be "known for centuries." One of the key tropes of Said's *Orientalism* is the idea that civilized, Western societies exist in time, while the Orient is traditional and thus timeless, unchanging, and often cruel. Civilization also depends on reason, while traditional societies trade in a different form of knowledge, often based in superstition, which too easily licenses brutality.[32] Torture is thus a threat to civilization because it threatens to push countries out of history, back into the timelessness of violent tradition. As will become clear in my discussions of extraordinary rendition and "black sites" in later chapters, the timelessness produced by torture is also part of the harm inflicted on the victim, who is taken out of legally cognizable space and placed in limbo, stripped of distinguishing features and abstracted in a perverse inversion of liberal citizenship, and left in the condition that Giorgio Agamben calls the *homo sacer* and that the CIA, with perhaps greater incisiveness, labels a "ghost."[33]

Conclusion

∾

This chapter has sketched the ways in which European law provides protections against torture and related conduct. Unlike the international law sources I discussed in chapter 1—which have uncertain avenues of enforcement—these protections are directly enforceable in cases brought by individual claimants. This steadily growing body of cases considers the nuances and problems that result from the effort to apply to the conduct of governments that are routinely violent an absolute ban on torture and cruel, inhuman, or degrading treatment. Further, the regular publication of the opinions of the Court of Human Rights reveals the violent conduct of state actors and thus furthers the goal of transparency that is commonly considered central to democracy and open societies.

At the same time, the existence of balancing tests and the steady stream of cases in which the court deliberately avoids finding systematic violations raise the possibility that the European Convention for the Protection of Human Rights operates most powerfully at a rhetorical level. With an absolute ban on torture and other forms of cruel conduct, a persistent conclusion that no European country practices this conduct in a systematic way, and a result that nearly all torture is by definition aberrational, the convention and its case law articulate standards of national and regional identity and lay claim to an ideal of (European) civilization as moral leadership, however tarnished that ideal may have become.

In the process, these legal documents also define and legitimize the institutional structures of the "new" Europe. The convention and cases certainly exhibit concern for the treatment and rights of individuals. The structure of the jurisprudence of the Court of Human Rights, however, indicates that these rights are important at least in part because they reinforce the regulatory power of an expanding set of local, national, and regional governments, as well as a larger framework of international structures. In other words, the individual right not to be tortured is as much an assertion about the nature of European citizenship as it is a legal claim.[34] Any consideration of torture in Europe—and of a related right not to be tortured—must take that dynamic into account.

CHAPTER THREE

Torture and State Violence in U.S. Law

U.S. Ratification of the Convention against
Torture and the ICCPR

The U.N. General Assembly adopted the International Covenant on Civil and Political Rights in 1966, and the United States signed it in 1977. When the Carter administration sent the ICCPR to the Senate in early 1978 for its advice and consent, it recommended a number of reservations, understandings, and declarations (RUDs) "designed to harmonize the treaties with existing provisions of domestic law." One of the most important was a declaration "that the treaties are not self-executing." Warren Christopher, U.S. deputy secretary of state, explained that without such a declaration, "the terms of the Convention might be considered as directly enforceable law on a par with Congressional statutes."[1]

In 1979, the Senate Foreign Relations Committee held hearings at which officials from the Justice Department and the State Department testified that the ICCPR would have no impact on domestic constitutional or statutory law. They also supported the declaration that the treaties would not be self-executing, in order to avoid "additional litigation in our own courts."[2] The Senate took no further action because the invasion of Afghanistan by the Soviet Union and the hostage crisis in Iran undermined the possibility of broad support.[3] A decade later, with the ICCPR still not ratified, the Senate took up the Convention against Torture.

President Reagan sent the Convention against Torture to the Senate in 1988. An accompanying memorandum analyzed the document and proposed several RUDs to address what it viewed as the convention's shortcomings. The idea that "torture" is a narrow category dominated the analysis. Thus, the memorandum contended that the convention "seeks to define 'torture' in a relatively limited fashion," such that "torture is at the extreme end of cruel, inhuman and degrading treatment or punishment" and "is usually reserved for extreme, deliberate and unusually cruel practices, for example, sustained systematic beating, application of electric currents to sensitive parts of the body, and tying up or hanging in positions that cause extreme pain." The administration also suggested that because mental pain and suffering is "a relatively more subjective phenomenon than physical suffering," application of the term *torture* should rely on "more objective criteria such as the degree of cruelty or inhumanity of the conduct causing the pain and suffering."[4] In keeping with this analysis, the administration proposed the following understanding: "in order to constitute torture, an act must be a deliberate and calculated act of an extremely cruel and inhuman nature, specifically intended to inflict excruciating and agonizing physical or mental pain or suffering."[5]

Even as it sought to confine the definition of torture, the administration also highlighted Article 2's "no exceptional circumstances" clause as "necessary if the Convention is to have significant effect, as public emergencies are commonly invoked as a source of extraordinary powers or as a justification for limiting fundamental rights and freedoms." Having made that point, however, the administration proposed an understanding that "relevant common law defenses, including but not limited to self-defense and defense of others," would remain available, under the rationale that such acts are simply outside the scope of torture because "specific intent to cause excruciating and agonizing pain and suffering" is lacking. Left unclear was whether this understanding would have made room for other common-law defenses—such as necessity—that might have been in greater tension with the nonderogable ban on torture.[6]

With respect to the regulation of cruel, inhuman, and degrading treatment (CIDT) in Article 16, the administration observed that the Convention against Torture "embodies an undertaking to take measures to prevent CIDT rather than a prohibition of CIDT." Even so, the administration expressed concern that "Article 16 is arguably broader than existing U.S. law." The administration proposed an understanding that "the term 'cruel, inhuman or degrading treatment or punishment' means the cruel, unusual, and inhumane treatment or punishment prohibited by the Fifth, Eighth, and/or Fourteenth Amendments to the Constitution of the United States."[7] Finally, the administration proposed an understanding to the convention's prohibition against extraditing a person to a country "where substantial grounds exist for believing that he would be in danger of being subjected to torture." The goal of the understanding was to conform the convention to existing U.S. immigration law, which prevents a person from being deported to a country where it is more likely than not that he or she would be persecuted. Accordingly, the proposed understanding declared that "substantial grounds" would exist only "if it is more likely than not that [the person] would be tortured."[8]

By the time the Senate Foreign Relations Committee took up the convention, President Reagan had left office, and the new Bush administration negotiated with the Senate over the proposed RUDs. The understanding on common-law defenses fell by the wayside—according to the administration, it "was widely misunderstood"[9]—and the administration also dropped the understanding that torture is limited to "extremely cruel and inhuman" acts that are "specifically intended to inflict excruciating and agonizing physical or mental pain." Yet even as they backed away from adjectives such as *excruciating* and *agonizing,* officials maintained that torture is limited to "barbaric cruelty," to "conduct the mere mention of which sends chills down one's spine: the needle under the fingernail, the application of electric shock to the genital area, the piercing of eyeballs, etc."[10]

For the Bush administration, the "greatest problem" with the convention was the concept of mental harm. A Justice Department official argued that mental suffering "is often transitory, causing no lasting harm." He suggested that the convention's approach was too vague.[11] To address these concerns, the administration proposed a new understanding that would narrow the kinds of mental suffering that counted as torture.

[M]ental pain or suffering refers to prolonged mental harm caused by or resulting from (1) the intentional infliction or threatened infliction of severe physical pain or suffering; (2) the administration or application or threatened administration or application, of mind altering substances or other procedures calculated to disrupt profoundly the senses or the personality; (3) the threat of imminent death; or (4) the threat that another person will imminently be subjected to death, severe physical pain or suffering, or the administration or application of mind altering substances or other procedures calculated to disrupt profoundly the senses or personality.

The point of this understanding was to shift the focus from "subjective" suffering to objective conduct and, in particular, to conduct "calculated to generate severe and prolonged mental suffering of the type which can properly be viewed as rising to the level of torture." Officials stressed that the understanding required "intentional acts . . . designed to damage and destroy the human personality," as opposed to "the normal legal compulsions which are properly a part of the criminal justice system—interrogation, incarceration, prosecution, compelled testimony against a friend, etc.—notwithstanding the fact that they may have the incidental effect of producing mental strain."[12]

The Reagan and Bush administrations sought to construct a sharp dichotomy between horrific acts that amount to torture and other forms of conduct. Torture would encompass only conduct that everyone assumed was already illegal and almost never practiced in the United States. In the process, more debatable categories of conduct would be relegated to the lesser category of cruel, inhuman, or degrading treatment, even as both administrations sought also to limit the scope of this category, which they viewed as ambiguous. Their efforts sought to raise the bar for establishing that either torture or cruel, inhuman, and degrading treatment had taken place, making sure that some of the conduct that arguably fell within the convention would now fall outside, at least under the understanding that the United States had of its obligations.

Several months after the hearing, the Foreign Relations Committee recommended that the full Senate give its advice and consent to ratification of the convention and the several RUDs negotiated among the administration, various senators, and other parties. Once again, the narrowness of the definition of the term *torture* was an important theme. Thus, the committee report declared, "For an act to be 'torture,' it must be an extreme form of cruel and inhuman treatment, cause severe pain and suffering, and be intended to cause severe pain and suffering."[13] On October 27, 1990, after a short debate, the full Senate gave its consent, with minor amendments.[14]

The final package of RUDs included the declaration that the convention is "not self-executing," so that it does not create any legal causes of action in the United States for individual claimants and may not create any domestic legal rights at all without congressional implementation.[15] The Senate also narrowed the convention's definition of torture. First, it adopted the understanding that "to constitute torture, an act must be specifically intended to inflict severe physical or mental pain or suffering." Although the meaning of this understanding is not completely clear, the Senate apparently meant the phrase "specifically intended" to describe an action taken with a mental state or level of intention more precise than simple knowledge that a particular act would cause severe pain. To be torture, an action would have to be taken with the express purpose of causing pain, which would insulate state violence accompanied by lesser levels of intention.[16] Second, the Senate adopted the proposed understanding on the definition of mental harm.[17] As I suggested already, this understanding provides that only four categories of conduct can result in mental suffering that is serious enough to constitute torture. No other practice, however severe the harm it causes, will qualify. These two definitional changes created more room for coercive practices by freeing state actors from concern about international law, perhaps especially during operations outside U.S. territory.

The Senate also agreed to the reservation—originally proposed as an understanding by the Reagan administration—that defined "cruel, inhuman or degrading treatment or punishment" as identical to conduct prohibited by the Fifth, Eighth, and Fourteenth Amendments of the U.S. Constitution.[18] In other words, "cruel, inhuman or degrading conduct" is unconstitutional conduct, and it follows that torture is unconstitutional as well. Significantly, the second Bush administration would later argue that this reservation limited the reach of Article 16 to actions in U.S. territory—as opposed to any territory under U.S. jurisdiction. Yet nothing in the hearings, report, or debate indicates any effort to achieve that result, and one official from the first Bush administration has explicitly denied any intent to do so.[19]

After the Senate agreed to the convention, the Bush administration asked it to reconsider the ICCPR. The administration proposed a revised group of RUDs. It explained that "a few provisions of the Covenant articulate legal rules which differ from U.S. law and which, upon careful consideration, the Administration declines to accept in preference to existing law." It also stated that "implementing legislation is not contemplated," because "existing U.S. law generally complies with the Covenant." The reservations—which "are in many respects, similar to those proposed by the Carter Administration"—declared that the ICCPR is not self-executing and that the ban in Article 7 on cruel, inhuman, or degrading treatment or punishment "means the cruel and unusual treatment or punishment prohibited by the Fifth, Eighth and/or Fourteenth Amendments to the Constitution of the United States." The primary reason for the reservation on Article 7 was to make "clear in the record that we interpret our obligations under . . . the Covenant consistently with those we have undertaken in the Torture Convention." The administration also noted that the reservation would ensure that decisions of the European Court of Human Rights and the U.N.'s Human Rights Committee would not apply domestically.[20]

The Foreign Relations Committee unanimously recommended adoption of the ICCPR as modified by the Bush administration. The committee's only independent statement was to stress that any changes in U.S. law should occur "through the normal legislative process." On April 2, 1992, the full Senate agreed, with no debate.[21] As with the Convention against Torture, nothing in the hearings or reports suggests that anyone in the administration or Senate raised questions about the phrase "within its territory and subject to its jurisdiction" in Article 2 of the ICCPR. As I explained in chapter 1, that phrase has become controversial because of its import for the extraterritorial obligations, if any, that the ICCPR imposes on signatories.

Congress subsequently enacted three statutes to implement the convention. First, the Torture Victim Protection Act (TVPA) provides a civil cause of action in the United States against people who torture under the auspices of a foreign government. Second, Section 2340 of Title 18 of the U.S. Code criminalizes torture committed outside the United States by U.S. nationals or persons later found in the United States.[22] Third, the Foreign Affairs Reform and Restructuring Act (FARRA) states,

> It shall be the policy of the United States not to expel, extradite, or otherwise effect the involuntary return of any person to a country in which there are substantial grounds for believing the person would be in danger of being subjected to torture, regardless of whether the person is physically present in the United States.[23]

All three statutes define the term *mental suffering* in ways that are essentially identical to the Senate's understanding of that term during the ratification process, rather than the more expansive views that the text of the convention or the ICCPR would support.[24] The statutes do not mention or provide any remedy for the infliction of cruel, inhuman, or degrading treatment or punishment. The distinction between that category and torture is therefore critical to the availability of criminal penalties under Section 2340, damages under the TVPA, and relief from extradition or removal under FARRA.

An additional statute, the Alien Tort Statute, gives federal courts jurisdiction over "any civil action by an alien for a tort only, committed in violation of the law of nations or a treaty of the United States." The statute has little force for treaties, because most of the ones that would be relevant—for example, the convention and ICCPR—have been declared not self-executing. But plaintiffs can bring claims under customary international law, as long as the rule under customary international law is clearly and definitely established.[25] Many claims under the statute involve torture, and U.S. courts have looked to the convention for a definition of torture.[26] Still unclear is the extent to which plaintiffs can bring claims based on cruel, inhuman, or degrading treatment that falls short of torture, because it is not clear whether the prohibition on such treatment is sufficiently clear and established.[27] It also remains to be seen whether or to what extent those cases will serve as the basis for analyzing torture claims against U.S. officials.[28]

In sum, both the Convention against Torture and the ICCPR were ratified with the declaration that they are not self-executing and with the reservation that they go no further than preexisting constitutional rights.[29] One could therefore conclude that both the act of advice and consent and the act of ratification were purely rhetorical. Both documents are "the supreme law of the land" under the supremacy clause of the Constitution, yet as ratified, they can hardly be called law if they have little or no legal effect.[30] Further, to the extent that they are law, they are defined as redundant—as a kind of nonlaw or at least as needless law.[31] Although the statutes give greater force to the prohibitions, they apply primarily to conduct that takes place outside the United States, which underscores the limited power of international human rights law in the U.S. legal system.

The Constitutional Law of Torture and State Violence

∾

The ratification by the United States of the Convention against Torture and the ICCPR with an understanding that cruel, inhuman, or degrading treatment is the equivalent of unconstitutional conduct raises the question of exactly what the constitutional prohibitions are on such conduct. The answer is, perhaps surprisingly, quite ambiguous. That ambiguity becomes even more significant in the context of the more general constitutional authority of the federal and state governments to use violence or coercion to enforce the law. At that point, it becomes difficult to deny the idea that rights function both to empower the state as much as to constrain it and to define citizens as much as to liberate them.[32]

Official Discretion

No federal statute spells out the specific powers of federal law enforcement officials and the limits on those powers, and the Supreme Court has not interpreted the Constitution to require such a statute.[33] As a result, the authority of these officials derives in large part from ideas about the nature of executive authority, common law, and constitutional restrictions on investigative techniques.[34] Thus, unless the Constitution prohibits a particular practice, law enforcement officials have broad discretion to investigate crimes, including the powers to search, seize, and interrogate people. Many state and local governments have adopted detailed procedures for arrests, use of force, and other practices, but these procedures still leave considerable room for discretion, and the Constitution has relatively little to say about its scope.

The Constitution may also make room for emergency powers that go beyond ordinary discretion. In *In re Debs*, for example, the Supreme Court ruled that the executive branch had authority to seek an injunction against a boycott linked to the 1894 Pullman strike and that the federal courts had the authority to grant the injunction, even though no federal statute had been violated or provided authority to seek or grant injunctions for such conduct. The Court reasoned that the Constitution gives Congress control over interstate commerce and the transportation of mail and that Congress had exercised its power by legislating in those areas. The Court explained, "The entire strength of the nation may be used to enforce in any part of the land the full and free exercise of all national powers and the security of all rights entrusted by the Constitution to its care. . . . If the emergency arises, the arms of the Nation, and all its militia, are at the service of the Nation to compel obedience to its laws." Indeed, the Court suggested that Debs was lucky only to have been enjoined and held in contempt rather than maimed or killed, because the government had the discretion to choose between "the club of the policeman and the bayonet of the soldier" and "the peaceful determination of judicial tribunals."[35]

The idea that the executive branch has inherent power to use violence to impose order has been qualified by more recent decisions, such as *Youngstown Sheet & Tube Co. v. Sawyer* and *Hamdan v. Rumsfeld*. Both cases stress the role of Congress, and *Hamdan* does so with particular reference to the executive branch's power to use violence against individuals.[36] Still, *Debs* has never been overruled, and it remains true that once the government obtains a judgment, state violence is available to enforce it. Moreover, the debate over the existence and extent of emergency powers in a liberal constitutional order persists in contemporary constitutional law and theory.[37]

Discretion and Rights

In 1886, the Supreme Court proclaimed an "indefeasible right of personal security, personal liberty, and private property," such that the rights articulated in the Fourth and Fifth Amendments "run almost into each other" and "should be liberally construed."[38] Under this conception, constitutional rights must be clear rules so that they can protect individual privacy and liberty from possibly arbitrary government authority. Contemporary constitutional analysis proceeds from entirely different assumptions. As Sanford Levinson recently explained in the context of the First Amendment, the textual enumeration of a right, even one prefaced with the command that "Congress shall pass no law" abridging it, does not make the scope of that right clear: "The fact is that 'no law' does *not* mean 'no law'; rather, it means, in our contemporary world, that the state must demonstrate what we call a 'compelling state interest' in order to justify the transgression of the stipulated norm." In *Anderson v. Creighton,* Justice Scalia, writing for the Court, noted with equal candor that "regardless of the terminology used, the precise content of most of the Constitution's civil liberties guarantees rests upon an assessment of what accommodation between governmental need and individual freedom is reasonable."[39]

Thus, the law of criminal procedure has moved from "indefeasible" and "liberally construed" rights to a focus on "reasonableness." The Supreme Court declared in *Schmerber v. California,* for example, that the Fifth Amendment privilege against self-incrimination "has never been given the full scope which the values it helps to protect suggest" and that the "proper function" of the Fourth Amendment "is to constrain, not against all intrusions as such, but against intrusions which are not justified in the circumstances, or which are made in an improper manner." Under contemporary doctrine, therefore, the word *right* is often simply the term for a balance of policies and interests that favors the individual claimant rather than the government, and police discretion has emerged as a legitimate interest with the power to shape evolving doctrine.[40] To borrow from Hannah Arendt, doctrines of criminal procedure no longer "function as stabilizing factors for the ever changing movements of men." Instead, they have become "laws of movement." For Arendt, this distinction represents the difference between positive law and totalitarian law, such that the reliance on "laws of movement" threatens "the living space of freedom."[41]

The Supreme Court's decision in *Terry v. Ohio* highlights the centrality of discretion and reasonableness to U.S. constitutional doctrine. The Court held that the Fourth Amendment permits police who have reasonable suspicion that a person may be engaged in criminal behavior to detain that person briefly and, if there is reason to believe that person may be armed, also to frisk him or her for weapons. The majority opinion never asked whether a statute authorized this kind of conduct. Instead, it assumed that police officers may stop and frisk potentially dangerous people unless the Constitution limits the officers' authority. The Court began with the assertion that "[n]o right is more sacred . . . than the right of every individual to the possession and control of his own person, free from all restraint or interference of others, unless by clear and unquestionable authority of law." Yet the Court immediately reformulated the idea of "clear and unquestionable authority of law" into a more flexible right "to be free from unreasonable governmental intrusion."[42] *Terry* moves from a conception of rights as near absolutes and from a need for clear legal authority to restrain liberty, on the one hand, to a willingness to balance interests and to accept reasonable restraints, even if they are not specifically authorized, on the other. This move occurs so quickly that it almost slips past unnoticed. Yet it exemplifies the shift from one view of rights and liberties to another, from a popular conception of strong rights to a more "realistic" idea of what they mean in practice.[43]

Reasonable Rights-Bearers

In the process of interpreting constitutional rights, the Supreme Court has defined the proper behavior of the rights-bearing subject. In *Florida v. Bostick,* the Court rejected a defendant's claim that he did not voluntarily "consent" to have his luggage searched when police officers boarded a bus on which he was riding. The Court recognized that Bostick did not feel free to leave the bus during the stop, but this fact alone did not mean that he had been seized by the police—which would have made his interaction with the police nonconsensual as a matter of law. Rather, according to the Court, "the appropriate inquiry is whether a reasonable person would feel free to decline the officers' requests or otherwise terminate the encounter." When Bostick argued that his consent could not have been voluntary because no reasonable person in his situation—someone carrying cocaine in his luggage—would consent to a search, the Court responded that "the 'reasonable person' test presupposes an innocent person."[44]

In *United States v. Drayton*, a post–September 11 case involving a bus search, the Court expanded on the characteristics of the reasonable innocent person. The Court began by stressing the "cooperative" nature of the interaction between police and passengers; suggested that the officers' uniforms were "cause for assurance, not discomfort"; and insisted that "[t]he presence of a holstered firearm thus is unlikely to contribute to the coerciveness of the encounter absent active brandishing of the weapon." As a result, the Court asserted that "bus passengers answer officers' questions and otherwise cooperate not because of coercion but because the passengers know that their participation enhances their own safety and the safety of those around them."[45]

The last part of the opinion rejected Drayton's claim that he should have been informed of his right not to consent to a search, because the failure to do so is simply "one factor to be taken into account" when assessing the reasonableness of police conduct. The Court concluded with the following comments on citizenship, police conduct, and the rule of law:

> In a society based on law, the concept of agreement and consent should be given a weight and dignity of its own. Police officers act in full accord with the law when they ask citizens for consent. It reinforces the rule of law for the citizen to advise the police of his or her wishes and for the police to act on that understanding. When this exchange takes place, it dispels inferences of coercion.[46]

Combined with *Bostick*, this passage from *Drayton* appears to hold that the normal or desirable rights-holder is the reasonable innocent person.[47]

Drayton stands solidly in a line of criminal procedure cases that, in Margaret Raymond's words, "defines rules that place the responsibility to protect rights on the defendants themselves" and "applies those rules so that the loss of rights is understood as the product of defendant-centered decisions like consent, compliance, or voluntary cooperation rather than police conduct."[48] Yet even as, in effect, these cases blame defendants for the loss of their rights, *Drayton* also declares that the reasonable innocent person best asserts his or her rights, whether or not he or she knows what they are, by refusing to invoke them and instead cooperating with state authority. Indeed, *Drayton* asserts that people are likely to feel increasingly "assured" and "safe" during interactions with an armed and uniformed police officer, with the implication that cooperation and refusal to assert rights becomes more voluntary and more consistent with good citizenship in such circumstances, not less. *Drayton* and cases like it suggest, in short, that one of the important functions of rights in a modern state is to manage one's subjugation to state power, which supports, in turn, the rule of law.

Extraterritoriality

An important aspect of the way in which rights define the citizen-state relationship is the manner in which the Constitution applies to U.S. officials' conduct outside the territory of the United States. In the Insular Cases, for example, the Supreme Court held that inhabitants of territory under U.S. sovereignty but not "incorporated" into the United States may claim not the full panoply of constitutional rights but only those deemed "fundamental." Exactly what that means remains unclear, especially after, first, the Court's subsequent cases that identify numerous fundamental aspects of the Bill of Rights that apply to the states through the due process clause of the Fourteenth Amendment and, second, the more recent detention cases.[49]

U.S. citizens have rights against the actions of U.S. officials on territory that is not controlled by the United States, but there are fewer constitutional constraints on U.S. officials overseas when they act against people who are not citizens.[50] Noncitizens held at Guantánamo Bay Naval Base—which is in Cuban territory—have the right to petition for habeas corpus, but it is not clear if this right extends to noncitizens held in other places outside the United States.[51] The Supreme Court has held that the Constitution has little to say about the manner in which foreign nationals residing overseas end up in the United States to face criminal proceedings. In response to a defendant's claim that he had been kidnapped by U.S. agents, the Court declared that it "need not inquire as to how respondent came before it."[52]

Plainly, these geographic limits bear heavily on the Constitution's relation to a criminal process and military infrastructure that contemplates investigation, seizure, detention, interrogation, and possibly adjudication on a global scale. Note, too, the apparent centrality of the border or citizenship to the reach of constitutional constraints but not to the reach of federal power. To the extent that borders are critical, everything outside the United States is an exceptional space. The alien who has not formally made it into the country, the "ghost detainee" held at an undisclosed overseas "black site," the resident of another country in which U.S. forces operate—all these inhabit a space that is in many respects without law from the U.S. perspective but in which U.S. power remains present. Enforceable rights may not exist in most of the world from the perspective of U.S. law, which leaves only the bare life and state power that Giorgio Agamben highlights in *State of Exception.* Importantly, this space of no rights may be less a reassurance that rights exist somewhere else than it is a harbinger of what might be a more general condition.[53]

There is an important caveat to the extraterritoriality issue. The Supreme Court's holding in *Hamdan v. Rumsfeld* that Common Article 3 of the Geneva Conventions applies by statute to U.S. actions against al Qaeda suggests that when the government acts extraterritorially, it must respect international law rights that are similar to those provided in the Constitution. Yet the enforceability of those rights remains to be seen. Before the Military Commissions Act of 2006, government officials could be prosecuted for violations of Common Article 3 under the War Crimes Act. After the Military Commissions Act, prosecutions are no longer possible for all of the conduct that would violate Common Article 3 as a matter of international law.[54] The possible application of Common Article 3 hovers over my analysis, but the Court is unlikely to interpret it to expand individual rights beyond those in the Constitution. U.S. courts may end up applying Common Article 3 as functionally equivalent to extraterritorial application of the Constitution, but I doubt they will ever apply it more broadly.

Reasonable Rights in Practice

Much of the conduct commonly characterized as torture is unconstitutional because it involves the application of excessive force in violation of the Fourth Amendment, the compulsion of incriminating statements in violation of the self-incrimination clause of the Fifth Amendment, the infliction of cruel and unusual punishment in violation of the Eighth Amendment, or a violation of due process rights under the Fifth and Fourteenth Amendments. While these general prohibitions are significant, their limits are equally important.[55] The text of the Constitution and the Supreme Court's interpretations of it are ambiguous enough to leave space for officials to read these rights narrowly as they make decisions about how to treat people. To the extent that the function of rights in a liberal system is to define the characteristics of the political subject and dictate the terms of the sovereign-subject relationship, this ambiguity—including its divergence from typical conceptions of how rights operate—is critical.

The Fourth Amendment provides a good example. Writing for a majority of the Court in *Anderson v. Creighton,* Justice Scalia stated that "the precise content of most of the Constitution's civil liberties guarantees rests upon an assessment of what accommodation between governmental need and individual freedom is reasonable." In *Atwater v. City of Lago Vista,* Justice Souter wrote that "courts attempting to strike a reasonable Fourth Amendment balance [will] credit the government's side with an essential interest in readily administrable rules."[56] In other words, the Fourth Amendment turns on reasonableness when the defendant's interests are at stake, while clear rules are appropriate when they serve government interests.

The Fourth Amendment's protection against unreasonable force in the context of a search or seizure (which includes arrests) regulates a wide variety of practices that inflict pain. Application of this standard requires assessing the reasonableness not just of the force itself but also of the official's belief about the need to use force.[57] In theory, the Fourth Amendment bars unreasonable force. But in practice, officials receive a great deal of latitude when they make decisions about how much force to use, because reasonable mistakes about whether to use force and how much force to use do not violate the Constitution. A police officer's belief that he must use deadly force to prevent the escape of a suspect, for example, will receive little second-guessing from courts.[58] This deferential review not only weakens the deterrent value of the excessive force rule; it also makes clear that the right to be free of excessive force is uncertain and fluid.

Outside the context of excessive force, the Fourth Amendment provides remarkably few restrictions on official conduct. The *Terry* doctrine has expanded, such that the Court now speaks of "a police officer's prerogative, in accord with *Terry*, to conduct a protective search of a person who has already been legitimately stopped."[59] When police officers execute a search warrant, they have a "categorical" authority to detain people on the premises for the duration of the search.[60] The authority to detain includes the power to restrain people with handcuffs or other "reasonable" force where the situation is "inherently dangerous." According to Justice Stevens, in such situations, "it may well be appropriate to use both overwhelming force and surprise in order to secure the premises as quickly as possible."[61] The categorical power to detain thus licenses increasing state violence. Even more, the use of force—even overwhelming force—is part of the baseline police conduct that the Fourth Amendment permits, subject only to a reasonableness assessment that favors the government as a matter of explicit doctrine. Further, if the warrant is valid, the use of unreasonable force to execute it may not prevent the admission into evidence of the things seized during the search.[62] In this way, force becomes conceptually separate from the legal processes to which it is attached, despite the physical injury that may take place in carrying out those processes.

Turning to interrogation, the Fifth Amendment's self-incrimination clause was drafted in part to prevent torture and related practices.[63] Today, most self-incrimination issues concern the admission in a criminal trial of allegedly coerced statements. Most of these issues fall, in turn, under the doctrine of *Miranda v. Arizona*, which holds, in essence, that before interrogating a suspect, police must inform that person of his or her rights to remain silent and to have the assistance of counsel. Failure to give the warn-

ings or the use of coercion that causes a suspect to waive his or her rights
will make any resulting statements inadmissible in court. Yet the Court also
held that suspects could waive their rights voluntarily, even though waiver
takes place in the same atmosphere of psychological coercion that characterizes police interrogation generally. Not surprisingly, most suspects
waive.[64]

Over the years, the Supreme Court has created several exceptions to the
Miranda doctrine, such as the "public safety" exception, which allows police
to question a suspect without giving the warnings—and also allows prosecutors to introduce the statement in court—if they have a legitimate concern about public safety.[65] Contemporary interrogators have also, in Welsh
White's phrase, "adapted to *Miranda*" by developing permissible methods
for obtaining waivers of the right to remain silent. While not physically violent, these methods are often extremely coercive in the ways in which they
deceive suspects and manipulate their fear, uncertainty, and deference to
authority.[66] For example, in one investigation, suspect Frank Miller "collapsed in a state of shock" after a psychologically manipulative interrogation. The court records report, "He slid off his chair and onto the floor with
a blank stare on his face. The police officers sent for a first aid squad that
took him to the hospital." Nonetheless, a federal court rejected Miller's
claim that the confession had been obtained by coercion and upheld its admission into evidence.[67] Put plainly, intense and psychologically coercive
interrogation is common, and U.S. interrogation law allows—perhaps even
condones—this kind of interrogation and the mental suffering it produces.

Admissibility of statements in criminal trials is also governed by the due
process voluntariness test, which the Court developed in the years before it
held that the self-incrimination clause applied to the states and before the
Miranda decision transformed the scope of the self-incrimination protection. A confession is involuntary in violation of due process if, under the to-
tality of the circumstances, "'a defendant's will was overborne' by the circumstances surrounding the giving of a confession," as long as those
circumstances include "coercive police activity."[68] Although this standard is
suggestive, the due process test provides little protection. Not only is the
voluntariness test famously difficult to apply, but few courts will find a confession involuntary under due process if the suspect received the *Miranda*
warnings, waived them, and thus apparently spoke free of Fifth Amendment compulsion.[69]

Going beyond the question of admissibility, some cases from the middle
of the twentieth century suggest that the privilege against self-incrimination provides substantive protection against coercive interrogation practices regardless of whether the government seeks to use that information in
court.[70] More recently, however, four justices stated clearly in *Chavez v.*

Martinez that the privilege against self-incrimination applies only to efforts to introduce coerced testimony in a legal proceeding and has no relevance to police conduct outside the court. Two concurring justices agreed that the privilege does not apply outside the courtroom, with the exception of extreme cases in which plaintiffs make "'powerful showing[s].'" Presumably, these justices had something like torture in mind, but given the facts of *Chavez*—in which a severely wounded man who believed he might be dying was interrogated relentlessly in a hospital emergency room by police who sought to take advantage of his pain and fear—their definition of torture is not expansive. Most forms of cruel, inhuman, or degrading treatment presumably would also fall short of providing a "powerful showing."[71]

The result is that judicial regulation of coercive interrogation when the government does not seek to introduce testimony in court relies on the substantive due process doctrine of the Fifth and Fourteenth Amendments, which provides two types of claims. The first claim is that specific government conduct "shocks the conscience." In *County of Sacramento v. Lewis,* the Court made clear, however, that official conduct does not shock the conscience unless it is "unjustifiable by any government interest." Three justices applied this doctrine in a very straightforward way in *Chavez:* "[T]he need to investigate whether there had been police misconduct constituted a justifiable government interest [allowing interrogation of Martinez] given the risk that key evidence would have been lost if Martinez had died without the authorities even hearing his side of the story." Only three justices explicitly disagreed.[72]

More generally, if "any government interest" will justify otherwise conscience-shocking behavior, the doctrine means only that the state must have a sufficient purpose when it tortures; it cannot do so arbitrarily. A recent district court decision applying the "shocks the conscience" test suggested just such a possibility. The court distinguished between torture "to extract evidence for the purpose of prosecuting criminal conduct" and torture "for the purpose of preventing a terrorist attack." The court concluded that "whether torture always violates the Fifth Amendment . . . remains unresolved from a doctrinal standpoint."[73] The extent to which "shocks the conscience" doctrine will consider whether the interests of individual claimants outweigh those of the government is also unclear. Even if the doctrine makes room for such an assessment, individuals likely will have difficulty proving their interests outweigh a public purpose articulated by the government in support of its actions.

The second claim available under substantive due process is that specific government conduct violates a fundamental right. Although this doctrine seems to provide stronger protection than the "shocks the conscience" test, it still makes room for exceptions. Conduct narrowly tailored to serve a compelling state interest is constitutional even if it violates what might otherwise be described as an individual's fundamental rights. When we add the sometimes-enforced requirement that the claimed right must be described with particularity, the doctrine becomes malleable enough to allow at least some coercive interrogation, especially under the compelling circumstances that many believe are presented by the war on terror.[74]

So far, I have considered rights that relate to investigation and prosecution of criminal activity. Once a defendant has been convicted of a crime, the focus shifts to punishment and the Eighth Amendment's ban on "cruel and unusual punishments." I provide a more detailed analysis of Eighth Amendment doctrine in chapter 6. Here, I simply want to highlight that the same kinds of ambiguity and deference that characterize the constitutional law of police investigation exist for punishment. The Constitution permits harsh and degrading prisons as long as inmates receive "the minimal civilized measure of life's necessities,"[75] and officials have a great deal of discretion in deciding how to manage and discipline a prison population.

Rights as Remedies

The preceding discussion indicates that the definition and application of rights in practice nearly always depart from the promises of liberal or constitutional theory. This disconnect expands when remedies come into play.[76] Criminal prosecutions of officials who violate constitutional rights are rare.[77] As a remedy, prosecutions fail to prevent harm, not only because they react to past events, but also because the paucity of prosecutions dilutes their deterrent value. By contrast, the exclusionary rule—another retrospective remedy—has more deterrent power because it is applied at trial and applied far more often. Despite continued criticism by the Supreme Court, the rule applies to most violations of the Fourth and Fifth Amendments when litigated in the course of a criminal case.[78] But the exclusionary rule has an important limitation. It applies only when the government seeks to introduce evidence in a state or federal judicial proceeding. It has no application to conduct outside the courtroom—however abusive that conduct may be—unless and until the government seeks to introduce the resulting evidence.

Other possible remedies exist, such as restraining official conduct in advance through legislation and administrative regulations. The federal government has statutory authority to seek injunctions against patterns or practices of law enforcement conduct that violate civil rights, but as with criminal prosecution, this power depends on the energy, resources, and commitment of executive branch officials.[79] Individuals may also seek injunctive relief against officials who violate their constitutional rights. But in *City of Los Angeles v. Lyons,* the Supreme Court held that a plaintiff may seek an injunction in federal court against violent official conduct only if he or she has "standing" to do so, which translates into proof that the plaintiff is suffering a continuing injury or faces a definite, imminent, and personal threat of future injury. There is no exception for people who have been harmed already and also seek damages. According to the Court, such people "are no more entitled to an injunction than any other citizen."[80] Whether or not these reasons are persuasive, most commentators agree that *Lyons* "makes it virtually impossible for the victim of police abuse to secure injunctive relief against a local government entity for practices of its police or sheriff's department."[81] A person tortured by government officials, therefore, may seek damages for harms already inflicted but lacks standing to seek an injunction absent a reasonable likelihood of being tortured again, which is difficult to prove in most cases.[82]

Despite their apparent utility, damages claims raise problems of their own.[83] First, in the context of a suit involving torture or related mistreatment by federal officials, concerns for national security and state secrets could lead to dismissal of the suit.[84] Second, claims against individuals confront doctrines of immunity. Absolute immunity, which applies primarily to judges, legislators, and prosecutors while they are performing those roles, prevents any suit for damages, no matter how egregious the conduct. Under the qualified immunity doctrine, a court must dismiss the claim if at the time the defendant acted, the conduct did not "violate clearly established statutory or constitutional rights of which a reasonable person would have known." Recovery is available only for violations of "clearly established" rights, and a right is not clearly established with respect to a specific claim unless "the contours of the right [are] sufficiently clear that a reasonable official would understand that what he is doing violates that right." "[I]n the light of pre-existing law," the Supreme Court has explained, "the unlawfulness must be apparent."[85]

For a damages claim involving torture or related mistreatment, the most likely sources of law are the Fourth Amendment and substantive due process. Under the Fourth Amendment, a court would ask whether an official's actions and beliefs about those actions were reasonable under the circumstances, which include the potential threat posed by the victim/plaintiff. For a substantive due process claim, the court would likely ask whether the official reasonably could have believed that his or her actions were serving "any government interest." As my discussion earlier in this chapter indicates, in either case, it will not be easy to say both that the conduct was unlawful and that the unlawfulness was "apparent."

State and Federal Criminal Law

ᐁ

Every state has statutes against murder, rape, assault, and kidnapping, and most acts of torture would fall within one of these prohibitions. Some states also recognize a distinct crime of torture or murder by torture or treat torture as an aggravating factor for purposes of the death penalty.[86] Many states recognize or provide tort or civil rights causes of action for damages as a remedy for official misconduct, and those claims are available for torture and related conduct.[87]

Federal criminal law provides a wide variety of avenues for pursuing torture claims.[88] The prosecution of some federal crimes depends on proof that the offense was committed within the special maritime or territorial jurisdiction of the United States. This jurisdiction includes U.S. vessels and aircraft; "the premises of United States diplomatic, consular, military or other United States Government missions or entities in foreign States"; and property "used for purposes of those missions or entities or used by United States personnel assigned to those missions or entities."[89] This jurisdictional statute has broad application.[90] Federal prosecutors used it, for example, in 2004 when they convicted David Passaro, a former army ranger working as a contractor for the CIA, for beating a local man to death during an interrogation at a U.S. army base in Afghanistan.[91]

All of these statutes support the claim that the ban on torture is a foundational commitment, written into the fabric of the rule of law in the United States. But no matter how clear the application of a particular criminal prohibition appears, it operates within a larger, mediating structure that alters and dilutes its meaning. This larger structure includes common-law principles of interpretation, defenses, and exceptions to liability that represent the multiple and sometimes competing goals of the criminal law that have grown up over time. For that reason, criminal prohibitions almost always include an unwritten "unless" that emerges from the effort to apply them to specific cases and that defeats efforts to create and maintain a clear and predictable body of criminal law.[92]

In the federal system, defendants ordinarily may raise traditional common-law defenses even if Congress has not included them in a statute.[93] Such doctrines as defense of self or others, duress, necessity, and reliance on official interpretations of law are thus presumptively available to defendants prosecuted for crimes in which torture is the underlying conduct—assuming, of course, that the defense applies to the specific facts.[94] The most obvious defense is necessity.

The Supreme Court indicated that necessity could be a defense to federal criminal charges in *United States v. Bailey*.[95] But in *United States v. Oakland Cannabis Buyers' Cooperative*, it rejected necessity as a defense to charges under the federal Controlled Substances Act. A five-justice majority went further and suggested—in tension with the general approach to defenses in federal criminal law—that necessity might never be available in federal court unless Congress expressly makes it available.[96] Notwithstanding this suggestion, lower federal courts treat necessity as an established and available defense, even if it is rarely successful.[97]

Necessity turns on the balance of harms or "choice of evils." As one federal court put it, necessity is "a utilitarian defense" based on "maximizing social welfare . . . where the social benefits of the crime outweigh the social costs of failing to commit the crime."[98] The defendant must prove some version of the following four elements:

(1) that he was faced with a choice of evils and chose the lesser evil; (2) that he acted to prevent imminent harm; (3) that he reasonably anticipated a causal relation between his conduct and the harm to be avoided; and (4) that there were no other legal alternatives to violating the law.[99]

For torture, the classic hypothetical of a "ticking time bomb"—in which a bomb is set to go off within a short period of time in an urban area and officials have arrested a person responsible for setting the bomb but who will not disclose its location—almost certainly satisfies these elements. The probable harm from the bomb likely outweighs the harm to an individual suspect,[100] and the harm is imminent if the time until the explosion is sufficiently short. The imminence factor also overlaps with the balance of harms. The Supreme Court of Israel, for example, declared that an explosion could be "imminent" for purposes of necessity "even if the bomb is set to explode in a few days, or perhaps even after a few weeks."[101] The third element, causation, is satisfied if officials have good reasons to believe that the suspect knows the location of the bomb. Finally, legal alternatives likely will be lacking if the explosion is truly imminent (and perhaps also if the harm is likely to be significant).

That said, my purpose is not to argue that courts should allow necessity claims in torture cases, although that result could be appropriate in extraordinary circumstances.[102] Nor am I claiming that it should be easy for a defendant to prevail on such a claim. Cases involving ticking time bombs are rare, if they exist at all, and the use of an extreme case to establish a rule risks distorting the application of the rule in typical cases.[103] Not all approaches to necessity are rigorously utilitarian. An alternative view maintains that necessity depends "on a concept of what is right and proper under the circumstances." Under this formulation, a defendant might still prevail on a necessity defense in a torture case, but the idea of balance of harms would lose at least some of its force.[104] The point I am trying to make in this discussion—and it is a point too easily overlooked when people assert that torture or other forms of state violence are criminal—is that necessity claims fit comfortably within the ordinary fabric of criminal law. The important corollary is a presumption that justification or excuse exceptions are part of the definition of any crime, including crimes involving torture.

One piece of the necessity analysis remains. *Oakland Cannabis* held that the necessity defense is not available if the legislature has "made a 'determination of values.'" The United States has ratified the Convention against Torture and the ICCPR, both of which ban torture and allow no derogations. Federal prosecutors easily could argue that the nonderogation provisions foreclose necessity claims. They could also point to the fact that during ratification of the convention, the Senate never adopted the proposed understanding on common-law defenses. They might even note the tenuous status of necessity defenses in international criminal law. In response, a defendant presumably would argue that because neither document is self-executing, neither document can override a preexisting defense.[105] Defendants could also claim that their conduct was not "torture" as defined by the convention and federal statutes and was no more than cruel, inhuman, or degrading treatment, to which the convention's nonderogation clause does not apply. As a result, they might argue, the necessity defense is available. Prosecutors could still rely on the ICCPR's nonderogable ban on cruel, inhuman, or degrading treatment, but that reliance would raise the difficult question of which document controls—and the outcome of that debate is far from clear.

A less obvious but potentially more fruitful defense to criminal charges is reasonable reliance on an official interpretation of law, which exists both at the common-law level and under the due process clauses of the Constitution. In its due process version, the defense holds that "citizens may not be punished for actions undertaken in good faith reliance upon authoritative assurance that punishment will not attach."[106] To gain its benefit, a defendant must show both actual "good faith reliance" on an official interpretation of law and that the "reliance was reasonable under the circumstances."[107] Thus, the defense is different from a claim of following orders or even a promise of no prosecution. The defendant must have had a basis for believing that the reason he or she would not be punished was because the conduct was legal. For example, a legal memorandum providing a reasonable (even if incorrect) explanation of the relevant legal landscape could provide the basis for the reliance defense. One of the functions of the federal government's torture memoranda was to prevent prosecution of federal officials who used coercive interrogation methods.[108]

Finally, the existence of statutes that ban torture does not mean that acts of official torture or abuse do not happen or even that preventive measures are in place to limit their occurrence (although measures have been implemented in some instances). Nor do they mean that every act of official torture or abuse leads to criminal prosecution. Individual actors in the criminal justice system possess a great deal of discretion at all levels and stages of a criminal proceeding, with the result that some acts of violence or even torture may not be investigated or prosecuted at all. Critically, when prosecutors do not seek criminal sanctions, it becomes more difficult to say that the acts of violence covered by the particular statute are illegal in a practical sense. Rather, they are illegal to the extent that the remedy of prosecution is sought and succeeds, and the legal prohibition becomes diluted when that remedy is sought haphazardly or not at all or when a jury acquits.

Regardless of official discretion to investigate or prosecute, these statutory prohibitions that include torture relegate it to the periphery as a formal matter, so that torture is always an exceptional circumstance as a matter of law. The prohibitions, in other words, define the permissible scope of state violence by reference to what is excluded. The exception of torture, then, is both outside the law, as a prohibited act, and inseparable from law, because it provides an organizing principle for it. Once torture has this central role, the question is whether the practice of the exception risks encompassing the rule or whether the practices that replace "torture" function equally well or better to enforce and circulate state power and dominance.

Conclusion: Legal State Violence and Political Identity

∾

A recent decision by the Supreme Court pulls together many of the themes in this chapter. A police officer observed 19-year-old Victor Harris driving 73 miles per hour in a 55-miles-per-hour zone. Harris did not respond to the officer's flashing lights and instead drove away at speeds up to 85 miles per hour, which put other drivers and pedestrians at risk. After 10 miles, Deputy Timothy Scott drove up behind Harris and used his car to push the rear bumper of Harris's car. Harris lost control of his car, crashed, and was left a quadriplegic.

Harris claimed he had been subjected to excessive force in violation of the Fourth Amendment, and he sought damages from the police officers involved in the chase. The Supreme Court rejected the claim. The Court stressed that the test for excessive force is whether the amount of force was reasonable, and it insisted that the rule is the same even when officers use "deadly force": "all that matters is whether Scott's actions were reasonable." The test for reasonableness required the Court to " 'balance the nature and quality of the intrusion on the individual's Fourth Amendment interests against the importance of the governmental interests alleged to justify the intrusion.'"[109]

The Court bracketed this assessment in two ways. First, it distinguished Harris from the people he put at risk.

> We think it appropriate in this process to take into account not only the number of lives at risk, but also their relative culpability. It was respondent, after all, who intentionally placed himself and the public in danger by unlawfully engaging in the reckless, high speed flight that ultimately produced the choice between two evils that Scott confronted. . . . By contrast, those who might have been harmed had Scott not taken the action he did were entirely innocent.

Second, in response to Harris's argument that "the innocent public equally [could] have been protected, and the tragic accident avoided, if the police had simply ceased their pursuit," the Court responded, "We think the police need not have taken that chance and hoped for the best. Whereas Scott's action—ramming respondent off the road—was certain to eliminate the risk that respondent posed to the public, ceasing pursuit was not." Indeed, argued the Court, "[a] police officer's attempt to terminate a dangerous high-speed car chase that threatens the lives of innocent bystanders does not violate the Fourth Amendment, even when it places the fleeing motorist at risk of serious injury or death."[110]

The Court confirmed, in short, that the Constitution does not interfere with the discretion of law enforcement officials to engage in conduct that threatens a person's life, as long as that conduct is reasonable. Among the circumstances in which potentially deadly force will be reasonable is when the victim is a wrongdoer who poses a threat to innocents. Further, the leeway that officials have to respond in such situations—that is, the range of conduct that courts will declare legally "reasonable"—increases in response not only to the number of people at risk but also to the relative guilt and innocence of the wrongdoer and those at risk. Finally, the Court specifically framed its analysis as evaluating "the choice between two evils," which is classic necessity language, except that in this instance, necessity worked to create or insulate state power rather than as a defense to illegal conduct. After all, Officer Scott's conduct was not illegal. It was consistent with the Constitution, in part because it was necessary.

Although *Scott v. Harris* is about "ordinary" police activity, the Court's conclusions are also suggestive for the issue of torture. One might even say that the case adopts the reasoning that drives the hypothetical of the ticking time bomb and that it writes that reasoning into the Constitution. Indeed, even if the Court were to say—as it very well might—that torture is unreasonable under this analysis, the fact remains that *Scott* and other cases hold that the legal category of "reasonable force" will often include killing and the infliction of grievous injury.[111] The Constitution creates room for "everyday" state violence—the ability of government officials to use "reasonable" amounts of violence against citizens to achieve government goals. While the Constitution and federal statutes, as well as state constitutions and state statutes, outlaw much of the conduct that falls into the category of torture, large swathes of discretion remain, including the discretionary ability to harm people.

As adopted by the United States, protections against torture that exist under international law reduce to preexisting constitutional protections that do not establish an absolute constitutional right not to be tortured or subjected to ill-treatment. Even when officials engage in conduct that might violate those rights, civil remedies are often unavailable. On the criminal side, remedies are largely subject to investigatory and prosecutorial discretion. The result is that any asserted right to be free of torture and related conduct risks being illusory, rhetorical, or hortatory in any specific case.

Courts are not bound to follow doctrines to their logical conclusions, of course. Even in *Chavez v. Martinez,* the justices seemed to say that "torture" is unconstitutional, and similar statements appear in other cases.[112] But although the Supreme Court is unlikely to approve something called "torture," constitutional doctrine is constructed in a way that leaves ample room for violent government action in cases of perceived necessity. Even if there is an absolute right not to be "tortured," the right may not extend to coercive interrogation that technically falls short of legal definitions of torture, when the government can provide reasons for its actions.

Debates over U.S. constitutional interpretation repeatedly transform into struggles over the identity of the nation itself. At the same time, however, the importance of the Constitution to national identity often leads people to assert that the Constitution has a meaning apart from the specific doctrines that it puts into practice.[113] Claims of this kind too easily allow commentators to ignore or minimize the enormous amount of ongoing state violence that the Constitution fails to restrain and even licenses. Similarly, commentators rarely recognize that this discretionary violence is both controlled and legitimized partly by individual rights. If the Constitution—the doctrines applied in courtrooms across the United States every day—operates in this way, American national identity must reflect that fact. National identity is not the only thing at stake. It follows from this analysis that American citizenship itself is defined to some degree—indeed, is constituted—as subjection or potential subjection to state violence within a structure of flexible and waivable rights.

CHAPTER FOUR

Torture, Rights, and the Modern State

As I stated in the introduction, this chapter breaks with the legal analysis in the previous chapters and turns to the relationship between torture, rights, and liberal governance. The starting point for my analysis is the idea that legal or human rights do not exist in a vacuum, are not inherent in nature or required by rational deduction, and do not function as trumps. In other words, I do not assume that Kantian, liberal, or natural law ideas of human rights—that such rights force the state to treat people as ends, not means; that they provide people with a sphere of liberty outside state power; or that they comprise "the right to be treated as human beings"—are correct as a descriptive matter.[1]

My analysis also goes against the grain of the standard, progressive account of international human rights, which sees them as an escape from state violence and a liberating regime of universal principles—indeed, as "a universal political ideology."[2] A well-known statement by Louis Henkin exemplifies this account.

> Human rights are universal; they belong to every human being in every human society. They do not differ with geography or history, culture or ideology, political or economic system, or stage of societal development. To call them "human" implies that all human beings have them, equally and in equal measure—regardless of sex, race, age; regardless of high or low "birth," social class, national origin, ethnic or tribal affiliation; regardless of wealth or poverty, occupation, talent, merit, religion, ideology, or other commitment.[3]

With respect to the more focused idea of universal human rights as law, Anthony D'Amato provides a wonderfully concise distillation of the prevailing view.

> Since the Holocaust of World War II, the Nuremberg trials, and Eleanor Roosevelt's superb drafting of a General Assembly resolution entitled, "The Universal Declaration of Human Rights" (1948), people are de-

manding direct access to public international law. Prior to 1945, a state could do anything it wanted to its citizens within its own territory, including murdering them, without any international accountability. Today, genocide, torture, enslavement, and other crimes, possibly extending to persecution and deportation, are illegal under customary international law even if they occur entirely within the territorial boundaries of a state and involve the state's own nationals. The law of human rights . . . is changing "international law" into "interpersonal law."[4]

In contrast to such views, I assume that rights as we know them today are a form of positive law, derive most of their power from sovereign authority, and exist only because of modern states.[5] As such, whether in the national or international context, rights are usually instruments of state or institutional power. More precisely, rights tend to serve the interests of states and international institutions, and one of those interests is defining the modern concepts of self and citizenship in relation to modern states and societies, as well as to an international legal and political order.

To the extent that rights discourse is constitutive, therefore, it fosters unexpected and even uncomfortable ideas of nation, community, citizen, and individual. Among other things, the idea of liberal rights requires the idea of the individual, whose identity, in turn, requires the state. As the European Court of Human Rights recently explained, the state is "the guarantor of individual rights and freedoms and the impartial organizer of the practice of the various beliefs and religions in a democratic society." To the extent that rights discourse is aspirational, it idealizes the nation, constitution, or political institution alongside the citizen, such that the citizen's identity is a legitimate political project. To quote the same court again, "the State has a positive obligation to ensure that everyone within its jurisdiction enjoys in full, *and without being able to waive them,* the rights and freedoms guaranteed by the Convention [on Human Rights]."[6] Important as well is that the constitutive and aspirational aspects of rights discourse also reflect the idea that liberal rights are universal.

Traditional accounts of rights as constraints on state power fail to explain not only the pervasiveness of torture and related practices but also the elasticity of legal rights in the face of torture. The approach I sketch here provides a better explanation of how legal discourse, including rights discourse, accommodates itself to and often supports the use of state violence. In other words, modern liberal states can respect rights and the rule of law even as they torture.

My argument is not that rights are inherently bad or ineffectual. Rights mark out areas that receive some degree of protection—or, more precisely, operate under a different kind of regulation—from state power and interference. Further, the resulting spaces (sometimes called the "public" and "private" spheres) can become locations for distinct forms of creative action (distinct but also controversial partly because of the kinds of activities supposedly best suited to the different spheres).[7] Finally, many people benefit from and enjoy the experience of having rights, and rights claims are useful tools for people living in modern states.

The point I am trying to stress is that rights are important parts of the citizen-state relationship (indeed, in many ways, they are constitutive of it) precisely because they are part of modern political structures. Rights thus have a double edge, for they confine even as they liberate, expose even as they protect, and confirm the power of states and other institutions every time they are invoked. An ever-expanding conception of rights thus brings with it an ever-expanding idea of state power. Each time that people exercise rights, whether against the state or against their fellow rights-holders, they also confirm the power of the state over them. Put differently, having rights is not the same thing as freedom from coercion and does not necessarily lead to it. Similarly, recognizing the utility of rights claims in a modern state is not the same as saying that either rights or the modern state are desirable.

Archetypes, Rights, and the Goals of State Violence

◡

The idea of rights that I just outlined leads to a complex view of such things as torture, not to mention of citizenship and the rule of law. Ideas of this kind are controversial in legal circles. Jeremy Waldron, for example, develops the apparently opposing idea that the ban on torture and the accompanying right to be free of it is an "archetype," by which he means

> the idea of a rule or positive law provision that operates not just on its own account, and does not stand simply in a cumulative relation to other provisions, but that also operates in a way that expresses or epitomizes the spirit of a whole structured area of doctrine, and does so vividly, effectively, publicly, establishing the significance of that area for the entire legal enterprise.

According to Waldron, the ban on torture is archetypal because of what it says about "the relation between law and force." It expresses "our determination to sever the link between law and brutality, between law and terror, and between law and the enterprise of trying to break a person's will." Not surprisingly, in this view, the absolute prohibition on torture is ultimately an archetype of the rule of law itself.[8]

Waldron's argument is powerful, and I suspect readers will agree that the ban on torture stands for something larger—for a commitment to democracy, human rights, and moral leadership. That conclusion is certainly correct. In the discourses of citizenship, rights, and democracy, the ban on torture has powerful rhetorical importance. It helps express what it means to be modern and progressive, and other writers have also stressed the idea that, by definition, liberalism and liberal rights reject the pain and cruelty of torture.[9] Waldron's argument also inoculates us against a simplified resort to violence on behalf of the state, and he rightly emphasizes the fragility and importance of this inoculation.

But whatever valuable role it may play, the ban on torture also operates within these discourses to condition our reaction to and perception of state violence. Waldron himself provides the text for this argument. Several years before he described the right not to be tortured as an archetype, he used it as an example of the way in which supposedly negative rights generate "waves of duties" that make it impossible "to sustain any simple division between negative and positive rights."

> The right not to be tortured, for example, clearly generates a duty not to torture. But, in various circumstances, that simple duty will be backed up by others: a duty to instruct people about the wrongness of torture; a duty to be vigilant about the danger of, and temptation to, torture; a duty to ameliorate situations in which torture might be thought likely to occur, and so on. Once it is discovered that people have been tortured, the right generates remedial duties such as the duty to rescue people from torture, the duty on government officials to find out who is doing and authorizing the torture, remove them from office, and bring them to justice, the duty to set up safeguards to prevent recurrence of the abuses, and so on. If these duties in turn are not carried out, then the right generates further duties of enforcement and enquiry with regard to them. And so on.[10]

The right not to be tortured, in short, demands much of the state, and these demands run against the assumptions of ordinary negative rights discourse. If the right depends on the success of these subsidiary rights and duties, the force or value of that right necessarily diminishes when some of them are ignored, forgotten, or denied. Failure to give effect to all of these related rights and duties makes the central right less effective and increases the likelihood that much of its function will be symbolic. So, too, these rights and duties mesh with the tendencies of the modern state. The right not to be tortured generates duties to instruct, intervene, assist, regulate, and control, which, in turn, generate rights to have these duties carried out.

There may be little difference, in short, between welfare rights and the right not to be tortured. Even more, the fact that the right not to be tortured rests on the fulfillment of these lesser obligations suggests that this archetypal right may be as contingent and controversial as welfare rights. Like them, the full right not to be tortured requires a substantive and robust theory of the state and state power.

Further, even as Waldron highlights the archetypal status of the right not to be tortured, he also admits we fail to satisfy the values of our archetypes. Police violence and abuse in prison sometimes happen, for example. But he appears to treat these events as aberrations or exceptions and suggests that the archetype itself gives us the ability to combat these "affront[s] to the deeper traditions of Anglo-American law."[11] He does not explore the possibility of exceptional circumstances or, more critically, the relationship between "ordinary" law and "exceptional" law, between normal conditions and states of emergency or exception.

As I have suggested already, my argument rests partly on the possibility that contemporary legal orders are already defined by ideas of the exception and commitments to violence. Succeeding chapters will confirm that the "deeper traditions" of liberal legal and political systems have always made room for brutal state violence and that the discourse of rights and the "archetypes" that revolve around it function to enable that violence as well as to prevent it, to channel it as well as to limit it. President Bush provided a glimpse of this relationship when he explicitly linked the killing of Abu Musab al-Zarqawi to "victory in the global war on terror" and creation of "the rule of law" in Iraq.[12]

This book thus approaches rights and legal doctrines in two different ways. In the preceding chapters on the law of torture, I have refused to treat the ban on torture and related legal doctrines as archetypes that flow through a collective legal consciousness. Instead, I have treated them simply as rules that people make, manipulate, change, apply, obey, avoid, and violate—as positive law in the most simplistic sense. I have also suggested that people who wish to combat such practices as torture might want to look beyond rights and rule-of-law discourse for the most useful tools. In this chapter, by contrast, I take seriously the idea that some legal doctrines and rights are archetypes—that they are mystical in the sense that Waldron identifies, as the things that "animate" law, form its "spirit," or serve as an "icon of the whole."[13]

In making these claims, Waldron is attempting to work within a liberal framework to address the concern that positivism fails to take adequate account of principles and structure. Archetypes, he suggests, give a principled structure to what might otherwise be mere rules vulnerable to skilled manipulation or simple override. His effort, moreover, came at a time of perceived crisis: some government officials and academics had argued that coercive interrogation is consistent with positive law, and other officials—perhaps in reliance on these arguments—had employed brutal methods to advance state interests. We can defeat these arguments and methods, Waldron argues, by insisting that the ban on torture is not simply positive law; it is part of the foundational law that animates the entire legal order. Without the ban on torture and related archetypes, there is no point to our law. By contrast, the archetype advances substantive goals, including having a "leadership position in human rights and the international rule of law."[14]

Carl Schmitt expressed a similar concern about positivism in 1932, when the Weimar Constitution was in crisis. Schmitt warned that in the liberal legislative state, "the way was open to an absolutely 'neutral,' value- and quality-free, formal-functional concept of legality without content." At some point, he contended, we must choose between a constitution of process and one of substance, and "the decision must fall for the . . . attempt to create a substantive order."[15] So, too, Schmitt understood the idea of legal archetypes. For him, sovereignty and law were grounded in the mystical or theological idea of the exception.

> The exception is more interesting than the rule. The rule proves nothing; the exception proves everything: It confirms not only the rule but also its existence, which derives only from the exception. In the exception the power of real life breaks through the crust of a mechanism that has become torpid by repetition.[16]

For Waldron, the archetype seems to function in a manner similar to the way the exception functions for Schmitt. Like the exception, it has an almost religious status—indeed, Waldron chose the term *archetype* to stress the "folkloric" status of the torture ban.[17] Further, like the exception, the existence of the archetype proves the force of law, even when it is in tension with positive law or attempted applications of it. Finally, like the exception, the archetype is both an ideal and a foundation that sits outside the ordinary legal and political order but also functions within it as law.

Waldron does not go as far as Schmitt in his substantive arguments, and he plainly seeks to maintain the fragile balance of liberal constitutionalism that Schmitt consciously attacked. Still, Waldron's arguments are representative of a liberal effort to understand torture legally, and that effort exposes certain weaknesses of liberal thought. One of my goals in this chapter is to demonstrate the ways in which liberal, critical, and authoritarian theorizing inevitably converge in contemporary political discourse.

Liberal Rights and State Power

ᐃᔭ

The conception of rights I am developing here has more in common with liberal thinking than readers might at first be willing to admit.[18] John Stuart Mill's argument for liberty depended partly on an instrumental claim. He explained that "different persons . . . require different conditions for their spiritual development." They require liberty to make their own choices so that they can "obtain their fair share of happiness" and "grow up to the mental, moral, and aesthetic stature of which their nature is capable." The goal, in other words, is not simply liberty for its own sake but liberty as a means to achieve a better, more sensible society.[19] To be sure, Mill also suggests that liberty is an end in itself, and some writers prefer to stress that part of his argument.[20] Rather than opt for one or the other statement as support for an idea of what "liberty" is for, I want, instead, to suggest that the tension in Mill between liberty as a means and liberty as an end is crucial, because it assumes the presence of a larger force (government or society) that demands and seeks to shape a particular kind of person, even as this person (the "individual") demands the ability to do the same.

Contemporary writers have expanded on the ways in which ideas of liberty and rights demand a powerful liberal state—the kind of state that, according to the European Court of Human Rights, must force people to have rights.[21] Scholars now recognize, in Stephen Holmes's words, that "only the state . . . can create the conditions under which individuals can successfully claim rights." Indeed, the necessary connection between state power and individual rights prompts Holmes to stress "the restrictive, or even anti-individualistic, element within liberalism itself." Once one accepts the idea that liberal rights are attached to "the individual viewed in abstraction from political, economic, familial, and religious roles, as well as from race and gender," Holmes is certainly correct.[22] The rights-holder—the individual citizen—is an abstraction, not a flesh-and-blood person who might be comprised of a variety of political, economic, familial, religious, racial, and gender identities. The only identity that counts is the one of possessing rights, which exists only in relation to a state.

It is also critical to recognize that claiming or being categorized as having one of these more specific identities risks making you less of a proper rights-holder, so that your rights are extended on sufferance, based on the expectation that someday you will be a complete, abstract individual. So, too, the insistence on abstraction suggests that divisive issues that implicate these identities may properly be excluded from political life. The sum total of these abstractions is not a diverse community but, instead, a society of undifferentiated but equal citizens defined precisely and only by the common fact of having rights. Because rights-holders are abstractions and because liberal rights are as much about restricting individuals as liberating them, a violation of rights is a harm as much to the state as to a particular person. As Holmes puts it, "[t]o violate rights in a liberal society . . . is to defy the authority of the liberal state."[23]

Joseph Raz similarly recognizes that liberal ideas of individual autonomy derive from state power. By definition, the coercion of the liberal state is unproblematic because, as he writes, "its coercive measures do not express an insult to the autonomy of individuals," as "they are motivated not by lack of respect for individual autonomy but by concern for it." Indeed, he insists that the state should foster "valuable autonomy," with the result that it may restrict the autonomy of some people and adopt "paternalist" measures "which encourage the adoption of valuable ends and discourage the pursuit of base ones."[24] Rights and autonomy must depend on state power as a matter of liberal theory as well as in practice, because only within the embrace of state power can we be guided toward "valuable autonomy"—an autonomy that is abstracted from our individual characteristics and serves the interests of the liberal state. For Holmes and Raz, rights help to define a certain kind of person: the abstract autonomous individual or citizen who is part of a state. Through their violation, rights also provide a condition precedent for state intervention in people's lives. Put differently, rights are about state power, not just in the sense of marking boundaries between individual and state, but also in a constitutive sense, as creators of state power and of the citizens who live under it.

Going further, the liberal idea of universal human rights requires rightsholders who can be defined as equal in formal terms. The creation of the abstract autonomous individual does not satisfy this need completely, because formal equality cannot exist apart from its substantive underpinnings. As Uday Mehta observes, the liberal idea of universalism presumes a particular set of social structures and conventions, and those who do not share these structures are implicitly excluded from the group of equal rights-holders.[25] The process of exclusion is not a simple decision of who is in or out. The dilemma facing a liberal state that excludes and does not provide equal rights can provoke efforts to make people equal. Whether or not those efforts proceed from good intentions, they often take the form of sustained domination or violence for the purpose of turning those who are excluded into the abstract individuals who will eventually have rights that are recognizable within a liberal order.

For example, Mill may have denied the general proposition that "any community has a right to force another to be civilized,"[26] but he made clear that his ideas about liberty do not apply to "backward states of society," because "despotism is a legitimate mode of government in dealing with barbarians."[27] Mill supported British colonial rule in India, with the argument that some people "must be governed by the dominant country, or by persons delegated that purpose by it." He explained, "This mode of government is as legitimate as any other, if it is the one which in the existing state of civilization of the subject people most facilitates their transition to a higher stage of improvement."[28] Liberal theory thus has included, perhaps from its inception, a particular stance toward governing people deemed incapable of having equal rights or of being full participants in political life.

To get at the characteristics of this stance toward those people defined as not ready for rights, Mehta's description of the "common liberal response" to the problems of empire is worth quoting at length. Mehta argues that liberalism functions

> to articulate the modalities of governance that exist . . . in the temporizing between educating Indians but *not yet* deeming them worthy of autonomy, in the penumbra between crafting responsible government but *not yet* giving Indians self-government—in the morally, politically, and rationally justified ambivalence of liberalism for the *time being* remaining imperial.

According to Mehta, "[t]his project is infinitely patient, perhaps even secretly counting on its own extended incompetence, of not getting *there* and hence permanently remaining in between." He further contends, "By the nineteenth century virtually every liberal justification of empire is anchored in the patience needed to serve and realize a future. And that future is invariably expressed through the notion of progress." Seen in this way, "[i]mperial power is simply the instrument required to align a deviant and recalcitrant history with the appropriate future."[29] Put more bluntly, imperial violence is both a mechanism for achieving liberal progress and an exemplification of liberal values in action.

Despite a rhetorical commitment to a contrary view—exemplified by the Declaration of Independence in the United States, the Declaration of the Rights of Man and Citizen in France, and the Universal Declaration of Human Rights internationally—rights are not held equally and universally by all people. The status of having rights distinguishes one group of people from other groups that have fewer rights or none at all. This is true at the conceptual level as well as at the level of description. For example, drawing on Kant and Rawls, Jeffrie Murphy argues that rights and the institutions that enforce them depend on reciprocity, so that one can only claim a right if one is "prepared to recognize and respect [one's] obligation to defer to others' rights in similar kinds of circumstances."[30]

To make this point, Murphy highlights a hypothetical person characterized by a "lack of moral feeling," by "his failure to be motivated by a recognition of the rights of others and the obligations he has to them." Such a person "is in no position to claim rights for himself," because "[h]e violates a condition for the possibility of reciprocity which is . . . a presupposition for the intelligibility of the whole obligation-rights game." Such people, Murphy contends, should be seen, from a moral point of view, as animals, not persons, who are in "no position to claim any rights on grounds of moral desert or respect." He argues, "We can act wrongly with respect to them, but they cannot be wronged. They can be injured, but they can be done no moral injury." Indeed, they are "morally dead."[31]

Murphy is writing about psychopaths.[32] But depending, perhaps, on how one interprets the requirement that the person without rights be "constitutionally incapable of real participation in cooperative social institutions or practices," this reasoning retains its force if we substitute the foreigner, the internal threat, or the terrorist in place of the psychopath. Murphy's reasoning generalizes—or can be generalized—as a way of defining who counts as a person, in moral terms, and who does not, as well as a way of determining what rests on that distinction.

Nor is this reasoning neatly confined to the moral realm. For his part, Murphy distinguishes his moral claims from what the legal and political systems actually ought to do with such people.[33] Others, however, may see less need to draw that distinction. Indeed, Murphy's moral reasoning has striking (even if arguably superficial) similarities with the rhetoric of contemporary political discourse. Consider the ways U.S. officials—to take examples from only one country—use the term *terrorist* as a way of defining a shifting and amorphous group of people characterized by their lack of civilization, their inhuman nature, and their bestiality. In the words of President Bush, Vice President Cheney, and other officials, terrorists are "fanatics," "brutal," "barbaric," "evildoers," "uncivilized," and "animals."[34] In the introduction, I presented examples of political rhetoric in which various political and media figures sought to define Arabs, Muslims, or the Middle East as fanatical, exotic, and in need of correction. One purpose of this rhetoric is precisely to classify terrorists, their supporters, and even larger groups as "incapable" of participating properly in the social institutions or practices that are central to liberal democracy.

Statements like these do more than provide examples of the Orientalist discourse that runs through the war on terror. They also underscore Carl Schmitt's claim that "[t]he concept of humanity is an especially useful ideological instrument of imperialist expansion." Schmitt explains that implicit or explicit monopolizing of the term *humanity* "probably has certain incalculable effects, such as denying the enemy the quality of being human and declaring him to be an outlaw of humanity."[35] When translated into an explicitly political context, Murphy's reasoning about psychopaths' moral death and lack of rights supports this deployment of "humanity" by providing a basis for concluding that others who share the qualities of the psychopath are without rights. Animals, barbarians, psychopaths, and the like simply do not have traditional negative rights or political identity in a liberal order.

Finally, no contemporary account of rights is complete without considering their biopolitical functions and potential. This aspect of rights is easiest to see in the context of positive or welfare rights. Many contemporary liberal theorists have gone beyond the idea of rights as restraints on state power, so that the liberal ideal of being left alone has morphed into a guarantee of basic political status, limits on inequality, and a right to be cared for. Indeed, this transformation of the role of liberal rights is a direct response to the need for shared social structures that will achieve a future of equal rights, even if that future is always receding.

Thus, in his essay "Two Concepts of Liberty," Isaiah Berlin cautions against "positive" conceptions of liberty, but he also quite logically questions the value of freedom "without adequate conditions for [its] use."[36] Although John Rawls avoids the possibility of positive rights to assistance, he plainly admits the importance of economic and social factors to a workable definition of liberalism. Indeed, his second principle of justice requires an active and extensive government role in regulating forms and degrees of economic and social inequality.[37] By not only articulating the second principle of justice but also making it play an important role in ensuring the "fair value" or usefulness of political liberties, Rawls goes a long way toward a conception of welfare rights.[38]

Jeremy Waldron has taken the analysis further, as I noted earlier. Waldron argues that "we are unlikely to sustain any simple division between negative and positive rights of the sort that liberals have often tried to work with," in large part because so-called negative rights almost always protect "a basic human interest" and, in so doing, generate "waves of duties."[39] Noting that "the liberal idea of rights proclaims the value of high-spirited individuals leading their lives proudly and independently, on their own terms," Waldron writes that this idea "amounts to the demand that we should organize our lives together, our use of material resources, and our forms of cooperation and exchange, so that such proud and independent lives are available for all."[40] Indeed, as Waldron explains, "[r]ights to decent subsistence . . . are fundamental to our conception of the dignity and the inherent claims of men and women, endowed with needs as well as with autonomy, in a world that contains the resources that might (if others let them) enable them to live."[41]

Most recently, Martha Nussbaum has advanced a theory of justice that seeks to recognize and incorporate groups, such as the physically or mentally disabled, that are often excluded implicitly or explicitly from traditional liberal theories of justice and rights. Nussbaum proposes that "a substantive account of certain abilities and opportunities" should be "the relevant benchmark to use in asking whether a given society has delivered a minimal level of justice to its citizens."[42] Among the "capabilities" she lists are "life," "bodily health," and "bodily integrity." She goes on to describe these capabilities as "one species of a human rights approach."[43]

Nussbaum's account is ambiguous about whether these capabilities equate with positive rights. On the one hand, she insists that capability is distinct from functioning, so that "[w]here health is concerned, . . . people should be given ample opportunities to lead a healthy lifestyle, but the choice should be left up to them."[44] On the other hand, with respect to the issues facing disabled people, she insists that "the role of care in a conception of justice" should be "fundamental."[45] Moreover, she argues that implementing this approach is "a public task, which requires public planning and a public use of resources."[46] Nussbaum's arguments thus accord with Waldron's assertion that the distinction between negative and positive rights is unsustainable. But her analysis goes further, to insist that a just society requires a distribution of resources that will result in decent care, such that everyone will be able as much as possible to participate equally in the social and political community. She thus stakes a powerful claim to a liberal society in which positive rights are foundational.

Contemporary law makes room for a positive right to be protected, cared for, or treated—as my discussion of the Universal Declaration of Human Rights in chapter 2 makes clear. Article 25 insists, "Everyone has the right to . . . medical care and social services, and the right to security in the event of . . . sickness, disability, [or] old age." In the same way, the International Covenant on Economic, Social and Cultural Rights asserts "the right of everyone to social security, including social insurance," and "the right of everyone to the enjoyment of the highest attainable standard of physical and mental health." The recent Convention on the Rights of Persons with Disabilities makes similar assertions.[47] Academic legal commentary in the United States tends to support these claims, and there has been some headway in European law.[48] Positive rights do not have much purchase in U.S. constitutional law, but the presence of an entrenched (even if contingent) welfare state indicates the extent to which some level of welfare rights exist in the United States, and constitutional law offers some protection for the interests created by the welfare state.[49]

In the Kantian world that Murphy sketched in his essay on psychopaths, people have rights—including the right to punishment—if they are "normal." Precisely because they are not normal, deviants are not entitled to these rights. The psychopath thus has forfeited the moral right to a particular kind of intervention in his or her life, an intervention that is designed to affirm moral worth. But Murphy recognizes and contemporary theorists confirm that the psychopath still gets something from the state, another form of intervention that is keyed to his or her moral worth, even if it is something less, in moral terms, than the punishment a normal person receives. Further, as I suggested earlier, these arguments about moral rights and duties are not hermetically sealed. They slip easily into the political realm (to the extent that we even want to speak of the moral and political as separate). Deviants thus not only have moral (even if unequal) rights but plainly also have extensive political rights in a modern liberal state. Those rights are simply the opposite of negative rights; they are explicitly positive rights to treatment and control.

In short, for people who cannot care for themselves in what we would call a normal way, contemporary liberal approaches tend to recognize a right to be treated, controlled, and detained. This means that welfare rights often include a right to be coerced—that is, to be a subject of state violence. For people unable to take care of themselves—be they psychopaths or, perhaps, terrorists—the decent liberal response is rational violence, containment, and, where possible, treatment.

This right to control and treatment also generalizes to anyone who cannot fully exercise the more traditional package of rights. Roy Porter explains,

> In a rational, democratic and progressive society, medicine should not be restricted and reactive; it should assume a universal and positive presence, it should address the totality of pathological tendencies in the community and correct them through farsighted policies, the law, education and specific agencies.[50]

By now, the biopolitical nature of the positive right to care should be clear. Welfare rights quite explicitly reflect Foucault's claim that modern sovereignty takes the form of a power "to 'make' live and 'let' die."[51] Consider, for example, Sheldon Wolin's observation that the U.S. welfare state has increased the power of the government over—and, indeed, helps to define— marginal groups who "are kept suspended between hope and despair but not plunged into desperation." Wolin asks, "[W]hat are the political implications of humanitarianism, of classifying citizens as needy and of making them needful objects of state power?"[52]

My point is not that there are no differences between torture and such things as medical care. But to the extent that we take seriously the idea of universal rights, including universal positive or welfare rights to care, treatment, and subsistence, these rights will extend broadly into the entire population. At that point, rights discourse faces the problem of describing, on its own terms, the difference between officially sanctioned care that is sometimes violent and painful, and officially sanctioned "torture."

International Rights and International Violence
❧

As I suggested earlier, the approach to rights I have sketched raises important questions, not just about the idea of liberal rights or their functioning in particular legal systems, but also about the idea of international human rights. If rights simply reduce to the actual ways in which people are treated and to their ability to claim meaningful protections and remedies, the international law of human rights appears weak. Enforcement structures are noticeably lacking, and human rights violations are rampant across the globe. So, too, because most of the more specific rules of international law are written by people acting on behalf of national governments, those rules will serve the goals of those governments, with the result that human rights will be protected only within a web of state interests. Brian Tamanaha suggests that "the most powerful states, and less powerful states when it matters most to them, . . . disregard international law . . . when they considered it necessary for perceived national interest or to preserve the regime in power." He contends that this is particularly true for human rights, which have "a largely paper or symbolic presence, at least in those states that reject them or respect them least."[53]

Still, as many international law scholars are fond of pointing out, most nations conform to the norms of international law, including human rights law, most of the time. Enforcement and compliance, although often weak, nonetheless take place in a variety of ways, such that one can speak meaningfully of international law as a source of norms that national governments weigh and consider in the course of developing policies. The fact that countries so often seek to justify their conduct as consistent with international law also suggests the importance of international law. Peter Malanczuk explains, "While international law is clearly weaker than municipal law from the viewpoint of independent enforcement, it still provides the external relevant terms of legal reference for the conduct of states in their international relations."[54] Recent developments in international law—such as the creation of the ICTY and the ICC—have made possible the direct and concrete enforcement of some international humanitarian and human rights norms through such traditional processes as criminal trials. International law provides a structure, language, and set of norms for international relations and for the ways people are treated by their own and by other countries. To have any meaning or effectiveness, it also builds on and depends on the existence and interests of nation-states and on the citizen-state relationship.[55]

Consider, then, the functions of international human rights law. Human rights discourse often appears to define rights simultaneously as universal and as the ultimate symbol of rational, Western, progressive ideals. Seen in the latter way, human rights are also something to be imposed on countries assumed to have no awareness or practice of rights—so that there are countries that by definition understand and respect rights and countries that by definition do not. This way of thinking about international human rights turns them into a colonial and imperial project. Importantly, moreover, the effort to transcend geographic particularity by defining human rights in universal terms cannot escape this accusation. As Jordanna Bailkin points out, to the extent that human rights discourse claims to be "placeless," it is all the more imperial.[56]

I am not making a simple claim of cultural relativism. Nor do I want to suggest that the West must accept responsibility for imperialism and "make amends," particularly when those amends will likely take the form of further intervention and control. Human rights norms are part and parcel of modernity and the politics of nation-states throughout the world. Indeed, as I noted in chapter 1, one way of thinking about rights is as the canary in the coal mine, such that an appearance or increase in rights claims alerts us to an expansion of modern state power—although the analogy is limited, because rights claims are ultimately part of that expansion, not merely an indicator of it. It is also worth remembering that in many countries, human rights norms function as much or more as rhetorical devices than as effective constraints on behavior. Thus, it is sometimes difficult to identify the countries in which these norms have the most practical effect. Finally, I am not claiming that international human rights are pernicious or hypocritical. To the contrary, in a world of modern nation-states, rights can help insulate some citizens from some forms of state violence.

My argument, instead, is twofold. First, I want to emphasize the points made repeatedly by a host of writers operating from a variety of critical and postcolonial perspectives: we cannot pretend that rights discourse and the liberal individualism it rests on are neutral, universal, or necessarily separate from the experience of modernity or from U.S. and European economic and political dominance—whether as a matter of history or of contemporary realities. Nor can we say that liberal rights are in fact liberating in some objective sense, even for those who have them. To the contrary, liberalism and the idea of rights developed alongside and in dependence on colonialism, imperialism, and modern systems of production and trade, and they serve the interests of the modern state.[57]

Second, I want to highlight the way in which international law and international human rights discourse serve to license state violence. An oft-cited example is the fact that the laws of war—including international humanitarian law—justify state violence even as they struggle to place limits on it.[58] Another example comes from chapter 1, which closed with a reference to a U.N. Security Council resolution requiring states to increase counterterror activities. Inderpal Grewal extends the point implicit in these examples.

> The U.S. government has used human rights as a key tool of its claims to exceptionality, while European governments have incorporated them into racialized demarcations of liberal democracy from non-Western barbarian or totalitarian rule all through the latter half of the twentieth century and into the twenty-first century.[59]

Along the same lines, chapter 2 noted how European human rights law tends to efface state responsibility for torture, while chapter 3 discussed the complex relationship between rights and state violence in U.S. constitutional discourse. The next chapter will describe how British concerns about compliance with the European Convention on Human Rights provided a justification for continued torture of Kikuyu prisoners.

Human rights concerns also support the war on terror. Amy Farrell and Patrice McDermott have described how the goal of "liberating" Afghan and Iraqi women became a justification for the U.S. invasion of both countries. Tarik Kochi has explained the ways in which foundational assumptions of contemporary international law continually license violence in the name of promoting peace and protecting universal human rights, even as, "for those who must face and suffer from this violence, a war in the name of humanity might appear, more accurately, as terror in the name of human rights."[60]

Conclusion

∼

My claim in this chapter is not that we must discard rights discourse. Perhaps one can reject the utopian and imperial aspects of liberalism and still declare oneself a liberal. Some writers might even argue that this is precisely the point of most liberal theories, when they are read correctly.[61] Certainly that is one way of understanding Waldron's argument about archetypes. Many readers—perhaps most—probably believe that liberal rights are, on balance, a good thing; that the development of international human rights protection is worth the effort; and that the alternatives are not so clearly superior as to justify serious exploration.[62]

Nonetheless, the fact remains that liberal rights inscribe people into state power as citizens or individuals whose critical political characteristic is the possession of rights. Where rights are wanting, people are at the mercy of the state. Where people have rights, they must exercise and assert them within the mechanisms of state power. As I pointed out in chapter 3, the most appropriate way to exercise rights in a liberal state is sometimes by waiving them or remaining ignorant of them. The law of international human rights, by expanding the network of obligations, further places people under the protection and control of the states in which they live and at risk of violence in the name of their rights.

Seen in this way, one must consider how far apart contemporary liberal theory is from more critical approaches to rights and the liberal state. While many liberal theorists claim that opposition to cruelty is foundational to liberalism and moral leadership, Lisa Silverman notes that this opposition sometimes takes the form of self-indulgent pity and sentimentality. Karen Halttunen demonstrates how the creation of the concept "sadism" is tightly integrated with the rise of a humanitarian sensibility. Giorgio Agamben controversially suggests that "[t]he 'imploring eyes' of the Rwandan child, whose photograph is shown to obtain money but who 'is now becoming more and more difficult to find alive,' may well be the most telling contemporary cipher of the bare life that humanitarian organizations, in perfect symmetry with state power, need."[63]

With respect to the definition of the liberal rights-holder, Stephen Holmes stresses the importance of the abstracted individual and the need to exclude some issues from the political sphere. Contrast Carl Schmitt's contention that "[i]n the domain of the political, people do not face each other as abstractions, but as politically interested and politically determined persons, as citizens, governors or governed, politically allied or opponents." Schmitt's point is that ultimately these specific interests will emerge in some forum, so that the insistence on a political realm of abstract rights, equality, and narrowly focused debate means that "political equality will be devalued to the extent that it approximates absolute human equality." He explains,

> Substantive inequalities would in no way disappear from the world and the state; they would shift into another sphere, perhaps separated from the political and concentrated in the economic. . . . Under conditions of superficial political equality, another sphere in which substantial inequalities prevail (today, for example, the economic sphere) will dominate politics.[64]

In fact, such liberal theorists as Holmes, Rawls, and Michael Walzer have recognized and sought to grapple with this problem, particularly with the limits of rights discourse for dealing with issues of distributive justice in a liberal society.[65] Meanwhile, of course, even the most casual observer of American politics realizes that the economic realm exerts an enormous amount of influence on the political.

Consider, too, the emphasis that Holmes and Raz place on the importance of rights to the state itself and on the role of the state in shaping the understanding and experience of autonomy, as well as the concern Nussbaum and Waldron express for positive rights. These ideas overlap with—although they are by no means the equivalent of—Foucault's idea of biopolitics, in which government regulation and disciplinary networks combine to produce not only "a system of rights that were egalitarian in principle," in which "the will of all [could] form the fundamental authority of sovereignty," but also a social structure that "provide[s], at the base, a guarantee of the submission of forces and bodies."[66] The implications of these ideas are not so different from Agamben's claim that "the spaces, the liberties, and the rights won by individuals in their conflicts with central powers always simultaneously prepared a tacit but increasing inscription of individual's lives within the state order."[67] Similarly, Holmes's assertion that a violation of individual rights is also defiance of the liberal state resonates with Ruth Miller's description of the ways in which modern states interpret crime—particularly crimes against bodily integrity—as invasions of national borders as much as bodily borders.[68] I am claiming, in other words, that as contemporary liberal theory accommodates itself to the realities of the biopolitical state, the differences between these ostensibly disparate approaches to modernity begin to seem like issues of emphasis only.

Finally and perhaps most critically in the context of this book, when Murphy develops the idea that psychopaths are moral animals without rights—so that "[w]e can act wrongly with respect to them, but they cannot be wronged. They can be injured, but they can be done no moral injury"—his application of Kant prefigures Agamben's analysis of "the politicization of bare life as such" and, in particular, Agamben's identification of the *homo sacer*, "who may be killed and yet not sacrificed," as central to modern politics.[69] That analysis dovetails, of course, with Schmitt's point about the ways in which the term *humanity* functions to deny the humanity and rights of one's enemies. Here, liberal and critical theory converge descriptively to create and recognize, respectively, categories of people—exemplified but not exhausted by the categories of terrorist "animals" and so-called ghost detainees—who stand in an exceptional state that renders them vulnerable to injury, including torture or death, even as the infliction of injury is itself not culpable.

To conclude, my discussion in the previous chapters of the international, European, and U.S. law of torture reflects my concern about tensions in the nature of rights and within legal structures that purportedly exist to control state violence. My discussion of the ways in which modern states continue to practice torture—which immediately follows—will demonstrate how these tensions play out on the bodies of people subjected to state violence. This chapter interrupts and therefore highlights these tensions. It also goes a step further to suggest that the operation of rights does not reflect tensions between theory and practice or between liberal theory and state power and that, rather, the control over people's lives exercised by the modern state—including sometimes violent domination—is consistent with and perhaps even the fulfillment of rights discourse and liberal ideology.

CHAPTER FIVE

❦

Torture in Modern Democracies

This chapter surveys episodes in the modern use of torture by countries in Europe, as well as by Canada and Israel. By using the word *modern,* I am suggesting that this chapter will discuss relatively recent uses of torture (for the most part, since World War II), as well as that the countries I am discussing define themselves as progressive, developed, and bureaucratic. These states define their relationships with their citizens and residents through such things as individual rights, voting, and the provision of welfare benefits. Each country is a signatory to the Convention against Torture and the ICCPR, and the European countries are signatories to the European Convention on Human Rights and the European Convention for the Prevention of Torture. Each has thus committed itself to respect human rights without regard for such things as ethnicity or citizenship.

My goal here is threefold. First, by weaving together examples of the frequent use of torture or related forms of abuse by each country and the willingness by some countries to send people to near-certain abuse in other countries, I provide support for my claim that torture is not a form of aberrational conduct in democratic societies but is instead pervasive. I do not provide a complete account of how liberal democracies have used torture in recent decades.[1] Nor do I engage much in this chapter with other forms of state violence that serve similar goals as those served by torture. For example, my discussion of Northern Ireland largely centers on the use of the so-called five techniques in 1971 and not on the larger patterns of violence that characterized the maintenance of British rule there. Similarly, when I discuss Israel, I will concentrate on the interrogation of people suspected of terrorism and not on the other forms of coercion and violence that the government has employed over the years. The ease with which my accounts can be supplemented and expanded by numerous media stories, human rights reports, and scholarly studies not only confirms the pervasiveness of state violence—including torture—in modern democracies but also suggests that it may be essential to them. Second, my consideration of each county will allow me to isolate strands of reasoning that are common to all of them—in particular, forms of racism and colonialism; concern about law; and ideas of emergency, exception, and necessity.[2] These common themes provide support or explanation for acts that many would maintain are contrary to the moral underpinnings of liberal, democratic societies. Third, for several of these countries, my narrative will include some of their actions in the contemporary war on terror. These actions further underscore the fact that torture in modern democracies, while arguably commonplace, is also hidden and therefore almost always capable of being characterized or explained as exceptional.

France
⌒

The case of France is particularly interesting for the strong parallels between the French approach to torture in Algeria and the U.S. approach to torture after September 11, 2001. My focus is on French torture in a colonial context, but torture has also been part of twentieth-century French policing. Thus, Darius Rejali notes that "[i]n Vietnam in the 1920s, *as in France,* police sweated and beat criminals during interrogation."[3] French police used torture, including water and electricity, in at least six cases in 1947 and 1948.[4] The 1999 *Selmouni* case was cited as a central example in chapter 2. French officials' use of torture against political prisoners in Algeria and Vietnam before and after World War II thus reflects both the imperial context of torture and a more general attitude toward using violence to maintain order.

During the struggle to maintain control of the French colony in Southeast Asia in the late 1940s and early 1950s, French forces developed counterinsurgency techniques that included the use of torture to obtain information, and they encouraged their allies among the Vietnamese to do the same. General Jacques Massu claimed that torture was used only by the Vietnamese themselves, who supposedly employed "ancient methods practiced among them." Douglas Porch demonstrates, however, that the "fairly typical pattern" of coercive interrogation during the French war in Vietnam involved small groups of French and Vietnamese forces, although it is possible that French troops supervised or encouraged their Vietnamese colleagues to take the lead in inflicting abuse.[5] If so, France followed a practice that, as we will see, the British also employed: allow or encourage abuse by "natives" on other natives, and so retain the ability of colonial officials to deny responsibility for deplorable but allegedly "traditional" methods of treating prisoners. The existence of such timeless practices among the colonized people ensures that they alone bear the blame for these practices and also becomes an argument that they remain uncivilized and thus in need of continued colonization—indeed, even in need of violent correction.

By 1954, when the insurgency in Algeria began, General Massu and other French military personnel were trained and prepared to apply their Vietnam experiences to the effort to suppress the Front de Libération National (FLN).[6] Police in Algeria were also able to draw on similar methods of abuse.[7] On April 3, 1955, the French National Assembly declared a state of emergency in Algeria and gave the government "special powers" to undertake "any exceptional measure required by the circumstances with a view to the reestablishment of order." By the time the state of emergency was declared, the government already had access to a report, discussed shortly, that substantiated early complaints about the use of torture. Thus, as Rita Maran points out, they could reasonably have anticipated that the legislation would only accelerate the use of abusive tactics. Article 16 of the Constitution of the Fifth Republic, which was adopted in 1958 as the conflict still raged and in full awareness of the excesses already committed by French forces, set the conditions for normalizing the state of emergency that had already been legislated under the Fourth Republic.

> Where the institutions of the Republic, the independence of the Nation, the integrity of its territory or the fulfillment of its international commitments are under serious and immediate threat, and where the proper functioning of the constitutional public authorities is interrupted, the President of the Republic shall take the measures required by these circumstances, after formally consulting the Prime Minister, the Speakers of the houses and the Constitutional Council.[8]

Throughout this period, French police and military forces sought to gather information, intimidate the non-European majority, and defeat the FLN by detaining large numbers of Algerians (one estimate claims that 40 percent of the men in the Casbah in Algiers were detained) and freely employing torture on them, most famously during the Battle of Algiers. The specific tactics included beatings, electric shock, submerging suspects in water, and prolonged standing. French forces also freely killed Algerians who may or may not have aided the FLN (which, of course, was waging its own violent campaign that included the targeting of French "civilians" of all ages), and they engaged in "indiscriminate bombing of villages in rebel-controlled areas and . . . resettlement of populations in French camps." Porch reports that "[a]lmost 4,000 people in French custody 'disappeared,'" and General Paul Aussaresses appears to accept that 24,000 were arrested or detained and that more then 3,000 "were missing." Importantly, the mistreatment of Algerians, specifically including torture, was not the spontaneous decision of forces on the ground. Instead, it was approved by commanding officers and—according to some commentators and participants—reflected a higher-level policy decision to use any means necessary to end the conflict. Nor was torture confined to the Algerian *départements;* French police also tortured Algerians in other parts of France. Torture, in short, was not an isolated phenomenon. It was part of an overall strategy to intimidate, dominate, and control not only the FLN but the entire non-European population of Algeria. Many French officers maintained that the strategy worked in the sense that suspects provided information, although charting the overall impact of torture on the war effort is far more complex.[9]

In a careful analysis, Darius Rejali agrees that torture sometimes resulted in useful information, but he also demonstrates that it produced false positives far more often.[10] As for the impact of torture on the Battle of Algiers, he suggests that the policy of mass arrests (which "create[d] a general feeling of terror"), selective violence against suspected FLN operatives, and an informant system were chiefly responsibly for the victory.[11] To the extent that torture played a role, it was largely as an "indispensable . . . method of intimidation"—that is, as "'a political form of violence'" that reinforced French power.[12] Yet torture did not destroy the FLN, and it almost certainly helped turn large numbers of Algerians against French rule.[13]

Just as significant as the widespread implementation of the torture policy was the response of the French political and intellectual establishment. Some officials and public figures deplored the use of torture and other abuses, but the overall reaction was mixed.[14] Although torture was a policy established by commanders and implemented by soldiers at all ranks, few were ever brought to trial or convicted of any crime. High-ranking politicians in the Fourth Republic—such as François Mitterand, minister of the interior—predictably condemned the use of torture, but their response to early allegations that it had in fact been used was simply to call for an investigation.

The result was the Wuillame Report of March 1955, which found that the allegations of police abuse in Algeria were essentially correct. Significantly, the report largely avoided the word *torture* and instead employed euphemisms for techniques it characterized as "old-established practice" that "in normal times" were only used "on persons against whom there is a considerable weight of evidence of guilt." Torture was thus part of the ordinary apparatus of colonial oppression in Algeria and was expanded during the struggle against the FLN. The report also found that the results obtained through these methods were "magnificent," and it therefore declined to "cast aspersions on a body of civil servants who can, in their defense, point to so many acts of devotion to duty, even heroism." The report did, however, suggest a more controlled use of "special procedures." It apparently served its purpose simply through the fact of being prepared, and the officials who ordered its preparation took no action in response to it.[15]

Other official responses to the use of torture were equivocal. In 1958, near the end of the Fourth Republic, Michel Debré, then a senator and soon to be de Gaulle's minister of justice, admitted, "There is torture in Algeria." But he explained that it occurred "because we have no State." "When we have a State again," he argued, "things will change." For Debré, in other words, torture could be explained away or minimized by linking it to a condition of statelessness in France or perhaps even to a state of nature, which Algeria, as a colonized space, already was by definition.[16] Yet the claim of statelessness is odd, because the trappings of state power—particularly the military and police—continued to function even if there was "no State" in some formal or political sense. What Debré might perhaps have meant is that there was no politically legitimate legal authority to manage the deployment of state violence. If that is so, the problem he was attempting to articulate was not that the state had disappeared; rather, to paraphrase Carl Schmitt, the state remained, but the law had receded.[17] Put simply, the problem that produced torture was, for Debré, the declared state of exception that had displaced the experience of normal political authority. Yet this statement risks being disingenuous, because the state of exception would soon be incorporated into the new constitution that would produce the government he was about to join. In a state partially constituted by a state of exception, what exactly would change?

De Gaulle's minister of information, André Malreaux, similarly admitted that torture had been part of the conflict in Algeria, when he asserted a short time later, "No act of torture has been produced . . . since the visit to Algiers of General de Gaulle." Again, a political rupture was taking place, which, for Malreaux, meant that the sins of the old regime would die with it. By 1960, de Gaulle was able to assert breezily, "The French Army is carrying out in Algeria what France expects of it," and he made clear that the situation in Algeria was simply one of many issues facing the government. Throughout this period, abuse of Algerians continued.[18] In short, the conflict and the violent treatment of Algerians that was integral to it was entirely normalized and had become just another issue to be managed pragmatically in the new political order.

Rita Maran's study of the French social and political response to the use of torture in Algeria is invaluable for the way in which she situates that response within a larger picture of French culture. According to Maran, the torture of Algerians reflected what seems, at first, a perverse fulfillment of the *mission civilisatrice*. Algeria was technically part of metropolitan France, in that it comprised three *départements*—as Mitterand said in 1954, "Algeria is France." But it was also a colony, and the majority of its population, although citizens, had little meaningful opportunity to participate in French rule. Thus, the application of the *mission civilisatrice* to Algeria—simultaneously France and a colony of France—was particularly interesting. Maran explains,

> Within the notion of the civilizing mission are simultaneously contradictory and symbiotic meanings. One reflects prevailing colonialist attitudes of the era in which the civilizing mission came into usage, of superiority and inferiority of certain categories of human beings. Another reflects the self-perception of France as a culture exceptionally well-endowed with an understanding of rights that derived from the works of French enlightenment philosophers. . . . The further assumption was that France—by virtue of its status as an enlightened civilization—had a duty to disseminate these concepts safely.

She goes on to suggest that this ideal of France as the purveyor of enlightenment was easily able to coexist with torture, because torture became a necessary tactic in the struggle to preserve enlightenment values and French citizenship against foreign pollution. In this way, national values became identified with a larger but more amorphous set of Western and Christian values to be defended against "[t]heir Muslim opponents . . . whether Islamic or Communist," and the need to hold the line on behalf of the West justified harsh tactics in the service of that greater good.[19]

One might also add, as Mark Sanders has written, that "any 'civilizing mission' is constantly at odds with a compulsion, irreducible to mere instrumentality, to limit the access of specific populations or subpopulations to it." Among other things, access is limited by violence, by what Anupama Rao describes as "the cultures of terror [that] were essential to the task of colonial governance." As she explains, "The colonial state often understood itself as struggling to institute a neutral and rational 'rule of law' in a situation where ruling over the racially inferior and culturally backward often demanded the imposition of forms of physical and symbolic violence."[20] Seen in this way, the violent campaign to destroy Algerian nationalism and maintain French rule ably reflected both aspects of the *mission civilisatrice*.

These ideas also fed a sense of grievance on the part of French forces. Because they represented civilization, they perceived themselves as unable to respond in kind to the atrocities committed by an enemy that was unfamiliar and inscrutable; their hands were "tied behind their backs." Torture was a way of leveling the playing field; it made possible the gathering of information that would allow a targeted response to indiscriminate terrorist atrocities. Perhaps more important, it was always, by definition, a response to worse practices on the other side. As General Aussaresses put it, "the use of this kind of violence, which is unacceptable under normal circumstances, could become inevitable in a situation that clearly defied every rule"—that is, where the opponent does not play by civilized rules. Some participants, such as Aussaresses's commanding officer, General Massu, also contended that the use of torture was carefully managed, not indiscriminate, and that the enemy exaggerated its use for propaganda purposes. Less self-interested commentators have concluded that "[t]he groundswell of antigovernment feeling in France that destroyed the Fourth Republic can in large part be directly attributed to the unrestrained, government-condoned, illegal acts of the French Army."[21] In other words, the widely publicized practices of the army revealed the violence that had always been necessary to colonialism, including in Algeria, and they upset the balancing act that comprised the *mission civilisatrice,* with the result that a large segment of "public opinion" demanded a different or at least less visible course.

The ideals of the *mission civilisatrice* also supported other efforts to justify the use of torture. In addition to such things as the Wuillame Report and the arguments of military personnel, media sources, such as *Le Figaro,* sought to explain away the use of torture by suggesting that the allegations were overblown and that, in any event, one could not expect strict adherence to legalities during such a conflict. One had, instead, to keep one's eye on the larger goal of "defend[ing] . . . high civilizing values against a blazing fire of barbarism."[22]

Even for many of those who opposed the use of torture, the reason was as much because they believed it contradicted French values and the country's "role as bearer of civilization and culture" as because of the harm it caused. The underlying fact of colonialism was accepted as reflecting "the fundamental benevolence and superiority of the French spirit and France's role in the world as a disseminator of civilization."[23] The solution, in other words, was to maintain France's position without torture.

These responses to detention, abuse, torture, summary execution, and other practices continue to resonate in France. As Vivian Curran has documented, France's Court of Cassation has defined the concept of the crime against humanity in a way that prevents French defendants from "being deemed to have committed crimes against humanity in Algeria in the name of France." President Chirac rejected calls to apologize for France's use of torture or even to admit that it took place. Referring to conduct that "may have been carried out," he insisted that he would "do nothing to detract from the honour of those French soldiers" who fought in Algeria. According to Curran, there is "a small minority in France today that believes France's war in Algeria had legitimate and just goals, and refuses to yield the entire terrain of victimhood to Arab Algerians."[24]

Since the war in Algeria, France has been involved in periodic charges before the European Court of Human Rights (e.g., those in the *Selmouni* case) and has cooperated with Spain and the United States in efforts to combat terrorism.[25] Beginning in the 1980s, France extradited, deported, or expelled significant numbers of Basque militants and refugees to Spain. In 1986, Amnesty International criticized France for taking these actions, because France had reason to know that the people sent back to Spain might be tortured and because officials had acted without obtaining assurances that there would be no torture. The U.N. Committee against Torture raised similar concerns in 1998 about "[t]he practice whereby the police hand over individuals to their counterparts in another country, despite the fact that a French court has declared such practices to be illegal."[26] As my discussion of Spain will indicate, these charges and concerns were warranted.

Current French law gives enormous powers to law enforcement officials, and these officials have relied heavily on "preemptive arrests, ethnic profiling, and an efficient domestic intelligence-gathering network." French officials have also cooperated extensively with the CIA in the apprehension, rendition, and interrogation of suspected terrorists. French investigators visited Guantánamo Bay Naval Base to obtain information about detainees with French connections, and the French government detained a large number of suspects after the terrorist attacks of September 11, 2001, often in cooperation with the CIA. Although I am not aware of evidence that suggests that these detainees were abused in French custody or sent to third countries for abuse, the fact that the French government was willing to take advantage of information extracted at Guantánamo suggests that it is not squeamish about the manner in which terrorism suspects are treated. Indeed, such cases as *Selmouni* suggest that mistreatment of suspected terrorists by the French government would not be a shock.[27]

The United Kingdom

~

The abuse of suspected Irish Republican Army (IRA) militants by British troops and the Royal Ulster Constabulary has been widely discussed among legal academics. Far less attention has been paid to a larger pattern of abusive treatment and torture on the part of British colonial authorities in the twentieth century. For example, the "five techniques" that were at issue in the *Ireland v. United Kingdom* case before the European Court of Human Rights—wall-standing for hours, hooding, continuous loud and hissing noise, sleep deprivation, and restricted food and water—were not innovations developed specifically for that conflict. The five techniques were among the methods (others included beating, flogging, electricity, and hot eggs) used "by the British authorities to cope with situations involving internal security problems"—that is, unruly colonial subjects—"in Palestine,

Malaya, Kenya, Cyprus, British Cameroon, Brunei, British Guiana, Aden, Borneo/Malaysia, and the Persian Gulf." They were "standard procedures authorized by the Joint Directive on Military Interrogation in Internal Security Operations Overseas." The joint directive, in turn, used the idea of a state of emergency as a rationale for these methods: "Persons arrested or detained during Internal Security operations or in near emergency are likely to be valuable sources of intelligence. They may be the only sources of intelligence at a time when it is urgently required."[28]

Notably, the emergencies during which these methods were used often had a legal basis. During the 1950s, the British government frequently filed official derogations from the European Convention on Human Rights when it faced colonial difficulties.[29] What distinguished the deployment of the five techniques during the emergency in Northern Ireland may simply be the use of these practices against colonized subjects who were also Europeans.

The use of torture as an integral part of British colonialism became public as early as 1855, with the *Report of the Commissioners for the Investigation of the Alleged Cases of Torture in the Madras Presidency*. That report, in Anupama Rao's words, "drew attention to torture as a structural problem of policing, rather than an aberrant and extraordinary instance." Yet the report was not an inquiry into the practices of British officials in India. Instead, it was an exposé of the actions of the native police whom they oversaw. Torture in the colonial setting was outsourced to the local population, who comprised the bulk of the police forces, which allowed colonial authorities to dismiss any abuses, no matter how common, as aberrational in a different sense—as a persistent native practice that departed from civilized British norms. Indeed, the report ultimately blamed most of the torture on the traditional practices of the police and distinguished those practices from "the upright morality of their British superiors." According to the report, disgust at the use of torture was not directed at the British rulers; rather "the whole cry of the people . . . is to save them from the cruelties of their fellow Natives."[30]

The systematic use of torture in India became associated with other disagreeable traditional practices that had to be eradicated to achieve the societal reform and imposition of a homogenous rule of law that characterized the colonial project. In this way, as Rao observes, "it was the presence of native policemen, rather than the role of the police in a colonial regime, that came to be problematized." For their part, colonial authorities were simultaneously able to deny responsibility for torture and other abuses, rely on the confessions that torture produced, and present themselves as protectors and reformers who saved the local population from its own malefactors. Indeed, the 1855 report became a justification for a more intrusive colonial regime that would—it was claimed—result in reform of the police and the criminal law. Radhika Singha suggests that the question of torture was merely one area in which this dynamic played out.

> The principle of European supervision over Indian subordinates also served a rhetorical function, that of associating the former with an avowedly transcendent, rule-governed public legality, through which the oriental excesses of the latter were monitored. The issue of torture in revenue and police work provided one such ideological terrain for claims to be protecting Indians against despotic native functionaries.

Rao's assessment of the report and of the way in which British administrators managed other complaints about torture—that they are examples of "discourses of improvement [that] masked the attempts to impose more coercive forms of rule over citizen-subjects"—thus appears accurate.[31]

I want to stress as well that the debate over torture in colonial India reflects two important themes of this book. One theme is that modern states "outsource" torture to local subordinates, thus maintaining the ability simultaneously to use torture, deny responsibility for it, and affirm the superiority of the civilized world. The second is that this dynamic of denial of and reliance on torture is central not just to the colonial project but also to the more general modern project of defining citizens and their relationship to the state. The creation of a colonial rule of law in India required defining the native population, discovering its traditional practices, and then managing that population partly through the criminal law, which, in turn, comprised a shifting mix of traditional and colonial elements. The goal, as Singha observes, was to create "an equal abstract and universal subject" whose actions had consequences for and infringed on the rights not just of other individuals but of the public as a whole. In the context of the criminal law, achieving this goal meant "reorder[ing] the identity of the offender in a more uniform and standardized way as the object of punishment."[32]

Let us move now from the relatively early days of the British Empire to its waning years. When it capitulated to the independence movement in India, Britain left behind, according to Anandswarup Gupta,

> a Police Force with a very small Indian leadership and a subordinate body, which had been studiously trained in the use of brute force and in which extortion, corruption and malpractices had been tolerated with a callous indifference to the welfare and the dignity of the Indian citizen and had been allowed to acquire the sanctity of a tradition.

Britain's withdrawal from India was not accomplished in an orderly or peaceful way. Beginning in the early 1930s, the government enacted and invoked a series of "emergency" laws that empowered police and soldiers to use violence to suppress the independence movement. During five months in 1942 alone, "[a]bout 60,000 people were arrested. 52,000 were convicted by Special, Ordinary, and Military Courts, 18,000 were detained without trial and 940 were killed and 1,941 injured in actions by the police and troops."[33] The years leading up to independence, in short, were exceptional as a matter of law, yet at the same time, the forces of law and order employed methods that were different, if at all, only in degree from their normal training and repertoire.

At the time Britain was relinquishing its colonial authority in India, it was also occupying portions of Germany after the allied victory in World War II. British forces set up camps and other facilities or used former concentration camps to house more than two million German prisoners, whether former members of the armed forces or suspicious civilians. Conditions in many of the camps were appalling, and in at least a few cases, British forces mistreated and even tortured the people under their control. They also made wide use of the death penalty, often without any meaningful review of sentences and with no effort to achieve consistency across cases. Further, military intelligence officials operated a special facility in London at which they interrogated large numbers of German prisoners. The interrogations were often coercive. Many of the prisoners were "systematically beaten, deprived of sleep, forced to stand still for more than 24 hours at a time and threatened with execution or unnecessary surgery." Others were "starved and subjected to extremes of temperature in specially built showers," while others "later complained that they have been threatened with electric shock torture or menaced by interrogators brandishing red hot pokers."[34]

A few years later, the use of torture by British colonial officials expanded in Kenya. Caroline Elkins notes, "White racial supremacy in Kenya had long manifested itself in various kinds of primitive settler justice, including public floggings, beating deaths, and summary executions." These and other practices became systematic in response to the Mau Mau uprising in the early 1950s—at roughly the same time that France was using torture in an effort to suppress Algerian nationalism. According to official documents, British forces established detention camps for "the rebellious Kikuyu . . . to civilize them." "Behind the barbed wire," writes Elkins, "colonial officials were reportedly giving the detainees civics courses and home-craft classes; they were teaching the insurgents how to be good citizens and thus become capable of running Kenya sometime in the future." In fact, the camps were locations of brutality and terror into which nearly one and a half million people were crowded, with families often separated, and where torture and summary execution were part of the normal routine.[35]

Critically, in October 1952, before the camps could be established or other steps taken, British officials declared a state of emergency in Kenya. They did not lift it until 1960. During the emergency, British forces pushed well over half of the Kikuyu population into overflowing transit and detention camps, in which sanitation was almost nonexistent, diseases multiplied, and deaths were common. They also implemented forced labor; tried suspected Mau Mau adherents in emergency courts (which cut procedural corners and freely handed down death sentences); indulged in summary executions; massacred groups of Kikuyu; and made torture into a pervasive, routine practice.[36]

The project of transferring the entire Kikuyu population into camps was known as "the pipeline" and consisted of attempting to obtain information, separating out the "bad" natives from the rest, and "rehabilitating" them. This task overwhelmed the colonial bureaucracy, and brutal force became the currency of the regime. Part of the pipeline process was "screening," which initially took place as people were sorted in the camps. Screening, it turns out, was often a euphemism for torture. David Anderson writes that "some 'screening teams' . . . were renowned for physical violence to extract confession, and in some places this certainly amounted to institutionalized torture." Court records also disclose "frequent allegations of beatings and worse."[37]

Elkins collected numerous mutually supportive accounts of prolonged and severe beatings, being bound to a chair and beaten or burned with cigarettes, electric shock, shoving objects (e.g., "[b]ottles (often broken), gun barrels, knives, snakes, vermin, and hot eggs") into men's rectums and women's vaginas, skin searing, castration, squeezing breasts and testicles with pliers, dragging people behind cars, and rape. Inevitably, these practices generalized beyond the initial screening process and became part of the repertoire of camp administration and discipline. Torture was sometimes carried out in public, before other Kikuyu who had been or were soon to be detained. It thus became a spectacle of domination and terror. Quasi-independent settler groups also set up their own screening centers—known to and "tacitly approved" by official authorities—at which similar practices took place.[38] Becoming civilized was thus a process—or perhaps more precisely a violent ritual—that worked on the body as well as the mind or spirit, and in it, failure was fatal.

None of these routine, violent practices were admitted by the British government, which insisted to the British public and the wider world that any abuses were aberrations and would be investigated. They also reminded their audience of the brutality of the Mau Mau, thus invoking the standard argument about the savage colonized "other" as support for practices that were equally or more savage, even if also rationalized in the context of a colonial bureaucracy. Insisting on the use of force as a necessary response to the other side's brutality also dovetailed with the legal regime created by the state of emergency. As one interrogator put it, "I did not believe in obtaining information under threat of violence, although there are cases where such methods are necessary, such as in an emergency." Few British officials were ever disciplined for these abuses—most of which had been approved by their superiors at least in outline—and the governor explained he did not want to undermine morale by prosecuting those who went too far.[39]

International law also played a role in the British government's policies. Officials were only too aware of the constraints created by the recently adopted European Convention on Human Rights. The government invoked the derogation clause of Article 15 and, of course, never admitted to the torture and inhuman or degrading treatment that was nonderogable under the convention. Yet the government worried that keeping so many people detained for so long would lead to questions about its compliance with the convention, especially once the emergency seemed to be nearing an end. The Mau Mau uprising included an oath-taking procedure, and those who took the oath were bound not to reveal it. Much of the "rehabilitation" process in the camps turned, therefore, on forcing people to confess the oath, both to break them psychologically and to make them vulnerable to Mau Mau reprisals and thus force them to accept British "protection." (By forcing confessions from nearly everyone, the British also defined "innocent" Kikuyu as Mau Mau adherents in need of rehabilitation and ensured that the identity of "trustworthy" natives might depend precisely on the experience of being tortured.)

As the end of the emergency neared, in short, the Kikuyu who remained in the camps obtained rights against the British government under the convention—rights that might soon be protected from suspension. The government thus insisted on more confessions, so that the remaining detainees could be processed through the pipeline. The predictable result was an increase in the intensity of torture and other abuse.[40] The constraints of international law and the rights held under it by the Kikuyu thus played a double role in the conflict. The government was unwilling to flout the law too blatantly for too long, and it worried that the patience of the international community might soon come to an end, so it placed temporal limits on the use of camps. Yet at the same time, the constraints of international law played a causal role in the increased use of brutality to force "confessions" from the remaining detainees. One way of describing this dynamic is as a perverse and cynical misuse of international norms by the British government. But this episode also reveals concretely how international human rights norms can have a more complex and troubling, though also entirely foreseeable, relationship to state violence, along the lines I suggested in chapter 4.

Soon thereafter, the use of coercion by British forces during interrogation of suspected insurgents in Cyprus played a role in the Greek government's decision to file suit against the United Kingdom before the European Commission of Human Rights. Among the claims were detailed allegations that British forces subjected 51 Cypriots to "torture or maltreatment."[41] The litigation ended before the commission could issue a decision on torture, as part of the political settlement of Cyprus's status.[42] Nonetheless, the case documented that abuse continued to have a place in the British approach to resisting anticolonial movements.

Let us return now to the five techniques and other practices used in Northern Ireland. In August 1971, in response to several months of IRA violence, the British government adopted a policy of "internment"—that is, the arrest and detention of people known or suspected to be associated with the IRA. British soldiers arrested roughly 350 people, with many more to follow over the subsequent months and years. About a third of those detained in that first sweep were released within 48 hours, but the rest were held for considerably longer periods.[43]

All of the detainees were interrogated, and many of them were also abused in various ways by the soldiers and policemen who held them in custody. The mistreatment included beatings, harassment by police or military dogs, being thrown out of helicopters believing they would fall to their deaths (although in fact they were only a few feet off the ground), performing rigorous physical exercise for hours at a time, and running over rough ground with bare feet. A smaller group of 12 or 14 detainees were treated to more severe abuse, under the label "interrogation in depth." Over the course of several days, this group was subjected to intense beatings with batons, kicking, being hooded and run into walls or posts, as well as the five techniques. Prisoners who were unable to endure the five techniques—for example, if they fell or collapsed while wall-standing—were beaten or kicked. After the abuse, they were detained for as long as three years without charges or meaningful hearings.[44]

Accounts of this mistreatment soon found their way into newspapers, and the government commissioned an investigation. The Compton Report of November 1971, officially known as the *Report of the Enquiry into Allegations against the Security Forces of Physical Brutality in Northern Ireland Arising out of Events on the 9th August, 1971*, vindicated the government by accepting its version of events and its explanation that many of the techniques were appropriate security measures. The report stressed the limited nature of the abuse and the emergency situation that made it necessary, when it noted that the five techniques were used in "the interrogation of a small number of persons arrested in Northern Ireland who were believed to possess information of a kind which it was operationally necessary to obtain as rapidly as possible in the interest of saving lives." Indeed, according to the report, the five techniques "assist[ed] the interrogation process by imposing discipline" on it.[45]

During the same period, government officials sought to justify the army's actions. The defense minister characterized those subjected to the five techniques as "thugs and murderers"—even though many of them had no serious IRA association and were never charged with any crime. The home secretary declared that the army's methods were justified by the need to subdue the IRA, while the junior defense minister maintained that they resulted in "invaluable" information—a claim that the European Court of Human Rights appears to have accepted in the subsequent *Ireland v. United Kingdom* litigation. Years later, the commander of the army in Northern Ireland, General Harry Tuzo, defended the techniques in the classic language used to refer to the lesser of two evils: "you have to choose between inflicting acute discomfort and humiliation, because it is that of course, on a few people in order possibly to save life and safeguard the well-being of perhaps a million people." As in Kenya, a legal patina helped give credibility to these justification arguments. Parliament passed a series of emergency measures that effectively placed Northern Ireland under emergency rule for many years, and the government sent the Council of Europe several notifications of its intention to derogate from the provisions of the European Convention on Human Rights in light of the situation in Northern Ireland.[46]

The Compton Report was followed by an inquiry into the kinds of interrogation techniques that ought to be used in the future. The *Report of the Privy Counsellors Appointed to Consider Authorised Procedures for the Interrogation of Persons Suspected of Terrorism*—usually called the Parker Report—appeared in January 1972. The majority of the commission noted that the five techniques had been developed and used elsewhere, and they accepted the army's claims that the techniques were justified based on information obtained. But one member of the commission, Lord Gardiner, filed a minority report objecting that the techniques were illegal and unjustifiable.[47] In response to the Parker Report—particularly the minority report—Prime Minister Edward Heath declared that the five techniques would no longer be used. John Conroy speculates that Heath's action was not humanitarian but political, particularly that it was a response to the suit that the Republic of Ireland had filed against the United Kingdom only a month before the Parker Report was issued.[48]

The lawsuit appears to have solidified popular opinion on the government's side, at least if the leading newspapers are any guide. The *Daily Mail* said that the five techniques were "necessary and nothing to be ashamed of," while the *Daily Express* emphasized that the army was dealing with "fanatics," against whom extreme measures were apparently justified. Other papers, such as the *Daily Telegraph* and the *Times*, noted that the techniques were not as bad as other methods that could have been employed, thus echoing the Parker Report's conclusion that these methods provided "discipline" for the interrogation process.[49] Seen slightly differently, these editorials asserted that the United Kingdom's abusive practices were more civilized than the tactics used by their opponents, so that the five techniques became markers of appropriate conduct instead of abuse.

The European Commission of Human Rights reviewed the claims of 228 people and found that the five practices, used together, amounted to torture and that several other practices also violated Article 3. Dissatisfied with the commission's failure to order prosecutions that would establish individual responsibility for use of the five techniques, Ireland appealed to the European Court of Human Rights. In response, the United Kingdom did not contest the finding that it had violated Article 3. Instead, it argued that because it had ceased using the five techniques, the court should decline to hear the case on the ground that "the objective of [the] application has been accomplished [and] adjudication on the merits would be devoid of purpose." The court rejected this argument and addressed the question whether British forces had violated Article 3's prohibition on torture and inhuman or degrading treatment.[50]

The court's decision on the Article 3 issues modified the commission's judgment in favor of the United Kingdom—even though the United Kingdom had not sought to litigate that issue at all. In a landmark ruling, the court held, in *Ireland v. United Kingdom,* that the techniques were inhuman and degrading but did not rise to the level of torture. The court explained that the techniques were inhuman because they caused "if not actual bodily injury, at least intense physical and mental suffering to the persons subjected thereto" and "also led to acute psychiatric disturbances during interrogation." The techniques qualified as degrading treatment because "they were such as to arouse in their victims feelings of fear, anguish and inferiority capable of humiliating and debasing them and possibly breaking their physical or moral resistance."[51]

The court insisted, however, that the five techniques were not torture. The difference between torture and inhuman or degrading treatment, the court explained, "derives principally from a difference in the intensity of the suffering inflicted." Because torture is an "aggravated" form of inhuman treatment that carries "a special stigma," the term *torture* should be reserved for "deliberate inhuman treatment causing very serious and cruel suffering." Although the five techniques were harsh and illegal, they did not "occasion suffering of the particular intensity and cruelty implied by the word torture." The court also ruled that the treatment of many other detainees was inhuman as well, although it declared that detaining people "in extreme discomfort" and making them "perform irksome and painful exercises" did not violate Article 3, even though it was "discreditable and reprehensible." Finally, the court ruled that it could not order punishment of the individuals responsible for the abuses. That was a matter for national courts, which, of course, were unlikely to take action once the conduct had been downgraded from torture to inhuman and degrading treatment.[52]

The court's decision has endured significant criticism from commentators who believe that the British practices were clearly torture, and the court's jurisprudence has changed to some degree, as I discussed in chapter 2. In its time, however, the decision was received as a triumph in Britain, and newspapers again defended the government's position and celebrated its victory. Moreover, while the case was on appeal from the commission to the court, newspapers revealed that soldiers were still receiving training in the five techniques, and the minister of defense defended the practice on the ground that the training would prepare soldiers for the tactics of "an unscrupulous enemy."[53]

More to the point, the court's decision exemplifies the kind of political balancing that Fionnuala Ní Aoláin has identified as characteristic of its approach to torture.[54] The United Kingdom's hands were slapped, but it was not labeled a torturer, and the issues in the litigation would hopefully be laid to rest by the government's pledge not to use the five techniques in the future (or, only to use them in emergencies). Significantly, the court's opinion devotes a significant amount of space to describing the depredations of the IRA and the emergency situation that existed, thus providing some rhetorical support for the justification arguments that were common in domestic British politics. But the court stopped short of accepting a justification rationale that would excuse the United Kingdom entirely— and doing so would have been difficult given the absolutist phrasing of Article 3 and the nature of the conduct. Still, the court's insistence on reaching the definitional issue and its decision that the five techniques are not torture plainly create an important dichotomy—not just a continuum—in Article 3, between the particularly serious category of torture and the illegal but less serious categories of inhuman or degrading treatment.

The idea of a strong dichotomy between torture and inhuman treatment was available the moment the European Convention on Human Rights was written, and it began to emerge in the Greek Case, but *Ireland v. United Kingdom* confirmed its importance. From then on, countries that wanted to mistreat detainees during interrogations could reasonably expect that they would receive greater latitude in emergency circumstances and that they could play a definitional game over the proper characterization of their conduct. Perhaps, they could argue, we have mistreated a few people, but we were in a tight spot, and at least we did not torture. Further, the convention and its interpretation in *Ireland v. United Kingdom* were known to the drafters of the U.N. Convention against Torture when they adopted a similar distinction between torture and lesser but still illegal forms of treatment. All of this strengthens my claims in chapter 1 that international law intentionally makes room for and implicitly encourages litigation over the proper characterization of abusive conduct and that one of the purposes of such arguments is to create a partial safe harbor for countries that take exceptional measures in the face of an emergency. It is therefore not surprising that the five techniques and the argument over their classification became the template for official coercion in other countries, such as Israel and the United States.[55]

Some commentators have suggested that in the wake of *Ireland v. United Kingdom,* the British government placed less emphasis on military solutions and made a more concerted effort to exert civilian control over the response by British forces to the IRA. Whether or not that is true, complaints about the treatment of detainees and others suspected of IRA connections or sympathies continued. Rejali suggests that with the five techniques unavailable, the Royal Ulster Constabulary "developed clean beating into a high art."[56] Another area of controversy was the purported existence of a shoot-to-kill policy with regard to the IRA, especially after officials shot and killed six unarmed Catholic men in 1982 and after British forces shot and killed three IRA members in Gibraltar in 1988 under uncertain circumstances. Investigations into these incidents have suffered from lack of cooperation and even obstruction from the authorities, and the final report on the 1982 incident remains secret.[57]

According to a recent report, Britain currently has one of the worst human rights records in Europe: "More than 100 findings have been lodged against Britain to which the Government has not adequately responded." After the escalation of the war on terror after September 11, 2001, the conduct of British officials has been drawn further into question. In a 2004 report, the European Committee for the Prevention of Torture and Inhuman or Degrading Treatment or Punishment declared that the government's detention and treatment of "foreign terror suspects" "could be considered as amounting to inhuman and degrading treatment." In response, the government "categorically reject[ed] the view that any of the detainees were held in conditions amounting to inhuman and degrading treatment," insisting that "the detainees received humane and decent treatment, and the appropriate levels of medical and psychological care." Yet in December 2004, the House of Lords ruled that the policy of indefinitely detaining aliens without trial violated the European Convention on Human Rights, and Parliament began to resist the government's detention policies.[58]

Intelligence officials in the United Kingdom apparently colluded with officials in Bangladesh, Dubai, Morocco, and Pakistan who would use torture or other coercive methods and then question suspects on behalf of the United Kingdom or deliver the suspects for questioning by U.K. officials.[59] The government also sought to deport "suspected international terrorists and extremists who incite hatred" to countries that are said to have "poor human rights records"—although it was not clear whether the deportees would be detained and interrogated in those countries on behalf of Britain or the United States. British officials cooperated with the CIA's rendition program, although the extent of that cooperation, particularly whether it included assisting renditions to countries that might use coercive tactics, remains unresolved at the time I write.[60] Significantly, the government warned British judges not to follow case law from the European Court of Human Rights that forbids such deportations, and it unsuccessfully urged the court to reconsider this issue and allow states to "balance the right of the individual not to be tortured against the interests of the state in national security."[61] British forces in Iraq were also implicated in the mistreatment of prisoners, and one judge dismissed abuse charges against several soldiers because he found that their superiors "did indeed sanction the use of hooding and stress positions."[62]

Also noteworthy is the decision by the House of Lords in December 2005 not to allow the admission in judicial proceedings of evidence obtained in other countries through torture. On that issue, the lords were unanimous, but on a four-to-three vote they also ruled that evidence is admissible unless proven to have been obtained by torture. Lord Hope's opinion was very clear on this point: "[A] court must exclude evidence if it concludes on the balance of probabilities that it was obtained by torture. In other words, if [the tribunal] is left in doubt as to whether the evidence was obtained in this way, it should admit it." The lords also refused to extend their analysis to evidence obtained by "[i]ll-treatment falling short of torture." In the words of Lord Bingham, "[s]pecial rules have always been thought to apply to torture, and for the present at least must continue to do so." Yet he took care to note that "it would of course be within the power of a sovereign Parliament (in breach of international law) to confer power . . . to receive third party torture evidence"—meaning, in short, that there is no judicial power to override a clear statutory statement in favor of torture.[63]

Finally, the lords disclaimed any general effort to prevent the government from using information obtained by torture or perhaps even from using torture itself. Lord Nicholls bluntly stated that "if the use of such information might save lives it would be absurd to reject it," because "the government cannot be expected to close its eyes to this information at the price of endangering the lives of its own citizens." Lord Bingham was more circumspect but went at least as far.

> I am prepared to accept . . . that the Secretary of State does not act un-lawfully if he certifies, arrests, searches, and detains on the strength of what I shall for convenience call foreign torture evidence. But by the same token it is, in my view, questionable whether he would act unlaw-fully if he based similar action on intelligence obtained by officially-au-thorised British torture. If under such torture a man revealed the where-abouts of a bomb in the Houses of Parliament, the authorities could remove the bomb and, if possible, arrest the terrorist who planted it.[64]

The result boils down, in sum, only to a prohibition on the admission in ju-dicial proceedings of evidence proven to have been obtained by torture, with no prohibition on evidence proven to have been obtained by lesser forms of coercion or on the use in other contexts of information obtained by torture. Although the question before the lords was limited to the ad-mission of evidence obtained by torture, their reasoning swept more broadly, in a direction that undermined a general prohibition on torture. The decision thus accords with the opinion of the Foreign Office's legal ad-visor that the Convention against Torture does not prohibit receiving or possessing information obtained by torture, even though both it and U.K. law bar admission of that information as evidence in court.[65] While U.K. law clearly provides a right not to be tortured, the contours of the right re-main unclear and exist at the sufferance of Parliament and the needs of the state.[66]

Spain

ᵔ

Torture appears to have been relatively common in Spain under Franco. My focus, however, will be on the use of torture in post-Franco, democratic Spain. I will leave unexplored abuses that can be explained away as "pre-democratic," including the several centuries of pervasive violence that char-acterized Spanish colonialism overseas. At least in the context of Basque separatism and terrorism, torture has persisted as part of the Spanish gov-ernment's counterterror strategy. Spain, one might say, was a modern state under Franco and continues to be one today, although its greater self-con-sciousness today about its modernity may lead to more of a bad conscience about torture and thus to a stronger effort to deny its use.

Police and army personnel committed abuses against members or sus-pected members of the Basque group Euskadi Ta Askatasuna (ETA), or

Basque Homeland and Liberty, under the Franco regime. That conduct continued during the transition to democracy. Little effort was made to reform the police and army, so the police and security apparatus of the Franco regime remained in place to combat ETA violence. The socialist government that came to power in 1982 acquiesced in established practices. Indeed, high-ranking members of the government, such as the director of state security and the undersecretary and the minister of the interior, apparently participated with lower-ranking police and military officials in some counterterror activities against the ETA. Roughly 30 people were killed in operations by the anti-ETA organization Grupos Antiterroristas de Liberación (GAL), and a similar number were injured—and credible allegations exist of torture in an unknown number of cases in addition to two confirmed cases.[67]

Paddy Woodworth argues that Prime Minister Felipe Gonzalez not only tolerated the operations of the GAL but may also have played a more important role. What seems clear is that the Socialist Party obstructed investigations into counterterror activities, including those of the GAL. Nonetheless, investigations and trials took place and resulted in convictions of high-ranking political figures—although the Council of Ministers granted partial pardons to several defendants. Woodworth provides the following explanation for the Socialist Party's willingness to tolerate and even participate in abuse of ETA members: "At the time, few members of the opposition, and few people in the media, actively opposed the use of death squads. Some applauded the GAL's campaign, and public opinion was also generally passive when not actually supportive."[68]

The use of torture and coercion has not been limited to the violence perpetrated by the GAL. Joseba Zulaika and William Douglass provide statistics about and narratives of torture of Basques by Spanish police. For example, they note that 84 percent of roughly 500 ETA activists in prison claimed they were tortured in 1993. They also contend that more than 60 people were tortured during anti-ETA operations in June 1994. Finally, they draw on Basque sources to observe, "During the 1980s, it was estimated that 85 percent of the tortured people in the Basque Country were subsequently released without charges." Luis Núñez Astrain provides similar figures, along with the following summary: "Between 1982, the year of the [Socialist Party's] electoral victory, and 1990, a total of 484 cases were reported." He also suggests that many others were tortured and failed to come forward for fear of reprisal.[69]

Allegations of torture have continued to surface under both socialist and center-right governments. In 1983, a report by a Spanish human rights organization said torture was "something more than an episodic event although it was not a part of a system or organized strategy." Another commentator reached roughly the same conclusion in 1993: "[T]orture, rather than being an organized system, seems to be just one of the consequences of prolonged detention and interrogation."[70] Of course, to conclude that torture is something that just happens to people who are detained and interrogated is both revealing and cramped—revealing because it categorizes torture as a normal consequence of antiterrorism practices, cramped because it portrays torture as unorganized and thus as attributable to no one and persistently aberrational.

More recent reports continue in the same vein. In 1999, Amnesty International stated that it "accepts that torture is not practiced systematically in Spain [but] shares the concern of the CAT, as expressed in its Concluding Observations on Spain's third periodic report, that the complaints of acts of torture and ill-treatment it continues to receive are 'frequent.'" Amnesty International's report went on to provide details on allegations by "terrorism suspects" that they were "held incommunicado for between three and five days" and subjected to "asphyxiation by the placing of a plastic bag over the head ('la bolsa'), and to repeated kicks and blows of the hand on the head or testicles." The report continued,

> One detainee alleged that he was severely beaten while wrapped in a blanket. Several claim they had been forced to bend repeatedly up and down. In one case an ETA suspect claimed that electrodes were applied to his penis, stomach and chest. In some cases allegations referred to sexual abuse, such as the placing of a pistol, a stick or fingers in the anus and vagina and to sexual harassment. There were also references to immersion of the head in water ("la bañera") and to threats of execution, rape, application of electric shocks, miscarriage or injury to partners and relatives. In several of these cases allegations were supported by medical evidence, particularly with regard to marks or injuries left by beating, although other allegations are, by their nature, almost impossible to substantiate.

The report also summarized concerns expressed throughout the 1990s about lax investigation and punishment of violations.[71]

Amnesty International's 2004 report noted that the European Court of Human Rights was hearing a case involving 15 Catalans who "alleged they had been subjected to physical and mental torture and inhuman and degrading treatment on their arrest and in custody . . . in mid-1992." It also reports charges that several directors and employees of a Basque newspaper "had been tortured by asphyxiation with a plastic bag (bolsa), exhausting physical exercises, threats and simulated execution." Amnesty International further noted that the government had increased to 13 days the time in which someone can be held incommunicado in police custody or in prison—which is precisely the situation that an earlier commentator said would increase the likelihood of torture simply as a "consequence."[72] The 2005 report revealed that the Court of Human Rights had not found a violation of the European Convention on Human Rights in the case involving the 15 Catalans, but the court had criticized Spain for failing to investigate the allegations and had noted a lack of detailed information that would have allowed it to determine whether the allegations were true—a "nuanced" decision that seems to fit with Ní Aoláin's analysis of the court's torture jurisprudence. The report also notes numerous allegations of abuse and torture in prisons, particularly of Muslims.[73]

More significantly, in February 2004, the U.N. special rapporteur on torture concluded, as had others before him, that "torture or ill-treatment is not systematic in Spain," but that "the system as it is practiced allows torture or ill-treatment to occur, particularly with regard to persons detained incommunicado in connection with terrorist-related activities." The rapporteur went out of his way, however, to stress that although torture may not be a "regular practice" in Spain, the frequency of abuse and mistreatment "is more than sporadic and incidental." He also detailed allegations of mistreatment that mirror those from the 1999 Amnesty International report.

> Suspects were arrested and transferred to Madrid. During transfer they were allegedly handcuffed, hooded, forced to keep their head between their knees and beaten. They were reportedly held incommunicado by the police or the Civil Guard for three to five days, when they were reportedly subjected to torture or cruel, inhuman or degrading treatment. Former detainees described the following methods of treatment during incommunicado detention: hooding, forced nudity, physical exercise, being forced to stand for prolonged periods facing the wall, sleep deprivation, disorientation, the "bolsa" (asphyxiation with a plastic bag), sexual humiliation, threatened rape, and threats of execution.

From 1999 to 2003, 178 complaints of this kind of mistreatment were filed against Spanish civil guards, and 38 of those complaints related to antiterrorism operations. Finally, the rapporteur criticized the government for its "reluctance to discuss the occurrence and extent of the practice of torture in Spain" and its tendency to assert that torture claims are false and part of an ETA strategy, although he did note 16 convictions for the use of torture during the 1999–2003 period. Some of those convicted of torture were later pardoned.[74]

These reports suggest a pattern in which the Spanish government asserts that people who make allegations of torture are likely to be terrorists, because terrorists make these kinds of false allegations, even as the government sometimes brings prosecutions against officials who use torture. One could almost say not only that the function of torture is to mark someone out as a terrorist but also that only terrorists (and perhaps easily deluded human rights activists) will talk about its use. In this way, torture has multiple effects as a tool of state power. As a practice, it harms individuals for the purpose of dominating them and draining them of any information. As a topic of political discourse, it is a badge of suspicion and disloyalty to the nation and so functions to define the permissible scope of what can be said about the government. Both of these effects presumably have the further result of intimidating the population in a way that plays on their nationalism—that is, by defining a good citizen as someone who is not tortured and who does not talk about its use on others. Finally, the occasional prosecution of a low-ranking official who uses torture provides the additional effect of reassuring the population that democratic Spain is not a country that tortures and that any abuses are merely aberrations.[75]

Israel
∾

The government of Israel has gone the furthest of the countries discussed in this chapter to justify its use of torture—although neither the government nor the courts that have sometimes blocked the government's efforts have been willing to describe Israeli interrogation practices as "torture." Also, as a self-consciously modern nation-state, Israel has administered coercion in a way that characterizes the rationality of contemporary governance and reveals the violence that is always underneath or bound up with it. The result has been widespread use of coercion but also candor about its use, at least as compared with other countries.

As early as 1977, media reports revealed that the General Security Service (GSS) used coercive tactics, such as "repeated cold showers, beatings, confinement in refrigerator cells, and electric shock." In the 1980s, after publicity surrounding the deaths of two Palestinians who were in custody, as well as the torture of a Circassian Israeli officer who had been convicted of treason, the government created a commission, chaired by the former president of the Supreme Court of Israel, Moshe Landau, to investigate potentially illegal actions of the GSS. The Landau Commission's report—known as the *Report of the Commission of Inquiry into the Methods of Investigation of the General Security Service regarding Hostile Terrorist Activity* or the Landau Report—was completed in 1987, but only portions of it were released.[76]

The available portions of the Landau Report described the interrogation of a suspected terrorist as "a difficult confrontation between the vital need to discover all he knows, based on a well-founded assumption, usually from classified sources, and the will of the person interrogated to keep silent and conceal what he knows or to mislead interrogators by providing false information."[77] Reading between the lines, the hypothetical suspected terrorist is not an ordinary person—let alone a scared, humiliated, or broken one— but is instead a defiant zealot who has the will to resist, conceal, and mislead. The interrogation of such a person is not just an effort to obtain critical information but is also a contest between civilization and its outside threats, where the role of the nation is to bend or break the will of those who challenge it. Given this construction of the terrorist and of the stakes involved in interrogation, the Landau Commission had little trouble concluding that Israel's codified version of the necessity defense provides legal authority for interrogators to use coercive tactics.

The commission supported its decision with a classic argument in favor of the balance of harms or the lesser of two evils.

> To put it bluntly, the alternative is: are we to accept the offence of assault entailed in slapping a suspect's face, or threatening him, in order to induce him to talk and reveal a cache of explosive materials meant for use in carrying out an act of mass terror against a civilian population, and thereby prevent the greater evil which is about to occur? The answer is self-evident.

In a portion of the report that remained classified, the commission provided guidelines for when coercion could be used on a suspect. Publicly, at least, the commission insisted that coercion "must never reach the level of physical torture or maltreatment of the suspect or grievous harm to his honour which deprives him of his human dignity."[78] This phrasing is another example of the definitional game at work, this time in the course of insisting that the mistreatment is entirely legal because necessary and that, in any event, it does not rise to the level of torture.

Although the Landau Report was controversial, its recommendations created a bureaucratic framework for what the Landau Commission called "a moderate degree of physical pressure." The Supreme Court of Israel has provided a good summary of how this treatment became routine.

> The decision to utilize physical means in a particular instance is based on internal regulations, which requires obtaining permission from various ranks of the GSS hierarchy. The regulations themselves were approved by a special Ministerial Committee on GSS interrogations. Among other guidelines, the Committee set forth directives pertaining to the rank authorized to allow these interrogation practices. . . . Different interrogation methods are employed depending on the suspect, both in relation to

what is required in that situation and to the likelihood of obtaining authorization. The GSS does not resort to every interrogation method at its disposal in each case.[79]

The Landau Report and the bureaucratic structure that it helped create were intended to rationalize and control the use of coercion, but GSS investigators often ignored its strictures. Evidence presented to the Supreme Court indicated that GSS investigators tortured as many as 85 percent of detained Palestinians in the 1990s. In 1987–94, between 16 and 25 Palestinians died after being subjected to coercion. Israeli officials also insist that they have discovered a wealth of useful information through coercive methods, although there is reason to doubt their assertions.[80]

Over the next several years, Palestinians who were coercively interrogated or who feared coercive interrogation frequently sought relief from the Supreme Court in its capacity as the High Court of Justice. Although the court would sometimes issue an injunction against the use of force and sometimes deny it, the court avoided the underlying issue of whether the use of force was permissible. In 1996, the court issued an order to prevent the use of force in a particular interrogation, but it lifted the order the next day, after the GSS claimed that it sought from the suspect information that might prevent future terrorist attacks. According to the suspect's attorney, this sequence of decisions reflected a practice of "grant[ing] injunctions only when the state made no objection, and allow[ing] the use of physical pressures when the state sought it."[81] To the extent that the court's approach to coercive interrogation during the 1990s actually fit that description, it turned the law of remedies on its head. The availability of a remedy in these cases turned on whether or not the remedy would be meaningful—which would not be surprising by itself. The twist is that the remedy was denied when it would be meaningful—that is, when the injury would be serious and perhaps irreparable—and granted when it would be meaningless, because there would be no injury to remedy. The most obvious explanation of these cases—which is also the explanation that the court later denied—is that only people who have no relevant information have a right to be free from coercive interrogation.

The 1996 incident attracted widespread attention. The United Nations opened an investigation into Israel's use of force in interrogations, and both the Committee against Torture and the special rapporteur on torture concluded that these practices, especially when used in combination—as they often were—constituted torture. They also rejected any argument that necessity or exceptional circumstances could justify the use of coercion.[82]

Soon thereafter, the High Court of Justice began hearings in a new case brought by two Israeli human rights groups and six Palestinians who were suspected of involvement in terrorist activities and had been subjected to coercion. In *Public Committee against Torture in Israel v. State of Israel,* they sought a declaration from the court that the abusive methods used against them were illegal. The methods, which were similar to the five techniques used by the British, included "forceful shaking . . . which causes the neck and head to dangle and vacillate rapidly"; the "Shabach position," in which a suspect is first bound in an uncomfortable position on a chair tilted forward and is then hooded and subjected to loud music for a prolonged period; the "frog crouch," in which suspects were forced to crouch on their toes for five-minute intervals; intentional tightening of handcuffs to cause pain and suffering; and sleep deprivation.[83]

The court ruled in favor of the plaintiffs and against the government. Beginning from the baseline that restraints on liberty are not permitted in the absence of "clear statutory authorization," the court declared that the interrogation methods at issue were illegal because the Knesset had not authorized them. It also recognized that, under international law, investigations and interrogations must be "free of torture, free of cruel, inhuman treatment of the subject and free of any degrading handling whatsoever." Finally, the court rejected the government's claim, based on the findings of the Landau Commission, that torture was authorized in advance by the necessity defense.[84]

These holdings are significant, but the decision is more complex than a simple description of its primary holdings would suggest. First, the court was circumspect in the way it described the coercive practices at issue. It used such terms as *physical means, pressure methods,* and *physical force,*[85] presumably because the word *torture* was simply too ominous, too loaded with political and legal consequences on the domestic and international stages. In brief, the court took advantage of the definitional game; some methods may be illegal, but that does not mean they are torture, and it may not be necessary even to decide that issue.

Second, the court based its decision on the Knesset's failure specifically to authorize these practices. It did not hold that these or any other coercive techniques were categorically illegal regardless of what the Knesset thought. Thus, in the final pages of its opinion, the court declared that "[e]ndowing GSS investigators with the authority to apply physical force during the interrogation of suspects suspected of involvement in hostile terrorist activities" was a question that "must be decided by the legislative branch," subject to review by the court to ensure that such an intrusion on liberty "is enacted for a proper purpose, and to an extent no greater than is required."[86]

Third, although the court rejected the claim that coercion was authorized in advance by the necessity defense, it declared its willingness "to accept that in appropriate circumstances, GSS investigators may avail themselves of the necessity defence, if criminally indicted." In other words, coercive treatment that may rise to the level of torture will not result in a conviction—and is therefore not illegal in the most pragmatic sense—if it was considered necessary under an analysis of the balance of harms. Indeed, the court went further and declared that in the classic scenario of the "ticking time bomb," coercion might be justified "even if the bomb is set to explode in a few days, or even in a few weeks."[87]

So, too, the court wove its holdings into a rhetorical fabric that celebrated Israel as a democracy under siege yet committed to the rule of law. In the first numbered paragraph of the opinion, the court said, "The State of Israel has been engaged in an unceasing struggle for both its very existence and its security, from the day of its founding." In the final paragraphs, the court returned to that theme, when it admitted that its decision "does not ease dealing with" the difficult security situation facing the country. But the court sought to cast these difficulties and its holding in a positive light: "This is the destiny of democracy, as not all means are acceptable to it, and not all practices employed by its enemies are open to it. Although a democracy must often fight with one hand tied behind its back, it nonetheless has the upper hand." According to the court, "preserving the Rule of Law and recognition of an individual's liberty . . . strengthen its spirit and allow it to overcome its difficulties."[88]

The court, in short, defined Israel as a state born out of and engaged in a constant struggle, so that it is defined by and draws meaning from the ongoing emergency it faces. The fact that the country is a democracy only increases the state of emergency, because the available ways of responding to challenges are limited by having to fight "with one hand tied behind its back." Democracy, in other words, by its very nature makes emergencies more likely or at least more dangerous. Notice, too, how the court's effort to provide reassurance—that the benefits of the rule of law and individual liberty outweigh the peril of fighting with one hand behind one's back—ends up defining and deploying those benefits in a martial sense. The rule of law and individual liberty are important to the nation as a whole because they produce vitality in the face of obstacles that impede national actualization: they "strengthen its spirit and allow it to overcome its difficulties."

Finally, this rhetoric defines Israel as a victim, cast in an unfair position as it faces an emergency. While it resists temptation and fights with one hand tied behind its back, its enemies use unacceptable methods. Yet the point of stressing this unfairness is ultimately to highlight national virtue. In keeping with the other countries discussed in this chapter, Israel conceives of itself as civilization struggling with barbarians. By prevailing against the odds while also preserving democracy, the rule of law, and individual liberty, the country constitutes itself as progressive and modern.

The court summarized this view in a more recent case: "The State's fight against terrorism . . . is also law's fight against those who rise up against it. . . . 'The state fights in the name of the law and in the name of upholding the law. The terrorists fight against the law, while violating it.'"[89] Yet for all its invocation of the rule of law against the chaos of terrorism, the court has also criticized ostensibly controlling sources of law when they risk impeding necessary state action: "[T]he provisions of international law that exist today have not been adapted to changing realities and the phenomenon of terrorism that is changing the form and characteristics of armed conflicts and those who participate in them."[90] The rule of law, therefore, cannot be too constraining; the court remains free to adapt international legal principles to "new realities" and, in the process, to uphold legislation that gives more scope to state violence.

In the immediate aftermath of *Public Committee against Torture,* such groups as Amnesty International certified that "the GSS ceased systematic use of these interrogation tactics," although they contended that torture still took place. After the Second Intifada began, however, the GSS adapted to the court's decision in a way that allows it to use coercive methods more systematically. Remember that the court allowed coercion after the fact under the necessity defense. The court appears to have meant that this defense could be raised in a criminal proceeding, but the GSS used it to effect a limited return to the idea of necessity justifying torture in advance. GSS interrogators simply informed suspects who were considered particularly important that they are "ticking bombs." Having defined the suspect as a kind of living emergency—a literal embodiment of the state of exception—officials are then free to employ coercive methods. By July 2002, more than 90 people had been defined as "ticking bombs" and tortured.[91]

Recent methods of coercion include the frog crouch and a modified version of the Shabach position, in which an ordinary chair is used and the victim's head remains uncovered. New methods—or perhaps simply methods that were not before the court in *Public Committee against Torture*—include the "banana bend," in which the detainee sits in a backless chair with one person in front who strikes the detainee in the stomach while another person "tips the detainee's back to a 45 degree angle for periods of up to half an hour." Interrogators also use the "horse position," in which victims, with hands and legs bound behind them, are leaned against a wall with only their heads touching it. When they fall, they are hit and placed back up against the wall. "Double cuffing" is common: "[T]he interrogatee's arms are bound with two sets of handcuffs, one at the wrist and the second in the middle of the joint. The cuffs press hard on the bones, and when the fingers swell with blood, the investigators squeeze them vigorously." "Ticking bomb" detainees are also subjected to "slaps and blows, threats and curses, sleep deprivation, exposure to extreme heat and cold, hand and foot cuffing for extended periods, isolation and denial of access to a lawyer for unlimited periods."[92] A U.N. special rapporteur has noted, however, that "no individual interrogator has been the subject of criminal charges since the 1999 Supreme Court decision, despite the existence of mechanisms facilitating the reporting of abuse by persons under interrogation."[93]

According to the Public Committee against Torture, the attorney general has granted "ticking bomb" status each time the GSS has sought such authority, the Supreme Court of Israel has refused to hear petitions that could result in prohibiting the use of these methods, and the State Prosecutor's Office has declined to prosecute officials who use torture.[94] The U.N.'s special rapporteur on human rights and counterterrorism recently criticized this process after a visit to Israel.

> The Special Rapporteur was shocked by the unconvincing and vague illustrations . . . of when such "ticking bomb" scenarios may be applicable. He was troubled by the process by which individual interrogators would seek approval from the Director of the ISA for the application of special interrogation techniques, potentially rendering this as a policy rather than a case-by-case, ex post facto, defence in respect of wrongful conduct. He was furthermore concerned by the lack of truly independent and impartial investigation mechanisms following the application of such methods.[95]

The case of Israel, in short, is much the same as those of England, France, and Spain, except that the debate has been more public. This public debate reveals that both the rule of law, which requires torture to occur only in "ticking bomb" situations, and respect for individual rights, which requires depriving people of liberty only for good reasons, easily coexist with the emergency but also routinized use of torture, which protects the civilized but fragile state from barbarous enemies.

Outsourcing Torture: Italy, Sweden, and Canada
∾

I have suggested that one characteristic of torture by liberal democracies is its hidden quality. The use of "rendition" is one way to hide torture. Rendition involves transferring a person from one country to another to face trial or imprisonment, and it tends to entail much less legal process (if any at all) than extradition or deportation.[96] Beginning in the 1990s, under the Clinton administration, the United States has also engaged in a practice known as "extraordinary rendition," which involved arranging the transfer of a person found outside the United States to the custody of another country for purposes of detention, interrogation, and sometimes trial. After the attacks of September 11, 2001, the use of extraordinary rendition—a phrase that suggests an emergency situation—skyrocketed. Often, the countries that received the detainees were also countries characterized by the U.S. State Department as having "poor human rights records." Indeed, credible claims by the detainees of mistreatment and sometimes torture in the course of interrogation suggest that they were sent to these countries precisely because rough treatment would be part of the interrogation process.[97]

Although the United States has been the prime mover in the effort to transfer prisoners from one country to another for purposes of interrogation, European countries have participated in these transfers. I have already discussed Britain's efforts to deport people to countries in which they might be mistreated and its possible cooperation with the CIA. Canada, Italy, and Sweden have also been involved in the transfer of people to countries in which they were tortured, and their actions appear to have been in response to or in cooperation with U.S. antiterror activities. Several other European states acquiesced in or indirectly aided the CIA program.[98]

In February 2003, a Muslim cleric known as Abu Omar, who was already under investigation by Italian authorities, "was walking to a Milan mosque for noon prayers . . . when he was grabbed on the sidewalk by two men, sprayed in the face with chemicals, and stuffed into a van." In a phone call to his wife in April 2004, he said he had been taken to a U.S. air base and ultimately sent to Egypt, where he was tortured during interrogation. After a two-year investigation into Omar's disappearance, Italian prosecutors brought kidnapping charges against "25 past and present CIA operatives," and their trial in absentia is ongoing. But however else one may wish to characterize this event, it may not have been a violation of Italian sovereignty. According to one report, before Omar was kidnapped, "the CIA station chief in Rome briefed and sought approval from his counterpart in Italy." Interesting as well is that the Italian minister of justice criticized the prosecutors' attempt to have the CIA agents extradited to Italy. He suggested that these efforts were "linked to a type of anti-Americanism that unfortunately runs through the left."[99]

According to Dana Priest, this incident "offers an accidental glimpse into how U.S. and foreign intelligence agencies coordinate and communicate on sensitive counterterrorism matters in ways that are expressly kept secret, even from other parts of their governments." "This bifurcation between stated policies and secret practices," writes Priest, "has become more common since the Sept. 11, 2001 attacks." The incident also supports the view—reinforced by the conclusions of a Council of Europe report on rendition—that some European countries have taken a "don't ask, don't tell" approach to rendition and would prefer not to know about or explore the details of CIA flights in and out of their territory.[100]

The operation of this coordination and bifurcation in Sweden is particularly well documented. In December 2001, Sweden expelled two men—Ahmed Agiza and Muhammad Zery—suspected of having ties to terrorist groups. Agiza had been tried *in absentia* in Egypt, found guilty, and sentenced to imprisonment for being a member of a terrorist group. He subsequently sought asylum in Sweden. Both men were sent back to Egypt after the Swedish government received diplomatic assurances that neither man would be mistreated. Neither Swedish nor Egyptian officials effected the transfer. Instead, the CIA offered its services, and the Swedish government accepted them. The U.N. Committee against Torture, drawing from the conclusions of the Swedish Parliamentary Ombudsman, described the transfer as follows:

> [T]he expellees were apprehended by Swedish police and subsequently transported to Bromma airport. The American aircraft landed shortly before 9.00 p.m. A number of American security personnel, wearing masks, conducted the security check, which consisted of at least the following elements. The expellees had their clothes cut up and removed with a pair of scissors, their bodies were searched, their hands and feet were fettered, they were dressed in overalls and their heads were covered with loosely fitted hoods. Finally, they were taken, with bare feet, to the airplane where they were strapped to mattresses. They were kept in this position during the entire flight to Egypt. It had been alleged that the expellees were also given a sedative per rectum, which the Ombudsman was unable to substantiate during the investigation. The Ombudsman found that the [Swedish] Security Police had remained passive throughout the procedure.[101]

Agiza also claimed to have been badly treated by Swedish police and to have then been tortured by Egyptian state security officers who subjected him to electric shocks, kept him bound in solitary confinement, and did not allow him to use a toilet. Zery made similar allegations.

The Committee against Torture found that Sweden had violated its obligation under Article 3 of the Convention against Torture not to expel, return, or extradite a person to a country if there are substantial grounds for believing that the person would be subjected to state torture in that country. According to the committee, its prior reports on Egypt—as well as the publications of other organizations, not to mention the context of terrorism and the victims' prior interaction with the Egyptian government—should have put the Swedish government on notice that the men were likely to be tortured. The committee felt that the Swedish government should have done more to protect the men than merely seeking diplomatic assurances.[102]

Canada's role in the rendition of suspected terrorists is murkier. The case of Canadian citizen Maher Arar has received the most attention. Arar's name appeared in the U.S. National Automated Immigration Lookout System as a member of al Qaeda, based on information received from Canadian officials. U.S. officials subsequently seized him in September 2002, while he was changing planes in New York's Kennedy Airport on his way home to Ottawa. After holding and interrogating him for several days, U.S. officials sent him to Syria, the country of his birth, to be detained and interrogated further.

The Canadian consul visited Arar while he was detained in New York. Arar claimed that he told her that U.S. officials wanted to send him to Syria, and he claimed that she assured him that would not happen. Although Canadian officials later denied knowing that the United States would move Arar to Syria, they supplied a list of questions for U.S. officials to use in their interrogation of him. Shortly before Arar was detained, moreover, Canadian officials discussed the possibility that other Canadian citizens who had been interrogated in Syria would make claims of torture. They agreed that "minimal information will be put out due to the ongoing police investigation."[103]

In Syria, Arar was kept in a small, unlit cell and subjected to severe and abusive treatment. Arar later reported,

The beating . . . was very intense for a week, and then less intense for another week. The second and the third days were the worst. . . . One tactic they use is to question prisoners for two hours, and then put them in a waiting room, so they can hear the others screaming, and then bring them back to continue the interrogation.

The cable is a black electrical cable, about two inches thick. They hit me with it everywhere on my body. They mostly aimed for my palms, but sometimes missed and hit my wrists; they were sore and red for three weeks. They also struck me on my hips, and lower back. . . . They used the cable on the second and third day, and after that mostly beat me with their hands, hitting me in the stomach and on the back of my neck, and slapping me on the face. Where they hit me with the cables, my skin turned blue for two or three weeks, but there was no bleeding. At the end of the day they told me tomorrow would be worse. So I could not sleep.[104]

Another Canadian consul visited Arar several times while he was in Syrian custody, but he was not released and allowed to return to Canada for almost a year.

Most legal scholars would define this treatment as torture. Both a fact finder and a commission of inquiry concluded that "the treatment of Mr. Arar in [Syria] constituted torture as understood in international law."[105] The commission of inquiry also made specific findings that Canadian officials (1) provided apparently false information to the United States that Arar was associated with al Qaeda, (2) knew he had been detained by the United States and sought to assist the interrogation of him by U.S. officials, (3) assured him that he would not be sent to Syria, (4) knew he was in Syria, and (5) were unable to obtain his release until he had been there for a year.

Remember, too, that U.S. officials detained Arar based on information obtained from Canadian officials. That information, in turn, derived from Canadian surveillance of other Muslims who live in Canada, at least two of whom were detained by Syrian officials earlier in 2002, when they arrived in that country to visit family members. Both detained men were held in custody in Syria (and one was held in Egypt as well) for more than a year. Both claimed—as did a third—to have been tortured, and two of them also alleged that they were asked questions that could only have come from Canadian intelligence services. The commission of inquiry and a separate investigator determined that Syrian authorities detained two of the men partly because of information provided by Canadian authorities, that all three were tortured, and that Canadian officials sent questions to Syria for use during interrogations of two of the men, even though some officials were aware that the interrogations would likely be abusive.[106]

No Canadian officials have been punished for their roles in Arar's rendition or in the other interrogations of Canadian citizens or residents in Syria, although the head of the Royal Canadian Mounted Police resigned. The Canadian government also refused to apologize to Arar after the commission of inquiry issued its report, because doing so "might drive up the cost of a financial settlement"—although the government ultimately apologized as part of a multi-million-dollar settlement.[107] In short, the level of involvement of Canadian officials in the mistreatment of Canadian citizens and residents may not be as great as that of U.S. and Syrian officials, but it seems clear that some Canadian officials tolerated and cooperated with the actions of both countries, even when those activities included interrogation that they must have known would include abuse and even torture.[108]

Canadian law on the issue of torture has also responded to the pressure of terrorism. In *Suresh v. Canada,* the Supreme Court of Canada upheld the constitutionality of a provision of an immigration statute that "permits [deportation of] a refugee on security grounds even where the refugee's 'life or freedom' would be threatened by the return." The court summarized its ruling as follows:

Canadian jurisprudence does not suggest that Canada may never deport a person to face treatment elsewhere that would be unconstitutional if imposed by Canada directly, on Canadian soil. To repeat, the appropriate approach is essentially one of balancing. The outcome will depend not only on considerations inherent in the general context but also on considerations related to the circumstances and condition of the particular person whom the government seeks to expel. On the one hand stands the state's genuine interest in combating terrorism, preventing Canada from becoming a safe haven for terrorists, and protecting public security. On the other hand stands Canada's constitutional commitment to liberty and fair process. This said, Canadian jurisprudence suggests that this balance will usually come down against expelling a person to face torture elsewhere.

Later in its opinion, the court stated, "We do not exclude the possibility that in exceptional circumstances, deportation to face torture might be justified," but it insisted that such a case would be rare.[109] The *Suresh* court, in other words, admitted that individual constitutional rights are subject to balancing against state interests and that state interests will sometimes outweigh even the most fundamental individual rights. Where the state's interest is in fighting terrorism, moreover, courts will try to accommodate that interest—although they may, as in *Suresh,* attempt to create procedural roadblocks that will make it difficult for the state to act on those interests in all but the most compelling cases.

The *Suresh* court also took account of the ICCPR and of Article 3 of the Convention against Torture, which creates a nonderogable obligation not to "expel, return ('refouler') or extradite a person to another State where there are substantial grounds for believing that he would be in danger of being subjected to torture." Although the court stated that this prohibition "informs the content of the principles of fundamental justice" under the Canadian Charter of Rights and Freedoms, it nonetheless ruled that the government could deport a person "to face torture."[110] The nonderogable obligation, once translated through the interests of the state, became flexible. It is also interesting that the deportation of Arar from the United States to Syria—with some involvement of Canadian officials—took place four months after the court decided *Suresh.*

The Committee against Torture highlighted the Arar incident and the *Suresh* decision in its review of the report Canada submitted pursuant to the Convention against Torture. The committee expressed concern over "the failure of the Supreme Court of Canada . . . to recognise, at the level of domestic law, the absolute nature of the protection of article 3 of the Convention that is subject to no exceptions whatsoever." In its correspondence with the committee, the government of Canada stressed that "deportation to face torture" would take place only in a "very narrow" category of "exceptional circumstances."[111]

Canadian jurisprudence, in short, is exactly what one would expect from a liberal constitutional democracy, once one looks behind the rhetoric of free-floating absolute rights. Like its European counterparts and the United States, Canada is committed to individual rights, but only within the context of state power and necessity, so that rights are bound up with and constitutive of state power.[112] The rules against torture and other forms of abuse may be categorical in theory and sometimes in practice, but they also bend with the winds of reasonableness and can be violated with some frequency by state actors.[113] Especially in an exceptional or emergency situation, the rules become flexible, both in theory and in operation.

The most revealing aspect of the debate over extraordinary rendition is the easy acceptance of the claim that the countries on the receiving end are seasoned violators of human rights. Officials of these countries almost certainly employ methods that violate human rights on a regular basis. But the more important point is that these countries—such places as Egypt, Jordan, Morocco, and Syria—are already classified, before rendition takes place, as the locations at which human rights violations occur.[114] None of these countries, of course, is ordinarily considered Western or liberal. Yet all of these countries have spent years under European or U.S. dominance, and some of them could be defined today, to some degree, as client states. In roughly analogous legal terminology, they are, in many ways, agents of the United States or Europe.

The idea of colonies or, more generally, the Orient as "outside" and "unchanging" is common, so it should be no surprise that this idea appears in the rendition context as well.[115] Media and other accounts report that civilized and developed countries send people outside, to uncivilized countries, where they will be subjected to traditional forms of abuse. But torture in these countries is, of course, not simply something that happens. It takes place because one or another liberal democracy asks for it to happen—and at this stage in the relationship, it may be that both sides perfectly understand the act of rendition to be the equivalent of a request. Yet because the abuse takes place outside, responsibility is also displaced. So, although discussions of extraordinary rendition usually criticize the United States and its European allies, one almost never sees these countries accused of poor human rights records (although human rights groups document many of their abuses). The principal-agent relationship dissolves just before the point at which the acts of the agent are attributed to the principal. One senses, instead, a feeling of disappointment that liberal democracies have failed to conform to their own values and have employed the services of countries with poor human rights records. As for those other countries, there is no disappointment, because there is no expectation that they would act differently. They merely are what they are.[116]

My point in these paragraphs is not to fan the flames of moral outrage. I want only to explain why, in the context of rendition, the use of torture remains hidden in plain view. Rendition is an exceptional measure—U.S. officials themselves now call it "extraordinary rendition"—and it is practiced on noncitizens and particularly on Arabs or Muslims, who often are sent back to their countries of origin. The entire process rests on assumptions of difference and of a moral hierarchy among nations, extending from benevolent liberal democracies that exercise "leadership" on human rights down to countries that torture because that is what they have always done.[117] These understandings make it difficult to entertain alternative possibilities, such as that there may be little material difference in the human rights records of the countries on either side of the rendition. Put plainly, for citizens of liberal democracies, rendition means that they do not see torture, they did not do it, and it may not even have happened; extraordinary rendition means that, even if it did happen, it was justified by exceptional circumstances.

Conclusion

~

Throughout the twentieth century and into the present, liberal democracies have employed torture or relied on others to do it for them. The European and Israeli experience with torture demonstrates that it is not an aberration in democratic countries; that its use by modern states is intimately connected to racism, colonialism, concerns about law, and ideas of emergency, exception, and necessity; and that modern torture is usually hidden and therefore almost always deniable or exceptional. I want to develop two further points in this conclusion.

The first is the issue of legality. By and large, the countries I discuss have not claimed that their conduct is legal in any normal sense—according, that is, to ordinary rules of interrogation or for treatment of prisoners. Indeed, the claims that rules may be bent in emergencies and that harsh methods may sometimes be necessary or justified are more familiar to political discourse. Yet they are also appeals to law, albeit to the law of exception. Equally critical is that the law of exception is itself normal, even pedestrian. Lawyers know there is an exception to every rule, or at least that they are always permitted to argue for an exception and that such arguments will be seen as reasonable and sometimes prevail. What happens in the case of torture is an appeal to a metadiscourse of exception, which is associated with states of emergency. Because the idea of the exception is already part of the law, the claim of exception due to an emergency is also an appeal to law, even when it asks for or demands the suspension of law in some sense. In fact, the governments of England and France took care to follow legal forms that created a process for declaring emergencies and assuming emergency powers. Court decisions in Israel, in Canada, and arguably in England similarly recognize that torture or sending someone to be tortured may be appropriate based on a balance of harms.

Whether or not the actions of these countries are illegal in some sense, their actions also have a fundamental claim to legality in the basic sense of being authorized by legislation or upheld by judicial decision. If these actions remain illegal, the reason is that, whatever the legal forms employed, governments are simply not allowed to torture or engage in related forms of abusive treatment. This claim is founded on an appeal to the idea of legal rights against certain kinds of government action. As we have seen repeatedly, however, rights-based arguments against abusive treatment are not clear-cut. The combination of legal reasoning and emergency power can carry the day against rights claims, partly because such claims must be interpreted against the background of the state power that animates them and gives them purpose. Further, whether or not the claim of government necessity wins in court, its legal veneer provides surface plausibility in the political and social realms. If we add to that the fact that modern states try to hide their use of torture and tend to employ it against unpopular or marginal groups, whether at home or abroad, one can easily see the precariousness of any claim or assumption that a right against torture actually provides meaningful protection against state violence.

The second point I wish to make here elaborates on the argument I made at the close of the section on rendition and outsourcing torture. The colonial and hidden qualities of torture overlap. Abuses that happen overseas are not subject to the same rules, as if the world outside is always a state of exception or emergency; accordingly, such abuses are easily suppressed or forgotten. But as Ann Stoler has argued, colonies served as Europe's "laboratories of modernity," such that "those most treasured icons of modern western culture—liberalism, nationalism, state welfare, citizenship, culture, and 'Europeanness' itself" were "clarified among Europe's colonial exiles in Asia, Africa, and Latin America and only then brought home."[118] She and other writers have suggested that these "treasured icons" went hand in hand with—or gloved the hand of—violent repression. If so, one would expect a certain degree of difficulty in separating the good from the bad in the process of bringing the icons home. The next two chapters, on the use of torture by the United States, will provide an additional forum for testing that hypothesis.

CHAPTER SIX

☙

U.S. Torture at Home and Abroad

This chapter surveys instances in which officials in the United States have engaged in torture or similar conduct. In each instance, allegations of misconduct have been publicized widely and substantiated to some degree. Yet each time, the allegations have also been denied, minimized, or explained away. Torture and other mistreatment in the Philippines and Vietnam have been characterized as anomalous responses to worse atrocities committed against U.S. forces. After World War II, officials created special categories to describe prisoners who were held outside the protections of the laws of war, and they developed new techniques of coercion. In Vietnam and Latin America, abuses were easily portrayed as the excesses of local officials over whom U.S. forces lacked control—and so, again, as anomalous or simply unrelated to U.S. law and practice. With police and prison practices, abuse is often explained as a reasonable or understandable—even if unfortunate and sometimes illegal—response to the pressures of controlling violent people. Finally, immigration is often insulated within the sovereign power to control borders and, by extension, the bodies of people moving across them.

In describing these events, my goal is to reveal the ways in which the use of torture and other violence provides precedents for and prefigures the debate over the use of torture in the war on terror. Further, my juxtaposition of imperial and domestic violence should underscore the ambiguities of state violence, the way in which torture sits on a continuum with other forms of state violence, and the links between detention and violence. Most important, I hope to display some of the commonalities between police and military violence against populations inside or outside the territorial boundaries of the United States. In each case, for example, authorities define the victims of torture as in some way deviant, inferior, violent, or undesirable. The same is true for the war on terror, whether the United States acts inside or outside its formal borders.

Torture and Foreign Policy

◡

This section provides a brief overview of ways U.S. officials have used torture as a tool of conquest or foreign policy, beginning with the Philippine-American War. My choice of these episodes reflects my desire to focus on the period of time in which the United States has been an imperial power, and the Philippines provide a good starting point. Of course—to take two examples—the treatment of Native Americans and African Americans throughout U.S. history could provide additional episodes of state violence deployed to create and sustain a national identity. Torture, corporal punishment, population control or concentration, mass or reprisal killing, and summary execution come up again and again in accounts of slavery and the displacement of Native Americans, and they return in the examples I discuss here. The treatment of Native Americans in particular—linked as it is to decades of military conflict—may even have provided a template for the operations of U.S. forces in other countries, especially when counterinsurgency tactics became the chosen means of engagement.[1]

The Philippines

Beginning in 1896, Filipino revolutionaries sought independence from Spain, and they proclaimed a republic in 1899. At the same time, however, Spain was losing the Spanish-American War, and it ceded the Philippines to the United States in 1898. Hostilities between U.S. and Filipino forces broke out in 1899, and the McKinley administration moved quickly to assert control over its new colony. By the end of 1902, the Philippine-American War was largely over.

Before hostilities broke out, U.S. officials and newspapers sometimes portrayed Filipino forces in positive terms, at least by comparison to the Spanish forces who were the common enemy. During that period, Filipino leaders worked to establish a government that could claim sovereignty over the country, and some U.S. officials concluded that the people of the Philippines were "capable of self government."[2] Those conclusions changed as the United States sought to assert sovereignty over the islands. Officials and journalists began to portray Filipinos as uncivilized and "absolutely unfit for self-government."[3] They also depicted Filipino forces as brutal, with the result that the Philippines became defined as a torture nation peopled by "bandits" who employed guerilla tactics and attacked unoffending victims (usually U.S. soldiers).[4] Soldiers on the ground tended to agree with this characterization of their enemy: at best, the natives were "wayward and violent children who needed to be coerced into behaving properly"; at worst, they were an unscrupulous enemy that had forfeited the right to civilized tactics.[5] Either way, harsh tactics similar to those of "Injun warfare" were warranted.[6]

In short, as Paul Kramer asserts, the conflict in the Philippines quickly turned into "a war whose ends were rationalized in racial terms before domestic publics, one in which imperial soldiers came to understand indigenous combatants and noncombatants in racial terms, one in which race played a key role in bounding and unbounding the means of colonial violence, and in which those means were justified along racial lines."[7] This rhetoric of race did not simply define the Filipinos, of course. It also helped define American identity and civilization in explicitly racial terms. Perhaps because this kind of rhetoric went deeper than the conflict in the Philippines, supporters of the war were not the only ones who used images of race and civilization to support their arguments. Anti-imperialist writers also made free use of racial and other stereotypes. An editorial in the *Washington Post,* for example, opposed occupying the islands because "[t]here is no authority in the Constitution to shoot civilization into savages on that other hemisphere."[8]

The tactics of individual troops and their commanding officers reflected these attitudes. Some officers told their men to take no prisoners during certain operations, and one officer was told by his commanding general to kill every male capable of bearing arms, which he defined as every male over 10 years old.[9] More generally, torture (often in the form of the "water cure," which consisted of holding a person down and pouring water into his mouth and nose), mass or reprisal killing, property destruction, and concentration camps became common tactics, especially after more than 50 U.S. soldiers were killed and their bodies mutilated at Balangiga.[10] Brian Linn confirms not only that the use of torture "steadily increased" over the course of the war but also that the army loosened its judicial processes, "which now proceeded with far more dispatch and sent prisoners to the gallows with far more regularity."[11]

As Linn summarizes the army's tactics, U.S. forces destroyed thousands of houses and over a million tons of crops and confiscated large numbers of horses and cattle. When the war was over, some areas of the Philippines were "systematically devastated," and large segments of the population were impoverished and thus entirely dependent on the colonial government.[12] In addition to destroying property to punish the population and deny resources to guerillas, U.S. forces also tried to control the population in certain areas through "concentration." General Arthur MacArthur ordered forces on Marinduque "to regard all the male population over fifteen years of age as enemies." He demanded that "whenever it is possible to round them up and treat them as prisoners of war, it should be done, and they should thus be held until the situation is entirely cleared up." Concentration also took the form of "separat[ing] civilians into towns or 'protected zones,' outside of which everyone was regarded as an enemy."[13] Andrew Birtle writes that to enforce this policy on Marinduque, "the Army destroyed almost all of the houses outside the six concentration zones."[14]

"[P]eople forced into the camps," reports Linn, "were overcrowded and suffered from food shortages and sanitation that ranged from poor to appalling." Linn also suggests that "malnutrition, poor sanitary conditions, disease, and demoralization may have cost as many as 11,000 Filipino lives and made the population susceptible to the cholera epidemic of 1902."[15] By the end of the conflict, 200,000 or more Filipinos had died, with a presumably comparable figure injured and an even larger number left without homes or adequate resources.[16] The army apparently considered these tactics successful, because concentration of the population was taught as an acceptable occupation strategy until the eve of World War II.[17]

The revelation of these tactics to a domestic public through letters and newspaper articles led to an uproar. The Anti-Imperialist League published a collection of soldiers' letters in 1899 that included numerous descriptions of shooting and killing unarmed, fleeing, or helpless Filipinos.[18] At roughly the same time, a representative of the International Committee of the Red Cross concluded that "American soldiers are determined to kill every Filipino in sight."[19] One soldier wrote of using the water cure "on 160 Filipinos, all of whom save twenty-six had died from the ordeal."[20] As stories of mistreatment accumulated, Massachusetts senator George Hoar demanded an investigation, and supporters of the war complied by referring the matter to the existing committee on the Philippines, chaired by Senator Henry Cabot Lodge (also of Massachusetts, but a supporter of the war).

The first witness in the investigation was William Howard Taft, the governor of the Philippines and a future president and chief justice of the United States. He admitted that U.S. forces had used the water cure to obtain information. The next witness, General R. P. Hughes, admitted that soldiers frequently burned homes to deter attacks and punish guerillas (by punishing their families).[21] Several soldiers described giving the water cure to Filipino prisoners, and at least one testified that his commanding officers were aware of its use.[22]

While the committee was conducting its investigation, the U.S. secretary of war, Elihu Root, published a report purporting to describe the results of an investigation into "charges of cruelty . . . toward natives of the Philippines." The report admitted that 44 genuine cases existed, but it justified the mistreatment by stating that Filipino forces acted "with the barbarous cruelty common among uncivilized races, and with general disregard for the rules of civilized warfare." The report continued,

That the soldiers fighting against such an enemy, and with their own eyes witnessing such deeds, should occasionally be regardless of their orders and retaliate by unjustifiable severities is not incredible. Such things happen in every war, even between two civilized nations, and they always will happen while war lasts.[23]

About the use of the water cure, Secretary Root adopted a set of arguments that prefigures the responses of present-day political figures. The gist of his arguments was that such activity did not happen; that if it did happen, it was the fault of someone else (probably a native); and that in any event, it was not so terrible.[24] The vehicle for these arguments was a letter written by Brigadier General Frederick Funston, which Root quoted prominently and at length.

It is my belief that the "water cure" was very rarely, if ever, administered by American soldiers. It was a matter of common knowledge that occasionally the Macabebe Scouts, when not under the direct control of some officer, would resort to this means of obtaining information as to the whereabouts of concealed arms and ammunition. They did this, however, on their own responsibility and without orders from their superiors. ... The so-called "water cure," as it has been described to me by Macabebe soldiers, was by no means so severe an ordeal. .... It occasions nothing more than a few moments of strangling, and never resulted fatally.[25]

The revelations of torture and other forms of abuse led to a few prosecutions, most of which resulted in acquittals. Military officials confirmed that the water cure ordinarily violated the laws of war, but they took care to stress that they were not ruling on cases of "emergency" or "exceptional circumstances." Convicted soldiers—including at least one who used the water cure—received minor sentences, and President Theodore Roosevelt commuted the one significant sentence handed down for a charge of murder.[26]

At least two officers who were court-martialed for murdering Filipinos mounted serious legal defenses based on General Orders No. 100, also known as the Lieber Code, in honor of Francis Lieber, who drafted it for the Union during the Civil War to codify a set of standards—the "law in war"—for the conduct of military operations. The code tends to receive uncomplicated plaudits for "articulat[ing] humanitarian principles that have since become basic concepts of international law,"[27] and it certainly exhibits humanitarian principles, partly by providing qualified rights for combatants. Thus, it seeks to prohibit "cruelty" and states that "[i]t is against the usage of modern war to resolve, in hatred and revenge, to give no quarter." Yet the code also accommodates principles of "military necessity" and emergency—for example, by providing that "a commander is permitted to direct his troops to give no quarter, in great straits, when his own salvation makes it impossible to cumber himself with prisoners."[28]

The Lieber Code takes a similar approach to civilians and insurgents. It "envisioned a reciprocal relationship between the population and the Army." Birtle explains, "As long as the population did not resist military authority it was to be treated well. Should the inhabitants violate this compact by taking up arms and supporting guerilla movements, then they were open to sterner measures."[29] The code thus exhibits a "double logic" that rests on an inclusion of certain categories of combatants (e.g., regular soldiers and peaceful citizens), who are entitled to the code's protections, and an exclusion of other categories (e.g., guerillas and hostile citizens), who are not entitled to protection and, instead, are subject to retaliation and other treatment according to principles of military necessity.[30] Going further, the intersection of the code's structure with the colonial project inevitably generated the conclusion that savage behavior by people known to be civilized (e.g., abuses committed by U.S. soldiers) was aberrational, while savage behavior by people known or suspected of being savages (e.g., guerillas or military-aged members of the subject population) confirmed the entire community's lack of rights.

For example, when General MacArthur officially adopted tougher tactics against Filipino fighters in 1901, his justification paraphrased Article 82 of the Lieber Code: "[M]en who participate in hostilities without being part of a regular organized force . . . divest themselves of the character of soldiers and if captured are not entitled to the privileges of prisoners of war."[31] He meant that nonuniformed fighters who employed guerilla tactics and who at least sometimes wounded or captured American prisoners were necessarily beyond "the pale of the law" and were "enemies of humankind." Instead of being protected fighters, they were criminals and murderers, which meant they could be treated summarily—and executed—under the laws of war.[32]

Within this structure, a defense based in the Lieber Code was a wise choice for the officers court-martialed for murdering Filipinos. One of the officers was acquitted, and the other—the general who ordered the killing of all males over 10 years old—was convicted only of "conduct to the prejudice of good order and military discipline." His punishment was immediate retirement. In imposing this punishment, President Roosevelt stressed "the cruelty, treachery, and total disregard [by Filipinos] of the rules and customs of civilized warfare," and he explicitly "approve[d] the employment of the sternest measures necessary to put a stop to such atrocities," even as he disapproved of "torture and of improper heartlessness in warfare on the part of individuals and small detachments."[33]

My discussion of the war in the Philippines has strayed beyond a targeted analysis of torture and related forms of abuse to include detention and concentration, killing, and destruction of property. Yet these tactics fit together to define the Philippines as a dependent colony of uncivilized natives in need of guidance. Torture was one of the processes by which the local population learned what civilization meant and what their relationship to it would be. It is also worth stressing that the dynamics of official and unofficial responses to the problem of fighting insurgents and to revelations of abuses by U.S. forces—media reports, reluctant congressional investigations, and limited criminal prosecution—have striking similarities to those surrounding the same issues in the war on terror. One clear similarity is that the public and political establishment quickly became bored with the topic and largely stopped paying attention. Indeed, an almost studied lack of attention by the general public and political figures—albeit with brief exceptions—underscores my account of torture as an integral part of U.S. military, intelligence, and foreign policy.

From the Allied Victory into the Cold War

Some of the brutality meted out by Allied forces—including U.S. forces—after the surrender of Germany in 1945 can be characterized and even arguably excused as a response to the tactics of Germany under Nazi rule. Nonetheless, the idea of collective guilt—that the surviving Germans were getting what they deserved—too easily helped create the sense that abuse was appropriate. This sense existed all the more because, as Giles MacDonogh notes, "[p]ropaganda had taught the soldiers that Germans—particularly German soldiers—were subhuman."[34]

Some of the violence—indiscriminate killing, rape, and destruction or theft of property—was perhaps a variation on the looting and pillaging that has often accompanied military victories. MacDonogh seems to take this view when he writes, "Understandably, civilians were shot as Germany was invested in the spring in 1945, either deliberately or by accident. This happened above all in the east, but it was a relatively frequent occurrence in the west as well."[35] Yet the violence of the occupation did not stop at the familiar. Just as the Bush administration adopted the terms *enemy combatant* and *detainee* to avoid the protections of national and international law during the war on terror, so, too, the Allies denied members of the disbanded German army the status of prisoners of war under the 1929 Geneva Convention relative to the Treatment of Prisoners of War. More than three million captured German soldiers were designated "surrendered enemy persons" or "disarmed enemy persons," which placed them outside the protections of international law and made them eligible for such things as forced labor.[36]

Many of these "persons" were housed in former death camps, and over a million perished—most in the east, but MacDonogh estimates that as many as 40,000 died in American custody. Starvation, beatings, and other forms of brutality were common in the revived camps, while higher-ranking officials, such as the former SS officers accused in the Malmédy massacre, were subjected to solitary confinement, extremes of heat and cold, and mock trials and mock executions, as well as kicks, beatings, and deprivation of food and sleep.[37] Perhaps, too, there was abuse by omission. In the general privation that inflicted the population following the war, hunger and starvation were seen by some occupying officials as a method of collective punishment.[38]

As the occupation wound down and the cold war began in the late 1940s and early 1950s, CIA officials began to gather information about the interrogation methods of communist countries. They became convinced that Russian and Chinese intelligence services had developed sophisticated tactics—such as brainwashing—that could undermine U.S. intelligence-gathering efforts. In response to this perception, CIA officials sponsored research into techniques for obtaining information from unwilling subjects, with a focus on psychological approaches. The eventual result was the *KUBARK Counterintelligence Interrogation* manual of July 1963, which sought to synthesize a science of counterintelligence interrogation. To that end, the manual proclaims that its guidelines are "based largely upon the published results of extensive research, including scientific inquiries conducted by specialists in closely related subjects," and its authors explicitly claim to be bringing "pertinent, modern knowledge to bear [on the] problems" of interrogation.[39] In keeping with this rhetoric, the manual contains a section titled "The Non-Coercive Counterintelligence Interrogation." The techniques in this section are designed to have an "unsettling effect" that "disrupt[s] radically the familiar emotional and psychological associations of the subject" and creates "feelings of guilt"—with the goal of generating cooperation instead of resistance.[40]

Yet the manual did not expect all interrogations to be free of pain. The introduction instructs interrogators to get "prior approval" "if bodily harm is to be inflicted" or "if medical, chemical, or electrical methods or materials are to be used to induce acquiescence," and the section immediately following the materials on noncoercive interrogation is titled "The Coercive Counterintelligence Interrogation of Resistant Sources." Indeed, according to the manual, if an interrogator believes that the suspect "has the skill and determination to withstand any non-coercive method or combination of methods," it is "better to avoid them completely" and proceed directly to coercive methods.[41]

In its discussion of coercive methods, *KUBARK* speaks in a modern tone, seeking to make clear, for example, that indiscriminate use of force is irrational. The manual explains, "The chan[c]es of success rise steeply . . . if the coercive technique is matched to the source's personality. . . . Moreover, it is a waste of time and energy to apply strong pressures on a hit-or-miss basis if a tap on the psychological jugular will produce compliance." Further, according to *KUBARK*, the goal of coercion is not to inflict pain but, instead, "to induce regression" and break down the prisoner's defenses, which will, in turn, create feelings of guilt and dependence in the prisoner as part of a relationship with the interrogator.[42]

The manual also addresses the concern that information obtained by coercion may not be reliable, and it does so by positing a more complex psychological relationship between the use of force and the production of information. Put differently, according to *KUBARK*, the goal of coercion in interrogation is only partly to obtain accurate information. Just as important is the process of putting the prisoner through a crisis, from which the prisoner emerges into a situation in which he or she will give truthful information.

> Psychologists and others who write about physical or psychological duress frequently object that under sufficient pressure subjects usually yield but that their ability to recall and communicate information accurately is as impaired as the will to resist. This pragmatic objection has somewhat the same validity for a counterintelligence interrogation as for any other. But there is one significant difference. Confession is a necessary prelude to the [counterintelligence] interrogation of a hitherto unresponsive or concealing source. And the use of coercive techniques will rarely or never confuse an interrogatee so completely that he does not know whether his own confession is true or false. He does not need full mastery of all his powers of resistance and discrimination to know whether he is a spy or not. Only subjects who have reached a point where they are under delusions are likely to make false confessions that they believe. Once a true confession is obtained, the classic cautions apply. The pressures are lifted, at least enough so that the subject can provide counterintelligence information as accurately as possible. In fact, the relief granted the subject at this time fits neatly into the interrogation plan. He is told that the changed treatment is a reward for truthfulness and an evidence that friendly handling will continue as long as he cooperates.[43]

Note how this discussion of breaking a subject frames the issues as "pragmatic." Yet *KUBARK* did not ignore moral questions altogether. Instead, it dealt with them in a rational manner, by compartmentalizing them as a topic for further research: "The profound moral objection to applying duress past the point of irreversible psychological damage has been stated. Judging the validity of other ethical arguments about coercion exceeds the scope of this paper."[44]

The manual then addresses several coercive tactics: "arrest, detention, deprivation of sensory stimuli through solitary confinement or similar methods, threats and fear, debility, pain, heightened suggestibility and hypnosis, narcosis, and induced regression." With respect to detention, the manual observes, "[M]an's sense of identity depends upon a continuity in his surroundings, habits, appearance, actions, relations with others, etc. Detention permits the interrogator to cut through these links and throw the interrogatee back upon his own unaided internal resources." As a result, the interrogator should manipulate "diet, sleep pattern, and other fundamentals" so the prisoner will not have "a routine to which he can adapt and from which he can draw some comfort—or at least a sense of his own identity." For its part, sensory deprivation is also useful, according to *KUBARK*, because it accelerates the production of anxiety and regression, which the interrogator can use to reinforce the prisoner's subservience and encourage the prisoner to see the interrogator as "benevolent" or as "a father-figure."[45]

Threats of coercion are useful, according to *KUBARK*, because they will often be more effective than actual coercion. Because "most people underestimate their capacity to withstand pain," the threat of pain can produce compliance. Threats also give the prisoner "time for compliance"; that is, the threat allows the prisoner "to protect [his] self-autonomy or 'will'" by complying and providing information "voluntarily." With respect to the infliction of physical pain, *KUBARK* observes, "whereas pain inflicted on a person from outside himself may actually focus or intensify the will to resist, his resistance is likelier to be sapped by pain which he seems to inflict on himself." The manual therefore advises against creating a simple contest between interrogator and prisoner. Instead, such tactics as forced standing are recommended as useful because they force the prisoner to be complicit in the infliction of pain. "Intense pain," by contrast, can be counterproductive, because it can lead to "false confessions, concocted as a means of escaping from distress."[46]

KUBARK also recommends judicious use of drugs, both as a tool to overcome resistance and as an excuse for suspects who want to justify their eventual cooperation. The manual assumes that a doctor will be available to help the interrogator determine appropriate doses, and it advises against using drugs "to facilitate the interrogative debriefing that follows capitulation." The manual explains, "Their function is to cause capitulation, to aid in the shift from resistance to cooperation. Once this shift has been accomplished, coercive techniques should be abandoned both for moral reasons and because they are unnecessary and even counter-productive."[47] In brief, physical pain, supplemented by threats and narcotics, is part of the coercive arsenal, but the focus is on psychological breaking and control of the prisoner to assist the collection of intelligence information, not on the infliction of physical pain per se.

Thus, in the competitive atmosphere of the cold war, CIA officials funded research into psychologically coercive interrogation tactics, not to replace physical coercion, but, rather, to supplement it. In so doing, they sought to create a science of coercive interrogation and new technologies of torture.[48] The results of that research were influential and became an international commodity, part of the global market in torture methods.

Vietnam

The Johnson administration justified the war in Vietnam not simply as a way to oppose communism but also as part of a struggle against "hunger, ignorance, and disease"—in other words, as a standard imperial civilizing mission.[49] When reports of abuse by U.S. forces began to filter out, the high purposes of the war at first made it difficult to accept that the claims could be true. For example, a 1965 editorial in *Time* magazine derided Senate majority leader Mike Mansfield's proposal for "an amnesty to prevent further 'barbarism and atrocities,'" because "he made it sound as if the U.S. and government forces in South Viet Nam were just as guilty of systematic torture and terrorism as the Viet Cong."[50] Yet by 1973, *Time* was able to refer almost casually—in words that anticipate Agamben's *homo sacer* and the war on terror's "ghost detainee"—to the existence of political prisoners who were "[v]ictims of torture on both sides [and] languish[ed] in a legal never-never land, protected by neither the Paris Accords nor even the status of common criminals."[51]

Many of these abuses had nothing to do with the CIA or *KUBARK*. It seems unlikely that methods from *KUBARK* could have been used on a large scale in Vietnam, given the level of training, judgment, and available time—not to mention secure facilities—that these methods require from interrogators. Other, more "traditional"—or perhaps, as we will see, simply French—methods of interrogation and abuse appeared as well. For example, a 1968 *Washington Post* article on interrogation included a picture of soldiers holding down a suspected Vietcong operative, "clad in the black pajamas typical of the Vietnamese peasant and the Vietcong," while one poured water onto a towel over the man's face. According to the article, "This induces a fleeting sense of suffocation and drowning which is calculated to make a suspect talk." The article noted that this incident was not unique: "The water technique is said to be in fairly common use among Allied troops in Vietnam. Those who practice it say it combines the advan-

tages of being unpleasant enough to make people talk while still not causing permanent injury."[52] The victim in the photograph is notable for his
lack of distinguishing characteristics. Not only is he anonymous, but he is a
Vietnamese everyman, clad in "black pajamas" that identify him as a peasant, as Vietcong, or both. No space exists between the enemy and the general population. They blur together; anyone in black pajamas is always the
subject of both protection and suspicion—and if suspicious, then also of
torture.

Recently declassified army files flesh out these statements (although it
also true that the military generally complied with the Geneva Conventions). In addition to the already well-documented My Lai and Son Thang
massacres, these materials substantiate several other incidents involving
U.S. Army forces, including massacres and other attacks on noncombatants, as well as 141 instances in which U.S. soldiers tortured civilian detainees or prisoners of war with fists, sticks, bats, water, or electric shock.[53]
These events underscore the distorted perception that some soldiers had of
the Vietnamese. One soldier testified: "It wasn't like [the Vietnamese] were
humans. . . . [W]hen you shot at someone you didn't think you were shooting at a human."[54] It is also notable that few of the soldiers involved in these
incidents received any significant punishment.[55]

U.S. forces and their proxies also used the infrastructure that French
forces left behind, such as the "tiger cages" at the Con Son Island penal
colony, in which three to five prisoners were confined together in cells as
small as five feet by nine feet, allegedly had lime dumped on them from
time to time, and were subjected to "bad food, insufficient water, frequent
beatings and being shackled for days on end."[56] This was not the only
French influence. A team headed by General Paul Aussaresses—who played
a central role in the torture of suspected FLN members during the Battle of
Algiers—helped train U.S. forces in counterinsurgency tactics at Fort Bragg
and Fort Benning.[57]

Nonetheless, the CIA played a special role in developing and implementing counterinsurgency strategies in Vietnam. CIA agents trained thousands
of South Vietnamese police officers in what Alfred McCoy calls "stringent
wartime measures," including interrogation tactics.[58] Beginning in 1963, the
CIA expanded South Vietnam's intelligence operations by training interrogators who would work at that country's National Interrogation Center
and at its provincial interrogation centers. Once again, the French influence
persisted. The Vietnamese interrogators "were already well versed in 'the
old French methods' of interrogation—namely water torture and use of
electricity." CIA officers attempted to retrain them in some of the more "sophisticated" methods from *KUBARK*.[59] Under CIA supervision, interrogations at the national center combined *KUBARK* and French methods, while

interrogations at the provincial centers tended to rely more on violence.[60] In addition to interrogation and counterintelligence activities, CIA agents also organized counterinsurgency groups "to use Viet Cong techniques of terror—assassination, abuses, kidnappings and intimidation—against the Viet Cong leadership."[61]

In 1967 and 1968, the CIA reorganized its efforts into the Phoenix program, which was "an attempt to combat . . . Vietcong support organizations by identifying their members, welcoming defectors, capturing members, and killing members."[62] According to McCoy, "[f]or all its technological gloss, the program's strategy remained grounded in [a] vision of physical and psychological counterterror," and under this vision, numerous prisoners were tortured in the provincial centers and "summarily executed without trial or due process." By the time the House of Representatives held hearings on Phoenix in 1971, CIA and South Vietnamese officials associated with the program had killed more than 15,000 suspected Viet Cong suspects.[63] The vast majority were almost certainly not Viet Cong operatives. As with the Battle of Algiers, torture compounded the inevitable problem of false positives.[64]

Mark Moyar's account of Phoenix maintains that most of the torture and killing was carried out by South Vietnamese forces trained by the CIA: "[I]t is clear that the large majority of South Vietnamese interrogators tortured some or all of the Communist prisoners in their care. . . . It should be noted that a significant minority of South Vietnamese, many of them in organizations administered by the CIA, did not torture prisoners regularly." Yet Moyar also notes, "CIA advisors in the Province Interrogation Centers, where many important nonmilitary prisoners went for questioning, watched over the Special Police interrogations there, hired their own South Vietnamese interrogators to work in the centers, and conducted some interrogations themselves through interpreters." Indeed, "almost all advisors" witnessed the use of violent interrogation methods, such as "beating, electric shock, and water torture," as well as the infliction of summary execution on suspected Viet Cong.[65]

In short, even if one would like to blame local officials for the bulk of the problem—that is, for the continued use of French methods that became conflated with traditional methods or vice versa—the fact remains that they did not act alone. The torture of suspected Viet Cong cannot be compartmentalized as the sovereign act of an independent South Vietnamese government. U.S. officials taught physically and psychologically coercive methods to South Vietnamese forces, who used those methods with the knowledge of their teachers. Despite the best efforts of many officials, the role of U.S. advisers became public—or at least publicly available. Therefore, the effort to outsource torture was only partly successful in Vietnam.

Evidence that U.S. personnel were directly involved emerged too easily, even if it was also quickly forgotten.

Latin America

U.S. involvement with the "dirty wars" in Latin America is often portrayed as a relatively simple matter of supporting dictatorial or oligarchic regimes that fought bloody campaigns against leftist, communist, or indigenous guerilla groups.[66] In this narrative, U.S. officials provided military and intelligence training, but they did not assist the abusive practices employed by these regimes. To the contrary, as James LeMoyne suggested in an influential 1988 *New York Times* article, "the Americans appear to have helped organize an army intelligence machine they could not control, or perhaps did not want to control." LeMoyne reported that CIA training sessions included warnings against the use of torture, and CIA documents dating from the Ford administration confirm that agents "were not to participate, directly or indirectly, in violations of human rights" and were to "make appropriate efforts to prevent or delay" human rights violations by officials in countries in which they were working.[67]

The clear message in stories like this is that U.S. officials stepped over the line in supporting specific regimes and officials in the use of brutal methods. The implicit message is that military and intelligence personnel in Latin American countries were already so violent in their treatment of prisoners and so inventive in their violence as to be beyond the control of American expertise. For example, LeMoyne specifically asserted, "The practice of 'disappearing' people is probably the most sordid invention of modern Latin American politics."[68] Put yet another way, human rights abuses were already happening and would have continued to happen. The United States either should not have intervened or should have been more careful about the terms of its intervention, but Latin American governments would have killed and tortured in any event.

But U.S. officials did not simply discover a society characterized by extreme brutality. Instead, they helped create a culture of violent practices that influenced the evolution of coercive interrogation as a tool of U.S. policy. To begin, U.S. involvement in Latin American politics did not start in the 1980s, with the Reagan administration. Peter Smith observes, "Between 1898 and 1934, the United States launched more than thirty military interventions in Latin America." Most of the time, "[m]ilitary forces would arrive amidst considerable fanfare; depose rulers, often with minimal force; install a hand-picked provisional government; supervise national elections [at which the winner was often pre-selected]; and then depart." Many of these operations were justified by a standard rationale of the white man's burden. Especially for the Roosevelt, Taft, and Wilson administrations, the people of Latin America were inferior and in need of benevolent but stern supervision.[69]

After World War I, spurred partly by scandals over human rights abuses committed by U.S. soldiers in Haiti and the Dominican Republic, U.S. policy makers moved away from military intervention, in favor of "alliance[s] with local military chieftans." This shift marked "the moment when the United States invented the Trujillos and Somozas, the military strongmen who would dominate Caribbean Basin politics for a generation."[70] By the end of the 1930s, long-term military dictatorships had emerged in Cuba, the Dominican Republic, El Salvador, Guatemala, and Nicaragua—as Smith comments, "precisely in those countries where the United States had intervened or meddled to the greatest degree." U.S. policy followed a general pattern of supporting military intervention and dictatorships in Latin America for the next 50 years, punctuated by occasional second thoughts at the end of World War II, early in the Kennedy administration, and during the Carter administration.[71] Thus, when one reads accounts which suggest that U.S. officials were unable to "control" the violence of their Latin American clients in one or another country, it is worth pausing to consider not only whether those comments reflect standard prejudices toward the region but also whether at least some of that violence derived from the more than 80 years of political instability that U.S. policy helped create there.

U.S. policy was not limited to general support or disapproval of specific regimes. During the cold war, U.S. military officials began to develop stronger ties with their counterparts in many Latin American countries.[72] Beginning in the early 1960s, under the Kennedy administration, CIA agents began training police officers in numerous countries, including Central and South American countries, just as they had trained police in Vietnam. In the early 1970s, congressional investigations looked into allegations that these programs had included instruction in torture, and in 1975, Congress cut funding for police training overseas.[73] By that time, however, according to McCoy, the agency had already "shift[ed] its torture training to the Army's Military Adviser Program." Defense Department officials, working through a secret program with the incredible name "Project X," determined to apply "Vietnam's lessons to South America," partly by developing "a complete counterinsurgency curriculum based on seven training manuals, all in Spanish, that addressed key tactical problems—including *Handling of Sources, Interrogation, Combat Intelligence,* and *Terrorism and the Urban Guerilla.*"[74]

The information in these manuals does not aspire to the scientific knowledge of *KUBARK*. To the contrary, army officials admitted that the *Handling of Sources* manual "refers to motivation by fear, payment of bounties for enemy dead, beatings, false imprisonment, executions and the use of truth serum."[75] Among other things, these tactics indicate not only that the strategy of "disappearing" political opponents may not have been a purely Latin American invention after all but also that the impetus to disappear opponents may not have been entirely homegrown.[76]

These materials remained in use until 1991, and the U.S. Southern Command distributed "as many as a thousand copies" "to military personnel and intelligence schools in five Latin American countries (Columbia, Ecuador, El Salvador, Guatemala and Peru)." The army's School of the Americas provided hundreds of copies to "military students from 10 Latin American countries attending intelligence courses," including students from "Bolivia, Colombia, Costa Rica, Dominican Republic, Ecuador, Guatemala, Honduras, Mexico, Peru, and Venezuela."[77] Although there appears to have been a hiatus during the Carter administration, the manuals were available in 1977 by mail order to "foreign officers nominated by their U.S. counterparts."[78] Thousands of military and police officials received training from the School of the Americas during this period, and graduates of the program include "some of the region's most notorious human rights abusers."[79]

In addition to these straightforwardly violent methods, the *KUBARK* approach survived in the 1983 *Human Resource Exploitation Training Manual*, which CIA officials used in Honduras and which may have been the template for similar courses in other countries. Large sections of the 1983 manual paraphrase or directly quote *KUBARK*. Like *KUBARK*, the 1983 manual advocates the primary use of psychological methods, but it also recognizes that coercive interrogation techniques can create "debility (physical weakness)," "dread (intense fear [and] anxiety)," and "dependence."[80]

Besides documentation about training in physically and psychologically coercive interrogation techniques, sufficient direct and circumstantial evidence exists to establish that U.S. officials were aware that interrogators in many Latin American countries supported by the United States were using rough and coercive methods on political and military prisoners.[81] Testimony of torture victims and anecdotal evidence indicate that U.S. officials sometimes were present during interrogations that included torture, although a CIA investigation declared with respect to Honduras that "[n]o evidence has been found to substantiate the allegation . . . that . . . any . . . CIA employee was present during sessions of hostile interrogation."[82] In this context, it is worth noting that although the CIA had promulgated human rights directives as early as the Ford administration, "no explicit CIA policy statement regarding interrogations has been found prior to 1985."[83] In sum, U.S. officials pioneered an approach of torture by proxy in Latin America. Further, the lack of any significant public furor when these practices were revealed in detail by journalists in the 1990s indicates that the idea of outsourcing abuse was quite successful as a political strategy.

So far, I have discussed the regular use of torture and other abuse by U.S. officials and—more recently—their U.S.-trained proxies from the Philippine-American War up to at least 1991. Time and again, the use of coercive tactics has been denied or minimized. Where abuse could not be denied, it was inevitably termed an aberration, and officials shifted responsibility for it onto the shoulders of low-ranking soldiers or onto allies operating outside of U.S. control and portrayed as difficult to control for cultural reasons. Each of these things—direct abuse, the use of proxies, denials, and efforts to shift responsibility—would return with the war on terror.

Torture in the Homeland

～

This section discusses the importance of physical abuse to domestic law enforcement and prison discipline. I also consider the structure of immigration law and detention. My goal is simply to demonstrate that arbitrary process, detention in difficult conditions, and deliberate abuse were part of the U.S. legal landscape well before September 11, 2001. These forms of abuse provided a direct source for many of the methods used by U.S. forces in Afghanistan, Iraq, and Guantánamo Bay.

"Domestic" Police Violence

In chapter 3, I described the constitutional law of police violence. I suggested that police officers have considerable leeway to use force, including deadly force, primarily because their conduct will be judged under a reasonableness test that avoids second-guessing the often difficult decisions of police work. Here, I elaborate on some of the historical and contemporary contexts of those legal doctrines.

Police violence was widespread in the late nineteenth and early twentieth centuries. Lawrence Friedman describes "a whole world of torture and abuse" in which "the police enjoyed an enormous amount of discretion as far as the lower levels of society were concerned." He continues, "Southern blacks were always fair game. And what the police did to drunks, hoboes, and the poor in general was largely invisible. It happened in the back alleys, in the station houses, on the streets, out of sight of the bright lights and boulevards of due process."[84] Police in many states also used their ability to detain and interrogate people as material witnesses—which sometimes meant they were actually detained as suspects.[85] The Wickersham Commission's 1931 report "Lawlessness in Law Enforcement" documented and exposed "in enormous and grisly detail the arbitrary coercive character of police practices in the USA."[86] The report revealed that police interrogators in many cities punched suspects, twisted their arms painfully, beat them with rubber hoses, or resorted to starvation and exhaustion.[87] These revelations galvanized efforts to reform police interrogation practices. Reform also gathered steam from Supreme Court holdings that certain confessions were involuntary in violation of the due process clause and from the *Miranda* decision requiring police to provide suspects with information about their legal rights—including a right to remain silent—prior to interrogation.[88]

Admittedly, police often must use force, and deciding whether a particular use of force was appropriate can be difficult. For example, a recent study by the Bureau of Justice Statistics reported that 2,002 people died "in the process of arrest" by state and local police from 2003 to 2005. More than half of those deaths were homicides, the vast majority of which were considered by authorities to have been justified under the circumstances[89]—although, of course, legal doctrine aids that conclusion. Notwithstanding the possibility of reading this report to suggest that most police violence is justified, it remains true that unnecessary police violence continues to be a significant problem in the United States today. Further, in the decades-old war on crime, a public willingness to accept police violence as the price of safe communities helps to mute concern over excesses; certainly, there is little if any public outrage over any but the most egregious events.[90]

In a report issued before the attacks of September 11, 2001, Amnesty International discussed numerous examples of police brutality, with a specific focus on its racial aspects. It concluded that "the overwhelming number of victims of police brutality, unjustified shootings and deaths in custody are members of racial or ethnic minorities." But the report continued, "[W]hile race is a key factor in police brutality, it is not the sole problem. Police use of excessive force and questionable shootings are reported with alarming regularity in a variety of situations, sometimes cutting across racial lines. . . . Suspects continue to die in police custody after being held in dangerous restraint holds or subjected to other force." Amnesty International recognized that "some police agencies have taken measures to tackle these problems," but it maintained that "police brutality and excessive force remains both persistent and widespread across the USA."[91]

Although many incidents of excessive force can be classified as aberrant, the sheer number of complaints suggests a different conclusion. Excessive force may not be a frequent event for any specific police officer or department, but it is on the menu of potential responses to suspicious behavior. Further, notwithstanding the fact that some acts of police violence are aberrational, others are systematic. The most notorious recent examples are the

Rampart scandal in Los Angeles and the widespread use of torture (includ-ing electric shock) and other abuse in the Chicago Police Department's Area 2.[92]

The problem of abusive conduct by law enforcement officers is not lim-ited to excessive force, whether isolated or systematic. Efforts to control po-lice violence have had significant successes. Police interrogation practices, in particular, have shifted from acceptance of physical methods to reliance on psychological tactics. But interrogation law has not responded with further regulation. Instead, it provides significant leeway for police to use coercive psychological tactics. It remains a fair question whether some of these meth-ods inflict severe mental suffering sufficient to qualify as torture on a sys-tematic basis and not simply with respect to particular individuals. Even if labeling them as torture is appropriate, the fact that these methods leave no marks makes this form of violence attractive as well as difficult to prevent.

Torture and Violence in U.S. Prisons

Once a defendant has been convicted of a crime, the focus shifts from in-vestigation and interrogation to punishment and the law that regulates it. Although there are many reasons for imposing criminal sanctions and many ways to impose them, punitive incarceration or its threat (through probation or suspended sentence) is the overwhelming choice in the con-temporary United States. During the last 30 years of the twentieth century, ideals of rehabilitation gave way to retributive and expressive rationales for punishment. The percentage of cases in which imprisonment was a com-ponent of the sentence increased, as did the length of prison terms, and the U.S. prison population increased by 500 percent between 1973 and 1997.[93] The Bureau of Justice Statistics reports,

> As of December 31, 2001, there were an estimated 5.6 million adults who had ever served time in State or Federal prison, including 4.3 million for-mer prisoners and 1.3 million adults in prison. Nearly a third of former prisoners were still under correctional supervision, including 731,000 on parole, 437,000 on probation, and 166,000 in local jails. . . . [A]n esti-mated 1 of every 15 persons (6.6%) will serve time in a prison during their lifetime.[94]

These numbers tell only part of the story. As the prison population in-creased, the understanding of the goals that prison and its related infra-structure should serve also changed. As David Garland observes, "[i]n the last few decades, the prison has been reinvented as a means of incapacitative restraint." He explains,

Probation and parole have de-emphasized their social work functions and give renewed weight to their control and risk-monitoring functions. Sentences that are higher than would be justified by retributive considerations are made available and even mandatory. Community notification laws publicly mark released offenders, highlighting their past misdeeds and possible future dangers. There is a relaxation of concern about the civil liberties of suspects, and the rights of prisoners, and a new emphasis upon effective enforcement and control.[95]

In other words, there is an emphasis on the idea of crime and the risk of crime as central to everyday life and experience in modern society, such that dealing with criminals—and dealing with them *as* criminals—is one of the overriding tasks of the state. At the same time, the fear remains that the government is failing to control crime, so that more efforts are needed, greater toughness is necessary, and individual security becomes paramount yet also elusive. The fear of crime and the war on crime are thus near-perfect analogues of the war on terror.

Not surprisingly in light of these developments, the prison conditions endured by this large part of the U.S. population are not good. In the early twentieth century, conditions were often very harsh, and not until the 1960s did a general effort to improve prison conditions gain momentum.[96] The doctrinal vehicle for these changes was the Eighth Amendment to the Constitution, which bans "cruel and unusual punishments." The Supreme Court has interpreted that language along two tracks, one dealing with physical violence and the other addressing general conditions of prison life. With respect to violence, the Court has interpreted the Eighth Amendment to prohibit the "unnecessary and wanton infliction of pain" in the course of incarceration or other punishment imposed as part of the criminal process.[97] Applied in any serious way, this standard outlaws abusive treatment of prisoners, including conduct that people likely would characterize as torture. For example, in *Hope v. Pelzer,* the Supreme Court ruled that Alabama corrections officials violated the Eighth Amendment when they left an inmate handcuffed to a hitching post in the sun with his hands above his head for seven hours as punishment for misbehavior on a work squad.[98]

Officially sanctioned violence has declined in most prisons over the past half century, but prisons remain harsh and violent. Indeed, the "unnecessary and wanton" standard for applying the Eighth Amendment explicitly leaves open the possibility of justifying the infliction of pain. "Unnecessary" uses of force are banned, but officials may still inflict severe pain on prisoners if that pain is related to a legitimate goal, such as maintaining prison discipline. In *Whitley v. Albers,* the Supreme Court said that officials are not liable for damages if "force was applied in a good faith effort to maintain or restore discipline" but that they will be liable if they act "maliciously and sadistically for the very purpose of causing harm."[99] Put differently, a prisoner seeking to establish in court that officials violated the Eighth Amendment by using too much force cannot succeed merely by proving a purpose to cause harm, because there might be legitimate reasons for such a purpose and because distinguishing a purpose to cause harm from mere knowledge that harm would result might be too difficult. A prisoner claiming an Eighth Amendment injury in a case involving use of force must instead prove a "malicious and sadistic" purpose. As with the Fourth Amendment, officials are likely to receive a great deal of latitude when prison order is— or "reasonably" appears to be—at stake and where a ruling against them would have the consequence of calling their fundamental decency into question and branding them as deviant.

Similar problems arise with contemporary claims about "conditions of confinement." Although inmates can challenge those conditions in court under the Eighth Amendment, the Supreme Court has held that they must prove two things to prevail. First, the conditions must be so bad that they deprive inmates of "the minimal civilized measure of life's necessities." Second, plaintiffs must show that prison officials were "deliberately indifferent" to those conditions, which requires proof that an official "knows of and disregards an excessive risk to inmate health or safety."[100] Thus, the Court has ruled that "an official's failure to alleviate a significant risk that he should have perceived but did not . . . cannot . . . be condemned as the infliction of punishment."[101] As the long history of litigation over prison conditions confirms, prisoners sometimes win such cases. But in recent years, at a time when public policy approaches to crime have turned increasingly punitive, the trend of court decisions has run against prisoner claims, and federal legislation has imposed significant procedural roadblocks.[102]

As if to underscore these doctrinal limitations, federal judges have taken care, from time to time, to express such sentiments as "Prisons are necessarily dangerous places; they house society's most antisocial and violent people in close proximity with one another." Judges have argued that "some level of brutality and sexual aggression among [prisoners] is inevitable no matter what the guards do . . . unless all prisoners are locked in their cells 24 hours a day and sedated."[103] They have explained that "forcibly keeping prisoners in detention is what prisons are all about," and they have claimed that "[t]o the extent that such conditions are restrictive and even harsh, they are part of the penalty that criminal offenders pay for their offenses against society."[104]

What, then, is the world with which these legal doctrines interact? The Bureau of Justice Statistics has compiled the following information:

- Ten percent of state inmates and 3 percent of federal inmates were injured in a fight.
- Two percent of deaths in state prisons from 2001 to 2004 were homicides, and 6 percent were suicides, while 32 percent of deaths in local jails during a similar period were suicides.
- The number of allegations of sexual violence is 2.91 per 1,000 inmates per year, with 54 percent of the allegations involving misconduct or harassment by staff.
- Fifty-six percent of state prisoners and 45% of federal prisoners have some kind of mental health problem, and 30% of state and federal prisoners "have symptoms of a mental disorder without a recent history."[105]

These numbers are incomplete, and their accuracy is debatable, as the bureau admits. They likely understate the level of violence in prison.[106] Recent litigation has also documented that prison conditions remain poor and that violence and abuse are common in many facilities. Responsibility for violence and abuse does not go entirely in one direction, but Jamie Fellner convincingly argues that wardens and other senior staff too often "failed to establish—and enforce—clear policies and expectations about how staff will treat inmates." Indeed, Fellner suggests that "some senior officials expressly or tacitly condone the abuse of inmates" in order to control prisoners and maintain good relations with staff. Violence thus becomes inevitable within the prison culture: "The 'default' culture in a prison is toxic. That is, the culture does not come automatically with respect for inmates as individuals with dignity and rights, or with a commitment that prison be as productive an experience as possible."[107]

The Texas prison system provides a good example. Litigation in federal court over the conditions in Texas prisons began in 1972. In 1999, a federal district judge found that conditions in the prison system violated the Eighth Amendment on several grounds. Among other things, the court documented the existence of "a prison underworld in which rapes, beatings, and servitude are the currency of power" and to which officials were deliberately indifferent. The court also reported, "[T]he pattern of 'slamming,' hitting, and kicking by corrections officers in the cellblocks . . . is so prevalent as to implicate the Constitution. Simply stated, the culture of sadistic and malicious violence that continues to pervade the Texas prison system violates contemporary standards of decency."[108]

Drawing from the court's finding of a violent and sexually charged prison culture in Texas, the issue of sexual assault in prison is worth considering in more detail. Congressional findings in the Prison Rape Elimination Act of 2003 included the "conservative" estimate that "thirteen percent of inmates in the United States have been sexually assaulted in prison."

They indicated that "young first-time offenders and inmates with mental illness are at the greatest risk for victimization."[109] Recent studies of midwestern prisons report, "[A]pproximately 20 percent of male inmates are pressured or coerced into unwanted sexual contact; approximately 10 percent are raped. Rates of sexual abuse in women's facilities, where the perpetrators are most likely to be male staff, seem to vary more by institution but are as high as 27 percent of inmates."[110]

Alice Ristroph extends this analysis by suggesting that "sexual coercion is intrinsic to the experience of imprisonment" in a way that goes beyond the paradigm of violent rape or assault. She explains,

> Each inmate will probably experience prison as a partly sexual punishment, even if he is neither raped nor rapist. He will receive extensive sexual harassment, and will likely engage in sexual harassment toward others. He will lose all privacy rights, including any semblance of sexual privacy, as his body is monitored, restrained, and regulated. And he will hold a place in a prison hierarchy based on his assignment to a sexual category.

As a result, "sex and sexual identities structure the prison experience in profound ways." Ristroph goes on to note that the official response to prison rape is often to propose more prisons in which inmates can be better controlled—that is, to "build more, and better, panopticons." These efforts will reduce violent prison rape, but they also "can be understood as further efforts to police the sexual, and to police through the sexual."[111]

The most stark example of the "better panopticons" that these and related efforts are producing is the rise of the so-called supermax prison, which is an extreme form of solitary confinement designed to "separate the most predatory and dangerous prisoners from the rest."[112] In *Wilkinson v. Austin,* the Supreme Court noted some of the common characteristics of supermax confinement: prisoners are confined in small single-inmate cells (e.g., 7 feet by 14 feet) for 23 hours every day; a light is on inside the cell at all times; inmates take all of their meals alone; the cell door is designed to prevent them from communicating with each other; and they receive one hour per day in an "indoor recreation cell."[113] Other courts have described additional conditions that exist in some supermax prisons. For example, in Wisconsin, supermax inmates are allowed no possessions except one religious text, one box of legal documents, and 25 personal letters. Inmates who violated the rules were placed in a behavior modification program. During the first stage of the program, the inmate was kept naked in the cell with no possessions for three days, was fed only with a composite food called nutria-loaf, and had no bedding (and so slept on a concrete slab). If those three days went well, the inmate proceeded to the next stage for at least seven days, which meant he was allowed to wear a one-piece smock without underwear, eat regular meals, and "receive hygiene items two times per day and . . . showers on regular shower days," but he still had to go without bedding. Bad behavior during this period resulted in starting the program over from the beginning.[114]

These conditions suggest that the Supreme Court's characterization of the supermax experience as "synonymous with extreme isolation" because the prisoner is "deprived of almost any environmental or sensory stimulus and of almost all human contact" is a dramatic understatement.[115] Yet such prisons exist in at least 30 states, as well as within the federal prison system, with more than 20,000 people confined in them as of 2000.[116] Although these facilities were designed to house the "worst of the worst," prisoners have been transferred to them for relatively minor infractions, and some commentators suggest that once a supermax is built, officials will manipulate the transfer policy in order to keep it full.[117] As Craig Haney points out, these prisons have clear "potential to inflict psychological pain and emotional damage," with such symptoms as "appetite and sleep disturbances, anxiety, panic, rage, loss of control, paranoia, hallucinations, and self-mutilations," as well as "suicidal thoughts and behavior." He asserts, "[T]here is not a single published study of solitary or supermax-like confinement in which nonvoluntary confinement lasting for longer than 10 days, where participants were unable to terminate their isolation at will, . . . failed to result in negative psychological effects."[118]

The supermax is perhaps the logical conclusion of what Garland describes as the new norm of incarceration: the idea of managing a population that is waste or surplus by warehousing it in prison.[119] Members of this population can be subjected to near-complete control over their movements and possessions, and they are subject to near-continuous surveillance. Further, law helps make such places possible by defining the "basic" or "fundamental" human needs that are the touchstone for a catalog of permissible policies and practices that take deprivation, discomfort, and trauma as a norm.[120] Indeed, the supermax inmate is almost a parody of the autonomous liberal political subject, for these inmates perform a mockery of (or take to its logical conclusion) the idea of the individual abstracted from all distracting social identities and contexts and placed in a hyperlegal relationship with sovereign authority.[121]

The development of supermax technology amid the apparent national emergency of the war on crime also provides an example of and symbol for a set of assumptions, infrastructures, and practices that were easily transferable to the newer emergency of the war on terror. This transfer took place on several levels, particularly with respect to the invasion of Iraq. Many members of the army reserve had civilian jobs in prisons, and they were assigned to places like Abu Ghraib "precisely because they had experience working in prisons." In these new settings, they naturally used some of the same techniques that they had used at home. At a higher level, military officials contracted with private prison consultants—often "former state directors of corrections" from states whose prisons have been involved in litigation over patterns of violence and abuse.[122] For example, the former director of the Texas prison system during part of the period that it was in litigation—and who, during his superintendence of that system as well as prisons in New Mexico and Utah, allegedly presided over policies that included strip-searching, rapid and violent reactions to rule infractions, and the use of restraint chairs—was hired in 2003 to help oversee the creation of prisons in occupied Iraq.[123] My point is not that this official was somehow responsible for the Abu Ghraib abuses but, rather, that people who were in charge of creating the kind of domestic prison system I have just described were considered natural choices to set up a similar system in Iraq.

A third level at which this transfer took place was within legal and political discourse, so that ideas of the rule of law, legitimacy, and sovereign power—not to mention notions of decent or acceptable conduct—had already evolved to make room for the kinds of practices that had become routine in maximum security and supermax prisons. If these methods were permissible for the worst of the worst at home, it followed that they were good enough for terrorists, war criminals, and the potentially violent others who were detained in counterterror efforts and who were assumed to populate such places as Iraq. The facilities, rules, and practices that exploded into public view at Abu Ghraib and Guantánamo are not so very different from those that have operated and continue to operate on a much larger scale within the United States, with the result that the appropriate descriptive narrative is one of continuity with the rule of law as a domestic practice. Some of the domestic prison practices that produce the rule of law also produce the kind of severe mental and physical pain and suffering that is central to the Convention against Torture's definition of torture—which simply underscores the point.

Immigration

I close this chapter with a discussion of immigration law and practice for three reasons. First, immigration law demonstrates the existence of a parallel (and "irregular") process that undercuts claims that due process is shared or extended widely in an equal way. Immigration supports obliquely and historically—not necessarily doctrinally—the use of novel or irregular processes for people detained in the war on terror. Second, immigration law reveals the use of camps and detention as a policy choice for dealing with people whose presence in the United States is undesirable in some sense. Third, immigration provides the primary area of U.S. law that considers and decides torture claims on a regular basis.

With respect to the processes attached to immigration—particularly the decisions about who may enter the country and who will be expelled (collectively known as "removal" under current law), the Supreme Court repeatedly has declared that "ordinary" standards of due process do not apply. For aliens seeking entry, the Court has said, "[W]hatever the procedure authorized by congress is, it is due process as far as an alien denied entry is concerned."[124] More generally, "Congress may make rules as to aliens," including permanent resident aliens, "that would be unacceptable if applied to citizens."[125] Although permanent residents may not be removed without some kind of hearing, the hearing does not come with the procedural protections one would find in a criminal case (because removal is not a criminal proceeding) or even in most civil cases.[126] This brief description does not begin to provide a sense of the procedural nightmare of immigration. Not only is the formal administrative and judicial process difficult to navigate, but the intricacies and arbitrariness of the immigration bureaucracy are the stuff of legend.[127]

Immigration cases are not criminal, but they have criminal overtones. Many people facing removal proceedings have committed a crime. More significant is the general tendency to think of the illegal or undocumented immigrant as a criminal—that is, increasingly to criminalize the effort to cross the border without proper permission and documentation. The number of people prosecuted for the misdemeanor of entering the United States illegally or for the felony of reentry after removal has risen sharply in recent years, and the vast majority of those convicted are sent to prison for significant terms.[128] Of course, a legal immigrant who commits a crime is likely to be removed—so that a change in immigration status is functionally one of the penalties handed out by the criminal justice system.[129]

The combination of crime and borders also influences procedure in the related context of international extradition. Extradition hearings—that is, hearings at which judges decide whether to uproot a person (whether citizen or alien) from the United States to face criminal charges in another country—do not look like ordinary court proceedings. The process repeatedly has been described as "sui generis,"[130] and the federal rules of criminal procedure, civil procedure, and evidence do not apply. The demanding country may rely on ex parte evidence, while the extraditee "cannot introduce evidence that contradicts the demanding country's proof; evidence to establish alibi; evidence of insanity; [or] evidence that the statute of limitations has run." The government's burden of proof is not an ordinary preponderance of the evidence standard (let alone beyond a reasonable doubt); rather, the standard is simply probable cause to believe that the extraditee committed the alleged crime.[131] After the hearing, the person facing extradition can seek habeas review in federal court, but review is often limited to three issues: whether the trial judge had jurisdiction, whether the offense is within the treaty, and "whether there was *any* evidence warranting the finding that there were reasonable grounds to believe the accused guilty."[132] The extradition process is so singular that federal courts do not even agree on exactly how a judge obtains the constitutional authority to hold an extradition hearing.[133]

The irregular procedures of immigration are tightly linked to the widespread use of detention as a means of managing the "removable" portion of the alien population. Thus, closing this chapter with a discussion of immigration also raises the topic of the camp. My discussion of the post–World War II abuse of German prisoners noted the use of the Nazi death camps to hold prisoners. But, of course, World War II also saw the creation of domestic concentration camps for Japanese Americans—famously, if indirectly, upheld by the Supreme Court.[134] Before that, beginning at the end of the nineteenth century, U.S. officials had already experimented with detention camps for Chinese immigrants, such as the facility on Angel Island for those seeking to enter the country: "Between 1910 and 1940, about 50,000 Chinese were confined—often for months and years at a time—in Angel Island's bleak wooden barracks, where inspectors would conduct grueling interrogations."[135] Congress also mandated "imprison[ment] at hard labor" for up to a year for Chinese immigrants already in the country who lacked valid identification (a provision that the Supreme Court struck down because the hard labor was imposed without a "judicial trial" and because the detention was not a punishment but simply a means of enforcing immigration law).[136] On the east coast, Ellis Island functioned primarily as a detention center in its last 25 years of operation.[137]

This history should make it unsurprising that detention camps (not "prisons"), with inmates described as detainees (not "prisoners") are an integral part of contemporary U.S. immigration law and policy. That became clear in late 1991 and early 1992, when thousands of people fled a military coup in Haiti. Federal officials followed an existing policy of intercepting these refugees at sea and screening them for "a credible showing of refugee status," which resulted in immediate repatriation for the vast majority. Yet officials quickly became overwhelmed by the volume of people, and they set up camps at Guantánamo Bay Naval Base, where more than 12,000 people were detained while they awaited further proceedings and probable repatriation.[138] In 1994, Guantánamo again became a detention center, this time for tens of thousands of Cuban and Haitian refugees, many of whom remained for more than a year.[139] Both times, the reason for using Guantánamo was not simply geographic convenience. Equally or more important was the fact that the camps were thoroughly under U.S. control but were not actually inside the United States, so the refugees had little chance of receiving the rights that attach to people who make it onto U.S. soil. Instead, they were subject to detention and military control with little concern for due process.[140]

Significantly, however, detention is not something that happens only in emergency situations; it is part of the typical immigration process. Detention for a significant period of time is a fact of life for large numbers of removable aliens, including asylum seekers. In 2002, for example, the average daily immigration-related detention population was 20,000, and the total number of people in immigration detention in a given year is roughly 200,000.[141] Approximately 3,000 people who had been found removable were being held in indefinite detention in 2001, when the Supreme Court ruled that an alien can only be detained until "there is no significant likelihood of removal in the reasonably foreseeable future."[142] As a result of that decision, the number of people in indefinite detention has fallen, but long-term and sometimes indefinite detention continues for people who are classified as "specifically dangerous."[143] Conditions in immigration detention centers vary widely, but they are generally like prisons, and the detainees—the term *detainee* often includes minors or entire families—are often treated as badly as or worse than criminals.[144] On some occasions, guards at these centers use physical abuse to maintain order. For example, in the 1990s, guards at Miami's Krome Detention Center used forced standing, as well as "slapping, beating, pointless exercises, and humiliation."[145]

I recognize that rational, well-intentioned policymakers easily could conclude that detention is appropriate for people who have been found removable and appear to be flight risks, particularly if they have serious criminal records. For a policymaker, the use of detention facilities or camps is not per se bad. To the contrary, the problem with the camp as a tool of modern statecraft is precisely that it is so often a reasonable option. My goal is simply to underscore that such places as the detention facilities at Guantánamo Bay are not aberrant or unprecedented in the United States today. Along with more traditional prisons, camps are a recurring tool for any modern state that seeks to manage and control diverse populations, including populations that the state determines to be undesirable.

Immigration is also important because most U.S. jurisprudence on torture has developed in the immigration context, through the adjudication of cases in which otherwise removable immigrants contend they will be tortured if returned to their country of origin.[146] Until recently, these claims arose in the context of efforts to withhold removal based on a threat of physical harm or to obtain asylum based on a well-founded fear of persecution. The kinds of conduct that qualify as threats or persecution go well beyond torture or other physical abuse, but they are limited to actions taken because of or on account of "race, religion, nationality, membership in a particular social group, or political opinion."[147] As a result, under the immigration statutes, a person could prove he or she was tortured yet nonetheless fail to obtain asylum or withholding of removal.[148]

In 1998, Congress passed the Foreign Affairs Reform and Restructuring Act, which declared that the United States would not "expel, extradite, or otherwise effect the involuntary return of any person to a country in which there are substantial grounds for believing the person would be in danger of being subjected to torture." The act also directed federal agencies to craft regulations to implement this policy and thereby also implement portions of the Convention against Torture.[149] Because of this directive, Department of Homeland Security regulations now require withholding or deferral of removal if an alien can prove "it is more likely than not that he or she would be tortured if removed to the proposed country of removal."[150]

Immigration courts hear roughly 30,000 cases every year in which aliens raise claims under the Convention against Torture. The "grant rate" for these claims fluctuates between 2 and 4 percent—for example, in 2006, immigration courts granted relief under the convention in 587 of the 31,364 cases in which aliens made torture claims.[151] Federal courts have been more welcoming to claims under the convention, and they frequently reverse or vacate the decisions of the immigration courts.[152] Still, the sheer number of cases being decided by immigration courts makes it impossible for federal courts to engage in meaningful review of every adverse decision. Federal court review also reflects both the ambiguities of the Convention against Torture and the restrictions created by the U.S. ratification process. In a recent case, for example, the U.S. Court of Appeals for the Ninth Circuit determined "it is not clear" that beatings of demonstrators by police "would rise to the level of torture," and it denied relief on that issue.[153] Several courts have also denied relief because the treatment the alien would face in the receiving country—such as atrocious prison conditions—is only cruel, inhuman, or degrading and does not rise to the level of torture, and they have made clear that under U.S. immigration law, "torture" requires specific intent—that is, a motive or purpose to inflict pain, rather than knowledge or willful blindness.[154] These holdings may be inevitable. Expansive definitions of torture in the context of police or prison violence would risk calling into question the legitimacy of those actions in the United States.[155]

Conclusion

～

This chapter has outlined the history and current practice relating to torture by U.S. officials and their proxies. The next chapter, on the use of torture in the war on terror, will pick up—sometimes explicitly and sometimes implicitly—on each of the themes that I have developed. The contemporary use of torture by U.S. forces relies on the interaction of military and foreign policy with ideas of race and civilization, reliance on outsourcing, development of psychological methods, and the precedents of domestic detention, control, interrogation, and violence.

CHAPTER SEVEN

Torture in the War on Terror

This chapter considers the use by U.S. forces of torture and other coercion in the war on terror. I do not ask the question asked in so many editorials, talk shows, and articles in the aftermath of the Abu Ghraib scandal: how "could [it] have been possible to commit such atrocious horrors against other human beings"? As in earlier chapters, I seek instead, in Agamben's words, "to investigate carefully how—that is, thanks to what juridical procedures and political devices—human beings could have been so completely deprived of their rights and prerogatives to the point that committing any act toward them would no longer appear as a crime."[1]

My discussion builds on the legal, historical, and political materials I discussed in the introduction and previous chapters, with the goal of narrating the relationship among these things and the way abuse reemerged as a part of U.S. foreign policy. My focus is on legal and, to some extent, political discourse, and I do not claim to provide a complete account; nor do I seek to determine individual responsibility for the abuse that I describe.[2] Throughout this chapter, I will also relate the official response to terrorism—particularly the tendency to torture—to the growing reliance in the United States on models of emergency government and to the shifting nature of liberal rights as an aspect of modern government.

The Framework of Emergency and Antiterror Legislation

Well before the terrorist attacks of September 11, 2001, U.S. law and practice accommodated emergency power in a wide array of situations. By the 1970s, the federal statute books contained roughly 470 pieces of legislation that provided the executive branch with emergency power in particular circumstances.[3] Major statutes include the National Emergencies Act and the International Economic Emergency Powers Act.[4] The Insurrection Act allows the president to use military force under certain conditions to restore order in response to "a natural disaster, epidemic, or other serious public health emergency, terrorist attack or incident, or other condition in any State or possession of the United States," as well as an actual insurrection.[5] The Foreign Intelligence Surveillance Act links emergency and national security by allowing a court to issue secret warrants for foreign intelligence wiretaps.[6]

To the extent that emergency powers highlight discretion and minimize constraint, the structure of contemporary federal law may even be based on an emergency powers model. The growth of a regulatory and administrative state has gone hand in hand with the development of legislation in which Congress declares broad policy goals and then delegates relatively unconstrained power to administrative agencies to use their discretion and expertise to craft precise rules that can be changed at the judgment of the executive branch.[7] Well before terrorism and the war on terror became central issues, the vast amount of executive branch discretion over the shape of federal law meant that the U.S. legal system included a large amount of what Hannah Arendt called the "law of movement," which she claimed is central to "totalitarian" law.[8]

Terrorism was also a subject of federal legislation prior to the September 11 attacks. In 1986, Congress passed the Omnibus Diplomatic Security and Antiterrorism Act, which "for the most part ... provides encouragement to and authority for the Executive Branch to act on ... various terrorism-related topics." The Antiterrorism and Effective Death Penalty Act of 1996 adopted more of a preventive tone and "develop[ed] a series of federal crimes aimed at terrorist acts generally and the interdicting of support for terrorist organizations."[9] Taken together, these statutes combine a desire for executive responsiveness and prevention with a more traditional focus on criminal law solutions. This uneasy balance came under pressure after the September 11 attacks.

Reacting to 9/11

∾

After the September 11 attacks, the FBI began a massive investigation that mobilized "more than 4,000 FBI special agents and 3,000 support personal."[10] On September 17, Attorney General John Ashcroft instructed all U.S. attorneys that the federal response included an effort "to prevent future terrorism by arresting and detaining [immigration] violators who 'have been identified as persons who participate in, or lend support to, terrorist activities." He maintained, "Federal law enforcement agencies and the United States Attorneys' Offices will use every available law enforcement tool to incapacitate these individuals and their organizations.'"[11] During the investigation, federal officials detained more than 1,200 noncitizens on immigration charges, on "terrorist-related criminal charges," or as "material witnesses" who might have information relevant to grand jury investigations into terrorist activity.[12] Detention often lasted for several months while legal proceedings were under way, and most of these people were held at detention centers in New York and New Jersey.

For the first several days and for several weeks in many cases, immigration detainees at Brooklyn's Metropolitan Detention Center were placed in restrictive custody. Tight restrictions continued even after the initial period. The Justice Department's Office of the Inspector General later summarized the harshness of these conditions as including

> inadequate access to counsel, sporadic and mistaken information to detainees' families and attorneys about where they were being detained, lockdown for at least 23 hours a day, cells remaining illuminated 24 hours a day, detainees placed in heavy restraints whenever they were moved outside their cells, limited access to recreation, and inadequate notice to detainees about the process for filing complaints about their treatment.[13]

The inspector general also found evidence of "a pattern of physical and verbal abuse by some correctional officers."[14] The physical abuse—which was substantiated by videotapes—was described as follows by the Office of the Inspector General:

> [S]ome MDC staff members slammed and bounced detainees into the walls at the MDC and inappropriately pressed detainees' heads against walls. We also found that some officers inappropriately twisted and bent detainees' arms, hands, wrists, and fingers, and caused them unnecessary physical pain; inappropriately carried or lifted detainees; and raised or pulled detainees' arms in painful ways. In addition, we believe some officers improperly used handcuffs, occasionally stepped on compliant detainees' leg restraint chains, and were needlessly forceful and rough with the detainees.[15]

Although this conduct probably does not rise to the level of torture as defined by U.S. or international law, it easily qualifies as cruel, inhuman, or degrading treatment under international law and as a violation of U.S. standards of due process.

In brief, patterns of abuse quickly emerged in the immediate law enforcement response to 9/11. These patterns would grow as military and intelligence officials became involved, as the scope of the response to 9/11 grew, and as justifications began to emerge for inflicting abuse. A critical step took place when the administration decided that traditional criminal investigation and prosecution was an inadequate response. Ashcroft's September 17 statement made clear that within law enforcement circles, the response would be as much preventive as reactive. Outside the Justice Department, administration officials began using military terms in talking about the attacks and the appropriate level of response to them. One administration lawyer later explained that feelings were "raw" and that "[e]veryone was expecting additional attacks." He went on to describe "a consensus that we had to move from retribution and punishment to preemption and prevention," explaining that "[o]nly a warfare model allows that approach."[16] Indeed, on the day Ashcroft signaled a shift to a preventive model, Bush signed an order that "gave the CIA broad authorization to disrupt terrorist activity, including permission to kill, capture and detain members of al Qaeda anywhere in the world."[17] The rationale for the program was self-defense, which echoes the emerging preventive and military model.[18] Perhaps to buttress the case for military action, some officials consciously began to describe terrorists and those who might support them as "evil," "barbaric," and "uncivilized."[19]

Congress quickly went along with the emerging war paradigm. On September 18, it passed a broadly worded authorization for use of military force (AUMF), which did not go as far as the executive branch wanted but nonetheless empowered the president

> to use all necessary and appropriate force against those nations, organizations, or persons he determines planned, authorized, committed, or aided the terrorist attacks that occurred on September 11, 2001, or harbored such organizations or persons, in order to prevent any future acts of international terrorism against the United States by such nations, organizations or persons.[20]

This language suggested not the enforcement of law but, rather, the use of force within constraints—"necessary and appropriate"—that have overtones of emergency, exception, and war.

Even as Congress was rushing to pass the AUMF, attorneys in the Justice Department's Office of Legal Counsel (OLC) were analyzing the president's power to respond to the attacks. They concluded not just that the president has inherent authority to use military force in response to emergencies but also that the ability to make such decisions was an area of essentially exclusive executive power. Indeed, they asserted that Congress's passage of the AUMF demonstrated its "acceptance of the President's unilateral war powers in an emergency situation like that created by the September 11 incidents."[21] Again, the emerging model was one of decisive action freed from ordinary law and legislative processes. In the meantime, Bush declared that "a collection of loosely affiliated terrorist organizations known as al Qaeda" was responsible for the September 11 attacks, and he made several demands on the government of Afghanistan, including the delivery to the United States of Osama bin Laden and other al Qaeda leaders.[22] The government of Afghanistan rejected these demands, and U.S. military forces began operations against Afghanistan in early October.

As military operations achieved initial success and the criminal investigation continued to grow, stories began to circulate that investigators were growing frustrated with their inability to obtain information from certain suspects. With ordinary, ostensibly humane tactics failing to provide useful information, some officials began to contemplate physical coercion, and a public debate about the use of torture began. Commentators questioned whether there should be a policy of coercion by U.S. investigators or whether U.S. officials should turn to security forces in other countries that would apply these kinds of pressures.[23] At this time, too, Alan Dershowitz published a widely discussed newspaper editorial asserting that torture was inevitable and proposing that rule-of-law principles required the use of "torture warrants" instead of the ad hoc authorization he predicted would take place within the executive branch.[24]

Structuring a State of Emergency

⟶

The scope of the emergency—or at least the scope of the federal government's definition of and response to it—became clearer a little more than a month after the attacks. First, on October 23, the OLC determined that the Posse Comitatus Act, 18 U.S.C. § 1385 (1994), which generally prohibits the domestic use of the Armed Forces for law enforcement purposes absent constitutional or statutory authority to do so, "does not apply to, does not prohibit, a Presidential decision to deploy the Armed Forces domestically for military purposes," including "to prevent and deter terrorism."[25] Three days later, the USA PATRIOT Act became law.[26] This act expanded the powers of law enforcement officials to investigate criminal activity, whether or not that activity is defined as terrorist.[27] Subsequent legislation confirmed that counterterrorism and national security concerns had expanded and enveloped other areas of government activity, with the consequence that new organizational structures were necessary.[28]

In the space of four days, the executive branch suggested that military forces be used for domestic purposes, while Congress passed legislation allowing criminal investigators to cooperate more fully with intelligence activities. My argument is not that the opinion based on the Posse Comitatus Act is incorrect (there is at least some statutory basis for the conclusion)[29] or that the aspects of the USA PATRIOT Act I mentioned are misguided (although I disagree with some of the act's provisions). Nor am I claiming that the convergence of the military and the police was entirely new. My point is that the deliberate use of legislation and formal legal opinion to invoke a war model while a massive criminal investigation was under way indicates that these two functions converged not only increasingly but increasingly easily. The lines between military and police activity blurred.

The post-9/11 dismantling of barriers between the military and the police and among criminal investigation, intelligence collection, and military action—which, in turn, built on developments already in place—underscores that policing in modern states has become more like military action, while military action increasingly "become[s] virtually indistinguishable from police activity."[30] Legal structures for controlling violent state actions seem less likely to make distinctions between the two. Instead, they allow government actors to switch from war fighting to crime control and back again in their efforts to maintain order.

The war-crime distinction blurred further—and its impact on individuals caught up in the war on terror became clearer—on November 13, 2001, when Bush issued an executive order that authorized the imprisonment and trial before a military commission of noncitizens "at an appropriate location designated by the Secretary of Defense outside or within the United States" if "there is reason to believe that such individual" was a member of al Qaeda, had "engaged in [or] aided . . . acts of international terrorism" intended "to cause injury to or adverse effects on the United States, its citizens, national security, foreign policy, or economy," or had harbored someone described in the first two categories. The order explicitly provided for detention of any person who met one of the three criteria, whether or not that person was to be tried by a military commission. As authority for this order, the president relied on his inherent powers, as detailed in the September 25 memo, as well as on the AUMF and statutes that refer to the possible existence of military commissions.[31]

Defense Department officials subsequently began a protracted process of drafting rules to govern the commissions. The resulting rules, which were intentionally more flexible than those that govern criminal trials in federal courts, provided a broader scope for the admission of evidence obtained under circumstances that would disallow it in an ordinary criminal proceeding. In particular, the rules allowed the admission of evidence obtained by coercion if it "would have probative value to a reasonable person."[32]

Creating Camps

∽

Military victory in Afghanistan produced large numbers of enemy prisoners. This situation and the effort to capture suspected terrorists for trial before military commissions led to an extensive debate within the administration about what to do with these people. Were they prisoners of war, criminal defendants, or officials or agents of state sponsors of terrorism? Whatever their category, where would the administration put the increasingly large number of people? Tightly connected with both questions was the debate over how to treat them, which was both an argument about the specific legal rules that would apply and an assessment of the kinds of conduct or conditions appropriate for people who might be terrorists or who might have useful knowledge about terror activities.

The Bush administration did not develop a clear process for deciding what prisoners fell into what category. Instead, a shifting series of ad hoc procedures developed. Along the way, it became clear that most of the people in detention were not terrorists. As a result, the administration changed its strategy and began using the label *enemy combatant* for its prisoners, with the clear implication that these people could be held for the duration of hostilities.[33] The administration did not immediately pursue military commissions for the most important prisoners, because "interrogation was given priority over prosecution."[34]

On the issue of where to put these enemy combatants, officials quickly seized on Guantánamo Bay Naval Base, which, just a few years earlier, had housed thousands of refugees whose admission into the country previous administrations had wanted to prevent. On December 28, OLC attorneys produced a memorandum concluding that any person held at Guantánamo is "outside" the United States and therefore also outside the habeas corpus jurisdiction of the federal courts.[35] Notably, the memorandum relied on the generally favorable outcome of litigation over using Guantánamo to house refugees from Cuba and Haiti.[36] Left unstated was the broader conclusion that the only applicable law at the base would be a combination of military law and simple sovereign authority. Two weeks later, the first group of prisoners arrived at Guantánamo. They were housed initially in Camp X-Ray, itself the site of one of the former refugee camps.

Executive Authority and the Geneva Conventions

∽

The Guantánamo solution addressed only part of the problem. It did not deal with all of the people in U.S. custody, and it did not provide clear rules for their treatment, beyond the implicit suggestion that any set of rules would be sufficient for people not under the protection of normal law. Lawyers at the White House, the Justice Department, the State Department, and eventually the Defense Department began to debate the extent to which—if at all—the Geneva Conventions, other sources of international law, or domestic constitutional and statutory law would apply. Again, a chief concern was the ability of U.S. officials to carry out successful interrogations of people whom they believed might have useful information.

Bush made an initial determination in January 2002, even as the OLC was drafting a memorandum that evidenced the concern about interrogation. It addressed the legal issues "by focusing on the War Crimes Act, 18 U.S.C. § 2441," specifically on whether the prisoners could "claim the protection" of the treaties that act incorporates and applies against U.S. officials. OLC lawyers sought to establish as official policy the conclusion that had been implicit in the December 28 memorandum: that the only law that clearly applied to people in U.S. military custody was the sovereign authority of the commander in chief. More specifically, they contended that the Geneva Conventions did not apply to a conflict with a "failed state," such as Afghanistan, which meant that they also would not apply to people fighting on that side of the conflict. As a result, the authors concluded, "neither the federal War Crimes Act nor the Geneva Conventions would apply to the detention conditions [and therefore also the interrogation conditions] of al Qaeda prisoners."[37]

State Department lawyers responded by arguing that the administration was not limited to a choice between applying or not applying the Geneva Conventions. Instead, they argued, a middle path was available that would stay within traditional international law frameworks while ensuring flexibility. That path was to determine that the conventions applied to the conflict with Afghanistan "but that members of al Qaeda as a group and the Taliban individually or as a group are not entitled to Prisoner of War status under the Convention." Part of the State Department's goal was to provide "the strongest legal framework for what we actually intend to do" and to protect U.S. forces, but Secretary of State Colin Powell also provided the pragmatic argument that recognizing the conventions while withholding them from most of the individuals who might claim their protection would allow "flexibility" while also presenting "a positive international posture" and preserving "U.S. credibility and moral authority by taking the high ground."[38]

White House counsel Alberto Gonzales supported the OLC, and he made clear that interrogation concerns played a large role in the debate over application of the Geneva Conventions. "The nature of the war," he wrote, "places a high premium on . . . the ability to quickly obtain information from captured terrorists and their sponsors in order to avoid further atrocities against American civilians." He continued, "In my judgment, this new paradigm renders obsolete Geneva's strict limitations on questioning of enemy prisoners." Further, a decision that the conventions did not apply would mean that the War Crimes Act would not cover the actions of U.S. personnel.[39] Implicit in this analysis was not only the claim that U.S. officials should have broad authority to interrogate without fear of prosecution but also an idea of necessity or balancing of harms, with an overtone of the "ticking bomb." The possible enormous harm of "further atrocities against American civilians" easily outweighed whatever harm might result from giving officials the tools "to quickly obtain information from captured terrorists."

Ultimately, the president reached several conclusions that tracked the arguments made by the OLC. The most important was that he had constitutional authority "to suspend Geneva as between the United States and Afghanistan." Having invoked his power to suspend the law, he exercised that power precisely by "declin[ing] to exercise it at this time" and "reserv[ing] the right to exercise this authority in this or future conflicts."[40] The result was that the Geneva Conventions would apply, if at all, through the sovereign decision; their status as applicable law would always depend on an act that was itself the suspension of law. In this way, President Bush not only declared his sovereign authority but also founded an important aspect of the legal order for the war on terror, in terms that explicitly created a state and law of exception.

Echoing the views of the White House counsel, President Bush also underscored the idea that war and crime blurred in the context of terrorism: he contended that "the war on terrorism ushers in a new paradigm" that "requires new thinking in the law of war."[41] This new paradigm and the overall response to the September 11 attacks were automatically placed in the "war" category. Those attacks were certainly criminal, and an enormous criminal investigation was under way. But none of the memoranda on the rules that might apply to al Qaeda members, if not to Taliban soldiers, suggested that the model of criminal investigation and prosecution should dominate or be a presumptive response. They did not venture the possibility that military operations should supplement or serve the goal of criminal prosecution (which is one way the accelerated blurring of war and crime could have been conceptualized).

Against this background, the rest of the president's memorandum came closer to the State Department's views of how the Geneva Conventions would apply in this exceptional order. He decided to apply the conventions "to our present conflict with the Taliban," and he only then declared that all "Taliban detainees are unlawful combatants and, therefore, do not qualify as prisoners of war." He also determined that "because Geneva does not apply to our conflict with al Qaeda, al Qaeda detainees also do not qualify as prisoners of war." Finally, he directed that all persons detained by U.S. armed forces be treated "humanely and, to the extent appropriate and consistent with military necessity, in a manner consistent with the principles of Geneva."[42]

On the issue of the specific rules that would apply to prisoners, the State Department prevailed, but the larger context of the memorandum makes clear that these conclusions—including the directive on humane treatment—took the form of unfettered exercises of sovereign discretion not to suspend the normal law. They were not admissions of legal obligation. Even the directive on humane treatment explicitly included its own exceptions. It applied only to people held by the armed forces, not to people in the custody of other federal entities, such as the CIA. Humane treatment is also not the same thing as the treatment required by the Geneva Conventions. Rather, it has the potential to be less, and it meets the standards of the conventions only "to the extent appropriate and consistent with military necessity"—the same standard that guides the president's use of force under the AUMF.[43]

Refining the Law of Interrogation

❧

Shortly after President Bush's decision regarding the application of the Geneva Conventions to post-9/11 investigations, OLC lawyers turned explicitly to interrogation. Traditional rules for criminal investigations made a brief appearance in the first OLC interrogation memorandum, which considered the relevance of *Miranda v. Arizona*'s holding that people in police custody must be informed of their rights to remain silent and consult with an attorney.[44] The memorandum concluded that *Miranda* would not bar the admission of unwarned statements in military commission proceedings and that military interrogators did not have to be overly concerned about giving the warnings when they sought intelligence information—partly because "the Fifth Amendment does not confer rights upon aliens outside the sovereign territory of the United States."[45]

The more important memo appeared five months later. By then, administration officials had already decided to use coercive methods, and prisoners at Guantánamo had begun to complain of mistreatment.[46] Military officials in Joint Task Force 170 were under pressure from the secretary of defense, Donald Rumsfeld, to obtain intelligence information, and they had begun to explore options beyond the army field manual, which authorized 17 interrogation methods designed to put a degree of psychological pressure on a suspect, though it also insisted on compliance with the Geneva Conventions and listed stress positions, threats of torture, and abnormal sleep deprivation as examples of torture.[47] Officials in the Defense Department's Office of General Counsel and Defense Intelligence Agency "arranged for SERE instructors to teach their techniques to the interrogators at GTMO" on several occasions.[48] The acronym *SERE* stands for "survival, evasion, resistance, escape" and refers to a harsh method of training soldiers to resist captivity and torture. Darius Rejali summarizes the training as follows:

> In the SERE program, American soldiers were hooded, deprived of sleep, starved, stripped of clothes, exposed to extreme temperatures and painful noise, choked with water (the Dutch method), and subjected to harsh interrogation including humiliation, sexual embarrassment, and desecration of religious symbols and books.[49]

Not surprisingly, once trained in these methods, some military interrogators at Guantánamo put them to use.[50] In particular, two of the SERE methods—"sexual embarrassment" and "desecration of religious symbols"—later emerged as leading tropes in the discussion of U.S. torture.

At roughly the same time, CIA agents—acting under the authority of Bush's September 17 order—also received SERE training and set up their own operations at Guantánamo and other places to conduct independent interrogations.[51] CIA operatives were also working, often in cooperation with intelligence agencies in other countries, to locate suspected al Qaeda members who could be detained (perhaps by kidnapping) and then interrogated. Some of these people were sent, or "rendered," to Egypt or Jordan for interrogation by officials in those countries. Others were held by the CIA at secret locations, called "black sites," in Afghanistan and, by mid-2002, in Thailand and Eastern Europe. In March 2002, CIA interrogators received permission to use several "enhanced interrogation techniques," including shaking, slapping, standing, cold temperatures, and waterboarding. Senior administration officials, sitting as the National Security Council's Principals Committee, were briefed on and approved the use of at least some of these techniques on specific prisoners. Still, as the program expanded, many CIA officials raised concerns "about the legality, morality, and practicality of holding even unrepentant terrorists in such isolation and secrecy, perhaps for the duration of their lives." The agency asked for a clear statement of the rules that would govern its programs involving rendition and black sites.[52]

The OLC's response appeared in late July and early August 2002. OLC first provided oral advice to the CIA that certain coercive interrogation methods were legal. It followed that advice with two memoranda. The first, known colloquially as the "torture memo," addressed "the standards of conduct under the Convention Against Torture and Other Cruel Inhuman or Degrading Treatment or Punishment as implemented by [18 U.S.C. §§ 2340–2340A] . . . in the context of the conduct of interrogations outside of the United States."[53] Recall that earlier memoranda had already concluded that Guantánamo was as much "outside" the United States as Afghanistan and (eventually) Iraq, which means that the legal regime described in the memo could apply to interrogations that took place there, including at the CIA "trailer operation," as well as to interrogations at other locations outside the United States, such as in Afghanistan and at the black sites. Also important is that the OLC's interpretation of this statute would effectively control the ability of future prosecutors to bring charges against interrogators for criminal conduct related to an interrogation, because it is difficult to bring charges against a government official who relied reasonably and in good faith on an OLC opinion.[54]

Federal statutes and international law prohibit torture; international law also prohibits cruel, inhuman, or degrading treatment or punishment; and the Constitution limits the government's ability to use violence, as with the Supreme Court cases holding that the due process clauses prevent state action that shocks the conscience. I have already highlighted the ambiguities and political compromises built into these prohibitions. With its conclusion that international and domestic law place few constraints on the aggressive interrogation of suspected terrorists outside the United States, the torture memo exploited and, in some cases, distorted and expanded those ambiguities.

For example, the torture memo argued that the prohibition on torture does not restrict the use of interrogation tactics that are not specifically intended to cause severe pain—which is exactly the position the Senate took in its advice-and-consent resolution to the Convention against Torture and that Congress passed into law when it enacted Section 2340 of Title 18 of the U.S. Code. Further, the memorandum exploited uncertainty over the definition of "severe" pain by analogizing to a federal statute (unrelated to torture or state violence of any kind) that defined it as pain of a level "that would ordinarily be associated with a sufficiently serious physical condition or injury such as death, organ failure, or serious impairment of bodily functions."[55] With respect to international law, the OLC used the ambiguities and structure of the Convention against Torture to carve out a large space for coercion. The memorandum stressed that the convention "not only defines torture as involving severe pain and suffering, but also makes clear that such pain and suffering is at the extreme end of the spectrum of acts." The memorandum also emphasized the convention's distinction between torture and the lesser category of cruel, inhuman, or degrading treatment or punishment.[56] To the extent that any specific interrogation method might violate the law, the torture memo suggested that the defenses of necessity and self-defense would apply. Finally, the memorandum argued that the federal criminal prohibition on torture could not be enforced if doing so would "regulate the President's authority as Commander-in-Chief to determine the interrogation and treatment of enemy combatants."[57]

In short, the OLC determined that existing legal rules provide substantial room for coercive interrogation and that, in any event, no law can regulate the president's choice of interrogation methods during a war, because the conduct of war is an aspect of sovereignty reserved exclusively to the president, who has the power to suspend the law in such situations. Many commentators have shown how the torture memo goes beyond the ordinary parameters of reasonable legal argument in several areas, such as the narrow definition of torture and the power of the president to disregard federal law.[58] No one involved in drafting the Convention against Torture or the relevant federal statutes would have thought that torture encompassed only pain similar to that caused by organ failure, and it is unlikely that participants in this process thought that the president could suspend or unilaterally narrow application of these prohibitions.

Amid the commentary, however, few have admitted that parts of the torture memo are defensible under existing law. In several areas—congressional delegation of authority to the executive branch; the broad power of the executive over foreign affairs issues; the compromises written into the Convention against Torture and, even more, into the Senate's resolution of advice and consent; the existence and scope of inherent executive authority in emergency situations; and whether the executive branch is a unitary entity headed by the president—the memo's analysis cannot simply be dismissed. It may go too far on these points, but it is not an aberration. Instead, it exploits tendencies and tensions in the law and pushes for greater centralization and discretion, including the power to suspend or limit rights that many writers would claim are foundational or even archetypal.[59]

Implementing the New Law of Torture
~

CIA Interrogation and Rendition

The OLC wrote the companion to the torture memo specifically for the CIA. It discussed the legality of ten techniques that the CIA wanted to use on a high-ranking member of al Qaeda, Abu Zubaydah. The techniques were

(1) attention grasp, (2) walling, (3) facial hold, (4) facial slap (insult slap), (5) cramped confinement, (6) wall standing, (7) stress positions, (8) sleep deprivation, (9) insects placed in a confinement box, and (10) the waterboard.[60]

OLC concluded that these methods, whether used singly or in combination, would not violate U.S. law because they "would not inflict severe physical pain or suffering," would not cause "any prolonged mental harm," and would not be inflicted with "specific intent" to cause mental or physical suffering.[61] In the aftermath of this advice, the Principals Committee also continued to meet at the White House for briefings on specific interrogation plans.[62]

By 2003, 14 CIA personnel had received training in these techniques, and they used them on more than a dozen people. At least four people died in the custody of the CIA or its contractors, and Bush later confirmed that "the CIA used an alternative set of procedures" in its interrogations. According to the president, "the procedures were tough, and they were safe, and lawful, and necessary."[63] The Red Cross was more blunt in its assessment of the allegations made by CIA prisoners: they described "treatment and interrogation techniques—singly or in combination—that amounted to torture and/or cruel, inhuman or degrading treatment."[64] Once again, the idea of necessity, where security and fear outweigh the harm to people already believed to have information or at least to be enemies, drives the formation of policy. Necessity, in turn, is a tool of the exception and the sovereign power manifest in it.

The director of the CIA admitted to "fewer than" 100 people in the CIA's terrorist detention program, but whether he meant to refer only to people held at CIA facilities or to anyone held under CIA auspices is uncertain.[65] In addition to establishing black sites, the CIA also transferred people to the military or intelligence forces of other countries. The people held in these related programs came from a variety of countries, and the CIA obtained them in a variety of ways. Some were captured by U.S. forces; some were handed over by the military and intelligence forces of other countries; and some were kidnapped by the CIA. The agency created a special group—the rendition team—to carry out kidnappings, which followed a "standard procedure."

> Dressed head to toe in black, including masks, they blindfold and cut the clothes off their new captives, then administer an enema and sleeping drugs. They outfit detainees in a diaper and jumpsuit for what can be a day-long trip. Their destinations: either a detention facility operated by cooperative countries in the Middle East and Central Asia, including Afghanistan, or one of the CIA's own covert prisons—referred to in classified documents as "black sites."[66]

Without laboring over the obvious, this "standard procedure" seems designed to overwhelm, thoroughly control and dominate, and begin the process of breaking the person subjected to it.

With the OLC memoranda in hand, the CIA expanded its black sites to additional countries, where it held at least 30 "ghost detainees."[67] The use of black sites expanded again with the war in Iraq. The CIA held at least 30 people at Abu Ghraib and conducted interrogations there, sometimes alongside military interrogators.[68] Suspects who were less valuable were sent to other countries to be held at facilities "operated by the host countries, with CIA financial assistance and, sometimes, direction."[69] People held in these places faced a variety of conditions and treatment. Some were simply held incommunicado, but others were subjected to treatment—such as beating and electric shocks—that probably qualifies as torture under any likely definition of the word.[70]

Rendition began as an alternative to the legal formalities of extradition proceedings and the unwillingness of some countries to hand over suspects. Beginning in the 1980s, on a few occasions, U.S. forces seized people in other countries and brought them back to the United States to face criminal charges.[71] During the Clinton administration, the idea of "extraordinary rendition" developed. In as many as 70 cases prior to 9/11, U.S. officials arranged, conducted, or assisted the seizure of a person in another country, where the goal was not to bring the person to the United States for trial but, rather, to send him to a third country for detention, interrogation, or trial.[72] After the September 11 attacks, extraordinary rendition for the purpose of interrogation greatly increased, with estimates of the number of people subjected to it ranging from roughly 70 to "hundreds" and even "several thousand."[73]

These CIA programs raise issues that go to the heart of the tensions in international and U.S. regulation of torture.[74] For rendition, the Convention against Torture provides, "No State party shall expel, return ('refouler') or extradite a person to another State where there are substantial grounds for believing that he would be in danger of being subjected to torture."[75] The convention does not specify whether it includes transfers entirely outside the territory of the signing state or only transfers of a person from the signing state's territory to the territory of another. The State Department has argued that this provision "does not impose obligations on the United States with respect to an individual who is outside the territory of the United States," and it has also argued that the convention does not apply to "U.S. detention operations in Guantanamo, Afghanistan, and Iraq [that] are part of ongoing armed conflicts."[76] Congress trumped the first argument—but perhaps not the second—by declaring that U.S. policy forbids "the involuntary return of any person to a country in which there are substantial grounds for believing the person would be in danger of being subjected to torture, regardless of whether the person is physically present in the United States."[77]

The State Department and the Department of Homeland Security have issued regulations to implement this policy in the context of extradition and removal, as I described in chapter 6.[78] No published regulations exist, however, for extraordinary rendition. U.S. officials have claimed to satisfy the statute by obtaining diplomatic assurances from the receiving country that it will not torture the person subjected to rendition. This process is entirely administrative, and the person affected by rendition obviously has no opportunity to participate.[79] In light of the treatment meted out to some of these people, such assurances have limited worth except to the extent that they serve as a marker that—however informal the actual process—officials nonetheless complied with legal forms.

Some of the complexity of diplomatic assurances arises from the fact that not all of the mistreatment suffered by people subjected to extraordinary rendition rises to the level of torture. The Convention against Torture's rendition prohibition applies only to torture, and the same is true of the federal statute. Neither document clearly prevents the United States from sending people to countries in which they will face cruel, inhuman, or degrading treatment that does not rise to the level of torture. It follows that the government does not need to obtain diplomatic assurances in such cases either. Once again, the difficult boundary between torture and cruel, inhuman, or degrading treatment becomes crucial, and the argument over extraordinary rendition easily reduces to categorization against a background presumption that people will suffer at least some degree of pain.

Still, the Convention against Torture also specifies that its provisions are "without prejudice to the provisions of any other international instrument . . . which prohibits cruel, inhuman or degrading treatment or punishment or which relates to extradition or expulsion."[80] The International Covenant on Civil and Political Rights bans torture and cruel, inhuman, or degrading treatment, with no possibility of justifying either category of conduct. Although the ICCPR does not mention rendition, the U.N. Human Rights Committee has interpreted that ban to include a prohibition on "expos[ing] individuals to the danger of torture or cruel, inhuman or degrading treatment or punishment upon return to another country by way of their extradition, expulsion, or refoulement."[81]

By contrast, U.S. officials have argued that "the obligations assumed by the United States under the Covenant apply only within the territory of the United States." The Bush administration also insisted that the law of war governs "the legal status and treatment" of people held in "Afghanistan, Guantanamo, Iraq and other places of detention outside the United States."[82] In other words, even if the ICCPR applies to the transfer of a person from the United States to another country, it does not apply to U.S. involvement in transfers that take place entirely outside the United States, particularly during wartime.[83] Administration officials also rejected the

Human Rights Committee's interpretation of the ICCPR to cover renditions, extraditions, and removal in any form.[84] In sum, the Bush administration claimed that the ICCPR simply does not apply to rendition.[85] The administration's claim that the ICCPR does not govern military operations or activities outside the United States presumably applies equally to "ghost detainees" held at black sites. As for the State Department's suggestion that the Convention against Torture's nonderogable prohibition of torture has little application to military activities, it is not clear how or whether that analysis extends to CIA activities.

The administration further suggested that the Convention against Torture's prohibition against cruel, inhuman, or degrading treatment has little or no impact overseas. First, Article 16 applies only in "any territory under [the] jurisdiction" of a state party, and the State Department contends that such concepts as "de facto control"—which many international lawyers embrace—do not satisfy this standard.[86] Second, the Justice Department emphasized the Senate reservation that equates cruel, inhuman, or degrading treatment with conduct "prohibited by the Fifth, Eighth, and/or Fourteenth Amendments to the Constitution," and it correctly observed that the Fifth Amendment has the most obvious application to the treatment of people detained by U.S. forces. But the Justice Department also pointed out that the Supreme Court has held that "the Fifth Amendment does not apply to aliens in U.S. custody overseas," with the result that nothing a U.S. official does overseas can violate it. Thus, the convention's prohibition on cruel, inhuman, or degrading treatment, as defined by the reservation, cannot apply to the conduct of U.S. forces overseas.[87] Finally, the Justice Department noted that the Fifth Amendment "protects against treatment that, in the words of the Supreme Court, 'shocks the conscience,' meaning . . . 'only the most egregious conduct,' such as 'conduct intended to injure in some way unjustifiable by any government interest.'"[88] Although the Justice Department did not develop the argument, it is an easy step to say that coercive interrogation that is short of torture and that is intended to elicit useful information is not "unjustifiable by any government interest," with the result that it is not banned by the Fifth Amendment and does not violate the Convention against Torture as accepted by the United States.[89] The distinction between torture, on the one hand, and cruel, inhuman, or degrading treatment, on the other, remains controlling.

To summarize, the Justice Department provided the CIA with legal authority to operate a parallel system for capturing, detaining, and coercively interrogating suspected terrorists. This parallel system was arguably outside normal constitutional or statutory law and was plainly intended to be exempt from or take advantage of the ambiguities in international agreements on detention and interrogation. Yet the seemingly lawless space of black sites and extraordinary rendition was not itself outside of law. The existence of these facilities and this program and the use of coercive interrogation techniques within it were entirely lawful in the sense that they were validated by executive decisions based on legal opinions that not only upheld the president's sovereign authority to make these decisions (and, in so doing, to suspend the normal law) but also regulated specific procedures. The legal rules and interpretations developed in the context of CIA interrogation would impact the conduct of U.S. armed forces overseas.

Military Operations at Guantánamo

The combination of SERE training and the torture memo created a general framework for interrogation at Guantánamo and other locations. In the last half of 2002, task force members "had begun using abusive techniques with some detainees," which involved "physical contact, degrading treatment (including dressing detainees in female underwear, among other techniques), the use of 'stress' positions, and coercive psychological pressures."[90] Much work remained to be done, however, to create a structure for interrogations and also to set up a long-term detention center for dangerous people in the middle of a naval base.

Pressure from senior Pentagon officials played an important role in the use of tactics that went beyond the army field manual.[91] By October 2002, partly in response to that pressure, and partly out of concern that they did not have authority to use the new techniques, interrogators and their supervisors at Guantánamo sought approval for a package of 19 methods, including the use of stress positions, isolation, "deprivation of light and auditory stimuli," hooding, "20 hour interrogations," "removal of clothing," and "using detainees' individual phobias (such as fear of dogs) to induce stress." The third and most severe category of requested techniques, perhaps inspired by CIA activities on the base, included

(1) [T]he use of scenarios designed to convince the detainee that death or severely painful consequences are imminent for him and/or his family.

(2) Exposure to cold weather or water (with appropriate medical monitoring).

(3) Use of a wet towel and dripping water to induce the misperception of suffocation.

(4) Use of mild, non-injurious physical contact such as grabbing, poking in the chest with the finger, and light pushing.[92]

An accompanying analysis concluded that all of these methods were legal but that some of them—including all of the most severe methods—"must undergo a legal, medical, behavioral science, and intelligence review prior to their commencement." The basis for the legal conclusion was the "legitimate governmental objective" to obtain information and the lack of any "purpose of causing harm or . . . intent to cause prolonged mental suffering."[93]

Interrogators received preliminary approval to use these methods from General James Hill of the U.S. Southern Command. When he requested permanent authority from the Joint Chiefs of Staff, Hill admitted that he had doubts "whether all the techniques in the third category are legal under U.S. law." "I am particularly troubled," he explained, "by the use of implied or expressed threats of death of the detainee or his family."[94] The chairman of the Joint Chiefs of Staff, General Richard Myers, received the request but neither approved nor rejected it. Myers also prevented his legal counsel from completing a legal review of the proposal, apparently because the general counsel of the Defense Department, William Haynes, did not want a full review.[95]

One month later, after consulting with some Pentagon officials as well as with the Justice Department, Haynes recommended approval of most of the methods. With respect to the third category, he recommended only the "[u]se of mild, non-injurious physical contact." Though he declared that the other methods "may be legally available," he added, "[W]e believe that, as a matter of policy, a blanket approval of Category III techniques is not warranted at this time." The secretary of defense, Donald Rumsfeld, approved the recommendation several days later.[96]

Three things stand out in this process. First, the legal analysis boiled down to the argument that coercive measures are permissible if there are reasons to use them. This analysis dovetails with ideas of emergency power and executive authority, but it also has a strong affinity with the ordinary constitutional law of investigation and punishment, as I suggested in chapters 3 and 6. Second, Rumsfeld's approval of coercive methods was not simply the ad hoc decision of a political partisan. To the contrary, although pressure for tough tactics and useful information came from above, the request went up the traditional chain of command, from people in the field to the highest levels of the military and their political superiors. Not everyone in that chain agreed with the result, and the ordinary process was short-circuited at the very top, but the overall process has more than a passing resemblance to ordinary bureaucratic decisions that implement desired policy objectives.[97] Third, although Rumsfeld certainly expanded the methods available to military interrogators, he did not go as far as the CIA. Military interrogators did not receive authority to use cold temperatures or the water method, and the use of "mild non-injurious physical contact" approved by the secretary does not, on its face, rise to the level of shaking or slapping (although the line between these methods is not clear and perhaps would have been impossible to sustain).[98]

While the Defense Department was mulling the approval of new methods, FBI agents at Guantánamo were becoming concerned about abusive interrogation tactics.[99] An FBI lawyer at Guantánamo forwarded to his superiors in Washington a memorandum that contained a legal analysis very different from the one prepared by the military lawyer in Washington. The list of techniques he described is also slightly different from the one forwarded up the chain of command. It includes two additional methods: "gagging with gauze" and "either temporarily or permanently" sending the prisoner "to Jordan, Egypt, or another third country to allow those countries to employ interrogation techniques that will enable them to obtain the requisite information." The FBI lawyer suggested that many of the methods—although, strangely, not gagging or isolation—were unconstitutional or could violate the criminal prohibition on torture by U.S. officials.[100] The memorandum also does not make clear who was using these techniques—whether military officials working with the FBI, task force members, CIA officials, or some combination. Senior FBI officials took these concerns to other officials in the Justice Department.[101]

After the navy's general counsel, Alberto Mora, lodged persistent objections, Rumsfeld rescinded his advance approval of most of the techniques—including all of the most severe—on January 15, 2003, and he set up a working group to review the issue of interrogation.[102] General Hill and the new commander at Guantánamo, Major General Geoffrey Miller, supported the continued use of the suspended techniques, based on their belief that they were helping interrogators obtain useful information.[103] Less than two months later, the working group submitted a report that began with the following premise: "Due to the unique nature of the war on terrorism . . . , it may be appropriate . . . to authorize as a military necessity the interrogation of . . . unlawful combatants in a manner beyond that which may be applied to a prisoner of war who is subject to the Geneva Conventions."[104] The supporting legal reasoning draws heavily from the OLC's post–September 11 memoranda, including the torture memo and a March 2003 memorandum that OLC deputy assistant attorney general John Yoo prepared for the working group. The March memorandum repeats the earlier torture memo's conclusions—most notably the earlier memorandum's expansive executive power and sovereignty claims—but it expands the analysis to encompass and dismiss the relevance of several other federal criminal statutes and jurisdictional issues.[105] The effect of this second torture memo was to trump the concerns of some members of the working group by putting the weight of the Justice Department behind the conclusion that prohibitions on torture and related forms of conduct did not apply to military interrogations carried out overseas and that those interrogations might be legal even if the prohibitions did apply.

Consistent with the conclusions and implicit recommendations of the OLC's torture memoranda, the working group's report stated that the Geneva Conventions did not apply, that the Convention against Torture and the ICCPR had limited relevance, and that customary international law could always be displaced by "a 'controlling' executive act."[106] It argued that the rights of the Fifth and Eighth Amendments did not apply outside the United States and, in any event, that they made room for conduct justified by legitimate government interests. Finally, it claimed that federal criminal statutes did not apply, because of the need to prove a specific intent to inflict pain (as opposed to a specific intent to obtain information) or the availability of necessity and self-defense claims.[107] According to the report, even if these statutes were generally applicable, the president could override them because he had "primary responsibility, and therefore the power, to ensure the security of [the] United States in situations of grave and unforeseen emergencies," which included the power to conduct successful interrogations to obtain "the intelligence he believes necessary to prevent attacks upon the United States."[108] The working group's report thus reinforced a conception of sovereign power lodged in a wartime president, with individual rights claims balanced by and often subordinated to the dictates of necessity and emergency.[109]

The report proposed a list of 35 acceptable interrogation techniques for people held outside the United States. Seventeen came from the army field manual; the rest reflect the methods that had been approved the previous year. Nine methods were labeled "exceptional techniques," and the report suggested that they should be used only in limited circumstances.[110] Rumsfeld rejected several methods—hooding, mild physical contact, threat of transfer, prolonged interrogation, forced grooming, prolonged standing, sleep deprivation, physical training, and face slap/stomach slap—and authorized the remaining 24 (only one of which—isolation—was "exceptional") for use at Guantánamo. He added that four of the methods could only be used in cases of military necessity and with advance notification to his office, but he also suggested that he might approve additional techniques in individual cases.[111] Personnel at Guantánamo received briefings about the working group's report and the new list of approved methods.[112]

While the Defense Department was establishing a new interrogation policy, officials at Guantánamo, under the new leadership of General Miller, were developing an integrated set of standard operating procedures for the expanding detention camp. The March 2003 document demonstrates that the treatment of prisoners at Guantánamo was carefully defined by a detailed set of rules that controlled their daily lives. The overall message is one of complete control and domination. Prisoners arrived masked, with earmuffs and restraints. Once at the camp, they were showered, subjected to a medical examination and a body cavity search, fingerprinted, forced to give blood and DNA samples, and placed into new restraints.[113] Next came a two-phase behavior management plan for new arrivals—which included isolation and deprivation of nearly all possessions—as well as the ongoing standards of conduct, a classification process based on cooperation, and a carefully calibrated disciplinary system.[114] These procedures were not without domestic precedent; many of them emulate the rigorous controls of the supermax prison.

The standard operating procedures confirm that the exceptional space of Guantánamo was not lawless, even though it lacked a normal legal framework. Rather, it was a space filled with incredibly detailed law about all aspects of the prisoners' lives: how they entered or left the facility; how they dressed, groomed, ate, and exercised; their medical care; their spiritual lives; and their interactions with guards and other officials, including during interrogation. This law emanated directly from the sovereign commander in chief and his staff, with only tenuous connection to a democratic process, and it was subject to change at regular and irregular intervals.[115] The following words from Giorgio Agamben seem apt: "In the camp, the state of exception, which is essentially a temporary suspension of the rule of law on the basis of a factual state of danger, is now given a permanent spatial arrangement, which as such nevertheless remains outside the normal order."[116] More important, Agamben's description of the Nazi death camps applies almost as well to Guantánamo's Camp Delta: "Insofar as its inhabitants were stripped of every political status and wholly reduced to bare life, the camp was also the most absolute biopolitical space ever to have been realized, in which power confronts nothing but pure life, without any mediation."[117]

These exceptional laws did more than maintain security and provide structures for gathering information. They also defined and created legal and political subjects. People detained at Guantánamo were "stripped of every political status and wholly reduced to bare life," but in the process, they were also remade into detainees, with a distinct legal and political identity. Many of the people who went into the camp may have been dangerous, may have been enemies of U.S. interests, and may have adopted political and religious views that seem extreme, but these things were almost certainly not the sum total of their existence. Once placed within the routines of the camp, however, only one identity became available: the dangerous, fanatical enemy detainee kept under strict control, who would attack U.S. citizens and facilities if released, but who also had information that he might be convinced or coerced to provide.[118] Further, this detainee had a legal status—even if it was a status outside the normal law—and was eligible for legal proceedings before a military commission. Even the detainee's death, whether or not it resulted from the judgment of a commission, was a managed legal and political event that involved a series of processes, investigations, and bureaucratic actions. Nothing else mattered, such that the bare life of the detainee was a coherent, rationally defined existence that turned entirely on his political and legal relationship to the war on terror.

The standard operating procedures also included rules for dealing with the Red Cross, such as providing that some prisoners would have "[n]o contact of any kind with the ICRC." In addition, they detailed methods for dealing with violations of camp discipline and with any threats posed by the prisoners—all of which, together with the approved interrogation methods, ensured that violence against the prisoners would continue as a matter of rule.[119] To the extent that one can assume that actual practices will go beyond the approved rule, these procedures also opened new space for violent practices not formally approved by the rules.

In fact, U.S. forces treated the Guantánamo prisoners violently. According to one account, "all the detainees were threatened with harsh tactics if they did not cooperate," and "about one in six were eventually subjected to those procedures."[120] The Red Cross concluded that "the American military has intentionally used psychological and sometimes physical coercion 'tantamount to torture' on prisoners at Guantánamo Bay." Personnel from the Criminal Investigation Task Force (CITF) tried to distance themselves from the interrogations carried out by Joint Task Force 170, and FBI agents working at Guantánamo continued to complain about the treatment meted out by their military colleagues.[121] An army report prepared in response to the FBI allegations substantiated several methods: wiping fake menstrual blood on prisoners and employing other forms of "gender coercion," playing loud music with strobe lights, extremes of heat and cold, sleep deprivation, short shackling (although allegedly only "in the early days"), using military dogs to frighten prisoners, using a leash on one prisoner and "forc[ing] him to perform a series of dog tricks," forced nakedness, "pour[ing] water over the subject" of an interrogation 17 times "as a control measure," prolonged standing, and threats against the life of at least one prisoner and his family. Notably, the report found that many of these techniques were consistent with Rumsfeld's April 2003 order and the report of the working group that he set up, although it also concluded that cumulative use could be "abusive and degrading."[122]

From Guantánamo to Afghanistan and Iraq

∽

In March 2004, army officials announced that they were bringing charges against 6 soldiers and investigating 11 others for the abuse of prisoners at Abu Ghraib prison. More than one report was already under way on the abuse and on detainee and interrogation operations generally, but the general tone—that this conduct was the work of "bad apples"—was already set. The report released by the army's inspector general in July bolstered this assertion, although, by then, other information had surfaced to undermine such claims.[123] In this section, I will discuss the migration of interrogation and detention practices among military forces, as well as the legal and political decisions that produced torture, abuse, and coercion in Afghanistan and Iraq, including at Abu Ghraib. My focus will be as much on the abuse and coercion that was normal as on the abuses—often specifically sexual— that form the usual public image of Abu Ghraib.

According to the report of former secretary of defense James Schlesinger, the army field manual was the baseline for interrogations in Afghanistan, but "more aggressive interrogation of detainees appears to have been ongoing" almost from the beginning of operations there, at least among some units, and some of those methods were later shared with the working group set up by Secretary Rumsfeld.[124] A former army interrogator has written that CIA operatives sometimes handed prisoners over to military forces at Kandahar Airport after they had been subjected to sleep deprivation, stress positions, and prolonged standing. He adds that interrogators in Afghanistan slowly came "to embrace methods we would not have countenanced at the beginning of the war." At Bagram Air Base, army interrogators began to use stress positions, as well as mock renditions designed to convince prisoners that they would be sent to countries and subjected to torture if they did not cooperate. The former interrogator noted that when new teams of interrogators arrived, they quickly learned the alternative methods and "did not regard [them] as a method of last resort but as a primary option in the interrogation playbook." "What was an ending point for us," he explained, "was a starting point for them."[125]

A January 2003 set of standard operating procedures for forces in Afghanistan included four techniques that went beyond the field manual: isolation, multiple interrogators, stress positions, and sleep deprivation.[126] Meanwhile, the informal catalog of coercive detention and interrogation tactics at Bagram expanded to include "removal of clothing," "exploiting fear of dogs, and sleep and light deprivation," as well as beating or slapping, shoulder dislocation, and sexual abuse.[127] With the invasion of Iraq, and despite the fact that the administration admitted that the Geneva Conventions applied to military operations there, interrogators began using similar methods on prisoners in that country—indeed, the standard operating procedures for interrogations in Iraq were based on the rules for Afghanistan.[128] As the Schlesinger Report found, "interrogators and lists of techniques circulated from Guantánamo and Afghanistan to Iraq" during 2002 and 2003.[129] One company of a military intelligence battalion that was using an enhanced set of techniques in Afghanistan was sent to conduct interrogations at Abu Ghraib, where they continued to use at least some of those methods and sought approval for more options.[130]

As resistance to the occupation took hold, military officials became less satisfied "with the amount of actionable intelligence resulting from the interrogation operations."[131] In August 2003, General Miller was sent from Guantánamo to Iraq to assess interrogation operations, particularly at Abu Ghraib, and after his visit, a training team from Guantánamo spent two months there.[132] Task force commanders decided to create a joint interrogation debriefing center at Abu Ghraib to centralize and improve intelligence collection, and they adopted an approach that used teams of interrogators, intelligence analysts, and interpreters—an approach that was already in use at Guantánamo. In his report on Abu Ghraib, Major General Fay concluded that this decision "introduced another level of complexity into an already stressed Abu Ghraib interrogation operations environment."[133]

Because the debriefing center was an innovation, no preexisting set of rules existed, and its procedures "were ad hoc in nature."[134] Despite the procedures available in the army field manual, this approach extended to the rules for interrogation. One source for procedures was Guantánamo. Miller had shared Rumsfeld's April 2003 memorandum approving interrogation tactics beyond those in the field manual, even though Rumsfeld had approved those methods only for Guantánamo. He also urged military police and military intelligence to work more closely together to set "the conditions for successful exploitation of the internees," and he suggested the use of military dogs for custody and control.[135] Brigadier General Karpinski later testified that Miller also told her that "you have to treat these detainees like dogs," and another Abu Ghraib interrogator claimed, "I was told by . . . the GTMO team that I was permitted to strip a detainee completely naked in the interrogation booth."[136]

At about the same time, an intelligence officer on the staff of Lieutenant General Sanchez, the commander of Joint Task Force 7, sent an email to several other intelligence officers in Iraq. The memo stated, "The gloves are coming off . . . regarding these detainees," and it asked for an "interrogation techniques 'wish list.'" Interrogators responded with lists that included exploiting "fear of dogs and snakes," as well as "open-hand strikes, closed-fist strikes, using claustrophobic techniques and a number of 'coercive' techniques such as striking with phone books, low-voltage electrocution and inducing muscle fatigue."[137]

On September 14, after consulting with his staff judge advocate general, Sanchez promulgated an interrogation and counterresistance policy for task force operations in Iraq. The 29 methods authorized by the policy drew heavily on the field manual (17 methods) and Rumsfeld's April 2003 approval (all 7 of the additional methods), but the policy also included 5 new methods ("presence of military working dogs" because it "exploits Arab fear of dogs"; sleep management; yelling, loud music and light control; deception, such as falsified documents and reports; and stress positions). These new methods are similar to some of the methods rejected by Rumsfeld but proposed by the working group he set up.[138] They are also similar to some of the methods that had been used in Afghanistan. Sanchez required prior approval for the same four techniques for which Rumsfeld required approval, as well as for yelling and stress positions—but not for dogs or sleep deprivation. Interrogators began using (or, in some cases, continued to use) these tactics.[139]

Sanchez sent a copy of the order to the commander of the U.S. Central Command, which apparently was unhappy with the policy and forced Sanchez to rescind it.[140] In October, he issued a new policy that listed the 17 methods approved by the army field manual. But the October policy no longer required prior approval for any of these techniques (including the field manual techniques for which Rumsfeld had required approval), and it also included the following statement:

> In employing each of the authorized approaches, the interrogator must maintain control of the interrogation: The interrogator should appear to be the one who controls all aspects of the interrogation, to include the lighting, heating and configuration of the interrogation room, as well as the food, clothing and shelter given to the security internee.[141]

This phrase comes from a 1987, superseded version of the field manual. More significantly, it can be read to open the door to many of the methods that were in the first order and that, on the surface, were excluded from the second. At the very least, as Lieutenant General Jones later commented, this passage "left certain issues for interpretation."[142]

Both versions of this policy made their way to interrogators. At Abu Ghraib, Captain Carolyn Wood prepared a chart listing the approved techniques and posted it "in numerous locations throughout the working area as a constant reminder." However, the second version of the chart did not remove the methods that were no longer authorized. Instead, Wood placed them in a separate column, under the heading "require CG's approval"— that is, General Sanchez's approval. She gave the following reason, "It was explained to me (I cannot remember by who, but the guidance was from higher) that those approaches removed from the 14 Sep version were not necessarily out of reach, that they had to be approved by the CG prior to use."[143] Her chart failed to mention several methods actually in use, such as "removal of clothing, forced grooming, hooding, and yelling, loud music and light control." It thus "left a question whether they were authorized for use without approval."[144]

What took place, in short, was the confusing development of an official policy on interrogations at Abu Ghraib and other locations in Iraq. Army officials sought to make the expanding facility at Abu Ghraib more professional. The model they adopted was Guantánamo (and, behind it, the working group set up by Rumsfeld), which had a set of operating and interrogation procedures based on familiar army doctrine, but which also incorporated new methods deemed necessary for a war on terror, even when, as in Iraq, that war had a conventional aspect. The use of Guantánamo as an example was not an effort to introduce sadism into interrogation; to the contrary, it was an effort to create a professional atmosphere and set of rules for effective interrogation.[145] Those rules took for granted that one aspect of military interrogation is complete control and domination over the physical and mental state of the person being interrogated, which, in turn, was nearly certain to generate pain and anguish among the prisoners.

As if to underscore these conclusions, the report of Vice Admiral A. T. Church III commented that "people unfamiliar with military interrogations might view a perfectly legitimate interrogation of [a prisoner of war], in full compliance with the Geneva Conventions, as offensive by its very nature."[146] Admiral Church may be correct—interrogation of this kind may be appropriate in wartime—but the practices approved for Guantánamo and Iraq reach an entirely different level. Put differently, even if some military police at Abu Ghraib had never engaged in and photographed their sexual and other violent abuse of prisoners, the people selected for interrogation there would have been subjected to coercion that often equated with cruel, inhuman, and degrading treatment and, in some cases, torture, precisely because interrogators were working from a set of rules that allowed such treatment.

Still, the manner in which these policies were developed, promulgated, and rescinded is also important. Not only did this process create confusion over what methods were allowed, but it raised the possibility that the published orders were a front for a looser, "gloves-off" set of approaches.[147] The fact that CIA interrogators were working at Abu Ghraib under what was clearly a more permissive set of rules contributed to the confusion, particularly when at least one CIA interrogation turned into a homicide.[148] When interrogators put these policies into effect in combination with their own experiences, information they obtained from other interrogators, and the formal and informal advice of Miller and the other members of the Guantánamo team, abuses became inevitable.

For example, Miller had suggested that military intelligence and military police should work together. Major General Taguba's report on Abu Ghraib found that, in practice, interrogators "actively requested that MP guards set physical and mental conditions for favorable interrogation of witnesses."[149] To that end, interrogators asked the guards to keep prisoners awake as part of the "sleep adjustment" method. Yet, according to General Fay, no one told the guards "how they actually should do the sleep adjustment." He noted, "The MPs were just told to keep a detainee awake for a time specified by the interrogator. The MPs used their own judgment as to how to keep them awake." Interrogators apparently also asked the guards to do more than merely keep prisoners awake, because the guards tried to assist in other ways as well: "What started as nakedness and humiliation, stress and physical training (exercise), carried over into sexual and physical assaults by a small group of morally corrupt and unsupervised Soldiers and civilians."[150]

An underlying theme in Fay's report is that while some forms of domination—such things as "sleep adjustment," "nakedness and humiliation, stress and physical training (exercise)"—are acceptable, the military police took these methods too far. But from the official point of view, the line between acceptable and unacceptable is often elusive: "Physical discomfort from exposure to cold and heat or denial of food and water is not as clear-cut and can become physical or moral coercion at the extreme."[151] Again, the deliberate attempt to cause discomfort or to manipulate the mental state of a detainee was acceptable; the approved methods of the field manual make that much clear. Thus, even interrogators working within the rules had to be careful about moving too much into the gray areas. They had to avoid extremes while also successfully controlling the prisoner and extracting any useful information. A similar but more general message emerges in the Schlesinger Report: that the working group set up by Rumsfeld set out a decent plan that succeeded at Guantánamo (as implemented by Rumsfeld's April 2003 approvals) and that confusion over interrogation policy and resulting problems with abuses might have been avoided if that report had been available from the beginning.[152] The assumption was that an ideal policy would allow controlled and thorough interrogation while also preventing abuses. The presence of coercion by itself was therefore not a sign of abuse.

Of course, the conduct at Abu Ghraib went beyond loose interpretations of the various policies by interrogators and guards. Much of the abuse that drove the scandal was more free-floating. In his report, General Taguba provided a list of conduct that he was able to document, which included

> punching, slapping, and kicking detainees; jumping on their naked feet;
> . . . forcibly arranging detainees in various sexually explicit positions for
> photographing; forcing detainees to remove their clothing and keeping
> them naked for several days at a time; forcing naked detainees to wear

women's underwear; forcing groups of male detainees to masturbate themselves while being photographed and videotaped; arranging naked male detainees in a pile and then jumping on them; positioning a naked detainee on a MRE Box, with a sandbag on his head, and attaching wires to his fingers, toes, and penis to simulate electric torture; ... placing a dog chain or strap around a naked detainee's neck and having a female soldier pose for a picture; a male MP guard having sex with a female detainee; using military working dogs (without muzzles) to intimidate and frighten detainees, and in at least one case biting and severely injuring a detainee.

He also provided a second list of conduct that various prisoners claimed had taken place, which "under the circumstances," he "found credible." This conduct included

breaking chemical lights and pouring the phosphoric liquid on detainees; threatening detainees with a charged 9mm pistol; pouring cold water on naked detainees; beating detainees with a broom handle and a chair; threatening male detainees with rape; allowing a military police guard to stitch the wound of a detainee who was injured after being slammed against the wall in his cell; sodomizing a detainee with a chemical light and perhaps a broom stick.[153]

Although these actions are not obviously linked to the interrogation policies, the conclusion does not follow that they were random violence. For example, Darius Rejali has observed that "positioning a naked detainee on a MRE Box, with a sandbag on his head, and attaching wires to his fingers, toes, and penis to simulate electric torture" is a recognized method of torture; it was used in Brazil and called "the Vietnam."[154] His point is that the guards did not make up all of their methods on the spot; they had a source—perhaps military intelligence personnel—for some of them. Thus, whether or not all of the abuses had a formal relationship to interrogation, one easily could conclude that many of them had some relationship to it.

Even if guards learned these methods from interrogators, the fact remains that they appear to have gone beyond the kinds of things that interrogators had in mind to "set the conditions" for interrogation. Generals Fay and Jones concluded that the violence and sexual abuse resulted from the individual propensities of "a small group of morally corrupt and unsupervised Soldiers and civilians." Similarly, the army's inspector general asserted that the abuses were "aberrations" and "unauthorized actions taken by a few individuals." The Schlesinger Report struck the same tone, suggesting that most of the Abu Ghraib abuses were "fostered by the predilections of the non-commissioned officers in charge."[155] These conclusions make sense to the extent that they mean that each form of abuse did not result from a specific order. Yet the assertion of deviance ultimately goes too far, for it contends not just that a few bad apples served at Abu Ghraib but that through some kind of unfortunate coincidence, a sizable group of deviants or sadists ended up serving together at the same prison, on the night shift, in the same block of cells, guarding the prisoners most likely to have useful information.

As other commentators have stressed, the explanation for the Abu Ghraib abuses must be more complex. Problems with staffing, organization, monitoring and reporting, and poor leadership played a role by helping to create the idea of a space partly out of bounds, an idea that may have been liberating at first but must ultimately have been extremely stressful for guards as well as prisoners.[156] Many of the guards had corrections experience, and in the absence of clear operating procedures, they fell back on the everyday violence of U.S. prison culture. Also critical were the social and psychological dynamics in which the guards lived and operated. The organizational problems helped create those dynamics, but other factors were at least as important—such things as the message that "the gloves were coming off"; the examples of everyday abuse by military and CIA interrogators; the fear created by the war on terror and the growing Iraqi insurgency; and the personal interactions of the guards with each other, with their superiors and other military personnel, and with the prisoners.

Susan Fiske, Lasana Harris, and Amy Cuddy explain how these dynamics could influence the actions of the military police: "Torture is partly a crime of socialized obedience. Subordinates not only do what they are ordered to do, but what they think their superiors would order them to do, given their understanding of the authority's overall goals."[157] Similarly, Philip Zimbardo notes, "[M]ost of us can undergo significant character transformations when we are caught up in the crucible of social forces. What we imagine we would do when we are outside that crucible may bear little resemblance to who we become and what we are capable of doing once we are inside its network."[158] Zimbardo treats these various factors generally as an example of the social construction of reality.[159]

I want to push the point a bit further. Just as the rules, procedures, and practices in place at Guantánamo and Abu Ghraib worked to construct a narrow and unitary political identity for the prisoners—the dangerous, fanatical enemy who is kept under strict control and may have useful information—the same was true for the guards and interrogators. Day after day, their job was to control and manage thousands of Iraqi prisoners jammed into an overcrowded prison, where fear, despair, and boredom ran together and legal rights were at their most basic if they existed at all. They were jailers in a dystopic landscape, in which the difference between guard and prisoner was not simply one of power or legal fiat but was also couched in ideas of nationalism, ethnicity, religion, and overall strangeness.

Certainly, the prisoners were in the condition of bare life, but so, too, were the guards. Agamben argues that one aspect of bare life in the biopolitical camp is "[t]he absolute capacity of the subjects' bodies to be killed," and he understandably links this to the experience of the prisoner. Yet his argument is meant to generalize. "Whoever entered the camp," he explained, "moved in a zone of distinction between outside and inside, exception and rule, licit and illicit, in which the very concepts of subjective right and juridical protection no longer made any sense."[160] The guards and prisoners were in a relationship of bare life, and as the prisoners took on a new identity, so, too, did the guards. The guards were legal and political actors within a military hierarchy, but one in which rules were incomplete or suspended. Their daily task was to set the conditions of a partly lawless space. In the process, their familiar identities were strained, and new identities competed for space—identities of the group, of a kind of sovereign embodiment of law, as the locus of power over the bare lives of the prisoners. This analysis applies more neatly to the guards at Abu Ghraib than to those at Guantánamo, but the guards at Guantánamo also took on new or more complicated legal and political identities as they worked within the standard operating procedures, as well as the informal procedures that grew up around them. In both cases, who they were and their role within a legal and political order not only changed but also became more encompassing.

Pushback and Retrenchment

ᓚ

The development of successive coercive interrogation policies took place amid a public debate that sharpened as prisoners arrived at Guantánamo and as stories began to leak about the treatment of people detained by U.S. forces. Political opposition to the administration's policies and conduct gained strength from protests against the invasion of Iraq, and the administration was not in lockstep. In December 2003, the new head of the OLC decided to withdraw the torture memo as well as the March 2003 memorandum on which the working group set up by Rumsfeld had relied, and he formally notified the Defense Department of his decision about the March 2003 document—although he also made clear that this withdrawal did not affect the techniques Rumsfeld had approved in April 2003.[161]

Still, it was Abu Ghraib that coalesced most of the opposition and forced changes in policy. On May 13, 2004, two weeks after the abuses became public, Sanchez issued a third interrogation policy for Iraq that "specifically prohibit[ed] the use of six interrogation techniques, including Sleep Management, Stress Positions, Change of Scenery, Dietary Manipulation, Environmental Manipulation, and Sensory deprivation," which, of course, suggests that these methods had continued to be used under the October 2003 order.[162] At roughly the same time, the torture memo leaked to the press. The OLC formally withdrew it in June 2004 and began work on a new document.[163]

The Supreme Court entered the fray that summer, with two cases that rejected some of the administration's most far-reaching claims of executive power. In *Hamdi v. Rumsfeld,* a plurality ruled that no statute allowed indefinite detention of citizen enemy combatants "for the purpose of interrogation," but it also ruled that the authorization for use of military force provided authority to detain enemy combatants, including citizens, for the duration of the conflict if they received sufficient process.[164] The plurality suggested that there is no inherent executive emergency power to detain indefinitely, but it said nothing about inherent power to detain for a limited period. A concurring opinion advanced the idea that the president may have "an emergency power of necessity . . . limited by the emergency" that would justify unauthorized executive detention and, presumably, interrogation of a citizen who is "an imminent threat to the safety of the Nation and its people."[165] The second case, *Rasul v. Bush,* held that aliens detained at Guantánamo could seek writs of habeas corpus in federal court to challenge their detention, and it left open the possibility that the same could be true anywhere in the world if a federal court has jurisdiction over the applicant's custodian.[166]

Together, *Hamdi* and *Rasul* affirmed a general right of access to federal courts, at least for procedural review. Still, the procedure endorsed by the *Hamdi* plurality heavily favored the government, and the likelihood that anyone held in military custody on suspicion of being an enemy combatant would be able to marshal persuasive arguments of innocence, even with the help of an attorney, was small.[167] In response to these decisions, the Defense Department created "combatant status review tribunals" to evaluate the prisoners at Guantánamo and an administrative review board to provide an annual update for each prisoner.[168] The tribunals found that the overwhelming majority of prisoners really were enemy combatants, with the result that their detention was appropriate.[169]

The administration also resisted efforts to obtain judicial review of these decisions. As this issue made its way through the courts, Congress passed the Detainee Treatment Act (DTA) in 2005, which sought to resolve the issue by preventing habeas cases and creating a limited form of review in the U.S. Court of Appeals for the D.C. Circuit for prisoners at Guantánamo and people convicted by military commissions. The court would be able to consider only two issues: whether the decision of the tribunals was consistent with standards and procedures developed by the secretary of defense and whether those standards and procedures were themselves consistent with federal law.[170]

In addition, the DTA mandates that Defense Department interrogations conform to the army field manual and states that "[n]o individual in the custody or under the physical control of the United States Government, regardless of nationality or physical location, shall be subject to cruel, inhuman, or degrading treatment or punishment" as that term was defined in the U.S. reservations to the Convention against Torture.[171] Another provision requires tribunals to determine "whether any statement[s] derived from or relating to" a prisoner were "obtained as a result of coercion," and tribunals are to assess any such statement's "probative value"—but not necessarily reject it. Finally, the act provides a defense for officials charged with using abusive interrogation techniques prior to its date of enactment.[172]

On the one hand, the DTA addresses the consequences of a two-tiered definition of coercion, by preventing military and political officials from saying that their interrogation methods are legal because they are degrading but not torture. It applies the cruel, inhuman and degrading treatment mandate to the CIA as well as the military. On the other hand, it ties the definition of degrading treatment to constitutional standards that themselves license a fair amount of coercion. The compromise was almost too much for the administration, and Bush signed the act with the statement that he would construe it "in a manner consistent with the constitutional authority of the President to supervise the unitary executive branch and as Commander in Chief and consistent with the constitutional limitations on the judicial power, which will assist in achieving the shared objective of the Congress and the President . . . of protecting the American people from further terrorist attacks."[173] Put more succinctly, the president suggested that the act's restrictions on interrogation could infringe his sovereign power over military and foreign affairs issues, and he took care to note that he was using that power in a manner necessary and appropriate to protect the country from harm.

At the end of 2004, the OLC issued a new interrogation memorandum repudiating much of the torture memo's analysis and concluding that interrogators could not engage in conduct that is "extreme and outrageous."[174] Exactly how this new analysis would generate different results was left unclear, however, and the memorandum responded to pressure from the attorney general by including a footnote that "reassure[d] the C.I.A. . . . that the Justice Department was not declaring the agency's previous actions illegal."[175] Two months later, under new leadership, the OLC issued three additional memoranda that "provided explicit authorization to barrage terror suspects with a combination of painful physical and psychological tactics, including head-slapping, simulated drowning and frigid temperatures."[176] One of the memoranda explicitly relied on the strength of the government's interest in doing what was necessary to prevent further terrorist attacks.[177]

But the legal opinions did not address the pressure the administration was facing over the CIA's black sites and program of extraordinary rendition. In mid-2005, the CIA pulled its prisoners from Europe. Shortly before enactment of the DTA, the secretary of state, Condoleeza Rice, announced that "as a matter of policy," the Convention against Torture's prohibition on cruel, inhuman, and degrading treatment "extend[s] to U.S. personnel wherever they are, whether they are in the United States or outside of the United States."[178] The act turned that policy into a legal mandate, although one with uncertain content, and the administration also continued its battle of interpretation with U.N. officials and human rights groups over the application of international law to the war on terror.[179]

For its part, the Defense Department took steps in a different direction. In March 2005—after the new OLC interrogation memorandum appeared—the department's general counsel rescinded the report of the working group set up by Rumsfeld, stating that it "does not reflect now-settled executive branch views of the relevant law" and should "be considered a historical document with no standing in policy, practice, or law to guide any activity of the Department of Defense."[180] Later that year, the deputy secretary of defense issued a memorandum requiring compliance with the DTA's prohibition on cruel, inhuman, and degrading treatment and forbidding any interrogation methods not contained in the army field manual— which effectively withdrew Rumsfeld's April 2003 approval of methods that went beyond the manual.[181]

The administration sought to hold firm on military commissions, but in *Hamdan v. Rumsfeld,* the Supreme Court declared the commissions illegal because the administration had ignored the statutory requirements for establishing tribunals of this kind. The Court appeared to hold that U.S. military action against al Qaeda was a "conflict not of an international character," occurring in the territory of a party to the Geneva Conventions, with the result that Common Article 3 of the conventions applied to it by statute. Common Article 3 requires trials before regularly constituted courts, and the Court found that military commissions failed that standard.[182] Along the way, the Court accepted the war model for confronting terrorism and the implicit hierarchy of rights that the war model creates. But the Court rejected the administration's most far-reaching executive power claims, insisted on compliance with Congress's determination that traditional standards of international humanitarian law must apply to military action, and went out of its way to mention that the administration's rules for commissions allowed admission of evidence obtained by coercion.[183] *Hamdan*'s holding on Common Article 3 also meant that U.S. personnel who violated its provisions could be prosecuted under the War Crimes Act as it then existed—which is one of the consequences the administration had sought to prevent.

After *Hamdan*, the military commissions could not operate, and CIA officials "refused to carry out further interrogations and run the secret facilities . . . until the legal situation was clarified."[184] In a speech on September 6, 2006, President Bush announced the transfer of 14 men from CIA custody to Guantánamo and declared, "The current transfers mean that there are now no terrorists in the CIA program." He admitted that *Hamdan*'s application of Common Article 3 to the conflict with al Qaeda "has put in question the future of the CIA program," because it raised the possibility that CIA officials could be prosecuted for violating it. But the president insisted that the need to obtain intelligence from suspected terrorists would remain critical.[185]

That same month, the army revealed a new field manual on interrogation. The document cites the Geneva Conventions more frequently than the superseded version, stresses the importance of treating prisoners humanely, and emphasizes the responsibility of commanders.[186] It also provides that "service members must treat all detainees captured during armed conflict consistent with the provisions of the [Geneva Conventions] unless a determination to the contrary is made"—although, of course, this suggests that the conventions will not apply at all to some prisoners.[187] The manual further stresses that people from "non-DOD agencies" "have no authority over Army interrogators" and that all interrogations "conducted by non-DOD agencies will be observed by DOD personnel."[188] Similarly, although the manual states that "close coordination must occur between MP and MI personnel in order to facilitate the effective accomplishment of the MP and MI missions," it maintains that "[t]he MPs do not conduct intelligence interrogations" and that they "will not take any actions to set conditions for interrogations (for example, 'softening up' a detainee)."[189]

Drawing on the DTA, the manual specifically prohibits cruel, inhuman, or degrading treatment and provides a nonexclusive list of prohibited interrogation methods. The prohibited methods include "forcing the detainee to be naked, perform sexual acts, or pose in a sexual manner"; "placing hoods or sacks over the head of a detainee"; "using duct tape over the eyes"; "applying beatings, electric shock, burns, or other forms of physical pain"; "waterboarding"; "using military working dogs"; "inducing hypothermia or heat injury"; "conducting mock executions"; and "depriving the detainee of necessary food, water, or medical care."[190] This list is similar to the May 2004 Sanchez order and implicitly confirms that these methods were used in Afghanistan and Iraq.

Finally, the new manual lists 18 permissible methods for all interrogations, as well as a "restricted interrogation technique called separation." The approved methods are the 17 from the 1992 field manual plus the "false flag" method, in which interrogators "convince the detainee that individuals from a country other than the United States are interrogating him, and trick the detainee into cooperating with U.S. forces."[191] Separation is a form of isolation that is meant to be less severe than sensory deprivation. The new field manual is thus an interesting combination of exhortations to comply with the Geneva Conventions and new methods that allow more psychological coercion and thus make compliance with the conventions more difficult.

In what seemed to confirm a strategy of partial retrenchment, the administration also sought congressional approval for its policies. The result was the Military Commissions Act of 2006 (MCA). The MCA codified much of the existing military commission instructions but nudged the process closer to the standards of the Uniform Code of Military Justice. It also confirmed the limited federal court review previously established by the DTA but extended the denial of habeas corpus and the substitution of limited D.C. Circuit review to include any alien detained by the United States as an enemy combatant.[192] In another rebuke to the administration's approach, the Supreme Court's decision in *Boumediene v. Bush* held that this aspect of the MCA was an unconstitutional suspension of habeas corpus.[193]

Other parts of the MCA remained in effect. For example, the statute allowed the CIA to restart the "ghost prisoner" program by redefining and narrowing the conduct that is subject to prosecution under the War Crimes Act.[194] The new version of the act provides a detailed list and definition of prohibited conduct—including "torture" and "cruel or inhuman treatment"—and declares that these limited definitions "fully satisfy the obligation" of the United States to implement Common Article 3.[195] The definition of "cruel or inhuman treatment" turns on whether the mental or physical pain inflicted or attempted was "severe" or "serious." The MCA defines "severe mental pain or suffering" as equivalent to the mental pain or suffering that would constitute torture under the federal torture statute, Section 2340 of Title 18 of the U.S. Code. The act says the same for "serious" mental pain, except that it need not be "prolonged." For its part, according to the MCA, "serious physical pain or suffering" involves "a substantial risk of death," "extreme physical pain," "a burn or physical disfigurement of a serious nature (other than cuts, abrasions, or bruises)," or "significant loss or impairment of the function of a bodily member, organ, or mental faculty."[196]

The new definition of cruel or inhuman treatment is far stricter than the definition of cruel, inhuman, or degrading treatment under the ICCPR or Convention against Torture. Those documents, as ratified by the United States, limit the scope of cruel, inhuman, or degrading treatment to conduct that is unconstitutional. By contrast, the new War Crimes Act only criminalizes a subset of unconstitutional conduct. Indeed, the subset is so small that it seems either to overlap substantially with the definition of torture or, instead, to narrow the definition of torture itself. Before the MCA, one might have thought that pain accompanied by serious physical disfigurement or "significant loss or impairment of the function of a bodily member, organ, or mental faculty" was exactly the kind of conduct that amounted to torture. But if this kind of treatment is only cruel or inhuman, the inescapable inference is that torture requires even more.

Further, the definition of the degree of pain required for torture simply refers to Section 2340, which, in turn, derives from the Senate's understandings about the meaning of torture in the Convention against Torture. The pressure that the new War Crimes Act puts on the definition of torture could put a parallel amount of pressure on the definition of torture in Section 2340. The new narrow definition of torture under the statutes also suggests a narrowing from the U.S. perspective of the conduct that the United States has pledged itself never to use, with a corresponding increase in the conduct that falls into the potentially "justifiable" category of cruel, inhuman, or degrading treatment. As if to cement these narrow interpretations, the MCA also bars the invocation of the Geneva Conventions as a source of rights "in any habeas corpus or other civil action or proceeding"; states that "the President has the authority for the United States to interpret the meaning and application of the Geneva Conventions," albeit in a way that does not "affect the constitutional functions . . . of Congress and the judicial branch of the United States"; and adds that "[n]o foreign or international source of law shall supply a basis for a rule of decision in the courts of the United States in interpreting those provisions."[197]

In February 2007, Bush signed an executive order establishing military commissions pursuant to the MCA, and the Defense Department initiated proceedings against people held at Guantánamo.[198] In July, he issued another order reestablishing the CIA's terrorist detention program. Relying on his authority under the MCA to interpret the Geneva Conventions, the president found that such a program complies with Common Article 3 so long as it does not include torture under Section 2340; any of the specific crimes in the new version of the War Crimes Act; cruel, inhuman, or degrading treatment as defined by the DTA and MCA; other "willful and outrageous acts of personal abuse done for the purpose of humiliating or degrading the individual in a manner so serious [as] to be outside the bounds of human decency"; and denigration of religion.[199] After the MCA, how-

202 ～ UNDERSTANDING TORTURE

ever, this set of restrictions, especially the one on "torture," is not as strong a constraint on CIA activities as it first appears.

Conclusion
～

The magnitude of U.S. engagement with torture, abuse, and coercion in the war on terror makes it impossible to address every important issue. I have omitted such things as the role of medical professionals in coercive interrogations, the use of private contractors to conduct interrogations, U.S. influence on the use of abusive tactics by the new Iraqi police and military, and the interaction of coercion and criminal prosecution.[200]

I have said enough, however, to establish that the discussion and analysis of torture and other forms of coercive interrogation in the war on terror led to a shift in legal and political discourse. Torture has been a tool of U.S. foreign policy for decades, but the extensive legal and political analysis of the past few years is something new and has tangible consequences. In early 2008, for example, the Bush administration told the U.N. Human Rights Committee that "having a CIA program for questioning terrorists will continue to be crucial to getting lifesaving information." The administration also publicly discussed the use of such methods as waterboarding, and it claimed repeatedly that carefully calibrated coercion leads to information that saves lives.[201] Thus, the pain and suffering of some people—those who have limited rights and exist in a condition of bare life—produces the safety of those assumed to have greater rights. Indeed, with the public justification of coercive interrogation, the practice of rights in the United States arguably expanded to include the right to torture the bodies and minds of perceived enemies in order to protect the body politic.

Perhaps the transparency of this debate is salutary. Indeed, this is essentially Alan Dershowitz's point in his discussion of torture warrants, and he is correct to the extent that this debate brings to the surface the rule of law's dependence on violence.[202] Yet the fact remains that legal norms have also shifted. The current state of the law opens more space for coercive conduct. Torture may not be legitimate, but cruel, inhuman, and degrading treatment seems to be. Some of this is expected to change under the Obama administration, but the anticipated retrenchment may not be as thorough as many people hope—and to the extent that some of this change happens through executive orders, it will further entrench ideas of executive control over detention and interrogation policy.[203]

Slavoj Žižek's observation about the debate over torture seems apt as the conclusion to this discussion of the discourse and practice of torture in the war on terror. He writes, "Such legitimization of torture as a topic of debate changes the background of ideological presuppositions and options much more radically than its outright advocacy: it changes the entire field while, without this change, outright advocacy remains an idiosyncratic view."[204] Advocating coercive interrogation is certainly no longer idiosyncratic, and its practice may have become constitutive.

CONCLUSION

༄

Living with Torture

Defining Torture

༄

The Convention against Torture characterizes torture as an exceptional act. By emphasizing, first, the amount of pain ("severe pain or suffering, whether physical or mental") and, second, the motivation behind the infliction of pain ("obtaining ... information or a confession," punishment, "intimidating or coercing," or discrimination), it implies that torture is different from other, less-regulated conduct, such as "other cruel, inhuman or degrading treatment or punishment."[1] Nonetheless, this legal definition is a compromise hammered out in negotiations among parties of diverging interests, and like other definitions of torture, it does not exhaust the questions of what torture is and how it operates. In concluding this book, I explore this issue not to develop a better or more specific definition but, rather, to suggest a broader understanding of torture's role in contemporary legal and political life.

As the convention recognizes, torture is not simply a method of interrogation or a form of punishment. Building on the convention's additional purposes of intimidation and discrimination, the impulse to torture may derive from the identification of the torture victim with a larger threat to social or political order.[2] More generally, gathering information or inflicting punishment are often the stated motives for torture, but they may not be its sole purpose. Rather, in Robert Cover's words, torture functions, in many cases, "to demonstrate the end of the normative world of the victim—the end of what the victim values, the end of the bonds that constitute the community in which the values are grounded." Cover continues, "The torturer and the victim do end up creating their own terrible 'world,' but this world derives its meaning from being imposed upon the ashes of another. The logic of that world is complete domination, though the objective may never be realized."[3]

This domination plays out in several ways. Intense pain, in itself, shapes and sometimes destroys human perception and personality. Even more, torture inverts typical conceptions about law and legal process by using punishment to gather evidence to justify punishment already inflicted.[4] When torture is legal in the sense of being an official policy, the victims' suffering and pain become irrelevant to the law—or, perhaps, relevant in a more encompassing way—precisely at their moment of greatest vulnerability.[5]

Torture is also "world-destroying" in its ability to subvert and degrade the ideas of agency, consent, and responsibility that shape liberal ideas of self and self-government. Once torture begins, the result is always the product of the victim's "choice." Victims who provide information have "chosen" to talk. Yet these words ascribe agency and responsibility to a victim whose ordinary subjectivity is compromised or broken.[6] If a victim resists, he or she will be tortured again—but again, the victim is responsible. According to the logic of torture, if the victim would only surrender to the torturer's domination, the pain would be over. By refusing to talk, the victim "consents" to more torture.[7]

The logic of choice, consent, and responsibility suggests an aspect of torture not explicit in legal definitions but clear in many accounts of torture as practice: escalation, such that the victim's resistance leads to more and greater pain. Importantly, however, escalation is not just about greater pain over time but also about beginning with a relatively milder amount of pain or coercion and with the possibility, even the expectation, of more. Torture encompasses this continuum; it can include not just the most intensely painful practices but also all the practices that use pain to punish or gather information, damage the victim's identity or worldview, or express the domination of the state and the torturer. Escalation thus becomes another way of describing the relationship between the power of the torturer and the victim's complex mix of agency and powerlessness. Both the torturer's ability to escalate the level of pain in response to the victim's reactions or choices and the victim's awareness of that ability are important components of torture's potential for domination and identity destruction.[8]

The idea of escalation thus suggests a legal conclusion: victims who "break" at the beginning of coercive or inhuman treatment have been tortured if they reasonably believe that progressively more painful treatment will follow. International law tries to establish that the purposeful infliction of severe pain, whether or not accompanied by the threat of escalation, is torture. But a practice that lasts only briefly and causes less than severe pain is also torture if it operates against a background (or threatened background) of total control and potential escalation, which, in turn, asserts the torturer's (and state's) dominance and unsettles or destroys the victim's normative world. From this perspective, torture includes the act of explaining to prisoners exactly what will transpire if they do not cooperate, accompanied by sufficient time for them to reflect on this future and, in so doing, to inflict severe mental pain or suffering on themselves. A thorough interrogation might follow to obtain information or simply to confirm the victims' self-torture and shattered political identity. This approach to torture broadens the Convention against Torture's carefully negotiated definition and further blurs the distinction between torture and cruel, inhuman, or degrading treatment or punishment.

None of these aspects of torture, however, necessarily place it in the category of the exception, as the convention implies. Or, if torture remains exceptional, the pervasiveness of practices that can be defined as torture or near torture suggests that what may once have been an exception has become the norm. The language of exception has become one of the normal languages of legal and political discourse.[9] As I discussed in the introduction, linking torture with other forms of domination provides an additional explanation for the effort to cabin it with narrow definitions. Broad definitions lead either to questions about the legitimacy of other, more accepted coercive practices or, conversely, to acceptance of coercion as a routine aspect of modern personal, social, and political arrangements. For these very reasons, however, the breadth of the approach or definition I have suggested may go beyond the ordinary terrain of legal efforts to regulate state violence, and its utility in a legal context is debatable.[10]

Pain or Purpose?

∾

Pain, for example, is difficult to measure, especially for legal purposes. The same practices will impact different people in different ways, and evaluating or comparing those effects is far from easy. When such writers as Elaine Scarry, Mordechai Kremnitzer, and Robert Cover discuss the impact of pain, for example, they end up writing not just about physical or mental agony but also about the effect of pain on the torture victim's identity or subjectivity. At that point, the discussion of pain has circled back on the purposes of torture.

The result is that the severity of pain ultimately fades as an effective analytical category. With the threat of escalation, the degree of pain actually inflicted by the torturer can be relatively small. The anguish or punishment that the victim of torture inflicts on himself or herself, perhaps in response to little outside coercion, is equally or more important.[11] Here, the insights of the *KUBARK* manual—that threats of coercion can be as effective as the real thing and that the most effective forms of coercion are the ones that implicate the victim in the infliction of pain—become central.[12] Without addressing the issue of escalation, but drawing on Kant and Scarry, David Sussman puts a theoretical spin on the *KUBARK* analysis when he insists that torture involves an "interpersonal relationship . . . that realizes a profound violation of the victim's humanity and autonomy." According to him, torture turns "the dignity of the victim as a rationally self-governing agent . . . against itself" by "tak[ing] the victim's pain, and through it [the] victim's body, and mak[ing] it begin to express the torturer's will." Sussman suggests, "My suffering is experienced as not just something the torturer inflicts on me, but as something I do to myself, as a kind of self-betrayal worked through my body and its feelings."[13] Similarly, Darius Rejali observes that "modern torturers" sometimes use physical pain "to touch the mind or warp a sense of self, and thereby shape the self-understandings of prisoners and dispose them to willing, compliant action."[14] For both writers, the "dignity" or "self" that is warped or turned against itself through torture functions as the rough equivalent of the victim's moral or political identity.

Creating Political Identity
∾

So far, then, torture is not only about severe pain or even about the reason for inflicting pain. Torture also includes the products of pain, and the relative importance of what pain produces also increases with the concept of escalation. To a large extent, the product of torture is the victim's ruined self, dignity, or political identity—that is, it is the remnant or absence that accompanies domination and destruction. But torture is also productive in a different sense; it has creative power amid its destructive impact. At least in the hands of modern states, torture destroys the victim's political identity but does not always stop with the act or results of destruction. Instead, the victim's identity is destroyed in order to create a new one defined more securely by the relationship with the torturer (and, behind the torturer, the state).

Kremnitzer stresses the victim's status as an object whose very "consciousness of himself" is destroyed. Scarry laments that through torture, "[w]orld, self, and voice are lost, or nearly lost," and she refers to torture as an "undoing" or an "uncreating."[15] Other commentators hint at a more complex result. Robert Cover suggests, for example, that the "[t]he torturer and the victim do end up creating their own terrible 'world,'" while Rejali notes that torture does not merely warp the self but also "shape[s] . . . self-understandings." Ñacuñán Sáez argues, "[T]he pain inflicted by contemporary torture does not break down a pre-existing subject. It does something more and something less than that: paradoxically, it produces the subject as already (or still) absent."[16] Most significantly for this discussion, Welat Zeydanlıoğlu argues that, for example, the torture of Kurds in Turkish prisons in the 1980s was part of maintaining not only physical but also ideological control over the prisoners—"a process of inscribing 'Turkishness' onto [their] bodies and minds." That is, the prisoners' dissident political and ethnic identities made it easy to categorize them as "enemies of the state," and "torture as turkification" aided "the project of creating a politically and ethnically homogenous nation."[17]

Torture, in short, includes the infliction or threat of pain for the purpose of substituting a new political identity for the one that it destroys. Yet including this process in a description of torture raises the possibility that the problem of torture collapses back into other forms of coercion and violence—unless one focuses only on severe pain. Unless severe pain in and of itself is the essence of torture, torture stands revealed as something that is harmful, in many instances, because it destroys a person's social or political identity and creates a new one in its place. As many writers have discussed, however, the manipulation, destruction, and creation of identity is one of the processes by which the modern state and modern institutions operate. The liberal state, after all, requires an individual "viewed in abstraction from political, economic, familial, and religious roles, as well as from race and gender."[18] This individual, moreover, must be "encouraged" to be autonomous in "valuable" ways.[19] Indeed, as I argued in chapter 4, being a member of a liberal political community creates a right to this abstract individual autonomy—that is, a right to be placed in and defined by this political arrangement. People who do not easily assume this role have the right to be coerced into it, which heightens and concentrates their status as individuals.[20]

The importance of psychological research to some forms of modern torture elucidates the similarity between these forms of torture and other processes of liberal governance. Thus, KUBARK states that the point of coercion is not to inflict pain but, instead, "to induce regression" and break down the prisoner's defenses, which, in turn, will create feelings of guilt and dependence in the prisoner as part of a relationship with the interrogator.[21] As I discussed in chapter 6, the goal of this process is only partly to obtain accurate information. Just as important is the process—described in KUBARK—of putting the prisoner through a crisis, from which he or she emerges into a new relationship with the torturer.

> Once a true confession is obtained, the classic cautions apply. The pressures are lifted, at least enough so that the subject can provide counterintelligence information as accurately as possible. In fact, the relief granted the subject at this time fits neatly into the interrogation plan. He is told that the changed treatment is a reward for truthfulness and an evidence that friendly handling will continue as long as he cooperates.[22]

Critically, this entire process requires a focus on the individual, because "[t]he chan[c]es of success rise steeply . . . if the coercive technique is matched to the source's personality."[23] At least in theory, *KUBARK* methods are tailored to each person being interrogated. The *KUBARK*-trained torturer treats each person as a unique individual, such that the end product will also be an individual, albeit one with a new political identity.

KUBARK does not represent an idiosyncratic approach. Consider Foucault's description of the purpose of questioning in nineteenth-century psychiatric practice.

> [T]he technique of psychiatric questioning . . . is not a way of getting information from the patient that one does not possess. Or rather, if it is true that, in a way, it really is necessary, by questioning the patient, to get information from him that one does not possess, the patient does not have to be aware that one is dependent upon him for this information. The questioning must be conducted in such a way that the patient does not say what he wants, but answers questions. Hence the strict advice: never let the patient spin out an account, but interrupt him with questions that are both canonical, always the same, and also follow a certain order, for these questions must function in such a way that the patient is aware that his answers do not really inform the doctor, but merely provide a hold for his knowledge, give him the chance to explain; the patient must realize that each of his answers has meaning within a field of an already fully constituted knowledge in the doctor's mind. Questioning is a way of quietly substituting for the information wormed out of the patient the appearance of an interplay of meanings which give the doctor a hold on the patient.[24]

Foucault further explains that the point of getting "a hold on the patient" is "fixing the individual to the norm of his own identity" and "pinning the individual to his social identity and to the madness ascribed to him by his own milieu."[25] But, of course, for the madman, the cure of being pinned to what the doctor determines is one's own identity is effectively the creation of identity. This becomes clear in Foucault's assertion that the doctor's role is "to impose reality, to intensify it, and add to it the supplement of power that will enable the doctor to get a grip on madness and reduce it, and therefore, to direct and govern it."[26] Yet this process of directing and governing the patient cannot simply lead to the recovery of a lost identity. Rather, it inevitably creates a new or hybrid identity.[27]

Foucault's description plainly resonates with the *KUBARK* method. Similarly, stripped of their horror at the material facts of torture, Cover's and Kremnitzer's descriptions of the effects of torture do not vary greatly from Foucault's description of psychiatric practice. My general point is that the practice of torture, in at least some of its versions, draws upon the same ways of understanding the self, the individual, and political life that have been central to other modern discourses.²⁸ For his part, Foucault expressly links the construction of an individual through such disciplinary practices as psychiatry with the construction of a juridical individual in liberal theory—the "abstract subject, defined by individual rights"—such that the two processes work together in "a kind of juridico-disciplinary pincers of individualism."²⁹

In addition, although Foucault does not emphasize this point, it is clear—in both his description of nineteenth-century psychiatric practice and in *KUBARK*'s description of the ideal interrogation—that liberal ideas of agency, choice, consent, and responsibility also play a role in or intersect with the disciplinary process.³⁰ In the process of undergoing treatment or coercion, of internalizing the norms or violence of the institution, and of responding to questions, the patient or victim participates in governing himself or herself. Especially under *KUBARK*, the self-inflicted nature of the anguish adds elements of agency and control back into the equation on the victim's side. The victim of torture, in short, is governing himself or herself and thereby participating in the creation of his or her new identity while he or she is being tortured.

At least for self-consciously modern states, therefore, my claim is that the creation of political identity is an important part of any definition or explanation of torture. When the British beat Kikuyu tribesmen into admitting that they had taken the Mau Mau oath, what mattered was less whether the victim had taken the oath and more that he said he had done so and that he was now dependent on the British not only for his safety but also for his political identity. When U.S. interrogators use stress positions and waterboarding on people at Guantánamo, what matters is not only the actionable intelligence they might obtain but also the fact that their victims will confess to something and, in so doing, will break themselves and their old political and social relationships and become dependent on their captors for the new identity of dangerous, imprisoned, fanatically religious terrorist.

The carefully detailed policies on respect for religious practices at Guantánamo play into this process. Whether or not they were particularly religious before, prisoners are already defined as such when they arrive and in how they are treated. As the camp strips away other aspects of their identities, being Muslim—particularly being devoutly or even fanatically so—remains and is reinforced by the experience of detention. Even episodes of deliberate disrespect for supposed Muslim practices or sensitivities work to deepen this particular identity. Sensitivity to difference in the treatment of prisoners (discussed in the introduction) also ascribes a political identity to them, and the addition of torture simply changes the ways in which that identity is imposed.

Thinking about torture in this way means that even when the information obtained through torture is inaccurate or merely duplicates what is already known, torture still "works" to the extent that it succeeds in creating these new identities.[31] Again, the creative function of torture suggests that some forms of it cannot be compartmentalized as exceptional practices. Instead, torture of this kind is simply another coercive tool of the state, and the point of these tools is largely the shaping and regulation of political identity.

As I suggested in chapter 7, torture and coercion also shape the identities of the guards and interrogators. Indeed, the sexual nature of some of the abuse at Abu Ghraib, Guantánamo, and other places—both in its sanctioned and unsanctioned forms—can be understood in this context. Extending the analogy to Foucault's discussion of psychiatric practice and to the *KUBARK* approach, an important aspect of the relationship between guards and prisoners was the search for a crisis or trauma that would produce the truth of the detention or interrogation.[32] I have already explored the effect of this trauma or crisis on the prisoners, but I want to suggest that the guards and interrogators were also caught up in it. The result was that even as they participated in the creation of new political identities for their prisoners, they also participated in the creation of new identities for themselves.

In this context, Private Lynndie England's claim that the abuses at Abu Ghraib were "just for fun" carries a special resonance.[33] The "fun" she described was not just an example of social or individual brutality or perversion. Within the relationship between guards and prisoners, for example, the overt deployment of sexual imagery and the use of photography to document it operated to highlight and control difference by exposing, containing, and demeaning a frightening "other."[34] Moreover, the abuses could be seen as a carnivalesque inversion of (military) authority and suspension of official rules by the guards—the creation of a temporary "second world and a second life outside officialdom"—in reaction to the stress of their experiences in Iraq and their position within a military hierarchy.[35] Finally, the "fun" Private England described includes the sexual activity among the guards that took place during the same period of time.[36] An apparent link thus existed at Abu Ghraib—as at Guantánamo and perhaps other places—between sex and torture, so that the abuses were not merely sexual in nature but also a form of sexual activity, which, in turn, raises the possibility that the sexual activity among the guards was a form of violence. Each of these explanations is consistent with the idea that the abusive conduct of the Abu

Ghraib guards was a response to crisis or trauma, even as this response also heightened the pain and trauma felt by the prisoners themselves.

For some commentators, the characterization of the Abu Ghraib abuses as "fun" and, particularly, the sexual aspect of the abuse demonstrate the special status—the exceptionality—of the abuse at Abu Ghraib. It was not "ordinary" torture and coercion, and it cannot be ascribed to the state. Yet sexual torture and humiliation has been a prominent part of the mistreatment meted out by U.S. forces in the war on terror. Further, the effort to draw a clear line between personal conduct—easily condemned as perverse, immoral, or disgusting—and the proper, upright conduct of the normal state actor fails utterly in this context. My discussion of political identity and the ways it can be created in the torture relationship ultimately draws on the modern state's ability to define, warp, or co-opt people's emotions, passions, and perversions, so that a guard who seemingly acts on a personal, sadistic whim when stripping a prisoner naked and putting him on a leash to be photographed in a position of subservience channels simultaneously the sovereign power of the state.[37] Indeed, the appearance of sexual activity amid the formation of political identity may simply reflect that in the crisis of the torture relationship, the guards will use their agency to "push their life, their real, everyday life, that is to say, their sexual life"[38] and will use their power over the prisoners to force them to participate in that life. All of this confirms again the way in which the formation of political identity through torture is perhaps not mutual but, indeed, almost certainly lopsided and also explicitly and intensely relational.

The role torture plays in the creation of political identity also goes beyond the victim and the guard/interrogator, even if, at each step, its power tends to diminish. In the context of crisis, normal patterns of identity and role become disrupted within a population, and in the norms of the emergency, anyone is theoretically a victim or an interrogator. Anyone, in other words, is simultaneously defined as capable of torturing or being tortured. Thus, Lisa Hajjar observes that torture is often linked to a discourse of national security, and she argues that "the discourse and politics of national security . . . establishes a class of innocents [and] operationalizes a politics of exclusion of categories of people deemed to threaten the national order." In the context of torture, according to Hajjar, "the politics of inclusion and exclusion manifest themselves as an extreme form of differentiation between the 'legitimate community' and 'enemies of the state.'"[39] Indeed, the stress that the war on terror has placed on the categories of "citizen" and "alien" results, to at least a significant extent, from this destabilization.[40]

Going a step beyond Hajjar, I would argue that the discourse of national security or emergency—of which torture is a component—also destabilizes the "legitimate community," not only by making its very survival contingent, but also by calling into question its defining characteristics. If the legitimate community strives to be the normal community, the emergency always undermines that quest for normality by threatening the terms under which the legitimate community can continue. One aspect of that threat is what might happen to members of that community or what they might be called on to do for the community. The emergency means that anyone, whether or not defined in advance as an enemy or a friend, is always at risk, always subject, among other things, to being tortured or to being forced to torture. This ongoing political trauma forces new identities—or perhaps reinforces existing identities—on a much broader group than those already involved in torture.

Finally, to the extent that the political life of the modern liberal democracy is characterized by ongoing emergency, this dynamic will also generalize in time as well as across a population. If the state is always engaged in the process of shaping political identity and does so more violently in times of emergency—including by making its population potentially subject to being tortured or being forced to torture—then to the extent that the emergency becomes the norm, the use of violence (including torture) to shape identity will also become the norm or, at least, will emerge as a perpetual potential.[41] This logic also means that when torture takes place, the new identities must include not just the fact of membership in a community that tortures but also recognition that one's rights, freedoms, or material well-being rest partly on those acts of torture. In the situation of perpetual emergency that some claim is normal contemporary political life, in other words, the state and its population are defined or constituted partly by torture.

Fragility and Resistance

∽

I do not mean to suggest that the political identities produced by torture are stable or monolithic. To the contrary, the harms of torture include not just the effort to create a new identity or the destruction or destabilization of former identities but also the fact that a new identity created through torture is often incomplete or unstable. Here again, the analogy to psychiatric practice holds, for the person cured of mental illness often relapses or remains in need of continued or even perpetual treatment.[42] Indeed, the state or torturer may not always care whether the new identity is stable—for them, it may be enough that the old identity is in shambles and that the new one existed or was imposed during the course of the torture.

But the instability of the political identity created by torture can play out in other ways as well. With respect to the community that tortures, the deployment of this violence can "corrosively delegitimize the state."[43] This delegitimization, in turn, will damage the political identity of that state's entire population, not simply those people defined as enemies or others.

With respect to the victims of torture, the effort to create political identity might fail or have unintended consequences because it runs into resistance. Hajjar suggests, for example, that "captured IRA members who were subjected to torture retained their agency because they comprehended their suffering as part of the national struggle, in which they were actively engaged."[44] A slightly different process takes place when a person subjected to torture discovers an agency or identity that he or she can put to creative uses in a way that departs from the torturer's goals. For example, people at Guantánamo who have been defined as fanatical Muslim terrorists could embrace that identity, and Kurds subjected to "Turkification" by torture could shape the process into one of "Kurdification." Under any of these scenarios, torture has yet another creative function because the torture victim is able to resist or exercise greater control in the relationship.

Readers should not conclude that I am discounting the pain and suffering that would accompany these acts of resistance. The person who embraces and creates a new political identity different, in greater or lesser ways, from the one the torturer seeks to impose may still emerge damaged, such that the new identity is a poor substitute for what was lost. Nor am I necessarily applauding the ability of the torture victim to reshape the torture narrative in a way that valorizes his or her political goals. Doing so at too general a level risks validating a different course of political violence, and sorting through the normative qualities of such acts is a task that goes well beyond the scope of this book. The effort to impose a political identity through the torture relationship will have a variety of consequences, some of which will be more favorable to the victim, even as all of this takes place against a background of pain and fear.

Understanding Torture
～

How, then, do we "understand" torture? Michael Taussig writes, "There is the effort to understand terror, in order to make others understand. Yet the reality at stake here makes a mockery of understanding and derides rationality."[45] I make no claim in this book to have understood torture in terms of the pain, terror, and despair that it produces, which is one of Taussig's central topics. At best, I have acknowledged that pain but focused, instead, on legal and political discourse and on the historical fact that torture persists among democracies. I have also advanced a claim about torture's potential to shape individual political identity. This potential can only deepen the concern, expressed by Taussig, that in the effort to understand torture, "[f]ascist poetics succeed where liberal rationalism self-destructs."[46]

People concerned about torture can point to a web of international and national laws that ban or regulate something called "torture." But it simply will not do to conclude that the kinds of abuse that people reasonably could label or experience as torture are therefore illegal. Similarly, it is true today that citizens of liberal democracies are unlikely to be rounded up, put in camps, and tortured by their own governments or to be beaten when in police custody as a matter of general practice or policy—although much of the truth of this statement depends on definitions. Yet this perception of safety cannot support a conclusion that torture is contrary to the values of those societies, that it does not persist as a problem in them, or even that torture is something that only threatens outsiders.

As I argued throughout this book, torture sits on a continuum with other forms of state violence, and violence is pervasive in and perhaps necessary to the maintenance of modern states. I also suggested that in this context, liberal and critical theories of rights have converged. This convergence emerges from the effort to uncover liberalism's authoritarian dimensions and to see those dimensions in liberal theory itself. Taussig's concern about fascist poetics resonates with the complexity of the modern liberal state's interaction with torture and with pain and violence generally. Indeed, the connections between torture and modern states indicate that the line between liberal rationalism and fascist poetics may be shifting or sometimes even illusory. Understanding torture requires the recognition that it exists as a potential part of every political relationship. If torture has a special horror, surely this is it, even if this horror is entirely prosaic.

Afterword

In January 2009, President Obama issued a series of executive orders on detention and interrogation policy. Among other things, the orders revoked Bush's 2007 post–Military Commissions Act order on CIA interrogation and declared that all interrogations of people in U.S. custody would comply with the Army field manual and Common Article 3 of the Geneva Conventions. In addition to reaffirming Obama's campaign promise to close the detention camp at Guantánamo Bay, the new administration also advanced a narrower view than the Bush administration of executive authority to detain illegal combatants. Finally, the administration began to review interrogation and detention policy, with the apparent goal of recalibrating the mix of war and crime approaches to terrorism and national security issues.

Nonetheless, the first six months of the Obama administration underscore the themes I have developed in this book, such that the administration's specific policy toward something called "torture" appears to matter much less than the pervasive structures of legal liberalism. In his inaugural address, for example, Obama asserted that the United States was involved in a war against terrorism. The fact that a number of his early decisions coincide with the previous administration's policies tends to bear out this assertion. Thus, even as officials continue to force-feed prisoners on hunger strikes, the Obama administration determined that conditions at the Guantánamo detention camp comply with international law. Rendition, in some form, remains a counterterrorism tool, and the administration has yet to reject the idea of indefinitely detaining suspected terrorists. Rather than seek a repeal of the Military Commissions Act, the Obama administration has endorsed the use of such commissions, although with some reforms and against a smaller pool of people. In litigation, the administration has endorsed the state secrets doctrine and opposed habeas corpus petitions brought by detainees. In signing statements Obama has suggested that his executive authority over foreign relations overrides certain provisions of federal law.

With respect to coercive interrogation, and despite the executive orders, the Obama administration has shown a clear preference for shifting debate to other issues. As I write in July 2009, a 2004 report by the CIA's inspector general remains classified (although it is expected to appear soon), and the

Department of Justice has yet to release a 2008 report by its Office of Professional Responsibility that is known to be highly critical of attorneys in the Office of Legal Counsel. Further, when he released several previously secret OLC memoranda on interrogation, Obama declared that officials who conducted interrogations while relying on those memoranda should not be punished. Any criminal inquiry by the Justice Department into interrogation abuses seems likely to be limited to whether officials went beyond the scope of the OLC memos. In the meantime, the Army field manual governs current interrogations, and it permits a significant amount of mental and emotional pressure—as well as the potential for physical discomfort during "isolation"—to be imposed on a suspect.

For the Obama administration, detention and interrogation abuses appear less pressing than other topics. The administration certainly faces many important issues and it must prioritize them. Yet its policies suggest that issues involving human or constitutional rights have no special status. The administration's actions thus accord with my argument that rights are simply one of many policy issues and tools for contemporary practitioners of governance in a liberal democracy. Officials must make statements about rights, pay some attention to them, and avoid too many public violations of them. But they take these actions less to protect or respect rights as such and more because of the larger role rights play in defining a liberal democracy and the rule of law.

Returning to the specific question of interrogation, the administration's decision to release the OLC memoranda, while also assuring officials who conducted coercive interrogations that they will not be prosecuted unless they went too far beyond the memos, has had some curious effects. Some administration officials and media commentators have expressed concern that prosecuting interrogators or their superiors would criminalize a policy disagreement with the Bush administration. But such a concern rests on the belief that the debate over coercive interrogation is primarily a matter of policy or, to the extent it is an issue of law, that it is simply a matter of legal interpretation without criminal overtones. Yet concluding that the use, or not, of practices such as waterboarding is a matter of policy—as opposed to seeing it as a decision whether or not to engage in criminal behavior—is one that has important consequences. Those consequences include, as Žižek insisted, the legitimation of the torture debate.

Further, even though the administration has disavowed the OLC memoranda, they will persist as meaningful legal documents so long as they continue to set the standard for evaluating past behavior. In other words, even as commentators and officials continue to deride them as shoddy or even illegitimate, the memoranda will remain legitimate in at least one important sense: prosecutions and convictions apparently will stand or fall based on what they mean and what they allowed. At stake here is not simply Žižek's concern about the terms of political discourse but also the content of legal rules. In addition to legitimizing the torture debate, the administration's reliance on the memoranda to guide criminal investigations risks legitimizing torture law.

Finally, it is worth stressing how decisions about detention and interrogation are being made in the Obama era. Although Congress has been involved to some extent in these decisions to change or continue Bush administration policies, most have been made by the president, pursuant to his status as commander in chief of the armed forces and the "one voice" of the nation in foreign affairs. These decisions have been made against the background of a continued assertion of war—in the midst of an ongoing emergency. Interrogation and detention decisions thus continue to be topics reserved primarily for the sovereign decision. To the extent that torture continues to be linked *both* to normal or everyday forms of state violence *and* to the state of emergency, it represents the continued potential for the sovereign decision to determine increasingly broad aspects of political life.

Notes

INTRODUCTION

1. Joan Sayre, review of *The Breaking of Bodies and Minds*, by Eric Stover & Elena O. Nightingale, *Contemporary Sociology* 16 (1987): 543; Daniel Chirot, review of *Torture and Modernity*, by Darius M. Rejali, *Contemporary Sociology* 23 (1994): 680.

2. Mark Bowden, "The Dark Art of Interrogation," *Atlantic Monthly*, Oct. 2003 ("the gloves came off"); Dana Priest & Barton Gellman, "U.S. Decries Abuse but Defends Interrogations," *Washington Post*, 26 Dec. 2002, A1.

3. For criticism of this dynamic, see Alice Ristroph, "Professors Strangelove," *Green Bag 2d* 11 (2008): 243.

4. Walter Pincus, "Silence of 4 Terror Probe Suspects Poses Dilemma for FBI," *Washington Post*, 21 Oct. 2001, A6; Jim Rutenberg, "Torture Seeps into Discussion by News Media," *New York Times*, 5 Nov. 2001, C1; Priest & Gellman; Dale Van Natta Jr., "Questioning Terror Suspects in a Dark and Surreal World," *New York Times*, 9 Mar. 2003, sec. 1, 14; Jess Bravin & Gary Fields, "How Do U.S. Interrogators Make a Captured Terrorist Talk?" *Wall Street Journal*, 4 Mar. 2003, B1. For human rights groups, see Amnesty International, *Amnesty International Criticizes U.S. Handling of Terror Suspects* (5 Mar. 2003); Human Rights Watch, *Reports of Torture of Al-Qaeda Suspects* (27 Dec. 2002).

5. Richard W. Stevenson, "Bush, on Arab TV, Denounces Abuse of Iraqi Captives," *New York Times*, 6 May 2004, A1.

6. *E.g.*, James Risen, David Johnston & Neil Lewis, "Harsh Methods Cited in Top Qaeda Interrogations," *New York Times*, 13 May 2004, A10; Neil A. Lewis, "Broad Use of Harsh Tactics Is Described at Cuba Base," *New York Times*, 17 Oct. 2004, A1.

7. Terence Hunt, "Bush Calls Human Rights Report 'Absurd,'" *Associated Press*, 31 May 2005; White House, *President Discusses Creation of Military Commissions to Try Suspected Terrorists* (6 Sept. 2006).

8. The 2005 report is at http://www.amnesty.org. In an accompanying press release, titled *Selective U.S. Prosecutions in Torture Scandal Underscore International Obligation to Investigate U.S. Officials*, Amnesty USA advocated an international investigation and the possible arrest of U.S. officials.

9. Jay S. Bybee, Assistant Attorney General, *Memorandum for Alberto R. Gonzales, Counsel to the President, re: Standards of Conduct for Interrogation under 18 U.S.C. §§ 2340–2340A* (1 Aug. 2002), in Karen J. Greenberg & Joshua L. Dratel eds., *The Torture Papers* (New York: Cambridge Univ. Press, 2005), 176.

10. *Working Group Report on Detainee Interrogations in the Global War on Terrorism: Assessment of Legal, Historical, Policy, and Operational Considerations* (4 Apr. 2003), in Greenberg & Dratel, 294.

11. *Convention against Torture and Other Forms of Cruel, Inhuman, or Degrading Treatment or Punishment*, art. 1 ¶ 1, art. 16 ¶ 1 (1984), 1465 U.N.T.S. 85.

12. Id., art. 2 ¶ 2.

13. Greek Case, *Yearbook of the European Convention on Human Rights* 12 (1969): 501.

14. Nigel S. Rodley, *The Treatment of Prisoners under International Law,* 2nd ed. (Oxford: Oxford Univ. Press, 1999), 104.

15. Lt. Gen. Ricardo S. Sanchez, *Memorandum re: CJTF-7 Interrogation and Counter-Realisation Policy* (14 Sept. 2003), in Jameel Jaffer & Amrit Singh eds., *Administration of Torture* (New York: Columbia Univ. Press, 2007), A-231.

16. *E.g.,* Alfred W. McCoy, *A Question of Torture* (New York: Henry Holt, Owl Books 2006), 127. For a possible source of "knowledge" about an apparently monolithic Arab culture and psychology, see the discussion in Jane Mayer, *The Dark Side* (New York: Doubleday, 2008), 167–68.

17. Headquarters, Joint Task Force—Guantánamo, *Camp Delta Standard Operating Procedures* (1 Mar. 2004), 6.2–6.3, ch. 16; Robert Burns, "U.S. Confirms Gitmo Soldier Kicked Quran," *Associated Press,* 3 June 2005; Pamela Hess, "Cause and Effect—Another Look at *Newsweek,*" *United Press,* 16 May 2005.

18. Carol D. Leonnig & Dana Priest, "Detainees Accuse Female Interrogators," *Washington Post,* 10 Feb. 2005, A1; Paisley Dodds, "Gitmo Soldier Details Sexual Tactics," *Associated Press,* 28 Jan. 2005; "Torture Policy," *Washington Post,* 16 June 2004, A26; Neil A. Lewis, "Red Cross Found Abuses at Abu Ghraib Last Year," *New York Times,* 11 May 2004, A13; Andrew Miga, "War on Terror; 'Stain on Our Honor'; Prez Backs Rumsfeld, Apologizes," *Boston Herald,* 7 May 2004, 5.

19. Uwe Siemon-Netto, "Analysis: Horror over Women Torturers," *United Press,* 6 May 2004. See also Seymour M. Hersh, *Chain of Command* (New York: HarperCollins, 2004), 23–24; McCoy, 129–30; Philippe Sands, *Torture Team* (New York: Palgrave Macmillan, 2008), 166–67.

20. See Joseba Zulaika & William A. Douglass, *Terror and Taboo* (New York: Routledge, 1996), 72, 104–5.

21. John F. Harris, "Bush Gets More International Support for U.S. 'Crusade' against Terrorism," *Washington Post,* 17 Sept. 2001, A1; Norman Podhoretz, "World War IV," *Commentary,* Sept. 2004, 47; Bill Powell, "Struggle for the Soul of Islam," *Time,* 13 Sept. 2004, 46. See also Nicholas D. Kristoff, "Martyrs, Virgins and Grapes," *New York Times,* 4 Aug. 2004, A17 (hoping for "reawakening of the Islamic world"); Max Rodenbeck, "Islam Confronts Its Demons," *New York Review of Books,* 29 Apr. 2004 (defining "authentic Muslim modernists" as skeptics of "the whole Islamic tradition").

22. Edward W. Said, *Orientalism* (New York: Pantheon, 1978), 1–2, 41. See also Zulaika & Douglass, 110; Lila Abu-Lughod, "Do Muslim Women Really Need Saving?" *American Anthropologist* 104 (2002): 783; Mahmood Mamdani, "Good Muslim, Bad Muslim," *American Anthropologist* 104 (2002): 766; Leti Volpp, "The Citizen and the Terrorist," *UCLA Law Review* 49 (2002): 1575.

23. "Coast Police Chief Accused of Racism," *New York Times,* 13 May 1983, A24.

24. Michel Foucault, *"Society Must Be Defended": Lectures at the Collège de France, 1975–1976,* trans. David Macy (New York: Picador, 2003), 256.

25. Charles Babington, "Senator Critical of Focus on Prisoner Abuse," *Washington Post,* 12 May 2004, A18.

26. See also Fred Hiatt, "Why Hawks Should Be Angry," *Washington Post,* 31 May 2004, A23 (quoting Senator Zell Miller of Georgia: "Why is it that there's more indignation over a photo of a prisoner with underwear on his head than over the video of a young American with no head at all?"); "Official: Abu Ghraib Like 'Animal House,'" *Rush Limbaugh Show,* 30 Aug. 2004 (comparing Abu Ghraib abuses to "hazing, an out-of-control fraternity prank, . . . Saturday night hijinks").

27. Stevenson; Michael Massing, "Trial and Error," *New York Times Book Review,* 17 Oct. 2004, 17.

28. Mark Bowden, "The Lessons of Abu Ghraib," *Atlantic Monthly,* July/Aug. 2004, 40. See also Reuel Marc Gerecht, "Against Rendition," *Weekly Standard,* 16 May 2005 (state-sponsored torture and killing "is the fate of many in the Muslim Middle East").

29. *Cf.* Human Rights Watch, *Ghost Prisoner* (Feb. 2007), 15 ("In retrospect, Jabour finds it hard to believe that he was paraded around naked in front of a group of men and women, but at the time he was so disoriented and upset that his lack of clothing seemed relatively minor.").

30. My analysis thus has broad similarities with Paul Kahn's *Sacred Violence* (Ann Arbor: Univ. of Michigan Press, 2008) and, more generally, with his *The Cultural Study of Law* (Chicago: Univ. of Chicago Press, 1999).

CHAPTER ONE

1. *Vienna Convention on the Law of Treaties,* art. 53 (1969), 1155 U.N.T.S. 331.

2. American Law Institute, *Restatement (Third) of Foreign Relations Law of the United States* (St. Paul: ALI, 1987), § 102(2) & comment c. See also Jean-Marie Henck-aerts, "Study on Customary International Humanitarian Law," *Int'l Review of the Red Cross* 857 (2005): 178.

3. Nicaragua v. United States of America, ICJ, No. 70, ¶¶ 184, 186 (1986).

4. *E.g.,* Theodor Meron, "Revival of Customary International Law," *American Journal of Int'l Law* 99 (2005): 820.

5. Filartiga v. Pena-Irala, 630 F.2d 876, 883–84 (2d Cir. 1980).

6. *E.g.,* A and Others v. Secretary of State, 2005 UKHL 71, ¶ 33 (opinion of Lord Bingham); Sosa v. Alvarez-Machain, 542 U.S. 692, 732 (2004); Al-Adsani v. United Kingdom, 34 EHRR 273, ¶¶ 60–61 (2001); Prosecutor v. Furundžija, ICTY, No. IT-95-17/1-T, ¶¶ 137–39 (10 Dec. 1998); American Law Institute, § 702(d); Council of Europe, *Guidelines of the Committee of Ministers of the Council of Europe on Human Rights and the Fight against Terrorism,* No. 4, Doc. 804/4.3 (app. 3) (11 July 2002). See also Jean-Marie Henck-aerts & Louise Doswald-Becj, *Customary International Humanitarian Law,* vol. 1 (Cambridge: Cambridge Univ. Press, 2005), 315–34.

7. *Filartiga,* 630 F.2d at 884 n.15. The Supreme Court adopted a more rigorous analytical method in *Sosa.*

8. Paul Kahn, *Sacred Violence* (Ann Arbor: Univ. of Michigan Press, 2008), 152; Amnesty International, *Combating Torture* (2003), 2; Amnesty International, *Take a Step to Stamp Out Torture* (2000); U.N. Commission on Human Rights, *Civil and Political Rights, Including the Questions of Torture and Detention: Torture and Other Cruel, Inhuman, or Degrading Treatment—Report of the Special Rapporteur,* ¶ 11, E/CN.4/ 2006/6 (23 Dec. 2005).

9. A. Mark Weisburd, "Customary International Law and Torture," *Chicago Journal of Int'l Law* 2 (2001): 81–99. *Cf.* Peter Malanczuk, *Akehurst's Modern Introduction to International Law,* 7th ed. (London: Routledge, 1997), 114.

10. Darius Rejali, *Torture and Democracy* (Princeton: Princeton Univ. Press, 2007).

11. *Cf.* Oona A. Hathaway, "The Promise and Limits of the International Law of Torture," in Sanford Levinson ed., *Torture: A Collection* (New York: Oxford Univ. Press, 2004), 201, 204.

12. Such a conclusion depends on citations to international agreements—not prac-

tice—as a source of customary international law and as proof of the norm's supposed peremptory status. *E.g.,* Henckaerts & Doswald-Becj, 315–34.

13. U.N. Commission on Human Rights, *Question of the Violation of Human Rights and Fundamental Freedoms . . . Transfer of Persons,* ¶ 3, E/CN.4/Sub.2/2005/L.12 (4 Aug. 2005); *Convention against Torture and Other Forms of Cruel, Inhuman, or Degrading Treatment or Punishment,* art. 3 (1984), 1465 U.N.T.S. 85.

14. The assertion draws some strength from U.N. Human Rights Committee, *General Comment No. 31,* ¶ 12, CCPR/C/21/Rev.1/Add.13 (26 May 2004). But the phrase "real risk" waters down the level of proof required by the Convention against Torture.

15. *E.g.,* George Letsas, *A Theory of Interpretation of the European Convention on Human Rights* (Oxford: Oxford Univ. Press, 2007), 21 (international human rights were "initially conceived as conditions of legitimacy of states vis-à-vis other states and the international community").

16. Helen Duffy, *The "War on Terror" and the Framework of International Law* (Cambridge: Cambridge Univ. Press, 2005), 7–9; Jacob Katz Cogan, "Noncompliance and the International Rule of Law," *Yale Journal of Int'l Law* 31 (2006): 189.

17. Duncan B. Hollis, "Why State Consent Still Matters," *Berkeley Journal of Int'l Law* 23 (2005): 8–9.

18. American Law Institute, § 102(3). See also *Nicaragua,* ¶ 183.

19. *Vienna Convention,* arts. 31–32.

20. Id., art. 30. See also U.N. International Law Commission, *Fragmentation of International Law: Difficulties Arising from the Diversification and Expansion of International Law,* A/CN.4/L.682 (13 Apr. 2006); Christopher J. Borgen, "Resolving Treaty Conflicts," *George Washington Int'l Law Review* 37 (2005): 587–90.

21. Duncan B. Hollis, "A Comparative Approach to Treaty Law and Practice," in Duncan B. Hollis, Merritt R. Blakeslee & L. Benjamin Ederington, eds., *National Treaty Law and Practice* (Leiden: Martinus Nijhoff 2005), 40–45.

22. *Vienna Convention,* art. 19(c). See U.N. Human Rights Committee, *General Comment No. 24,* ¶¶ 8, 14, CCPR/C/21/Rev.1/Add.6 (4 Nov. 1994); "Observations by the United States on General Comment 24," *Int'l Human Rights Reports* 3 (1996): 265; Elena A. Baylis, "General Comment 24," *Berkeley Journal of Int'l Law* 17 (1999): 277–329.

23. See *Convention (No. I) for the Amelioration of the Condition of the Wounded and Sick in Armed Forces in the Field,* art. 2 (1949), 75 U.N.T.S. 31; *Convention (No. II) for the Amelioration of the Condition of the Wounded, Sick, and Shipwrecked Members of Armed Forces at Sea,* art. 2 (1949), 75 U.N.T.S. 85; *Convention (No. III) Relative to the Treatment of Prisoners of War,* art. 2 (1949), 75 U.N.T.S. 135; *Convention (No. IV) Relative to the Protection of Civilian Persons in Time of War,* art. 2 (1949), 75 U.N.T.S. 287.

24. I assume here that the Geneva Conventions create individually enforceable rights, as the commentary on the conventions suggests; see Jean S. Pictet, ed., *The Geneva Conventions of 12 August 1949: Commentary,* 4 vols. (Geneva: International Committee of the Red Cross, 1952–60), 3:91, 4:76–79. But "only the participant states are qualified, through consultation between themselves, to give an official and . . . authoritative interpretation of an intergovernmental treaty" (Pictet, 1:7; see also 2:1, 3:1, 4:1). See also Hamdan v. Rumsfeld, 548 U.S. 557 (2006) (noting the issue but not resolving it).

25. *Convention (No. III) Relative to the Treatment of Prisoners of War,* arts. 4, 12, 13, 14, 17, 99.

26. *Convention (No. IV) Relative to the Protection of Civilian Persons,* arts. 4, 5, 27, 31, 45, 49, 100.

27. *Convention (No. III) Relative to the Treatment of Prisoners of War,* arts. 129, 130; *Convention (No. IV) Relative to the Protection of Civilian Persons,* arts. 146, 147.

28. Derek Jinks, "The Declining Significance of POW Status," *Harvard Int'l Law Journal* 45 (2004): 367 n. 1, 368–70, 374; Pictet, 4:54.

29. John Bellinger, "Unlawful Enemy Combatants" (17 Jan. 2007). But see *Protocol Additional (No. I) to the Geneva Conventions of August 12, 1949, and Relating to the Protection of Victims of International Armed Conflicts*, art. 44 (1977), 1125 U.N.T.S. 3.

30. *Convention (No. IV) Relative to the Protection of Civilian Persons*, arts. 4, 5; Pictet, 4:50. See also Jinks, "Declining Significance," 381–86; Derek Jinks, "Protective Parity and the Laws of War," *Notre Dame Law Review* 79 (2004): 1503–6; Prosecutor v. Delalić, ICTY, No. IT-96-21-T, ¶ 271 (trial) (16 Nov. 1998).

31. Pictet, 1:53, 3:39, 4:38.

32. The commentary on the Geneva Conventions speaks of applying legal protection "to *all* cases of armed conflicts" and declares that Common Article 3 "should be applied as widely as possible" (Pictet, 1:38, 49–50), but the latter statement is embedded in a discussion of internal conflicts. See also Pictet, 3:37, 4:36; Allen S. Weiner, "*Hamdan*, Terror, War," *Lewis & Clark Law Review* 11 (2007): 1009–11. The safest conclusion is that negotiators expected Common Article 3 to apply to internal conflicts but did not rule out broader application. Their intentions are unclear for conflicts that are neither between states nor "within the confines of a single country." Perhaps they would have endorsed such an application, but the basis for concluding that they actually did so is weak.

33. Prosecutor v. Delalić, ICTY, No. IT-96-21-A, ¶¶ 142–50 (appeal) (20 Feb. 2001); Jinks, "Protective Parity," 1507–10; Jinks, "Declining Significance," 399–409; Jordan J. Paust, "Post-9/11 Overreaction and Fallacies regarding War and Defense, Guantánamo, the Status of Persons, Treatment, Judicial Review of Detention, and Due Process in Military Commissions," *Notre Dame Law Review* 79 (2004): 1351; Jordan Paust, "Executive Plans and Authorizations to Violate International Law concerning Treatment and Interrogation of Detainees," *Columbia Journal of Transnational Law* 43 (2005): 817–18. See also *Hamdan*, 548 U.S. at 627–31.

34. *Protocol Additional (No. I)*, art. 1 ¶¶ 2 & 4, art. 44. See Nigel S. Rodley, *The Treatment of Prisoners under International Law*, 2nd ed. (Oxford: Oxford Univ. Press, 1999), 59.

35. *Protocol Additional (No. II) to the Geneva Conventions of August 12, 1949, and Relating to the Protection of Victims of Non-International Armed Conflicts*, art. 4 (1977), 1125 U.N.T.S. 609

36. *E.g.*, *Delalić* (appeal), ¶¶ 142–50; Michael J. Matheson, "The United States Position on the Relation of Customary International Law to the 1977 Protocols Additional to the 1949 Geneva Conventions," *American Univ. Journal of Int'l Law & Policy* 2 (1987): 420, 427.

37. *Protocol Additional (No. I)*, art. 44 (all members of the armed forces of the party to the conflict shall "be given protections equivalent in all respects to those accorded to prisoners of war by the Third Convention and by this Protocol," which include protection against rendition or transfer to countries that will not follow the Geneva Conventions). This language excludes illegal combatants not in a state's "armed forces"; they remain vulnerable to transfer except to the extent protection is inferred from Common Article 3 and Article 75.

38. *Convention (No. III) Relative to the Treatment of Prisoners of War*, art. 130; *Convention (No. IV) Relative to the Protection of Civilian Persons*, art. 147. See also Jinks, "Protective Parity," 1512.

39. The commentary on the Geneva Conventions does not define torture but insists on the breadth of the ban (Pictet, 4:223). The commentary on the First Protocol refers to the definition in the U.N. Declaration against Torture and mentions the ban in the

ICCPR. See Yves Sandoz et al., eds., *Commentary on the Additional Protocols of 8 June 1977 to the Geneva Conventions of 12 August 1949* (Geneva: Martinus Nijhoff, 1987), 873.

40. Mary Ellen O'Connell, "Affirming the Ban on Harsh Interrogation," *Ohio State Law Journal* 66 (2005): 1244.

41. *Protocol Additional (No. II)*, art. 1; *Rome Statute of the International Criminal Court*, art. 8 ¶¶ 2(d), 3 (1998), 2187 U.N.T.S. 90.

42. U.N. Commission on Human Rights, *Situation of Detainees at Guantánamo Bay*, ¶83, E/CN.4/2006/120 (15 Feb. 2006); George H. Aldrich, "The Taliban, al Qaeda, and the Determination of Illegal Combatants," *American Journal of Int'l Law* 96 (2002): 892–93; Silvia Borelli, "Casting Light on the Legal Black Hole," *Int'l Review of the Red Cross* 857 (2005): 45–46; Paust, "Post-9/11 Overreaction," 1342. For critical assessments, see Rosa Ehrenreich Brooks, "War Everywhere," *Univ. of Pennsylvania Law Review* 153 (2004): 680, 714–19; Duffy, 250–55; Margaret L. Satterthwaite, "Rendered Meaningless," *George Washington Law Review* 75 (2007): 1333.

43. *Hamdan*, 548 U.S. at 629–31. For the problem of defining al Qaeda, see Faisal Devji, *Landscapes of the Jihad* (Ithaca, N.Y.: Cornell Univ. Press, 2005), 19–20.

44. Duffy, 272.

45. See also Brooks, 724, 726.

46. See also David Kennedy, *Of War and Law* (Princeton: Princeton Univ. Press, 2006), 2; Devji, 156.

47. See Alex P. Schmid, "The Response Problem as a Definition Problem," in Alex P. Schmid & Ronald D. Crelinstein eds., *Western Responses to Terrorism* (London: F. Cass, 1993), 7–13; Colin Warbrick, "The European Response to Terrorism in an Age of Human Rights," *European Journal of Int'l Law* 15 (2004): 1002–3.

48. For assessment of the International Criminal Tribunal for Rwanda, see L. J. van den Herik, *The Contribution of the Rwanda Tribunal to the Development of International Law* (Leiden: Martinus Nijhoff, 2005), 274–82.

49. Allison Marston Danner, "When Courts Make Law," *Vanderbilt Law Review* 59 (2006): 20–22, 25–33. ICTY decisions do not bind other countries or international institutions, but they have become important sources for international humanitarian and human rights law. *E.g., Al-Adsani*, ¶¶ 30, 60 (torture); *Hamdan*, 548 U.S. at 631 n.63 (Common Article 3).

50. Prosecutor v. Tadić, ICTY, No. IT-94-1, ¶ 99 (2 Oct. 1995) (emphasis added). For a defense of this approach, see Meron, 821–29.

51. *Tadić*, ¶ 70. See also Prosecutor v. Kunarac, ICTY, Nos. IT-96-23 & IT-96-23/1-A, ¶ 56 (appeal) (12 June 2002).

52. *Delalić* (appeal), ¶ 73.

53. On the torture ban as a peremptory norm, see *Furundžija*, ¶¶ 137, 139; *Delalić* (appeal), ¶ 172 n. 225. On defining torture, see *Furundžija*, ¶ 111; *Kunarac* (appeal), ¶¶ 146–48.

54. Kadic v. Karadžić, 70 F.3d 232, 243 (2nd Cir. 1995).

55. Prosecutor v. Brđanin, ICTY, No. IT-99-36-A, ¶¶ 249, 251 (2 Apr. 2007). The appeals chamber made these observations in the course of holding that the definition of severe pain in the "torture memo" prepared by the U.S. Justice Department's Office of Legal Counsel—discussed in chapter 7—did not reflect customary international law.

56. *Kunarac* (appeal), ¶ 150. See also William A. Schabas, "The Crime of Torture and the International Criminal Tribunals," *Case Western Reserve Journal of Int'l Law* 37 (2006): 349–64; Nigel S. Rodley, "The Definition(s) of Torture in International Law," *Current Legal Problems* 55 (2002): 480–89.

57. *Kunarac* (appeal), ¶ 58. The trial decision in *Kunarac* declared that every person has a right to be free of torture inflicted by any source and that governments must

affirmatively protect people from torture inflicted by nonstate actors (Prosecutor v. Kunarac, ICTY, Nos. IT-96-23-T & IT-96-23/1-T, ¶¶ 479–81 (trial) (22 Feb. 2001)). The appeals chamber did not adopt this reasoning, but it remains a source for other courts and activists.

58. *Rome Statute*, arts. 5(1), 9, 25(2).

59. Id., art. 7.

60. Rodley, "Definition(s)," 481–84.

61. Id. See Henckaerts & Doswald-Becj, 317; *Kunarac* (trial), ¶ 495, n. 1210.

62. *Rome Statute*, art. 8.

63. *Official Journal of the International Criminal Court: Elements of Crimes*, arts. 7(1)(f), 8(2)(a)(ii)-1, 8(2)(c)(i)-4 (9 Sept. 2002).

64. Id., arts. 21(1)(b), 22(2).

65. Id., General Introduction ¶ 4.

66. *Rome Statute*, arts. 31–33.

67. Meron, 832.

68. Robert M. Chesney, "Leaving Guantánamo," *Univ. of Richmond Law Review* 40 (2006): 700–4; Duffy, 298–301. For the application of human rights law to war, see Borelli, 53–55; Paust, "Executive Plans," 820; Anna-Lena Svensson-McCarthy, *The International Law of Human Rights and States of Exception* (The Hague: Martinus Nijhoff, 1998), 214, 376–77. But see Michael J. Dennis, "Application of Human Rights Treaties Extraterritorially in Times of Armed Conflict and Military Occupation," *American Journal of Int'l Law* 99 (2005): 132–39.

69. *Universal Declaration of Human Rights*, preamble and arts. 15, 21–22, 25–26, 29, U.N. G.A. Res. 217A(III) (1948).

70. *Proclamation of Teheran, Final Act of the International Conference on Human Rights* (13 May 1968), U.N. Doc. A/CONF. 32/41, at 3; Rodley, *Treatment*, 70–71. The Vienna Declaration of the World Conference on Human Rights more modestly described the Universal Declaration as "the source of inspiration and . . . the basis for the United Nations in making advances in standard setting as contained in the existing international human rights instruments" (*Vienna Declaration and Programme of Action* (12 July 1993), U.N. Doc. A/CONF. 157/23).

71. *Universal Declaration*, arts. 3, 5, 9, 10.

72. For other international or multilateral legal instruments that address torture, see J. Herman Burgers & Hans Danelius, *The United Nations Convention against Torture* (Dordrecht: Martinus Nijhoff, 1988); Henckaerts & Doswald-Becj; Chris Ingelse, *The UN Committee against Torture* (The Hague: Kluwer, 2001); Rodley, *Treatment*.

73. *International Covenant on Civil and Political Rights*, arts. 4, 7 (1966), 999 U.N.T.S. 171. In General Comment No. 29 (U.N. Human Rights Committee, *General Comment No. 29*, ¶ 7, CCPR/C/21/Rev.1/Add.11 (31 Aug. 2001)), the U.N. Human Rights Committee declared, "Conceptually, the qualification of a Covenant provision as a non-derogable one does not mean that no limitations or restrictions would ever be justified." That comment should be read in context (the committee was discussing Article 18, on freedom of conscience and religion) and with General Comment 20's statement that the torture ban "allows of no limitation" or derogation (U.N. Human Rights Committee, *General Comment 20*, ¶ 3 (10 Mar. 1992)).

74. *International Covenant on Civil and Political Rights*, arts. 4, 8–10.

75. Id., arts. 2(2), 3.

76. See Ahcene Boulesbaa, *The U.N. Convention on Torture and the Prospects for Enforcement* (The Hague: Martinus Nijhoff, 1999), 107–18. Parties to the ICCPR's optional protocol recognize the Human Rights Committee's competence "to receive and consider

communications from individuals subject to its jurisdiction who claim to be victims of a violation by that State Party of any of the rights set forth in the Covenant" (*Optional Protocol to the International Covenant on Civil and Political Rights,* art. 1 (1966), 999 U.N.T.S. 302).

77. Svensson-McCarthy, 214; Legal Consequences of the Construction of a Wall in the Occupied Palestinian Territory, ICJ, No. 131, ¶¶ 105–6 (2004). See also U.N. Human Rights Committee, *Concluding Observations: Israel,* ¶ 11, CCPR/CO/78/ISR (21 Aug. 2003); U.N. Human Rights Committee, *General Comment No. 31,* ¶ 11.

78. Compare Dominic McGoldrick, "Extraterritorial Application of the International Covenant on Civil and Political Rights," in Fons Coomans & Menno T. Kamminga eds., *Extraterritorial Application of Human Rights Treaties* (Antwerp: Intersentia, 2003), 41–72, and Satterthwaite, 1358–65, with Dennis, "Application of Human Rights Treaties," 122–27, 130–31, 136–38. See also Borelli, 55–62.

79. U.N. Human Rights Committee, *General Comment No. 31,* ¶ 10. Compare Duffy, 283, with Gerald L. Neuman, "Counter-Terrorist Operations and the Rule of Law," *European Journal of Int'l Law* 15 (2004): 1028.

80. *Legal Consequences of the Construction of a Wall,* ¶¶ 108–9. The court also asserted that the drafting history of the ICCPR revealed that states "only intended to prevent persons residing abroad from asserting, vis-à-vis their state of origin, rights that do not fall within the competence of that State, but of the State of residence." See also McGoldrick, 66–67. For a contrary view, see Dennis, "Application of Human Rights Treaties," 123.

81. U.N. Human Rights Committee, *General Comment No. 20,* ¶ 4.

82. Ingelse, 229, 230. See also Svensson-McCarthy, 408–29; Rodley, *Treatment,* 86–90, 96–98, 102–3.

83. U.N. Human Rights Committee, *General Comment No. 31,* ¶ 8. See also U.N. Human Rights Committee, *General Comment No. 20,* ¶ 2.

84. U.N. Human Rights Committee, *General Comment No. 20,* ¶ 9.

85. U.N. Human Rights Committee, *General Comment No. 31,* ¶ 12 (emphasis added).

86. Id., ¶ 12. For a broader view, see Committee on International Human Rights of the Association of the Bar of the City of New York & Center for Human Rights and Global Justice at NYU School of Law, *Torture by Proxy: International and Domestic Law Applicable to "Extraordinary Renditions"* (2004), 54–55.

87. U.N. Human Rights Committee, *Concluding Observations: United States of America,* ¶ 16, CCPR/C/USA/CO/3 (15 Sept. 2006).

88. *Convention against Torture,* arts. 1, 2, 3, 15.

89. Id., arts. 2, 4, 17, 19–22; Boulesbaa, 293; *Optional Protocol to the Convention against Torture and Other Cruel, Inhuman, or Degrading Treatment,* arts. 1, 2, 11 (2002), U.N. G.A. Res. 57/199.

90. Boulesbaa, 74; Borelli, 55–62; Satterthwaite, 1367–70. Paragraph 1(a) of Article 5, on establishing jurisdiction over offenses, uses the phrase "any territory under its jurisdiction or on board a ship or aircraft registered in that State." A state might contend that reading Article 2 to include ships and aircraft renders paragraph 1(a) of Article 5 superfluous and that this specific language distinguishes the convention from general precedents on the meaning of jurisdiction. Yet Article 5 is the more specific provision on jurisdiction, and reading the two articles together and expansively may be the most reasonable approach. For commentary on jurisdiction, see Burgers & Danelius, 123–24, 131–32.

91. U.N. Committee against Torture, *Conclusions and Recommendations: United*

Kingdom of Great Britain and Northern Ireland—Dependent Territories, ¶ 4(b), CAT/C/CR/33/3 (10 Dec. 2004).

92. Burgers & Danelius, 122.

93. U.N. Commission on Human Rights, *Question of the Human Rights of All Persons Subjected to Any Form of Detention or Imprisonment, in Particular: Torture and Other Cruel, Inhuman, or Degrading Treatment or Punishment—Report of the Special Rapporteur,* ¶ 8, E/CN.4/1997/7 (10 Jan. 1997); U.N. Commission on Human Rights, *Civil and Political Rights, Including the Questions of Torture and Detention,* ¶¶ 38–41. For the similar U.S. position, see Rodley, *Treatment,* 322; 8 C.F.R. § 208.18(a)(3) (2009).

94. Burgers & Danelius, 47, 70; Ingelse, 206–8, 274; David P. Stewart, "The Torture Convention and the Reception of International Criminal Law within the United States," *Nova Law Review* 15 (1991): 460. On the meaning of *undertake,* compare Medellin v. Texas, 128 S. Ct. 1346, 1358–59 (2008) ("undertakes" suggests the need for "further action to give effect" to the relevant provision), with Carlos Manuel Vázquez, "Treaties as Law of the Land," *Harvard Law Review* 122 (2008): 661 ("in international law, an 'undertaking' is well recognized to be a hard, immediate obligation"); *Nicaragua,* ¶¶ 235, 261 .

95. See Burgers & Danelius, 2–3, 70–71; Ingelse, 78, 248, 245, 312; Rodley, *Treatment,* 50. See also U.N. Committee against Torture, *Communication No. 161/2000: Yugoslavia,* ¶ 9.6, CAT/C/29/D/161/2000 (21 Nov. 2002). Compare the special rapporteur's unexplained claim that the convention "does not permit derogation from its provisions" (*Civil and Political Rights, Including the Questions of Torture and Detention,* ¶ 36).

96. See *Kunarac* (trial), ¶ 473; Burgers & Danelius, 122, 150. For the lack of drafting history, see Boulesbaa, 37–38.

97. U.N. Committee against Torture, *General Comment No. 2,* ¶ 3, CAT/C/GC/2/CRP.1/Rev.4 (23 Nov. 2007). Compare Brad R. Roth, "Just Short of Torture: Abusive Treatment and the Limits of International Criminal Justice," *International Journal of Criminal Justice* 6 (2008): 215.

98. *Declaration on the Protection of All Persons from Being Subjected to Torture and Other Cruel, Inhuman, or Degrading Treatment or Punishment,* arts. 2, 3, 12 (1975), U.N. G.A. Res. 3452.

99. U.N. Committee against Torture, *General Comment No. 1,* ¶¶ 1, 3, 4, 5, A/53/44, annex IX (1997). Burgers & Danelius (124) argue for broader constraints on renditions. For criticism of the state action requirement, see Ingelse, 224–25, 299; see also Boulesbaa, 23–28.

100. U.N. Committee against Torture, *General Comment No. 2,* ¶ 19; U.N. Committee Against Torture, *Conclusions and Recommendations of the Committee against Torture: United States of America,* ¶¶ 20–21, CAT/C/USA/CO/2 (25 July 2006).

101. Burgers & Danelius, 117.

102. The committee sometimes adds that in light of the finding of torture, it "need not consider whether there was a violation of article 16, paragraph 1 [on cruel, inhuman, or degrading treatment]" (*Communication No. 172/2000: Serbia and Montenegro,* ¶ 7.2, CAT/C/35/D/172/2000 (29 Nov. 2005)).

103. *Communication No. 171/2000: Serbia and Montenegro,* ¶ 7.1, CAT/C/34/D/171/2000 (23 May 2005); *Communication No. 207/2002: Serbia and Montenegro,* ¶ 5.3, CAT/C/33/D/207/2002 (29 Nov. 2004).

104. E.g., *Communication No. 278/2005: Switzerland,* ¶¶ 6.3, 6.4, CAT/C/36/D/278/2005 (17 May 2006); *Communication No. 256/2004: Sweden,* ¶¶ 9.2, 9.3, CAT/C/36/D/256/2004 (17 May 2006); *Communication No. 254/2004: Switzerland,* ¶¶ 6.3, 6.4, CAT/C/35/D/254/2004 (5 Dec. 2005); *Communication No. 245/2004: Canada,* ¶¶ 8.1, 8.3, CAT/C/35/D/245/2004 (5 Dec. 2005); *Communication No. 238/2003: Norway,* ¶ 13.1,

CAT/C/35/D/238/2003 (5 Dec. 2005); *Communication No. 194/2001: France,* ¶ 9.2, CAT/ C/34/D/194/2001 (24 May 2005). For recent cases finding violations in the context of rendition or deportation, see *Communication No. 258/2004: Canada,* CAT/C/35/D/ 258/2004 (5 Dec. 2005); *Communication No. 233/2003: Sweden,* CAT/C/34/D/233/2003 (24 May 2005); *Communication No. 226/2003: Sweden,* CAT/C/34/D/226/2003 (27 May 2005); *Communication No. 195/2002: France,* CAT/C/34/D/195/2002 (24 May 2005). For denial of relief even though an applicant had been tortured in the country to which he would be deported, see *Communication No. 220/2002: Sweden,* ¶ 8.3, CAT/C/34/D/220/2002 (17 May 2005).

105. Pheng Cheah, *Inhuman Conditions* (Cambridge, Mass.: Harvard Univ. Press, 2006), 145–77. *Cf.* Marie-Bénédict Dembour, *Who Believes in Human Rights? Reflections on the European Convention* (Cambridge: Cambridge Univ. Press, 2006). Crucial issues remain, of course, such as (1) what it means to "benefit" from rights and (2) why people should look to law and government for the shape and definition of their identities and lives.

106. U.N. Security Council, *Resolution 1373,* S. Res. 1373 (28 Sept. 2001). See also U.N. Counter-Terrorism Committee, *Survey of the Implementation of Security Council Resolution 1373 (2001),* S/2008/379 (10 June 2008).

CHAPTER TWO

1. Council of Europe, *Convention for the Protection of Human Rights and Fundamental Freedoms,* arts. 3, 5 (1950), 213 U.N.T.S. 222.

2. Id., arts. 13, 15, 19, 34. Protocol 11 rewrote Article 19, which had provided for the commission and the court. For a good, brief description of how the ECHR operates under Protocol 11 (and the more recent Protocol 14), see Marie-Bénédicte Dembour, *Who Believes in Human Rights? Reflections on the European Convention* (Cambridge: Cambridge Univ. Press, 2006), 24–26.

3. Council of Europe, *European Convention for the Prevention of Torture and Inhuman or Degrading Treatment or Punishment* (1989), 27 ILM 1152.

4. Steven Greer, *The European Convention on Human Rights: Achievements, Problems, and Prospects* (Cambridge: Cambridge Univ. Press, 2006), 56. See also id., 20; George Letsas, *A Theory of Interpretation of the European Convention on Human Rights* (Oxford: Oxford Univ. Press, 2007), 31–36.

5. Nevmerzhitsky v. Ukraine, ECHR, No. 54825/00, ¶¶ 73, 79 (5 Apr. 2005); Z & Others v United Kingdom, ECHR, No. 29392/95, ¶ 103 (10 May 2001).

6. Dembour, 13. See also Greer, xvi, 38, 55.

7. Luzius Wildhaber, "The Role of the European Court of Human Rights: An Evaluation," *Mediterranean Journal of Human Rights* 8 (2004): 27; Luzius Wildhaber, "A Constitutional Future for the European Court of Human Rights?" *Human Rights Law Journal* 23 (2002): 163. Wildhaber admits that "this analysis of the Convention system is not universally accepted," but he insists that "given the current situation with the ever-rising case-load . . . the future of the system cannot be exclusively individual-relief based" ("Constitutional Failure," 163).

8. For discussion of accommodation clauses and the court's derogation jurisprudence, see Dembour, 47–49; Letsas, 80–98; Claire Ovey & Robin White, *Jacobs & White: The European Convention on Human Rights,* 4th ed. (Oxford: Oxford Univ. Press, 2006), 439–50; Anna-Lena Svensson-McCarthy, *The International Law of Human Rights and States of Exception* (The Hague: Martinus Nijhoff, 1998), 324–25.

9. Wildhaber, "Constitutional Future," 162. For other discussions—and criticisms—of the margin of appreciation doctrine, see Dembour, 37, 70–73; Letsas, 4, 80–98; Ovey & White, 53–54. As Ovey & White point out (53, 445–47), the doctrine applies with particular force to the issue of emergencies and derogations. *See, e.g.,* A and others v. United Kingdom, ECHR, No. 3455/05, ¶ 180 (19 Feb. 2009) ("the national authorities enjoy a wide margin of appreciation under Article 15 in assessing whether the life of the nation is threatened by a public emergency"; with respect to the threat posed by al Qaeda, "it was for each Government . . . to make their own assessment on the basis of the facts known to them"). For the doctrine's origins in Greece's complaints about British repression in Cyprus, see A. W. Brian Simpson, *Human Rights and the End of Empire* (Oxford: Oxford Univ. Press, 2001), 1000–1005.

10. N. v. United Kingdom, ECHR, No. 26565/05, ¶ 44 (27 May 2008).

11. Greer, 233–34.

12. A. R. Mowbray, *The Development of Positive Obligations under the European Convention on Human Rights by the European Court of Human Rights* (Oxford: Hart, 2004), 2. See also Letsas, 61–67; Ovey & White, 28–29, 84–86.

13. Dembour, 9.

14. Greer, 57, 171, 195–213.

15. Greek Case, *Yearbook of the European Convention on Human Rights* 12 (1969): 186. For early application of the three-tier approach by the court, see Tryer v. United Kingdom, ECHR, No. 5856/72, ¶ 29 (25 Apr. 1978). For general discussion of the Greek Case, see Ovey & White, 78–79.

16. *Greek Case,* 499, 501. See also Nigel S. Rodley, "The Definition(s) of Torture in International Law," *Current Legal Problems* 55 (2002): 470–71.

17. Nigel S. Rodley, *The Treatment of Prisoners under International Law,* 2nd ed. (Oxford: Oxford Univ. Press, 1999), 95–96. For the case law's effort to draw these distinctions, see id., 77–106.

18. Eren v. Turkey, ECHR, No. 32347/02, ¶ 35 (14 Oct. 2008); Boicenco v. Moldova, ECHR, No. 41088/05, ¶¶ 103, 109 (11 July 2006); Dıkme v. Turkey, ECHR, No. 20869/92, ¶ 73 (11 July 2000); Georgiev v. Bulgaria, ECHR, No. 61275/00, ¶ 36 (16 Oct. 2008). See also Ovey & White, 86–87.

19. A. v. United Kingdom, No. 100/1997/884/1096, ¶ 22 (23 Sept. 1998). See Mowbray, 43–46.

20. Soering v. United Kingdom, 11 EHHR 439, ¶¶ 88, 91 (1989). See also Chahal v. United Kingdom, ECHR, No. 22414/93 (15 Nov. 1996); Mamatkulov & Askarov v. Turkey, ECHR, Nos. 46827/99 & 46951/99 (4 Feb. 2005); Nnyanzi v. United Kingdom, ECHR, No. 21878/06 (8 Apr. 2008); NA. v. United Kingdom, ECHR, No. 25904/07 (17 July 2008). The deportation cases also include consideration of health care risks, particularly of people suffering from AIDS, but the Grand Chamber of the court recently insisted that relief in such cases would be very unusual (*N.,* ¶¶ 32–43).

21. *Soering,* ¶ 89; *Chahal,* ¶¶ 79–82. See also Greer, 234. *Chahal* also declared that "the activities of the individual in question, however undesirable or dangerous, cannot be a material consideration" in the decision to extradite. The court reaffirmed this rule in *Saadi v. Italy,* ECHR, No. 37201/06, ¶ 139 (28 Feb. 2008).

22. Selmouni v. France, 29 EHRR 25, ¶ 99 (1999); *Dkme,* ¶ 90.

23. *A and others,* ¶¶ 127, 134; Ciorap v. Moldova, ECHR, No. 12066/02, ¶ 63 (19 June 2007).

24. *N.,* ¶ 44; *Nevmerzhitsky,* ¶¶ 93–98; *Ciorap,* ¶¶ 76–77; Gäfgen v. Germany, ECHR, No. 22978/05, ¶¶ 98–106 (30 June 2008). See also Jalloh v. Germany, ECHR, No. 54810/00, ¶ 105 (11 July 2006) ("incriminating evidence . . . obtained as a result of . . . torture—

should never be relied on as proof of the victim's guilt"). Outside the Article 3 context, no reported ECHR decision has applied a convention right to prevent a deportation, although the cases hold out the possibility. See Lord Bingham's discussion in *EM v. Secretary of State* (2008 UKHL 64, ¶¶ 32–38 (22 Oct. 2008)), in which the House of Lords determined that Article 8 of the European Convention would be violated by a deportation but stressed that the case was "exceptional" (id., ¶ 58 (Lord Carswell)).

25. Ireland v. United Kingdom, 2 EHRR 25, ¶¶ 167–68 (1978).

26. Aksoy v. Turkey, 23 EHRR 553, ¶¶ 63–64 (1996); Bati et al. v. Turkey, 2004 ECHR 246, ¶¶ 120, 123 (2004); Akkoç v. Turkey, ECHR, Nos. 22947/93 & 22948/93, ¶ 115 (10 Oct. 2000); İlhan v. Turkey, ECHR, No. 22277/93, ¶ 85 (27 June 2000).

27. *Selmouni*, ¶ 100; *Akkoç*, ¶ 115; *İlhan*, ¶ 85. See also Malcolm D. Evans, "Getting to Grips with Torture," *Int'l & Comparative Law Quarterly* 51 (2002): 377; Mary Ellen O'Connell, "Affirming the Ban on Harsh Interrogation," *Ohio State Law Journal* 66 (2005): 1249; Rodley, "Definition(s)," 489–90 (endorsing a focus on purpose).

28. *Selmouni*, ¶ 101; A and Others v. Secretary of State, 2005 UKHL 71, ¶ 53 (opinion of Lord Bingham). See also David Hope, "Torture," *Int'l & Comparative Law Quarterly* 53 (2004): 826.

29. *Selmouni*, ¶¶ 102–3; Mikhayez v. Russia, ECHR, No. 77617/01, ¶¶ 20, 129, 135 (26 Apr. 2006).

30. Fionnuala Ní Aoláin, "The European Convention on Human Rights and Its Prohibition on Torture," in Sanford Levinson, ed., *Torture: A Collection* (New York: Oxford Univ. Press, 2004), 220, 223; *Akkoç*, ¶¶ 128–29.

31. Ní Aoláin, 222. See also Fionnuala Ní Aoláin & Colm Campbell, "The Paradox of Transition in Conflicted Democracies," *Human Rights Quarterly* 27 (2005): 203. For sovereign immunity, see Al-Adsani v. United Kingdom, 34 EHRR 273 (2001).

32. Edward W. Said, *Orientalism* (New York: Pantheon, 1978), 108–9, 317–18.

33. Giorgio Agamben, *Homo Sacer* (1995), trans. Daniel Heller-Roazen (Stanford: Stanford Univ. Press, 1998).

34. Refah Partisi v. Turkey, ECHR, Nos. 41340/98, 41342/98, 41343/98, & 41344/98, ¶ 70 (31 July 2001).

CHAPTER THREE

1. *Message from the President Transmitting Four Treaties Pertaining to Human Rights*, Sen. Exec. Doc. C, D, E, & F, 95th Cong., 2nd Sess. (1978), vi, viii, xv. For definitions of "reservations," "understandings," and "declarations," see Congressional Research Service, *Treaties and Other International Agreements: The Role of the United States Senate*, S. Rpt. 71, 106th Cong., 2nd Sess. 39 (2001), 125–126. For more detailed discussion of U.S. ratification of the ICCPR and Convention against Torture, see John T. Parry, "Torture Nation, Torture Law," *Georgetown Law Journal* 97 (2009): 1034–51.

2. *International Human Rights Treaties*, Hearings before the Senate Committee on Foreign Relations, 96th Cong., 1st Sess. (14, 15, 16, & 19 Nov. 1979), 26, 29–30, 36–37, 39–40, 42.

3. *International Covenant on Civil and Political Rights*, S. Exec. Rpt. 23, 102nd Cong., 2nd Sess. (1992), 2.

4. *Message from the President of the United States Transmitting the Convention against Torture and Other Cruel, Inhuman, or Degrading Treatment or Punishment*, S. Treaty Doc. 100–20, 100th Cong., 2nd Sess. (1988), 3–5.

5. Id., v, 4–5, 15.

6. Id., 5–6.

7. Id., 15–16.

8. Id., 6.

9. Prepared statement of Abraham D. Sofaer, legal advisor, U.S. Department of State, in *Convention against Torture,* Hearing before the Senate Committee on Foreign Relations, 101st Cong., 2nd Sess. (30 Jan. 1990), 11.

10. Prepared statement of Mark Richard, deputy assistant attorney general, U.S. Department of Justice, in *Convention against Torture* (hearing), 16.

11. Id., 17.

12. Id., 10, 17.

13. *Convention against Torture and Other Cruel, Inhuman, or Degrading Treatment or Punishment,* S. Exec. Rpt. 101-30, 101st Cong., 2nd Sess. (1990), 4, 7–8, 10.

14. 36 Cong. Rec. S17487–89 (27 Oct. 1990); *Resolution of Advice and Consent to Ratification of the Convention against Torture and Other Forms of Cruel, Inhuman, or Degrading Treatment or Punishment,* 136 Cong. Rec. S17491 (27 Oct. 1990).

15. Federal courts have held that the convention is not self-executing. See Cornejo-Barreto v. Seifert, 379 F.3d 1075 (9th Cir. 2004) (collecting cases), *vacated as moot,* 389 F.3d 1307 (9th Cir. 2004) (en banc).

16. *Resolution of Advice and Consent,* parts II(1)(a) & III(1). *Specific intent* is a common-law term for a high level of mens rea, as opposed to the more ordinary general intent. See also Renee C. Redman, "Defining 'Torture,'" *NYU Annual Survey of American Law* 62 (2007): 465–95.

17. *Resolution of Advice and Consent,* part II(1)(a).

18. Id., part I(1).

19. Abraham Sofaer, "No Exceptions," *Wall Street Journal,* 26 Nov. 2005, A11.

20. *International Covenant on Civil and Political Rights,* Hearing before the Senate Committee on Foreign Relations, S. Hearing 478, 102nd Cong., 1st Sess. (21 Nov. 1991), 8, 9, 10, 14, 112; 1992 S. Rpt., 2, 12.

21. 1992 S. Rpt., 4; 138 Cong. Rec. S4781 (2 Apr. 1992).

22. Torture Victim Protection Act of 1991, Pub. L. No. 102-256, 106 Stat. 73, in note, 28 U.S.C. § 1350 (2000). The definition of *United States* in Section 2340 means that some acts could be outside the United States for that statute but within the "special and maritime jurisdiction" of the United States for other federal criminal statutes.

23. Foreign Affairs Reform and Restructuring Act, Pub. L. No. 105-277, § 2242(a), (b), 112 Stat. 2681 (1998).

24. 18 U.S.C. § 2340(1)–(2); TVPA, 28 U.S.C. § 1350 note; FARRA, § 2242(f)(2).

25. 28 U.S.C. § 1350; Sosa v. Alvarez-Machain, 542 U.S. 692, 724–25, 732–33 (2004).

26. Filartiga v. Pena-Irala, 630 F.2d 876 (2nd Cir. 1980); Aldana v. Del Monte Fresh Produce, N.A., Inc., 416 F.3d 1242, 1251 (11th Cir. 2005).

27. Compare *Aldana,* 416 F.3d at 1246–47, with Aldana v. Del Monte Fresh Produce, N.A., Inc., 452 F.3d 1284 (11th Cir. 2006).

28. Julian Ku, "The Third Wave," *Emory Int'l Law Review* 19 (2005): 105. Claims for violations of treaty rights under Section 1983 of Title 42 of the U.S. Code usually founder on the self-execution issue, but the jurisprudence in this area is developing rapidly.

29. Federal courts have accepted the reservation that the ICCPR is not self-executing. Margaret L. Satterthwaite, "Rendered Meaningless," *George Washington Law Review* 75 (2007): 1365 n. 184.

30. For the controversies in the United States over whether treaties should be presumed self-executing and over the use of reservations against self-execution, see Curtis A. Bradley & Jack L. Goldsmith, "Treaties, Human Rights, and Conditional Consent,"

Univ. of Pennsylvania Law Review 149 (2000): 399; Carlos Manuel Vázquez, "The Four Doctrines of Self-Executing Treaties," *American Journal of Int'l Law* 89 (1995): 695. See also Medellin v. Texas, 128 S. Ct. 1346, 1356–67 (2008) (stopping short of adopting presumption against self-execution, but rejecting a presumption in favor of it).

31. Whether the Geneva Conventions are self-executing or confer individual rights in U.S. courts remains unclear. See Hamdan v. Rumsfeld, 548 U.S. 557, 627–28 (2006). The War Crimes Act (18 U.S.C. 2441) originally criminalized violations of obligations imposed by international agreements, such as the Geneva Conventions. The 2006 Military Commissions Act amended § 2441 to include torture and cruel or inhuman treatment as specific crimes, but it provided definitions that limit the conduct subject to prosecution, as chapter 7 discusses.

32. For more extended versions of the analysis in this section, see John T. Parry, "Terrorism and the New Criminal Process," *William & Mary Bill of Rights Journal* 15 (2007): 733; John T. Parry, "Constitutional Interpretation, Coercive Interrogation, and Civil Rights Litigation after *Chavez v. Martinez*," *Georgia Law Review* 39 (2005): 812–37; John T. Parry, "Judicial Restraints on Illegal State Violence," *Vanderbilt Journal of Transnational Law* 35 (2002): 73.

33. For statutes that provide grants of authority, see 28 U.S.C. §§ 533, 535, 538, 540, 540A, 540B. For delegation of investigatory authority to the FBI, see 28 C.F.R. § 0.85 (2006). See also 28 C.F.R. §§ 8.1, 8.2 (power to seize property). For other sources of FBI authority, see 18 U.S.C. §§ 3052, 3105, 3107; Federal Rule of Criminal Procedure 41(a) & (d).

34. *E.g., Sosa*, 542 U.S. at 2768; Atwater v. City of Lago Vista, 532 U.S. 318 (2001).

35. *In re* Debs, 158 U.S. 564, 579–83 (1895). See also Oren Gross & Fionniala Ní Aoláin, *Law in Times of Crisis* (Cambridge: Cambridge Univ. Press, 2006), 74–77; Henry P. Monaghan, "The Protective Power of the Presidency," *Columbia Law Review* 93 (1993): 1; Parry, "Judicial Restraints," 131–34.

36. Youngstown Sheet & Tube Co. v. Sawyer, 343 U.S. 579 (1952); *Hamdan*, 548 U.S. 557.

37. *E.g.*, Sanford Levinson, "Constitutional Norms in a State of Permanent Emergency," *Georgia Law Review* 40 (2006): 699; Jules Lobel, "Emergency Power and the Decline of Liberalism," *Yale Law Journal* 98 (1989): 1385; Michael Stokes Paulsen, "The Constitution of Necessity," *Notre Dame Law Review* 79 (2004): 1257.

38. Boyd v. United States, 116 U.S. 616, 630, 635 (1886).

39. Levinson, "Constitutional Norms," 718–19; Anderson v. Creighton, 483 U.S. 635, 643–44 (1987).

40. Schmerber v. California, 384 U.S. 757, 762, 768 (1966). See also Morgan Cloud, "A Liberal House Divided," *Ohio State Journal of Criminal Law* 3 (2005): 33; Silas J. Wasserstrom, "The Court's Turn Toward a General Reasonableness Interpretation of the Fourth Amendment," *American Criminal Law Review* 27 (1989): 119.

41. Hannah Arendt, *The Origins of Totalitarianism*, new ed. (New York: Harcourt Brace Jovanovich, 1973), 463, 464, 466.

42. Terry v. Ohio, 392 U.S. 1, 9 (1968).

43. These concerns also play out with the "private police," who outnumber the official police and exercise discretion outside the reach of most constitutional law. See David A. Sklansky, "The Private Police," *UCLA Law Review* 46 (1999): 1165–1287; Ric Simmons, "Private Criminal Justice," *Wake Forest Law Review* 42 (2007): 911.

44. Florida v. Bostick, 501 U.S. 429, 435–36, 438 (1991).

45. United States v. Drayton, 536 U.S. 194, 204–5 (2002).

46. Id. at 206–7.

47. See also Samson v. California, 547 U.S. 843 (2006) (searches of parolees); United States v. Knights, 534 U.S. 112 (2001) (searches of probationers); Wilkinson v. Austin, 545 U.S. 209 (2005) (procedural due process rights of prisoners).

48. Margaret L. Raymond, "The Right to Refuse and the Obligation to Comply," *Buffalo Law Review* 54 (2007): 1484. Raymond compares these cases to statutes that create duties of cooperation, such that defendants are often caught between the risk of failing to comply and the risk of waiving their rights.

49. *E.g.,* Downes v. Bidwell, 182 U.S. 244 (1901); Dorr v. United States, 195 U.S. 138 (1904). See Kal Raustiala, "The Geography of Justice," *Fordham Law Review* 73 (2005): 2501; Kermit Roosevelt III, "Guantánamo and the Conflict of Laws," *Univ. of Pennsylvania Law Review* 153 (2005): 2017; Gerald L. Neuman, "Extraterritorial Rights and Constitutional Methodology after *Rasul v. Bush,*" *Univ. of Pennsylvania Law Review* 153 (2005): 2073.

50. Reid v. Covert, 354 U.S. 1 (1957) (plurality opinion) (citizen); United States v. Verdugo-Urquidez, 494 U.S. 259 (1990) (action against noncitizen's property in Mexico not regulated by Constitution); Harbury v. Deutch, 233 F.3d 596, 602–4 (D.C. Cir. 2000) (denying Fifth Amendment claim of alleged torture under CIA auspices of noncitizen overseas), *rev'd on other grounds,* 536 U.S. 403 (2002); Arar v. Ashcroft, 414 F. Supp. 2d 250, 276–79 (E.D.N.Y. 2006) (due process rights of aliens, particularly those with connection to the United States, are "unresolved"), *aff'd,* 532 F.3d 157 (2nd Cir. 2008). The Court of Appeals for the Second Circuit granted a rehearing en banc in *Arar* on August 12, 2008, and had not issued a decision at the time I completed this manuscript.

51. *See* Boumediene v. Bush, 128 S.Ct. 2229 (2008).

52. United States v. Alvarez-Machain, 504 U.S. 655, 662 (1992). The Court conceded that a specific ban on kidnapping in an extradition treaty might lead to a different result.

53. Giorgio Agamben, *State of Exception,* trans. Kevin Attell (Chicago: Univ. of Chicago Press, 2005).

54. *See* Military Commissions Act, Pub. L. No. 109-366, § 6, 120 Stat. 2600 (2006).

55. Compare Seth F. Kreimer, "Too Close to the Rack and the Screw," *Univ. of Pennsylvania Journal of Constitutional Law* 6 (2003): 300, and Seth F. Kreimer, "'Torture Lite,' 'Full Bodied' Torture, and the Insulation of Legal Conscience," *Journal of National Security Law & Policy* 1 (2005): 187, with Marcy Strauss, "Torture," *New York Law School Law Review* 48 (2003): 201.

56. *Anderson,* 483 U.S. at 643–44; *Atwater,* 532 U.S. at 347.

57. Graham v. Connor, 490 U.S. 386, 388 (1989); Saucier v. Katz, 533 U.S. 194, 205 (2001).

58. Under *Tennessee v. Garner* (471 U.S. 1, 3 (1985)), use of deadly force required "probable cause to believe that the suspect poses a significant threat of death or serious physical injury to the officer or others." But in *Scott v. Harris,* 550 U.S. 372 (2007), the Court held that claims of deadly force turn on the same assessment of reasonableness as any other claim of excessive force.

59. Florida v. J.L., 529 U.S. 266, 274 (2000).

60. Michigan v. Summers, 452 U.S. 692, 702–3 (1981). See also Los Angeles County v. Rettele, 550 U.S. 609 (2007) (officers executing a search warrant acted reasonably when they ordered a naked couple out of bed, forced them to stand at gunpoint for a few minutes, and then permitted them to dress).

61. Muehler v. Mena, 544 U.S. 93, 98–100 (2005); id. at 108 (Stevens, J., concurring in the judgment). See also Illinois v. McArthur, 531 U.S. 326 (2001) (police may detain residents outside their home while waiting for approval of a warrant application).

62. See United States v. Ankeny, 490 F.3d 744 (9th Cir. 2007) (use of flash-bang de-

vices, rubber bullets, and other force to serve search warrants, burning the defendant and damaging a home, did not require exclusion of evidence obtained in the search, even if the methods were unreasonable).

63. Albert W. Alschuler, "A Peculiar Privilege in Historical Perspective," *Michigan Law Review* 94 (1996): 2651.

64. Miranda v. Arizona, 384 U.S. 436 (1966); Richard A. Leo, "The Impact of Miranda Revisited," *Journal of Criminal Law & Criminology* 86 (1996): 653–54.

65. New York v. Quarles, 467 U.S. 649 (1984). For the exceptions, see Wayne R. LaFave et al., *Criminal Procedure*, 4th ed. (St. Paul: West, 2004), §§ 9.5, 9.6.

66. Welsh S. White, *Miranda's Waning Protections* (Ann Arbor: Univ. of Michigan Press, 2001); Richard J. Ofshe & Richard A. Leo, "The Decision to Confess Falsely," *Denver Univ. Law Review* 74 (1997): 985–86; Richard A. Leo & Richard J. Ofshe, "The Consequences of False Confessions," *Journal of Criminal Law & Criminology* 88 (1998): 440–41.

67. Miller v. Fenton, 796 F.2d 598, 603 (3rd Cir. 1986).

68. Dickerson v. United States, 530 U.S. 428, 434 (2000); Colorado v. Connelly, 479 U.S. 157, 167 (1986).

69. *Dickerson*, 530 U.S. at 444; Missouri v. Seibert, 542 U.S. 600, 608–9; W. White, 39–48, 120–22.

70. *E.g.*, Chambers v. Florida, 309 U.S. 227 (1940); Ashcraft v. Tennessee, 322 U.S. 143, 160 (1944) (Jackson, J., dissenting). See also Brown v. Mississippi, 297 U.S. 278, 286 (1936) (interrogation obtained in violation of due process was "revolting to the sense of justice").

71. Chavez v. Martinez, 538 U.S. 760, 766–67 (2003) (plurality opinion); id. at 778 (Souter, J., concurring in the judgment) (quoting *Miranda*, 384 U.S. at 515, 517 (Harlan, J., dissenting)). Compare id. at 783 (Stevens, J., concurring in part and dissenting in part) (conduct was "functional equivalent of an attempt to obtain an involuntary confession from a prisoner by torturous means").

72. County of Sacramento v. Lewis, 523 U.S. 833, 849 (1998); *Chavez*, 538 U.S. at 775 (opinion of Thomas, J.), 787–88 (Stevens, J., concurring in part and dissenting in part), 796–99 (Kennedy, J., concurring in part and dissenting in part), 799 (Ginsburg, J., concurring in part and dissenting in part).

73. *Arar*, 414 F. Supp. 2d at 274. For the subsequent procedural history of the case, see *supra* note 50.

74. Washington v. Glucksberg, 521 U.S. 702, 721 (1997); *Chavez*, 538 U.S. at 775–76. Justice Thomas treated the "shocks the conscience" test and fundamental rights approach as distinct in *Chavez*, but *Lewis* suggested that the fundamental rights approach applies to legislative action and that the "shocks the conscience" test applies to executive action, which would weaken due process protection against coercion. See *Lewis*, 523 U.S. at 845–47 & n. 8.

75. Farmer v. Brennan, 511 U.S. 825, 837 (1994).

76. Daryl J. Levinson, "Rights Essentialism and Remedial Equilibration," *Columbia Law Review* 99 (1999): 857. See also Rajeswari Sunder Rajan, *The Scandal of the State* (Durham, N.C.: Duke Univ. Press, 2003), 6 ("Any understanding of state-citizen relations requires, therefore, attention to the microlevel workings of state regimes, as much as to the terms of liberal democratic principles in the constitutional provisions; nor is the distance and disjuncture between the two always reducible to the (inevitable) gap between practice and promise.").

77. Parry, "Judicial Restraints," 77–79, 121 n. 220. See also John Sifton, "United States Military and Central Intelligence Personnel Abroad," *Harvard Journal on Legislation* 43 (2006): 489–90 (few prosecutions in response to counterterror abuses).

78. Hudson v. Michigan, 547 U.S. 586, 594–97 (2006); Sanchez-Llamas v. Oregon, 548 U.S. 331, 347–49 (2006).

79. 28 U.S.C. § 14141; Parry, "Judicial Restraints," 75.

80. City of Los Angeles v. Lyons, 461 U.S. 95 (1983).

81. Harold S. Lewis Jr. & Elizabeth J. Norman, *Civil Rights Law and Practice,* 2nd ed. (St. Paul: Thomson-West, 2004), 473. See also Seth F. Kreimer, "Exploring the Dark Matter of Judicial Review," *William & Mary Bill of Rights Journal* 5 (1997): 501 n. 172.

82. Parry, "Judicial Restraints," 98–100.

83. Individuals may seek damages in federal court against state officials under Section 1983 of Title 42 of the U.S. Code and against federal officials under Bivens v. Six Unknown Named Agents of Federal Bureau of Narcotics, 403 U.S. 388 (1971).

84. El-Masri v. United States, 479 F.3d 296 (4th Cir. 2007); *Arar,* 414 F. Supp. 2d at 281–83 (see *supra* note 50). But see Mohamed v. Jeppesen Dataplan, Inc., 563 F.3d 992 (9th Cir. 2009) (interpreting the state secrets concept narrowly).

85. Wilson v. Layne, 526 U.S. 603, 614–15 (1999) (quoting *Anderson,* 483 U.S. at 640). See also Stump v. Sparkman, 435 U.S. 349 (1978) (discussing absolute immunity).

86. *E.g.,* California Penal Code §§ 189, 190.2 (14), 206.

87. State criminal charges against federal officials have limited utility because the official would likely remove the case to federal court under Section 1442(a)(1) of Title 28 of the U.S. Code and might seek dismissal based on a claim of immunity. See *In re* Neagle, 135 U.S. 1 (1890); Idaho v. Horiuchi, 253 F.3d 359 (9th Cir.) (en banc), *vacated as moot,* 266 F.3d 979 (2001).

88. 18 USC §§ 113 (assault), 114 (maiming with intent to torture), 241 (conspiracy against civil rights), 242 (deprivation of civil rights), 956 (conspiracy to kill, kidnap, maim, or injure persons or damage property in a foreign country), 1111 (murder), 1112 (manslaughter), 1117 (conspiracy to murder), 1201 (kidnapping), 1203 (hostage taking), 2241 (aggravated sexual abuse), 2242 (sexual abuse), 2244 (abusive sexual contact), 2245 (sexual abuse resulting in death), 2340 (torture committed outside the United States by U.S. nationals and non-U.S. nationals later found in the United States), and 2441 (war crimes of torture and "cruel or inhuman treatment").

89. 18 U.S.C. § 7(9).

90. United States v. Corey, 232 F.3d 1166 (9th Cir. 2000).

91. Indictment, United States v. Passaro, No. 5:04-CR-211-1, U.S. District Court for the Eastern District of North Carolina (17 June 2004). See also "Civilian Sentenced in Afghan Beating," *Associated Press,* 14 Feb. 2007. The Uniform Code of Military Justice is also relevant. It prohibits "flogging, . . . branding, marking . . . , or any other cruel or unusual punishment"; "[t]he use of irons"; "cruelty and maltreatment"; and more familiar crimes, such as conspiracy, murder, manslaughter, rape, and maiming (Uniform Code of Military Justice, 10 U.S.C. ch. 47, arts. 55, 93, 118, 119, 120, 124). See also id., arts. 81 (conspiracy), 133 (conduct unbecoming an officer), 134 (conduct prejudicial to good order and discipline of armed forces); Martin N. White, "Charging War Crimes: A Primer for the Practitioner," *Army Lawyer* (Feb. 2006): 1–11.

92. John T. Parry, "The Virtue of Necessity," *Houston Law Review* 36 (1999): 397.

93. United States v. Bailey, 444 U.S. 394, 415 n. 11 (1980).

94. For discussion of self-defense, see Miriam Gur-Arye, "Can the War against Terror Justify the Use of Force in Interrogations?" in Sanford Levinson, ed., *Torture: A Collection* (New York: Oxford Univ. Press, 2004), 183; Michael S. Moore, "Torture and the Balance of Evils," *Israel Law Review* 23 (1989): 323.

95. *Bailey,* 444 U.S. at 410, 415 n. 11.

96. United States v. Oakland Cannabis Buyers' Coop., 532 U.S. 483, 490–91 (2001).

97. For an overview of necessity in the federal courts, see Stephen S. Schwartz, "Is There a Common Law Necessity Defense in Federal Criminal Law," *Univ. of Chicago L. Rev.* 75 (2008): 1259.

98. United States v. Schoon, 971 F.2d 193, 196 (9th Cir. 1991).

99. United States v. Aguilar, 883 F.2d 662, 693 (9th Cir. 1989). Section 3.02(1) of the Model Penal Code provides a slightly different version.

100. The Model Penal Code commentary states that necessity is a defense to a homicide that results in a "net saving of lives" (id., comment 3).

101. Public Committee against Torture in Israel v. State of Israel, H.C. 5100/94, 53(4) P.D. 817, ¶ 39 (1999).

102. John T. Parry & Welsh S. White, "Interrogating Suspected Terrorists," *Univ. of Pittsburgh Law Review* 63 (2002): 743.

103. Kim Lane Scheppele, "Hypothetical Torture in the 'War on Terrorism,'" *Journal of National Security Law & Policy* 1 (2005): 285; Henry Shue, "Torture in Dreamland," *Case Western Reserve Journal of Int'l Law* 37 (2006): 231; Geoffrey C. Hazard et al., *The Law and Ethics of Lawyering*, 3rd ed. (New York: Foundation, 1999), 312.

104. *Schoon*, 971 F.2d at 200 (Fernandez, J., concurring); Parry, "Virtue," 437–46.

105. *Cf.* Jay S. Bybee, Assistant Attorney General, *Memorandum for Alberto R. Gonzales, Counsel to the President, re: Standards of Conduct for Interrogation under 18 U.S.C. §§ 2340–2340A* (1 Aug. 2002), in Karen J. Greenberg & Joshua L. Dratel eds., *The Torture Papers* (New York: Cambridge Univ. Press, 2005), 209 n. 23.

106. United States v. Laub, 385 U.S. 475, 487 (1967). See also John T. Parry, "Culpability, Mistake, and Official Interpretations of Law," *American Journal of Criminal Law* 25 (1997): 1.

107. United States v. Pennsylvania Indus. Chemical Corp., 411 U.S. 655, 675 (1973).

108. See also United States v. Barker, 546 F.2d 940 (D.C. Cir. 1976) (reversing conviction of two Watergate burglars in part because they claimed that White House officials told them they would not be violating the law).

109. *Scott*, 550 U.S. at 383 (quoting United States v. Place, 462 U.S. 696, 703 (1983)).

110. Id., 384–85.

111. Relying on *Tennessee v. Garner*, Mark Weisburd has argued that the choice between war and crime models for responding to terrorism matters, because different rules govern the ability to use deadly force (A. Mark Weisburd, "Al-Qaeda and the Laws of War," *Lewis & Clark Law Review* 11 (2007): 1066). *Scott v. Harris* has now displaced *Garner*. Whether or not the Court was thinking about terrorism in *Scott*, the case blurs the distinction between the war and crime models by opening more space for "necessary" force.

112. *Chavez*, 538 U.S. at 773 (opinion of Thomas, J.), 783–84 (Stevens, J., concurring in part and dissenting in part), 789 (Kennedy, J., concurring in part and dissenting in part). See also *Sosa*, 542 U.S. at 732; McKune v. Lile, 536 U.S. 24, 41 (2002).

113. *E.g.*, Henry P. Monaghan, "Constitutional Common Law," *Harvard Law Review* 89 (1975): 2–3 (some decisions go beyond what the Constitution requires and should be considered constitutional common law); Lawrence Gene Sager, "Fair Measure," *Harvard Law Review* 91 (1978): 1212–13 (some decisions underenforce constitutional norms that should be considered binding to their "full conceptual boundaries").

CHAPTER FOUR

1. *Universal Declaration of Human Rights by the World's Religions*, art. 1 (2000). See also Ronald Dworkin, *Is Democracy Possible Here?* (Princeton: Princeton Univ. Press,

2006), 35. For rights as trumps, see id., 31; Ronald Dworkin, *Taking Rights Seriously* (Cambridge, Mass.: Harvard Univ. Press, 1977), xi (also denying that rights "have some special metaphysical character"). See also George Letsas, *A Theory of Interpretation of the European Convention on Human Rights* (Oxford: Oxford Univ. Press, 2007), 110–17.

2. Lori F. Damrosch et al., *International Law,* 4th ed. (St. Paul: West, 2001), 586. See David Kennedy, *The Dark Sides of Virtue* (Princeton: Princeton Univ. Press, 2004), 277–79; Michael Ignatieff, *Human Rights as Politics and Idolatry,* ed. Amy Gutman (Princeton: Princeton Univ. Press, 2001), 53.

3. Louis Henkin, *The Age of Rights* (New York: Columbia Univ. Press, 1990), 2.

4. Anthony D'Amato, "International Law," in Kermit L. Hall et al., eds., *The Oxford Companion to American Law* (New York: Oxford Univ. Press, 2002), 426.

5. To some extent, my description of rights has some affinity with Jeremy Bentham's criticism of the Declaration of the Rights of Man and the Citizen, which Marie-Bénédicte Dembour associates with a "realist" view of rights. See Marie-Bénédicte Dembour, *Who Believes in Human Rights: Reflections on the European Convention* (Cambridge: Cambridge Univ. Press, 2006), 30–35.

6. Refah Partisi v. Turkey, ECHR, Nos. 41340/98, 41342/98, 41343/98, & 41344/98, ¶ 70 (31 July 2001) (emphasis added). The ECHR Grand Chamber endorsed this language when it affirmed. See Refah Partisi v. Turkey, ECHR, Nos. 41340/98, 41342/98, 41343/98, & 41344/98, ¶ 119 (13 Feb. 2003).

7. For a recent celebration of the public-private divide that seems to assert that only the public is political, see Thomas Nagel, "Progressive but Not Liberal," *New York Review of Books,* 25 May 2006, 45. Nagel's distinction between public and private—between the domains of politics and private choice—categorizes marriage as a "public institution" but categorizes religious belief and sexual morality as private (48 & n. 5). For useful criticism of notions of this kind, see Nancy Fraser, *Unruly Practices* (Minneapolis: Univ. of Minnesota Press, 1989), 113–43.

8. Jeremy Waldron, "Torture and Positive Law," *Columbia Law Review* 105 (2005): 1726–27. See also Seth F. Kreimer, "Too Close to the Rack and the Screw," *Univ. of Pennsylvania Journal of Constitutional Law* 6 (2003): 310–17.

9. See Lynn Hunt, *Inventing Human Rights* (New York: W. W. Norton, 2007), 70–112. See also Lisa Silverman, *Tortured Subjects* (Chicago: Univ. of Chicago Press), 168–72; David Luban, "Liberalism, Torture, and the Ticking Bomb," *Virginia Law Review* 91 (2005): 1428–35.

10. Jeremy Waldron, "Rights in Conflict," in *Liberal Rights* (Cambridge: Cambridge Univ. Press, 1993), 212–13. For a similar analysis, see Henry Shue, *Basic Rights: Subsistence, Affluence, and U.S. Foreign Policy,* 2nd ed. (Princeton: Princeton Univ. Press, 1996), 51–53.

11. Waldron, "Torture," 1728, 1738.

12. White House, *Statement by the President on Death of Abu Musab al-Zarqawi* (8 June 2006).

13. Waldron, "Torture," 1722–23.

14. Id., 1746.

15. Carl Schmitt, *Legality and Legitimacy* (1932), ed. & trans. Jeffrey Seitzer (Durham, N.C.: Duke Univ. Press, 2004), 23, 94.

16. Carl Schmitt, *Political Theology* (1934), trans. George Schwab, 2nd ed. (Chicago: Univ. of Chicago Press, 2005), 15.

17. Waldron, "Torture," 1725. Compare Dembour, 2 (arguing, from a more critical perspective, that human rights are an "article of faith").

18. See Mitchell Dean, "Powers of Life and Death beyond Governmentality," *Cultural Values* 6 (2002): 128 (seeking to "move the analysis of liberalism away from its status as a

moral philosophy that drives the design of institutions of state and more toward its practical and technical operation"). See also Michel Foucault, *The Birth of Biopolitics,* trans. Graham Burchell (New York: Palgrave Macmillan, 2008), 321 ("Undoubtedly liberalism does not derive from juridical thought"; "democracy and the Rule of law have not necessarily been liberal, and nor has liberalism been necessarily democratic or bound to the forms of law"); Paul Kahn, *Sacred Violence* (Ann Arbor: Univ. of Michigan Press, 2008), 116 ("The liberalism that supports faith is never free floating. . . . We are attached to 'our' liberalism, not to liberal systems wherever they appear.").

19. John Stuart Mill, *On Liberty* (1859) (Indianapolis: Bobbs-Merrill, 1956), 82–83.

20. *E.g.,* Kwame Anthony Appiah, "Liberalism, Individuality, Identity," *Critical Inquiry* 27 (2001): 316–18.

21. See also Jean-Jacques Rousseau, *On the Social Contract* (1762), trans. Judith R. Masters (New York: St. Martin's Press, 1978), 55.

22. Stephen Holmes, *The Anatomy of Antiliberalism* (Cambridge, Mass.: Harvard Univ. Press, 1993), 203, 230, 236. See also Michel Foucault, *Psychiatric Power,* trans. Graham Burchell (New York: Palgrave Macmillan, 2006), 57 (liberalism requires "the individual as abstract subject, defined by individual rights that no power can limit unless agreed by contract").

23. Holmes, 203. See also Stephen Holmes, *Passions and Constraint* (Chicago: Univ. of Chicago Press, 1995), 19, 202–35; Sotiros A. Barber, "Fallacies of Negative Constitutionalism," *Fordham Law Review* 75 (2006): 655. Compare Rajeswari Sunder Rajan, *The Scandal of the State* (Durham, N.C.: Duke Univ. Press, 2003), 1 (discussing ways in which citizenship is "a more total relationship" with the state).

24. Joseph Raz, *The Morality of Freedom* (Oxford: Clarendon, 1986), 157, 412, 423. See also George Crowder, "Two Concepts of Liberal Pluralism," *Political Theory* 35 (2007): 139.

25. Uday Singh Mehta, *Liberalism and Empire* (Chicago: Univ. of Chicago Press, 1999), 51–64.

26. Mill, *On Liberty,* 113.

27. Id., 14.

28. John Stuart Mill, *Considerations on Representative Government* (1861) (New York: Henry Holt, 1873), 345. See Mehta, 70–73; Jennifer Pitts, *A Turn to Empire* (Princeton: Princeton Univ. Press, 2005), 138–150.

29. Mehta, 30–31. See also Mark Sanders, "Extraordinary Violence," *Interventions* 3, no. 2 (2001): 247.

30. Jeffrie G. Murphy, "Moral Death," *Ethics* 82, no. 4 (1972): 291.

31. Id., 287, 291–95. *Cf.* Kahn, *Sacred Violence,* 39.

32. For Rawls's assessment of mental disabilities, see John Rawls, *Political Liberalism,* expanded ed. (New York: Columbia Univ. Press, 2005), 20, 300–303. See also Martha C. Nussbaum, *Frontiers of Justice* (Cambridge, Mass.: Harvard Univ. Press, 2006), 65–66, 130–135.

33. Murphy, 296–98. For the relationship between Kant's moral and political philosophies, see Nussbaum, 50; Patrick Riley, *Will and Political Legitimacy* (Cambridge, Mass.: Harvard Univ. Press, 1982), 131, 133; Jeremy Waldron, "Welfare and the Images of Charity," in *Liberal Rights,* 229.

34. *E.g.,* Dan Blaz, "Bush Warns of Casualties of War," *Washington Post,* 18 Sept. 2001, A1; "Bush's Remarks on U.S. Military Strikes in Afghanistan," *New York Times,* 8 Oct. 2001, B6; Mike Allen, "Bush Says Citizens Must Help in Fighting Terror," *Washington Post,* 9 Nov. 2001, A1; James Brooke, "Cheney Praises Japan's Stand against Abductors in

Iraq," *New York Times,* 13 Apr. 2004, A15; Greg Myre & Mona El-Naggar, "Death Toll Rises in Egyptian Bombings," *New York Times,* 24 July 2005, 1; Douglas Jehl, "C.I.A. Says Berg's Killer Was Very Probably Zarqawi," *New York Times,* 14 May 2004, A12; Paul Wolfowitz, "The First Draft of Freedom," *New York Times,* 16 Sept. 2004, A27.

35. Carl Schmitt, *The Concept of the Political* (1932), trans. George Schwab (Chicago: Univ. of Chicago Press, 1996), 54.

36. Isaiah Berlin, *Four Essays on Liberty* (London: Oxford Univ. Press, 1969), 123–24. For an argument that subsistence rights are necessary to negative rights, see Amy Gutman's introduction in Ignatieff, xii.

37. Rawls, *Political Liberalism,* 327.

38. See id., 324–29. See also Noah Feldman, "Cosmopolitan Law?" *Yale Law Journal* 116 (2007): 1038.

39. Waldron, "Rights in Conflict," in *Liberal Rights,* 212–13. In a different essay, entitled "Liberal Rights," Waldron argues that the duties generated by a "right to assistance" are sufficient, even though none is "a perfect duty incumbent on anyone in particular" (Waldron, *Liberal Rights,* 16).

40. Waldron, "Liberal Rights," in *Liberal Rights,* 13.

41. Id., 22. Following T. H. Marshall, Waldron suggests that welfare rights exist because of "the contingent fact that welfare guarantees have been established in this society," such that "they are now part of what we understand by citizenship" (Waldron, "Social Citizenship and the Defense of Welfare Provision," in *Liberal Rights,* 293). See also Shue, *Basic Rights,* 35–51, 155–57, 160.

42. Nussbaum, 74.

43. Id., 76, 78; see also 155 (analogizing to the Indian and U.S. constitutions).

44. Id., 80.

45. Id., 168; see also 87–88.

46. Id., 168.

47. *Universal Declaration of Human Rights,* art. 25, U.N. G.A. Res. 217A(III) (1948); *International Covenant on Economic, Social and Cultural Rights,* arts. 9, 12 (1966), 999 U.N.T.S. 171; United Nations, *Final Report of the Ad Hoc Committee on a Comprehensive and Integral International Convention on the Protection and Promotion of the Rights and Dignity of Persons with Disabilities,* A/61/611, annex 1, arts. 25, 28 (6 Dec. 2006).

48. *E.g.,* A. R. Mowbray, *The Development of Positive Obligations under the European Convention on Human Rights by the European Court of Human Rights* (Oxford: Hart, 2004); Jennifer Prah Ruger, "Toward a Theory of a Right to Health," *Yale Journal of Law & the Humanities* 18 (2006): 273–326; George P. Smith, II, "Human Rights and Bioethics," *Vanderbilt Journal of Transnational Law* 38 (2005): 1295–1321.

49. *See* Mathews v. Eldridge, 424 U.S. 319, 335 (1976); Jerry L. Mashaw, "The Supreme Court's Due Process Calculus for Administrative Adjudication in *Mathews v. Eldridge,*" *Univ. of Chicago Law Review* 44 (1976): 28–59. Compare the broader approach of the dissenting opinions in *DeShaney v. Winnebago County Dept. of Health and Human Services,* 489 U.S. 189 (1989).

50. Roy Porter, *The Greatest Benefit to Mankind* (New York: W. W. Norton, 1997), 632.

51. Michel Foucault, *"Society Must Be Defended": Lectures at the Collège de France, 1975–1976,* trans. David Macy (New York: Picador, 2003), 241.

52. Sheldon S. Wolin, *The Presence of the Past* (Baltimore, Md.: Johns Hopkins Univ. Press, 1989), 154, 161.

53. Brian Z. Tamanaha, *On the Rule of Law* (Cambridge: Cambridge Univ. Press, 2004), 128. See also Jack L. Goldsmith & Eric A. Posner, *The Limits of International Law*

(New York: Oxford Univ. Press, 2005). Compare Harold Hongju Koh, "Why Do Nations Obey International Law," *Yale Law Journal* 106 (1997): 2599; Mary Ellen O'Connell, "Affirming the Ban on Harsh Interrogation," *Ohio State Law Journal* 66 (2005): 1231.

54. Peter Malanczuk, *Akehurst's Modern Introduction to International Law*, 7th ed. (London: Routledge, 1997), 7. See also James D. Morrow, "When Do States Follow the Laws of War?" *American Political Science Review* 101 (2007): 559.

55. Pheng Cheah, *Inhuman Conditions* (Cambridge, Mass.: Harvard Univ. Press, 2006), 145–77.

56. Jordanna Bailkin, "The Place of Liberalism," *Victorian Studies* 48, no. 1 (2005): 83–84. See also Mehta, 120.

57. *E.g.*, Giorgio Agamben, *Homo Sacer* (1995), trans. Daniel Heller-Roazen (Stanford, Cal.: Stanford Univ. Press, 1998); Antony Anghie, *Imperialism, Sovereignty, and the Making of International Law* (Cambridge: Cambridge Univ. Press, 2005); Cheah; Kennedy, *Dark Sides of Virtue;* Mehta; Sundhya Pahuja, "This Is the World: Have Faith," *European Journal of Int'l Law* 15 (2004): 381; Ann Laura Stoler, *Carnal Knowledge and Imperial Power* (Berkeley: Univ. of California Press, 2002).

58. See James Dawes, *The Language of War* (Cambridge, Mass.: Harvard Univ. Press, 2002), 213–16.

59. Inderpal Grewal, foreword to Wendy S. Hesford & Wendy Kozol, eds., *Just Advocacy?* (New Brunswick, N.J.: Rutgers Univ. Press, 2005), viii. See also Inderpal Grewal, *Transnational America* (Durham, N.C.: Duke Univ. Press, 2005), 149.

60. Amy Farrell & Patrice McDermott, "Claiming Afghan Women," in Hesford & Kozol, 47–48; Tarik Kochi, "Terror in the Name of Human Rights," *Melbourne Journal of Int'l Law* 7 (2006): 130. See also David Kennedy, *Of War and Law* (Princeton: Princeton Univ. Press, 2006); Deborah M. Weissman, "The Human Rights Dilemma," *Columbia Human Rights Law Review* 35 (2004): 259. For recognition of this dynamic and an effort to address it, see Ignatieff, 37–43.

61. On the connections and interactions between liberalism and human rights discourse, including the possibility of advocating one but not the other, see Dembour, 6–8.

62. *E.g.*, Cheah, 172, 174; Leela Fernandes, "The Boundaries of Terror," in Hesford & Kozol, 70–71. See also Patricia Williams, *The Alchemy of Race and Rights* (Cambridge, Mass.: Harvard Univ. Press, 1991), 148–61.

63. Silverman, 174–75, 180; Karen Halttunen, "Humanitarianism and the Pornography of Pain in Anglo-American Culture," *American Historical Review* 100 (1995): 303; Agamben, *Homo Sacer,* 133–34. For criticism of Agamben's assertion, see Volker Heins, "Giorgio Agamben and the Current State of Affairs in Humanitarian Law and Human Rights Policy," *German Law Journal* 6 (2005): 845.

64. Holmes, *Anatomy,* 231; Holmes, *Passions,* 36–40, 236–66; Carl Schmitt, *The Crisis of Parliamentary Democracy* (1926), trans. Ellen Kennedy, 2nd ed. (Cambridge, Mass.: MIT Press, 1988), 11, 13.

65. Rawls, *Political Liberalism;* John Rawls, *A Theory of Justice* (Cambridge, Mass.: Harvard Univ. Press, 1971); Michael Walzer, *Spheres of Justice* (New York: Basic Books, 1983).

66. Michel Foucault, *Discipline and Punish,* trans. Alan Sheridan (New York: Pantheon, 1978), 222. See also Foucault, *"Society,"* 245–47; Michel Foucault, *Security, Territory, Population,* trans. Graham Burchell (New York: Palgrave Macmillan, 2007), 341–54.

67. Agamben, *Homo Sacer,* 121. See also Mitchell Dean, "Four Theses on the Powers of Life and Death," *Contretemps* 5 (Dec. 2004): 21–22 ("The more liberalism and modern rights movements seek to defend us from the dangers of bio-powers, it would seem, the more they make possible its extension.").

68. Ruth A. Miller, *The Limits of Bodily Integrity* (Aldershot: Ashgate, 2007).

69. Agamben, *Homo Sacer,* 8.

CHAPTER FIVE

1. Darius Rejali covers much of this ground in *Torture and Democracy* (Princeton: Princeton Univ. Press, 2007). For histories, see Michel Foucault, *Discipline and Punish,* trans. Alan Sheridan (New York: Pantheon, 1978), 3–69; Chris Ingelse, *The UN Committee against Torture* (The Hague: Kluwer, 2001), 23–31; John Langbein, *Torture and the Law of Proof* (Chicago: Univ. of Chicago Press, 1977); Edward Peters, *Torture,* expanded ed. (Philadelphia: Univ. of Pennsylvania Press, 1996); Lisa Silverman, *Tortured Subjects* (Chicago: Univ. of Chicago Press), 168–72.

2. See also Peters, 135–38; Kate Millet, *The Politics of Cruelty* (New York: W. W. Norton, 1994), 74–116. For the importance of not seeing torture in terms of a simple "home country"-colony dichotomy, see Rejali, *Torture and Democracy,* 565.

3. Rejali, *Torture and Democracy,* 146 (emphasis added).

4. Id., 159.

5. Douglas Porch, *The French Secret Services* (New York: Farrar, Straus & Giroux, 1995), 381–83; Marie-Monique Robin, "Counterinsurgency and Torture," in Kenneth Roth & Minky Worden eds., *Torture: Does It Make Us Safer? Is It Ever OK?* (New York: New Press, 2005), 46.

6. Robin, 49.

7. Rejali, *Torture and Democracy,* 160.

8. Rita Maran, *Torture: The Role of Ideology in the French-Algerian War* (New York: Praeger, 1989), 40; France, Constitution of 4 October 1958, art. 16. See also Anna-Lena Svensson-McCarthy, *The International Law of Human Rights and States of Exception* (The Hague: Martinus Nijhoff, 1998), 36–42 (discussing French approaches to states of emergency).

9. Porch, 380, 383–84; Gen. Paul Aussaresses, *The Battle of the Casbah* (New York: Enigma Books, 2005), 16–17, 19–20, 48–51, 76, 87, 101, 119–22, 124–29, 134–41, 144–46, 163. See also Lt. Col. James D. Campbell, "French Algeria and British Northern Ireland," *Military Review,* Mar./Apr. 2005, 3–4; Vivian Grosswald Curran, "Politicizing the Crime against Humanity," *Notre Dame Law Review* 78 (2003): 696–97; Maran, 47, 52, 99; Rejali, *Torture and Democracy,* 482; Antonio Vercher, *Terrorism in Europe* (Oxford: Clarendon, 1992), 241 (citing M. C. Hutchinson, *Revolutionary Terrorism* (Stanford: Hoover Institution Press, 1978), 122).

10. Rejali, *Torture and Democracy,* 480–93.

11. Id., 483.

12. Id., 487–88 (quoting Raphaëlle Branche, "Torture and Other Violations of the Law by the French Army during the Algerian War," in Adam Jones, ed., *Genocide, War Crimes, and the West* (London: Zed Books, 2004), 144).

13. Id., 493.

14. Maran, 50–51, 104–5, 117–18.

15. Id., 45–52, 117; Vercher, 241. See also Rejali, *Torture and Democracy,* 161.

16. For Debré's statements, see Maran, 55. *Cf.* Herman Lebovics, "The Uses of America in Locke's Second Treatise of Government," *Journal of the History of Ideas* 47, no. 4 (1986): 567–81.

17. Carl Schmitt, *Political Theology* (1934), trans. George Schwab, 2nd ed. (Chicago: Univ. of Chicago Press, 2005), 12.

18. For the statements of de Gaulle and Malreaux, see Maran, 55–56. Maran (57) also relates a story that "at a dinner with the officers of his sector," Colonel Marcel Bigeard (later a general) "reported having been told by de Gaulle: 'No more torture!'" and "then said to his colleagues: 'So I, sirs, I say to you: 'No more torture, but . . . go on torturing just the same.'"

19. Id., 12, 16, 78, 85, 87, 98; Peters, 135.

20. Sanders, 247; Anupama Rao, "Problems of Violence, States of Terror," *Interventions* 3, no. 2 (2001): 188, 193.

21. Aussaresses, 17; Campbell, 4; Maran, 79, 82, 86, 102; Peters, 133, 177.

22. Maran, 103 (quoting and translating the *Le Figaro* article).

23. Id., 50–51.

24. Curran, 688, 697, 706; "Algeria: Chirac Rejects 'Torture Apology,'" *BBC News*, 15 Dec. 2000.

25. Jeremy Shapiro & Bénédicte Suzan, "The French Experience of Counter-Terrorism," *Survival* 45, no. 1 (2003): 67.

26. Luis Núñez Astrain, *The Basques*, trans. Meic Stephens (Wales: Welsh Academic Press, 1997), 100–105; Paddy Woodworth, *Dirty War, Clean Hands* (New Haven, Conn.: Yale Univ. Press, 2002), 120–49, 411–12; U.N. Committee against Torture, *Conclusions and Recommendations of the Committee against Torture: France*, U.N. Doc. A/53/44, ¶ 143(d) (1998).

27. Craig Whitlock, "French Push Limits in Fight on Terrorism: Wide Prosecutorial Powers Draw Scant Public Dissent," *Washington Post*, 2 Nov. 2004, A1; Dana Priest, "Help from France Key in Covert Operations," *Washington Post*, 3 July 2005, A1; "Francais de Guantánamo: Affaire Renvoyée en 05/07," *Nouvel Observateur*, 27 Sept. 2006.

28. Vercher, 66. See also John Conroy, *Unspeakable Acts, Ordinary People* (New York: Alfred A. Knopf, 2000), 127. The five techniques may have been adapted from Soviet positional tortures (see Rejali, *Torture and Democracy*, 330–31).

29. A. W. Brian Simpson, *Human Rights and the End of Empire* (Oxford: Oxford Univ. Press, 2001), 877–81, 901, 1058–61, 1071.

30. Rao, "Problems of Violence," 192; Anupama Rao, "Torture, the Public Secret," *Economic & Political Weekly*, 5 June 2004; Radhika Singha, *A Despotism of Law* (Delhi: Oxford Univ. Press, 1998), 305 (quoting *Report of the Commissioners for the Investigation of the Alleged Cases of Torture in the Madras Presidency* (1855), part 1).

31. Rao, "Problems of Violence," 192; Singha, 69–70, 303. See also Peters, 137–38. The report appeared shortly before the British government explicitly and formally assumed imperial rule over India.

32. Singha, viii–ix, xvi. See also Sandria B. Freitag, "Crime in the Social Order of Colonial North India," *Modern Asian Studies* 25, no. 2 (1991): 227–61.

33. Anandswarup Gupta, *The Police in British India, 1861–1947* (New Delhi: Concept, 1979), xix, 518, 537–38, 541–42. For discussion of this legacy, see Anil Kalhan et al., "Colonial Continuities," *Columbia Journal of Asian Law* 20 (2006): 93.

34. Ian Cobain, "Revealed: UK Wartime Torture Camp," *Guardian*, 12 Nov. 2005, 1. See Patricia Meehan, *A Strange Enemy People* (London: Peter Owen, 2001), 70, 74–87; Giles MacDonogh, *After the Reich* (New York: Basic Books, 2007), 407, 412–15; Ian Cobain, "Revealed: Victims of UK's Cold War Torture Camp," *Guardian*, 3 Apr. 2006, 1.

35. Caroline Elkins, *Imperial Reckoning* (New York: Henry Holt, 2005), xii–xiii, xv, 42. British officials also used concentration camps during the Boer War. See Thomas Pakenham, *The Boer War* (London: Weidenfeld & Nicolson, 1979).

36. David Anderson, *Histories of the Hanged* (New York: W. W. Norton, 2005), 5,

293–96, 314–21; Elkins, 35–37, 45, 51–52, 54–55, 72–73, 75, 78–79, 98, 137–41, 143–45. Simpson (834–35) does not discuss torture, but he notes the reliance on mass detention as well as executions.

37. Anderson, 295–96.

38. Elkins, 65–66, 80, 99–101, 115–17, 136, 155–56, 207–9, 244–58, 312, 319–20, 326. See also Anderson, 299–300 (discussing the brutality of white police and the home guard).

39. Elkins, 65, 81–83, 275–76, 281–82, 291. See also Anderson, 300–301, 305, 309.

40. Elkins, 314–15.

41. Simpson, 929–1052. The second case brought by Greece turned specifically on allegations of torture. See id., 1020–21, 1024.

42. Id., 1051.

43. Ireland v. United Kingdom, 2 EHRR 25, ¶ 39 (1978); Conroy, 4.

44. *Ireland,* 2 EHRR ¶¶ 39, 96; Conroy, 4–7, 41, 130; Rejali, *Torture and Democracy,* 363–64.

45. Conroy, 41–43; Vercher, 67.

46. *Ireland,* 2 EHRR ¶¶ 68, 75, 78, 79, 98; Conroy, 3, 43, 46, 188, 258, 260.

47. Conroy, 44–46; Vercher, 67.

48. Conroy, 47, 125; Vercher, 67.

49. Conroy, 136–37, 261–63.

50. Ireland v. United Kingdom, *Yearbook of the European Convention on Human Rights* 19 (1976): 792–94; *Ireland,* 2 EHRR ¶¶ 98, 152.

51. *Ireland,* 2 EHRR ¶¶ 167–68.

52. Id., ¶¶ 167–68, 180–81, 186–87.

53. Conroy, 137, 187, 261; Nigel S. Rodley, *The Treatment of Prisoners under International Law,* 2nd ed. (Oxford: Oxford Univ. Press, 1999), 92–94.

54. Fionnuala Ní Aoláin, "The European Convention on Human Rights and Its Prohibition on Torture," in Sanford Levinson, ed., *Torture: A Collection* (New York: Oxford Univ. Press, 2004), 220–23.

55. Other reasons the five techniques could be used as a template are that methods of this kind leave no marks and that their use and impact are difficult to reconstruct, as Rejali stresses throughout *Torture and Democracy.*

56. Rejali, *Torture and Democracy,* 337.

57. Campbell, 3–4; John Stalker, *The Stalker Affair* (New York: Viking, 1988); John Stalker, "Guarded with the Truth," *Times,* 23 Feb. 1997, features section; Vercher, 384–86; McCann v. United Kingdom, 21 EHRR 97 (1995); Joseba Zulaika & William A. Douglass, *Terror and Taboo* (New York: Routledge, 1996), 158; "Britain Accused over Ulster investigations: European Ruling Sidesteps Issue of Unlawful Killing but Questions Deaths after Long-Term Surveillance: Case Two," *Guardian,* 4 May 2001, 9.

58. Robert Verkaik, "Britain in the Dock for Human Rights Failures after More than 100 'Guilty' Judgments Filed," *Independent,* 3 Oct. 2005, 6; Clare Dyer, "UK Treatment of Terror Suspects 'Inhuman,'" *Guardian,* 10 June 2005, 5; A and Others v. Secretary of State, 2004 UKHL 56; Patrick Wintour, "After Eight Years in Power Tony Blair Hears a New Word: Defeat," *Guardian,* 10 Nov. 2005, 1; "Britain Makes Glorifying Terrorism a Crime," *Gulf Daily News,* 14 Apr. 2006.

59. See Ian Cobain, "The Truth about Torture: Britain's Catalogue of Shame," *Guardian,* 8 July 2009, 7.

60. See Amnesty International, "UK: CIA Rendition Flights Used UK Airfields" (2005); Colin Brown, "U.S. Planes Carrying Prisoners Were Allowed to Land in Britain," *Independent,* 13 Dec. 2005, 16; Colin Brown, "Straw Faces MPs over Claims MI6 Deliv-

ered Suspect for Torture," *Independent,* 12 Dec. 2005, 9; Adam Zagorin, "Source: British Territory Used for U.S. Terror Interrogation," *Time,* 31 July 2008. See also Ian Cobain, "Torture: MPs Call for Inquiry into MI5 Role," *Guardian,* 15 July 2008, 1.

61. Clare Dyer, "Ministers Seek to Overturn Torture Rule in Deportations," *Guardian,* 3 Oct. 2005, 11; Alan Travis, "Clarke Confronts Judges on Terror Law," *Guardian,* 7 Sept. 2005, 2.

62. Peter Graff, "British Judge Says Headquarters Okayed Iraq Abuse," *Reuters,* 12 Mar. 2007. See Jamie Doward, "UK Link to Torture Jail's Rules," *Observer,* 20 Feb. 2005, 2; Audrey Gillan, "British Soldiers Found Guilty of Abuse," *Guardian,* 24 Feb. 2005, 1; Severin Carrell, "Army Colonel Facing Trial for War Crimes," *Independent,* 22 May 2005; Severin Carrell, "Behind Three Lines in a Secret Army Log Lies Real Story of an Alleged War Crime," *Independent,* 22 May 2005; *The Aitken Report: An Investigation into Cases of Deliberate Abuse and Unlawful Killing in Iraq in 2003 and 2004* (25 Jan. 2008).

63. A and Others v. Secretary of State, 2005 UKHL 71, ¶¶ 51, 53, 118. See also RB and Another v. Secretary of State, 2009 UKHL 10 (relying in part on *A and Others* to apply a relaxed standard for reviewing claim that alien would face a criminal trial tainted by torture if deported).

64. *And Others,* 2005 UKHL, ¶¶ 47, 68–69.

65. M. C. Wood, Legal Advisor, Memo to Linda Duffield re: Uzbekistan: Intelligence Possibly Obtained under Torture (13 Mar. 2003). See also "MI5 'Given Secret Prisons Data,'" *BBC News,* 23 Nov. 2005.

66. Compare Al-Skeini v. Secretary of State, 2007 UKHL 26 (U.K. Human Rights Act applies extraterritorially to conduct of U.K. forces when the victim of the conduct—such as a person held in detention by them—also has a connection with the United Kingdom, based on the degree of control exercised by U.K. forces). See also *A and Others,* 2004 UKHL ¶¶ 16–29, 115–20, 154, 165–66, 208 (public emergency existed in Britain after the 9/11 attacks, such that the government could derogate from the European Convention on Human Rights); Jones v. Ministry of Interior al-Mamlaka al-Arabiya AS Saudiya, 2006 UKHL 26 (rule of foreign sovereign immunity in civil cases includes immunity for officials of the foreign sovereign and applies equally to torture claims against officials of a foreign sovereign). *Jones* rejected the more permissive U.S. doctrine that officials of a foreign sovereign are not entitled to immunity for actions beyond the scope of their authority (id., ¶¶ 58, 99). Lord Bingham dryly remarked, "[T]here is no reason to think that the United States would now subscribe to a rule of international law conferring a universal tort jurisdiction which would entitle foreign states to entertain claims against US officials based on torture allegedly inflicted by the officials outside the state of the forum" (id., ¶ 20).

67. Woodworth, 66–67, 187; Zulaika & Douglass, 176, 205.

68. Woodworth, 7, 75, 409; Amnesty International, *Spain: A Briefing on Human Rights Concerns in Relation to the Basque Peace Process* (1999), 7–9. On the scope of ETA violence, see Woodworth, 11; Amnesty International, *Spain: A Briefing,* 12–13.

69. Zulaika & Douglass, 198–99, 201–7, 210–12; Astrain, 87, 99–100.

70. Vercher, 247.

71. Amnesty International, *Spain: A Briefing,* 4–6. See also Astrain, 91–93.

72. Amnesty International, *Report 2004—Spain* (2004).

73. Amnesty International, *Report 2005: The State of the World's Human Rights—Spain* (2005).

74. U.N. Commission on Human Rights, *Civil and Political Rights, Including the Question of Torture and Detention: Report of the Special Rapporteur on the Question of*

Torture—Addendum, Visit to Spain, E/CN.4/2004/56/Add.2, at 2, 10–11, 15, 19 (6 Feb. 2004); *Communication No. 212/2002: Spain,* CAT C/34/D/212/2002 (24 May 2005). Astrain (87–88) also criticizes the Spanish government's tendency to argue that torture allegations are false claims encouraged by the ETA.

75. The relative reluctance of Spanish authorities to confront domestic torture contrasts with the willingness of Spanish magistrates to investigate the use of torture by officials of other governments, including investigations of Bush administration practices. See Marlise Simons, "Spanish Court Weighs Inquiry on Torture for 6 Bush-Era Officials," *New York Times,* 29 Mar. 2009, A6; Giles Tremlett, "Spanish Court Opens Investigation of Guantánamo Torture Allegations," *Guardian.co.uk,* 29 Apr. 2009, http://www.guardian.co.uk/world/2009/apr/29/spain-court-guantanamo-detainees-torture. Recently, however, Spanish legislators voted to limit the ability of prosecutors to bring such cases. See Daniel Woolls, "Spanish Lawmakers Vote to Limit Cross-Border Justice Law Used to Indict Pinochet, bin Laden," *Associated Press,* 25 June 2009.

76. Conroy, 212–13; Lisa Hajjar, *Courting Conflict* (Berkeley: Univ. of California Press, 2005), 70; John T. Parry, "Judicial Restraints on Illegal State Violence," *Vanderbilt Journal of Transnational Law* 35 (2002): 88–89.

77. *Report of the Commission of Inquiry into the Methods of Investigation of the General Security Service regarding Hostile Terrorist Activity* (1987), *Israel Law Review* 23 (1989): 157–58.

78. Id., 174–75. See also Conroy, 213; Talal Asad, "On Torture, or Cruel, Inhuman, and Degrading Treatment," in Arthur Kleinman et al., eds., *Social Suffering* (Berkeley: Univ. of California Press, 1997), 296.

79. Public Committee against Torture in Israel v. State of Israel, H.C. 5100/94, 53(4) P.D. 817, ¶¶ 8, 16 (1999).

80. Michael Mandel, "Democracy and the New Constitutionalism in Israel," *Israel Law Review* 33 (1999): 306; Parry, "Judicial Restraints," 88 & n. 76; Jason S. Greenberg, "Torture of Terrorists in Israel," *ILSA Journal of Int'l & Comparative Law* 7 (2001): 546; Rejali, *Torture and Democracy,* 515–18.

81. *Public Committee against Torture in Israel v. State of Israel,* ¶ 17; Serge Schmemann, "Israel Allows Use of Physical Force in Arab's Interrogation," *New York Times,* 16 Nov. 1996, sec. 1, at 8.

82. Rodley, *Treatment,* 83–84, 94–95.

83. *Public Committee against Torture in Israel v. State of Israel,* ¶ 9–13, 30. For other coercive practices employed by Israeli forces prior to the court's decision, see Conroy, 212–14; Parry, "Judicial Restraints," 88 n.75; Rejali, *Torture and Democracy,* 355–57.

84. *Public Committee against Torture in Israel v. State of Israel,* ¶¶ 18, 23, 33–38.

85. Id., ¶¶ 1, 2, 8, 14, 17. For extensive analysis of *Public Committee against Torture in Israel v. State of Israel,* see Parry, "Judicial Restraints."

86. *Public Committee against Torture in Israel v. State of Israel,* ¶ 39.

87. Id., ¶¶ 32, 34.

88. Id., ¶¶ 1, 39.

89. Public Committee against Torture in Israel v. Israel, HCJ 769/02, ¶ 62 (11 Dec. 2005) (quoting Almandi v. Minister of Defense, 56(3) P.D. 30, 34 (2002)).

90. A v. State of Israel, CrimA 6659/06 (11 June 2008), ¶ 9 (upholding the statute providing for administrative detention of "unlawful combatants").

91. Amnesty International, *Torture in Israel* (2000); Elizabeth Olson, "Israel Denies Groups' Charge that It Is Torturing Detainees," *New York Times,* 21 Nov. 2001, A10; Shosh Mula, "Changed Position," *Yedioth Ahronoth,* "Shi'vah Yamin" *Weekend Magazine Sup-*

plement, 4 Apr. 2005 (translated for the Public Committee against Torture); Public Committee against Torture, *Back to a Routine of Torture* (n.d.), 9–10; Public Committee against Torture, *Ticking Bombs* (May 2007).

92. Mula. See also Public Committee against Torture, *Back to a Routine of Torture,* 45–47; Public Committee against Torture, *Shackling as a Form of Torture and Abuse* (June 2009); B'Tselem & HaMoked, *Absolute Prohibition* (May 2007); United Against ~~Torture,~~ *Getting Around the International Prohibition of Torture* (Dec. 2006), 26–27.

93. U.N. Human Rights Council, *Report of the Special Rapporteur on the Promotion and Protection of Human Rights and Fundamental Freedoms while Countering Terrorism: Mission to Israel, Including Visit to Occupied Palestinian Territory,* ¶ 19, No. A/HRC/6/17/Add.6 (16 Nov. 2007).

94. Public Committee against Torture, *Back to a Routine of Torture,* 12, 17–18.

95. United Nations, press release, "UN Special Rapporteur on Human Rights and Counter Terrorism Concludes Mission to Israel, Including Visit to Occupied Palestinian Territory" (10 July 2007).

96. Ethan A. Nadelmann, "The Evolution of United States Involvement in the International Rendition of Fugitive Criminals," *New York Univ. Journal of Int'l Law & Policy* 25 (1993): 857.

97. John T. Parry, "The Shape of Modern Torture," *Melbourne Journal of Int'l Law* 6 (2005): 516; Committee on International Human Rights of the Association of the Bar of the City of New York & Center for Human Rights and Global Justice at NYU School of Law, *Torture by Proxy: International and Domestic Law Applicable to "Extraordinary Renditions"* (2004); Steven Lee Myers & Neil A Lewis, "Rumsfeld Offers Assurances about Use of Military Courts," *New York Times,* 16 Nov. 2001, B10.

98. European Parliament, *Report on the Alleged Use of European Countries by the CIA for the Transportation and Illegal Detention of Prisoners,* Final A6-0020/2007 (30 Jan. 2007); Council of Europe, *Report on Alleged Secret Detentions and Unlawful Inter-State Transfers of Detainees Involving Council of Europe Member States,* Doc. 10957 (12 June 2006).

99. Craig Whitlock, "Europeans Investigate CIA Role in Abductions: Suspects Possibly Taken to Nations that Torture," *Washington Post,* 13 Mar. 2005, A1; Dana Priest, "Italy Knew about Plan to Grab Suspect," *Washington Post,* 30 June 2005, A1; "Italian Questions Prosecutor's Motives," *Associated Press,* 22 Nov. 2005; John Crewdson, "CIA Chiefs Reportedly Split over Cleric Plot," *Chicago Tribune,* 8 Jan. 2007, 1. Several Italian officials have denied that their government knew about or took part in the kidnapping. See "Berlusconi to Testify in C.I.A. Case," *Associated Press,* 14 May 2008.

100. Priest, "Italy Knew"; Michael Isikoff & Mark Hosenball, "'Don't Ask, Don't Tell,'" *Newsweek,* 8 Dec. 2005; Council of Europe, *Report on Alleged Secret Detentions,* ¶¶ 230–36.

101. U.N. Committee against Torture, *Communication No. 233/2003: Agiza v. Sweden,* ¶¶ 12.29–12.30, CAT/C/34/D/233/2003(20 May 2005).

102. Id., ¶¶ 2.6–2.8, 13.2–13.5; Craig Whitlock, "New Swedish Documents Illuminate CIA Action," *Washington Post,* 21 May 2005, A1.

103. See http://www.maherarar.ca; Commission of Inquiry into the Actions of Canadian Officials in Relation to Maher Arar, *Report of the Events Relating to Maher Arar: Analysis and Recommendations* (2006); Commission of Inquiry into the Actions of Canadian Officials in Relation to Maher Arar, *Report of Professor Stephen J. Toope, Fact Finder* (14 Oct. 2005); U.S. Department of Homeland Security, Office of the Inspector General, *The Removal of a Canadian Citizen to Syria,* OIG-08-18 (Mar. 2008); Scott Shane, "The Costs of Outsourcing Interrogation: A Canadian Muslim's Long Ordeal in

Syria," *New York Times,* 29 May 2005; quotation from Doug Struck, "Canadian's Lawyers Blame U.S.: Agents Accused of Sending Man to Syria for Torture in '02," *Washington Post,* 1 July 2005, A14.

104. http://www.maherarar.ca.

105. Commission of Inquiry, *Report of Professor Stephen J. Toope,* 1, 17; see also Commission of Inquiry, *Report of the Events Relating to Maher Arar,* 14, 187–88.

106. See Frank Iacobucci, *Internal Inquiry into the Actions of Canadian Officials in Relation to Abdullah Almalki, Ahmad Abou-Elmaati, and Muayyed Nurreddin* (2008); Commission of Inquiry, *Report of the Events Relating to Maher Arar,* 206–14. See also Daniel LeBlanc, "Calls Grow for Torture Inquiry," *Globe & Mail,* 8 Sept. 2005; Jeff Sallot, "Once a Muhajed Who Took Flying Lessons, Ahmad El Maati Seemed to Fit the Profile of a Terrorist," *Globe & Mail,* 29 Aug. 2005, A1; Jeff Sallot, "For the First Time, Abdullah Almaki Tells His Story," *Globe & Mail,* 27 Aug. 2005, A1.

107. "Cleared Terror Suspect Seeks Amends," *Oregonian,* 30 Sept. 2006, A6; see also Doug Struck, "Fallout from Abduction Continues for Mounties," *Oregonian,* 15 Dec. 2006, A5; "Torture Victim to Get Millions," *Oregonian,* 27 Jan. 2007, A8.

108. Canada's foreign ministry decided to rewrite a training manual after U.S. officials protested the inclusion of the United States "in a list of possible torture sites" (Charmaine Noronha, "Canada to Revise Manual, Terror At-Risk List," *MiamiHerald .com* (19 Jan. 2008)), which suggests that in Canada, as in other liberal democracies, whether a country should be accused of torture turns in part on Canada's relationship to that country.

109. Suresh v. Canada, 2002 SCC 1, ¶¶ 15, 58, 78. See also Mahjoub v. Minister of Citizenship and Immigration, 2006 FC 1503 (avoiding the exceptional circumstances issue); compare Saadi v. Italy, ECHR, No. 37201/06, ¶ 139 (28 Feb. 2008) (rejecting the position adopted in *Suresh*).

110. *Suresh,* ¶¶ 59–79.

111. U.N. Committee against Torture, *Conclusions and Recommendations of the Committee against Torture: Canada,* CAT/C/CO/34/CAN (7 July 2005), 2.

112. See Charkaoui v. Minister of Citizenship and Immigration, 2007 SCC 9 (suggesting a less accommodating approach to government interests, but stressing that national security and terrorism concerns receive significant weight when determining the process due a person who may be a "security threat"); Hape v. The Queen, 2007 SCC 26, ¶¶ 88, 99, 108–9 (the Canadian Charter of Rights and Freedoms does not prevent officials from engaging in extraterritorial searches that comply with international human rights law but that would violate the charter if the search took place in Canada, and evidence is admissible if consistent with the right to a fair trial); Canada v. Khadr, 2008 SCC 28 (the charter applies extraterritorially if officials participate in acts that violate international law, because there is no comity basis for deferring to the law of the other country—in this case, the United States at Guantánamo—such that Canadian officials must disclose relevant information to a defendant).

113. *Cf. Hape,* ¶ 109 (a defendant's right to a fair trial prevents introduction of evidence obtained by torture but not addressing executive conduct outside the courtroom); Michael Isikoff & Mark Hosenball, "Canada Tosses Terror Testimony Obtained through Waterboarding," *Newsweek,* 5 Mar. 2008 (Canadian security officials withdrew citations in court documents to information provided by the United States and obtained through waterboarding).

114. Dana Priest & Barton Gellman, "U.S. Decries Abuse but Defends Interrogations," *Washington Post,* 26 Dec. 2002, A1; http://www.amnesty.org/ailib/aireport/index.html; http://www.state.gov/g/drl/hr/c1470.htm.

115. *E.g.,* Edward W. Said, *Orientalism* (New York: Pantheon, 1978), 7, 57, 108–9, 317–18.

116. See also Page DuBois, *Torture and Truth* (New York: Routledge, 1991), 157.

117. Harold Hongju Koh, "A World without Torture," *Columbia Journal of Transnational Law* 43 (2005): 661; Jeremy Waldron, "Torture and Positive Law," *Columbia Law Review* 105 (2005): 1746.

118. Ann Laura Stoler, *Carnal Knowledge and Imperial Power* (Berkeley: Univ. of California Press, 2002), 146–47. See also Antony Anghie, *Imperialism, Sovereignty, and the Making of International Law* (Cambridge: Cambridge Univ. Press, 2005); Michael Hardt & Antonio Negri, *Empire* (Cambridge, Mass.: Harvard Univ. Press, 2000), 124–29; Uday Singh Mehta, *Liberalism and Empire* (Chicago: Univ. of Chicago Press, 1999).

CHAPTER SIX

1. Sources on the treatment of Native Americans and enslaved African Americans are numerous. For a recent brief account that emphasizes the construction of a civilization-savage dichotomy and links it to the war on terror, see Charles R. Venator-Santiago, "From the Insular Cases to Camp X-Ray," *Studies in Law, Politics, & Society* 39 (2006): 24–25, 32–35.

2. Paul A. Kramer, *The Blood of Government* (Chapel Hill: Univ. of North Carolina Press, 2006), 102 (quoting Admiral Dewey).

3. "Mr. Hull on the Filipinos: Iowa Congressman Says They Are Not Fit for Self Government—Spooner Bill a Mistake," *New York Times,* 29 Aug. 1901, 2.

4. *E.g.,* "Death for Luzon Bandits: Guerillas Caught by Col. Smith Will Be Shot or Hanged," *New York Times,* 13 Dec. 1899, 1; "Court to Try a Filipino: A Military Commission Will Sit in Judgment on a Bandit at Calambra To-day," *New York Times,* 21 Feb. 1900, 4; "Roosevelt Speaks to Republican Clubs," *New York Times,* 18 July 1900, 7; Frederick W. Eddy, "Obstacles to Order in the Philippines: Natives Abandon Open Warfare and Resort to Guerilla Methods," *New York Times,* 7 Oct. 1900; "Filipino Bandits' Methods: Gen. MacArthur's Remarks on Their Inhuman Ways—Several to be Hanged," *New York Times,* 14 Jan. 1901, 1; "Death for Filipino Bandits," *New York Times,* 4 Sept. 1901, 6. See also Brian McAllister Linn, *The Philippine War, 1899–1902* (Lawrence: Univ. Press of Kansas, 2000), 5; Stuart Creighton Miller, *Benevolent Assimilation* (New Haven, Conn.: Yale Univ. Press, 1982), 15, 91–93, 134, 245–48; Ruth A. Miller, *The Erotics of Corruption* (Albany: State Univ. of New York Press, 2008), 124–27.

5. Linn, *Philippine War,* 300. See also S. Miller, 179.

6. S. Miller, 179–80, 188, 195, 241. See also "Death for Luzon Bandits."

7. Kramer, 89. See also Kimberly Alidio, "When I Get Home, I Want to Forget," *Social Text* 59 (Summer 1999): 105; Oscar V. Campomanes, "Casualty Figures of the American Soldier and the Other," in Angel Velasco Shaw & Luis H. Francia, eds., *Vestiges of War* (New York: New York Univ. Press, 2002), 140.

8. "A War for Civilization," *Washington Post,* 15 Mar. 1906.

9. S. Miller, 188–89, 220, 230; Court Martial of General Jacob Smith, in Leon Friedman, *The Law of War,* vol. 1 (New York: Random House, 1972), 801.

10. S. Miller, 203–8, 211, 225–26, 238; Kramer, 141–42. See also Court-Martial of Major Edwin F. Glenn (Apr. 1902) , in Leon Friedman, 814; Reports regarding the Death of Father Augustine de la Pena, in Leon Friedman, 830; Evan Wallach, "Drop by Drop," *Columbia Journal of Transnational Law* 45 (2007): 494–501.

11. Linn, *Philippine War,* 223, 215. See also "Death for Luzon Bandits"; "Court to Try

a Filipino" (reporting the use of a military commission to try "a Filipino member of [a] guerilla band" and noting that "[t]he case is important as foreshadowing the policy of treating guerillas as bandits"); "Death for Filipino Bandits" (demonstrating the looseness of the terms *bandit* and *guerilla*).

12. Brian McAllister Linn, *The U.S. Army and Counterinsurgency in the Philippine War, 1899–1902* (Chapel Hill: Univ. of North Carolina Press, 1989), 157–58. See also Linn, *Philippine War*, 214–15; Andrew J. Birtle, "The U.S. Army's Pacification of Marinduque, Philippine Islands, April 1900–April 1901," *Journal of Military History* 61 (1997): 265, 268–69, 278–80.

13. Birtle, 263; Linn, *Philippine War*, 215. See also Kramer, 152–54.

14. Birtle, 278.

15. Linn, *U.S. Army*, 155. See also Birtle, 280.

16. Alidio, 109 (citing a contemporaneous estimate of 600,000); Campomanes (estimates a range from 100,000 to 1,000,000, with a consensus of 200,000 to 250,000); Kramer, 157 (250,000 is a conservative estimate); Ronald Spector, review of *Schoolbooks and Krags*, by John M. Gates, *Military Affairs* 37, no. 4 (Dec. 1973), 159 (100,000). I am not aware of figures for the number of Filipinos wounded, tortured, or left homeless.

17. Birtle, 281.

18. Anti-Imperialist League, *Soldiers Letters: Being Materials for the History of a War of Criminal Aggression* (Boston: Rockwell & Churchill, 1899). The introduction to the collection states, "As it is often unable to verify their statements, or even to identify the writers, [the league] disclaims responsibility for their truthfulness. The letters are given for what they are worth." See also Kramer, 445 n. 5 (the collection is "questionable as a primary document").

19. S. Miller, 194.

20. Id., 213. Miller suggests that few people actually died from the water cure.

21. Id., 213–15.

22. "Testified on 'Water Cure,'" *New York Times*, 22 Apr. 1902, 2; "The Water Cure Described: Discharged Soldier Tells Senate Committee How and Why the Torture Was Inflicted," *New York Times*, 4 May 1902, 13; "Tell of 'Water Cure' Cases: Witnesses Give Further Testimony before the Senate Committee on the Philippines regarding Filipino's Treatment," *New York Times*, 13 June 1902, 3. See also S. Miller, 213–15.

23. *Charges of Cruelty, etc., to the Natives of the Philippines*, S. Doc. 205, 57th Cong., 1st Sess. (19 Feb. 1902), 2. See S. Miller, 217. For a response, see Moorfield Storey & Julian Codman, *Secretary Root's Record* (Boston: Geo. H. Ellis, 1902). See also Linn, *Philippine War*, 221 (suggesting that the report's assertion was reasonable under sentiments prevailing at the time).

24. See also Kramer, 140–41, 146–50.

25. *Charges of Cruelty*, 3.

26. Linn, *U.S. Army*, 57–58; S. Miller, 218, 258–59; see Court-Martial of Major Edwin F. Glenn (one-month suspension from command and $50 fine for use of the water cure "not as an exceptional circumstance, but as the habitual method of obtaining information from suspected insurgents"); Court-Martial of Lieutenant Preston Brown (June 1902), in Leon Friedman, 820–29 (dismissal from the army and five years hard labor for murder, commuted by President Roosevelt to a reduction in rank on the first lieutenants list and temporary half pay). See also Reports Regarding the Death of Father Augustine de la Pena, 837 (the water cure "was not justified by military necessity," and "there did not exist, at the time of its commission, a condition of emergency so instant, imperious, and overwhelming in its character as to justify" its use).

27. "The History of International Law at Columbia" (6 Sept. 2007). See also James

Ross, "Bush, Torture, and Lincoln's Legacy," *America: The National Catholic Weekly* (15 Aug. 2005).

28. *Instructions for the Government of Armies of the United States in the Field*, prepared by Francis Lieber, LL.D. (Washington, D.C.: Government Printing Office, 1898; originally issued as General Orders No. 100, Adjutant General's Office, 24 Apr. 1863), arts. 16, 60. For military necessity, see arts. 14–16.

29. Birtle, 266. See also David Bosco, "Moral Principle vs. Military Necessity," *American Scholar*, Winter 2008. Compare Dianne Marie Amann, "Punish or Surveil," *Transnational Law & Contemporary Problems* 16 (2007): 878 (the Lieber Code "remains an 'extraordinarily enlightened' application of reciprocity and humanity—principles that animate contemporary humanitarian law—to international and to irregular wars").

30. Scott Michaelson & Scott Cutler Shershow, "The Guantánamo 'Black Hole': The Law of War and the Sovereign Exception" (12 Jan. 2004), http://world.mediamonitors.net/content/view/full/3849. See *Instructions for the Government of Armies of the United States in the Field*, arts. 15, 82, 84–85.

31. S. Miller, 163.

32. "Filipino Bandits' Methods."

33. Court Martial of General Jacob Smith, in Leon Friedman, 799–813 (Roosevelt quotation at 799, invocation of Lieber Code at 807). See also S. Miller, 227–32, 236, 238, 255.

34. Giles MacDonogh, *After the Reich* (New York: Basic Books, 2007), 235. See also Robert A. Pape, *Bombing to Win* (Ithaca, N.Y.: Cornell Univ. Press, 1996), 92–94, 103–4, 260–62, 269–72 (the British and U.S. air campaign made little effort to avoid extensive civilian casualties).

35. MacDonogh, 237; see also 240.

36. Id., 392–93. See also George G. Lewis & John Mehwa, *History of Prisoner of War Utilization by the United States Army, 1776–1945* (Washington, D.C.: Department of the Army, 1955), 237. The 1929 convention permits requiring POWs to work, but the allies nonetheless desired a parallel, unregulated system. See *Convention Relative to the Treatment of Prisoners of War*, § III (27 July 1929). Still, MacDonogh notes that the United States was more inclined to adhere to existing international humanitarian law standards than were the other Allies.

37. MacDonogh, 4, 394–95, 397–404, 406–7. These tactics were not the norm, particularly when the goal was to obtain useful intelligence. *E.g.,* Petula Dvorak, "A Covert Chapter Opens for Fort Hunt Veterans," *Washington Post*, 20 Aug. 2006, A1.

38. MacDonogh, 362–66.

39. *KUBARK Counterintelligence Interrogation* (July 1963), 1, 2 (redacted version). See also Alfred W. McCoy, *A Question of Torture* (New York: Henry Holt, Owl Books, 2006), 21–53; Michael Otterman, *American Torture* (London: Pluto, 2007), 42–58. The name *KUBARK* is code for the CIA in Vietnam. See Otterman, 54.

40. *KUBARK*, 65–66.

41. Id., i, 8, 82, 65.

42. Id., 83.

43. Id., 84; see also 85 (a prisoner who is about to break needs an "acceptable rationalization: a face-saving reason or excuse for compliance").

44. Id.

45. Id., 85, 86, 87, 90; see also 50 ("[A] subject who has finally divulged the information sought and who has been given a reason for divulging which salves his self-esteem, his conscience, or both, will often be in a mood to take the final step of accepting the interrogator's values and making common cause with him.").

46. Id., 90, 91, 94.

47. Id., 100.

48. Compare Darius Rejali, *Torture and Democracy* (Princeton: Princeton Univ. Press, 2007), 375–84 (there is no science of torture).

49. *Declaration of Honolulu,* parts III & IV (8 Feb. 1966). See also "Have Talking Cell, Will Travel," *Time,* 25 Feb. 1966 (Vice President Hubert Humphrey said that "two wars can be won—the war to defeat the aggressor and the war to defeat the ancient and persistent enemies, disease, poverty, ignorance and despair").

50. "A Small Something for Hanoi," *Time,* 10 Sept. 1965.

51. "The Other Prisoners," *Time,* 19 Mar. 1973. Many of the prisoners were held at Con San, and an earlier article had made clear that U.S. forces were involved to some extent with operation of that prison. See "The Cages of Con San Island," *Time,* 20 July 1970.

52. "Interrogation," *Washington Post,* 21 Jan. 1968, A1.

53. Nick Turse & Deborah Nelson, "Vietnam Horrors: Darker Yet," *Los Angeles Times,* 6 Aug. 2006, A1; Deborah Nelson & Nick Turse, "A Tortured Past," *Los Angeles Times,* 20 Aug. 2006, A1. For My Lai, see United States v. Calley, 48 C.M.R. 19 (1973); "Investigation of the My Lai Incident," Report of the Armed Services Investigating Subcommittee of the Committee on Armed Services, 91st Cong., 2nd Sess. (15 July 1970). For Son Thang, see Gary D. Solis, *Son Thang: An American War Crime* (Annapolis, Md.: Naval Institute Press, 1997). For discussion of the evidence of torture in Vietnam, see Rejali, *Torture and Democracy,* 172–74, 581–91.

54. Testimony of Scott Camil (spelled *Camile* in the transcript), *Winter Soldier Investigation* (31 Jan. 1971). Camil increasingly became an extremely controversial figure in the antiwar movement after his testimony, and by itself, his statement can only be suggestive.

55. Rejali, *Torture and Democracy,* 174. See also Gary D. Solis, "Military Justice, Civilian Clemency," *Transnational Law & Contemporary Problems* 10 (2000): 59–84 (sentences in cases that went to trial were fairly severe, but many cases were never investigated or prosecuted, while appeals and clemency led to significant reductions).

56. "Cages of Con San Island." See also "Other Prisoners"; Don Luce, "The Tiger Cages of Viet Nam," in *Torture, American Style,* Historians against War Pamphlet 3, 9, http://www.historiansagainstwar.org/resources/torture/luce.html; Robert N. Strassfield, "American Innocence," *Case Western Reserve Journal of Int'l Law* 37 (2006): 295–96.

57. Marie-Monique Robin, "Counterinsurgency and Torture," in Kenneth Roth & Minky Worden eds., *Torture: Does It Make Us Safer? Is It Ever OK?* (New York: New Press, 2005), 51–52.

58. McCoy, 61.

59. Otterman, 64. As noted earlier, when U.S. forces encountered the water cure in the Philippines, it was deemed a local or Spanish practice. For European use of water tortures, see Rejali, *Torture and Democracy,* 280–85.

60. McCoy, 63; Mark Moyar, *Phoenix and the Birds of Prey* (Annapolis, Md.: Naval Institute Press, 1997), 90; Otterman, 65–66.

61. John Ranelagh, *The Agency* (New York: Simon & Schuster, 1986), 439–40 (quoting former State Department official Wayne Cooper).

62. Id., 438. See Jennifer Van Bergen & Douglas Valentine, "The Dangerous World of Indefinite Detentions," *Case Western Reserve Journal of Int'l Law* 37 (2007): 459–67.

63. McCoy, 64–67; Rejali, *Torture and Democracy,* 470. William Colby told Congress that more than 20,000 were killed "under the program from 1968 to 1971," but he later claimed that most were combat deaths. See Ranelagh, 440 (citing William Colby & Peter

Forbath, *Honorable Men* (New York: Simon & Schuster, 1978), 270–71). Phoenix was not a combat operation, so it is hard to see how combat deaths could take place under its auspices—unless Colby meant to say that victims were killed in combat based on intelligence gleaned from Phoenix.

64. Rejali notes, "The most optimistic (i.e., most accurately selective scenario) is that about 4.7 innocent persons were killed for every Vietcong agent. In the intermediate case, we have about 10.3 innocents killed for every rebel participant" (*Torture and Democracy,* 471, quoting Stathis Kalyvas & Mathew Kocher, "Violence and Insurgency: Implications for Collective Action," unpublished manuscript, 10 Apr. 2006, 27).

65. Moyar, 88, 90–93, 100, 102–3.

66. For recent use of the term *dirty war* to describe certain forms of violence in Latin American countries in the 1970s and 1980s, see, e.g., Jennifer K. Harbury, *Truth, Torture, and the American Way* (Boston, Mass.: Beacon, 2005).

67. James LeMoyne, "Testifying to Torture," *New York Times,* 5 June 1988, sec. 6, at 45. See also Mireya Navarro, "Guatemalan Army Waged 'Genocide,' New Report Finds," *New York Times,* 26 Feb. 1999, A1; CIA, Inspector General, *Report of Investigation: Selected Issues Relating to CIA Activities in Honduras in the 1980s,* Doc. 96-0125-IG (27 Aug. 1997), 16.

68. LeMoyne.

69. Peter H. Smith, *Talons of the Eagle,* 2nd ed. (New York: Oxford Univ. Press, 2000), 50–52. See also Lars Schoultz, *Beneath the United States* (Cambridge, Mass.: Harvard Univ. Press, 1998); Theodore Roosevelt, "Fourth Annual Message to Congress" (6 Dec. 2004).

70. Schoultz, 253–56, 258.

71. Smith, 71, 130–88.

72. Id., 131.

73. McCoy, 73. See also LeMoyne; Strassfield, 298.

74. McCoy, 74, 86.

75. Werner E. Michel, Assistant to the Secretary of Defense (Intelligence Oversight), *Memorandum for the Secretary of Defense re: Improper Material in Spanish-Language Intelligence Training Manuals* (10 Mar. 1992), 2–3. See also Office of the Assistant Secretary of Defense/Public Affairs Office, *Fact Sheet concerning Training Manuals Containing Materials Inconsistent with U.S. Policy* (1992); Lisa Haugard, "Declassified Army and CIA Manuals Used in Latin America: An Analysis of Their Content" (18 Feb. 1997).

76. U.S. policy and U.S. officials are not the single source of the violent techniques used in Latin America during much of the twentieth century, but they are the source of many. See Rejali, *Torture and Democracy,* passim.

77. Michel, 1–2. See also McCoy, 86–88.

78. McCoy, 78, 88. See also Harbury, 37, 45.

79. Dana Priest, "U.S. Instructed Latins on Executions, Torture," *Washington Post,* 21 Sept. 1996, A1. See also Timothy J. Kepner, "Torture 101," *Dickinson Journal of Int'l Law* 19 (2001): 475. In 2000, the Defense Department reorganized the curriculum to include more courses on human rights and due process and renamed the school the Western Hemisphere Institute for Security Cooperation.

80. *Human Resource Exploitation Training Manual—1983,* L-3, L-4, L-5; see McCoy, 91–94, 99. In 1985, after congressional committees began another investigation, someone edited the manual: "Passages were crossed out and written over by hand to warn that the methods they described were forbidden. However, . . . the original wording remained clearly visible beneath the written changes" (Gary Cohn, Ginger Thompson, & Mark Matthews, "Torture Was Taught by CIA: Declassified Manual Details the Methods Used

in Honduras; Agency Denials Refuted," *Baltimore Sun,* 27 Jan. 1997, 1A). See also Tim Weiner, "C.I.A. Taught, Then Dropped, Mental Torture in Latin America," *New York Times,* 29 Jan. 1997, A11.

81. McCoy, 95–96. See also Kepner; LeMoyne.

82. Harbury, 31, 56–104; Dianna Ortiz, *The Blindfold's Eyes* (Maryknoll, N.Y.: Orbis Books, 2002), 31–33; CIA, *Report of Investigation,* 204 (the ellipses in the quotation indicate redacted material).

83. CIA, *Report of Investigation,* 18. The 1985 policy statement coincides with the clumsy hand editing of the *Human Resources Exploitation Manual.*

84. Lawrence M. Friedman, *Crime and Punishment in American History* (New York: Basic Books, 1993), 361–62.

85. Carolyn B. Ramsey, "In the Sweat Box: A Historical Perspective on the Detention of Material Witnesses," *Ohio State Journal of Criminal Law* 6 (2009): 681; Wesley McNeil Oliver, "The Rise and Fall of Material Witness Detention in Nineteenth Century New York," *NYU Journal of Law & Liberty* 1 (2005): 726.

86. Edward Peters, *Torture,* expanded ed. (Philadelphia: Univ. of Pennsylvania Press, 1996), 111.

87. Lawrence M. Friedman, *American Law in the 20th Century* (New Haven, Conn.: Yale Univ. Press, 2002), 209–10; Welsh S. White, *Miranda's Waning Protections* (Ann Arbor: Univ. of Michigan Press, 2001), 14–22.

88. Peters, 112; W. White, 21–22.

89. U.S. Department of Justice, Office of Justice Programs, Bureau of Justice Statistics, *Special Report: Arrest-Related Deaths in the United States, 2003–2005* (Oct. 2007), 1–2. The study also reported that "80% of law enforcement homicides involved the use of a weapon by the arrest subject" (id., 2).

90. *E.g.,* John Conroy, *Unspeakable Acts, Ordinary People* (New York: Alfred A. Knopf, 2000), 225–41; Lou Cannon, "One Bad Cop," *New York Times Magazine,* 1 Oct. 2000, 62.

91. Amnesty International, *Race, Rights, and Police Brutality* (1999), 3. See also Amnesty International, *Stonewalled: Police Abuse and Misconduct against Lesbian, Gay, Bisexual, and Transgender People in the U.S.* (2005).

92. James Sterngold, "Los Angeles Police Officials Admit Widespread Lapses," *New York Times,* 17 Feb. 2000, A16; James Sterngold, "Police Corruption Inquiry Expands in Los Angeles," *New York Times,* 11 Feb. 2000, A16; Conroy; Rejali, *Torture and Democracy,* 240–41.

93. David Garland, *The Culture of Control* (Chicago: Univ. of Chicago Press, 2001), 14.

94. http://www.ojp.usdoj.gov/bjs/crimoff.htm#prevalence (accessed 8 Nov. 2007).

95. Garland, 12; see also 8–20.

96. Lawrence Friedman, *American Law,* 92–95, 214–17; Lawrence Friedman, *Crime,* 158, 310.

97. Hudson v. McMillian, 503 U.S. 1, 6–9 (1992); Ingraham v. Wright, 430 U.S. 651 (1977); Estelle v. Gamble, 429 U.S. 97, 102 (1976).

98. Hope v. Pelzer, 536 U.S. 730 (2002).

99. Whitley v. Albers, 475 U.S. 312, 320–21 (1986). See also *Hudson,* 503 U.S. at 6.

100. Farmer v. Brennan, 511 U.S. 825, 837 (1994).

101. Id. at 838.

102. Seth F. Kreimer, "Too Close to the Rack and the Screw," *Univ. of Pennsylvania Journal of Constitutional Law* 6 (2003): 283–84; Margo Schlanger, "Inmate Litigation," *Harvard Law Review* 116 (2003): 1557; Prison Litigation Reform Act, Pub. L. No. 104-134, 110 Stat. 1321 (1996); Woodford v. Ngo, 548 U.S. 81 (2006).

103. *Farmer,* 511 U.S. at 858–59 (Thomas, J., concurring); McGill v. Duckworth, 944 F.2d 344, 348 (7th Cir. 1991).

104. *Hudson,* 503 U.S. at 26 (Thomas, J., dissenting); Rhodes v. Chapman, 452 U.S. 337, 347 (1981).

105. U.S. Department of Justice, Bureau of Justice Statistics, *Data Brief: Medical Causes of Death in State Prisons, 2001–04* (Jan. 2007), 1; *Special Report: Suicide and Homicide in State Prisons and Local Jails* (Aug. 2005); *Special Report: Sexual Violence Reported by Correctional Authorities, 2006,* 3; *Special Report: Mental Health Problems of Prison and Jail Inmates* (Sept. 2006), 1, 3; *Special Report: Medical Problems of Inmates, 1997* (Jan. 2001), 1.

106. *E.g., Medical Problems of Inmates,* 2; Jamie Fellner, "Torture in U.S. Prisons," in Roth & Worden, 174; Rejali, *Torture and Democracy,* 179, 242–43, 321.

107. Fellner, 179, 181.

108. Ruiz v. Johnson, 37 F. Supp. 2d 855, 916, 929 (S.D. Tex. 1999), *rev'd,* 243 F.3d 941 (5th Cir. 2001), *remanded,* 154 F. Supp. 2d 975 (S.D. Tex. 2001), *appeal dismissed,* 273 F.3d 1101 (2001). The court reaffirmed the 1999 findings in its 2001 opinion.

109. Mary Sigler, "By the Light of Virtue," *Iowa Law Review* 91 (2006): 570.

110. David Kaiser, "A Letter on Rape in Prisons," *New York Review of Books,* 10 May 2007, 22.

111. Alice Ristroph, "Sexual Punishments," *Columbia Journal of Gender & Law* 15 (2006): 140, 150, 160, 176.

112. Wilkinson v. Austin, 545 U.S. 209, 214 (2005).

113. Id. at 214. The Court concluded that inmates have a liberty interest in not being assigned to a supermax and that prison officials must develop and apply adequate procedures before making transfer decisions. For other rulings that aspects of supermaxes are unconstitutional, see Gillis v. Litscher, 468 F.3d 488 (7th Cir. 2006); Madrid v. Gomez, 889 F. Supp. 1146 (N.D. Cal. 1995).

114. See Scarver v. Litscher, 434 F.3d 972, 974 (7th Cir. 2006); *Gillis,* 468 F.3d at 489–91.

115. *Wilkinson,* 545 U.S. at 214. See Craig Haney, "Mental Health Issues in Long-Term Solitary and 'Supermax' Confinement," *Crime & Delinquency* 49 (2003): 130.

116. Jennifer R. Wynn & Alisa Szatrowski, "Hidden Prisons," *Pace Law Review* 24 (2004): 499; David C. Fathi, "The Common Law of Supermax Litigation," *Pace Law Review* 24 (2004): 676.

117. Wynn & Szatrowski, 506.

118. Haney, 130–32. See also Wynn & Szatrowski, 510–18.

119. Garland, 8–20. See also James E. Robertson, "Houses of the Dead," *Houston Law Review* 34 (1997): 1003.

120. See Joan Dayan, "Held in the Body of the State," in Austin Sarat & Thomas R. Kearns, eds., *History, Memory, and the Law* (Ann Arbor: Univ. of Michigan Press, 1999), 195–98, 213–14.

121. *Cf.* Stephen Holmes, *The Anatomy of Antiliberalism* (Cambridge, Mass.: Harvard Univ. Press, 1993), 230.

122. Michelle Brown, "'Setting the Conditions' for Abu Ghraib," *American Quarterly* 57 (2005): 982, 984. See also Rejali, *Torture and Democracy,* 315; Neil A. Lewis, "F.B.I. Saw Inmates Treated Harshly at Abu Ghraib," *New York Times,* 26 Oct. 2004 ("One agent reported seeing inmates stripped naked and put in isolation cells [which] seemed similar to what the agent had seen in prison strip-searches in the United States.").

123. Kim Cobb, "Ex-head of TDCJ Set Up Iraq Jail," *Houston Chronicle,* 16 May 2004, A1; Devlin Barrett, "Senator Criticizes Hiring of 4 Iraq Prison Officials," *Houston Chronicle,* 3 June 2004, A6. See also U.S. Department of Justice, Press Release, "Department of

Justice Sends 25 Advisors to Iraq in Support of Provisional Authority Effort to Reconstruct Criminal System" (20 May 2003).

124. United States *ex rel.* Knauff v. Shaughnessy, 338 U.S. 537, 544 (1950). See also Shaughnessy v. United States *ex rel.* Mezei, 345 U.S. 206 (1953).

125. Demore v. Kim, 538 U.S. 510, 522 (2003).

126. Kwong Hai Chew v. Colding, 344 U.S. 590 (1953).

127. For a somewhat anecdotal account, see Mark Dow, *American Gulag* (Berkeley: Univ. of California Press, 2004). For the enormous discretion of immigration officials and the often perverse incentives of immigration judges, see Daniel Kanstroom, *Deportation Nation* (Cambridge, Mass.: Harvard Univ. Press, 2007), 237–39.

128. U.S. Department of Justice, Bureau of Justice Statistics, *Special Report: Immigration Offenders in the Federal Criminal Justice System, 2000* (Aug. 2002), 1, 2, 6.

129. For the increasing merger of criminal and immigration law, see Juliet Stumpf, "The Crimmigration Crisis," *American Univ. Law Review* 56 (2006): 367.

130. United States v. Doherty, 786 F.2d 491, 498 (2nd Cir. 1986); Hooker v. Klein, 573 F.2d 1360, 1369 (9th Cir. 1978) (Chambers, J., concurring); Jhirad v. Ferrandina, 536 F.2d 478, 482 (2nd Cir. 1976).

131. First Nat'l Bank of New York v. Aristeguita, 287 F.2d 219, 226–27 (2d Cir. 1960) (citations omitted), *vacated as moot*, 375 U.S. 49 (1963). See 18 U.S.C. § 3184; John G. Kester, "Some Myths of United States Extradition Law," *Georgetown Law Journal* 76 (1988): 1441.

132. Fernandez v. Phillips, 268 U.S. 311, 312 (1925) (emphasis added). See John T. Parry, "The Lost History of International Extradition Litigation," *Virginia Journal of Int'l Law* 43 (2002): 153–58 (discussing efforts to loosen the habeas standard).

133. Parry, "Lost History," 125–50, 158–64, 168–69.

134. Hirabayashi v. United States, 320 U.S. 81 (1943); Korematsu v. United States, 323 U.S. 214 (1944); *Ex parte* Endo, 323 U.S. 283 (1944).

135. Bill Ong Hing, *Making and Remaking Asian America Through Immigration Policy, 1850–1990* (Stanford, Cal.: Stanford Univ. Press, 1993). See also Erika Lee, *At America's Gates* (Chapel Hill: Univ. of North Carolina Press, 2003), 217.

136. Wong Wing v. United States, 163 U.S. 228 (1896). See Kanstroom, 122–23; Lucy E. Salyer, *Laws Harsh as Tigers* (Chapel Hill: Univ. of North Carolina Press, 1995) (modern U.S. immigration doctrine derives from effort to control Chinese immigration).

137. Dow, 6. See also *Mezei*, 345 U.S. at 217 (Jackson, J., dissenting) (petitioner held two years on Ellis Island).

138. Sale v. Haitian Centers Council, 509 U.S. 155, 161–65 (1993) (upholding repatriation program against international law and federal statutory challenges).

139. Mireya Navarro, "For Guantánamo Refugees, Hope Fades as Time Passes," *New York Times,* 10 Dec. 1994, 1; Mireya Navarro, "Resources Strained at Guantánamo Bay," *New York Times,* 4 Sept. 1994, 12.

140. Harold Hongju Koh, "America's Offshore Refugee Camps," *Univ. of Richmond Law Review* 29 (1995): 139. Compare Cuban American Bar Association v. Christopher, 43 F.3d 1412 (11th Cir. 1995) (naval base at Guantánamo not U.S. territory), with Haitian Centers Council v. McNary, 969 F.2d 1326 (2nd Cir. 1992) (some constitutional rights apply to Haitians at Guantánamo because the base is under exclusive U.S. control). The Supreme Court vacated *McNary* as moot after it decided *Sale* (see 509 U.S. 918 (1993)). It decided years later that people held at Guantánamo may seek habeas corpus relief (Rasul v. Bush, 542 U.S. 466 (2004)).

141. T. Alexander Aleinikoff, David A. Martin & Hiroshi Motomura, *Immigration and Citizenship,* 5th ed. (St. Paul: West, 2003), 697. See Dow, 9 (23,000 in 2004). For dis-

cussion of detention of asylum seekers, see Aleinikoff, Martin, and Motomura, 991; Stephen H. Legomsky, *Immigration and Refugee Law and Policy*, 4th ed. (New York: Foundation, 2005), 1106.

142. Zadvydas v. Davis, 533 U.S. 678 (2001). See also Clark v. Martinez, 543 U.S. 371 (2005). For the 3,000 number, see Legomsky, 203.

143. Legomsky, 205–6. See also *Demore*, 538 U.S. 510 (refusing to limit detention of permanent resident aliens while removal proceedings are pending; 85% were detained an average of 47 days, and 15% were detained an average of four months).

144. Dow focuses on Miami's Krome Detention Center. The ACLU has challenged conditions for juveniles at the Hutto Detention Center in Texas. See http://www.aclu .org/immigrants/detention/hutto.html; Margaret Talbot, "The Lost Children," *New Yorker*, 3 Mar. 2008, 58. See also Reno v. Flores, 507 U.S. 292 (1993).

145. Rejali, *Torture and Democracy*, 321.

146. Aleinikoff, Martin, and Motomura, 995–1002. Although federal courts have faced an increasing amount of litigation under the Alien Tort Statute and the Torture Victim Protection Act, the immigration cases are more numerous. They are also more significant, because they consider torture claims in the heightened context of whether to send a person back to the country where the torture allegedly took place.

147. 8 U.S.C. §§ 1101(a)(42), 1231(b)(3)(A); Li v. Attorney General, 400 F.3d 157, 165–66 (3rd Cir. 2005).

148. Al-Saher v. INS, 268 F.3d 1143 (9th Cir. 2001).

149. Foreign Affairs Reform and Restructuring Act, Pub. L. No. 105-277, § 2242(a), (b), 112 Stat. 2681 (1998).

150. 8 C.F.R. § 208.16(c)(2). For people who have committed serious crimes, removal is deferred until conditions change in the country to which they would be removed. 8 C.F.R. § 208.17.

151. *E.g.*, U.S. Department of Justice, Executive Office for Immigration Review, *FY 2006 Statistical Year Book* (Feb. 2007), M1.

152. *E.g., Al-Saher*, 268 F.3d 1143; Kay v. Ashcroft, 387 F.3d 664 (7th Cir. 2004); Khouzam v. Ashcroft, 361 F.3d 161 (2nd Cir. 2004); Mouwad v. Gonzales, 485 F.3d 405 (8th Cir. 2007).

153. Ahmed v. Keisler, 504 F.3d 1183, 1201 (9th Cir. 2007). The court held that police beatings created a probability of persecution, but the dissenting judge disagreed. See id., 1201–3 (Rawlinson, J., dissenting).

154. *E.g.*, Auguste v. Ridge, 395 F.3d 123, 128, 154 (3rd Cir. 2005); Pierre v. Attorney General, 528 F.3d 180 (3rd Cir. 2008) (en banc). See Renee C. Redman, "Defining 'Torture,'" *NYU Annual Survey of American Law* 62 (2007): 465–95.

155. FARRA has played out differently for international extradition. U.S. law forbids courts from inquiring into the conditions or treatment that the extraditee will face in the receiving country. Some courts have suggested an exception on "humanitarian" grounds, but no court has ever denied extradition on this basis. See Prasoprat v. Benov, 421 F.3d 1009, 1016 (9th Cir. 2005); John Quigley, "The Rule of Non-Inquiry and Human Rights Treaties," *Catholic Univ. Law Review* 45 (1996): 1242–47. FARRA suggests a statutory exception but also provides that "no court shall have jurisdiction to review the regulations adopted to implement this section" and that "nothing in this section shall be construed as providing any court jurisdiction to consider or review claims raised under the Convention or this section . . . except as part of the review of a final order of removal" under U.S. immigration law (§ 2242(d)). Courts have split on whether FARRA expands federal court review or simply tells the secretary of state how to exercise non-reviewable discretion. Compare Cornejo-Barreto v. Siefert, 218 F.3d 1004 (9th Cir. 2000)

(federal courts may review the secretary of state's application of FARRA), and *Prasoprat,* 421 F.3d at 1016 n. 5 (same), with Cornejo-Barreto v. Seifert, 379 F.3d 1075 (9th Cir. 2004) (federal courts cannot review application of FARRA), *vacated as moot,* 389 F.3d 1307 (9th Cir. 2004) (en banc), and Mironescu v. Costner, 480 F.3d 664 (4th Cir. 2007) (same).

CHAPTER SEVEN

1. Giorgio Agamben, "What Is a Camp?" in *Means without Ends,* trans. Vincenzo Binetti & Cesare Casarino (Minneapolis: Univ. of Minnesota Press, 2000), 41.

2. For more detailed narratives of many of these events, see U.S. Senate Armed Services Committee, *Inquiry into the Treatment of Detainees in U.S. Custody,* 110th Cong., 2nd sess. (20 Nov. 2008); Jane Mayer, *The Dark Side* (New York: Doubleday, 2008); Philippe Sands, *Torture Team* (New York: Palgrave MacMillan, 2008). For detailed analysis of the legal advice provided by Bush administration lawyers, see Harold H. Bruff, *Bad Advice: Bush's Lawyers in the War on Terror* (Lawrence: Univ. Press of Kansas, 2009).

3. Jules Lobel, "Emergency Power and the Decline of Liberalism," *Yale Law Journal* 98 (1989): 1404, 1408.

4. 50 U.S.C. §§ 1601, 1702.

5. 10 U.S.C. § 333(a)(1)(A). See also 10 U.S.C. §§ 371–74 (the military may provide assistance and personnel to civilian law enforcement without a declared emergency).

6. For inherent or emergency power claims in the controversy over foreign and domestic surveillance, see, *e.g.,* U.S. Department of Justice, *Legal Authorities Supporting the Activities of the National Security Agency Described by the President* (19 Jan. 2006); Chita Ragavan, "The Letter of the Law: The White House Says Spying on Terror Suspects without Court Approval Is OK; What about Physical Searches?" *U.S. News & World Report* (27 Mar. 2006). See also John C. Yoo, Deputy Assistant Attorney General, *Memorandum for William J. Haynes II, General Counsel of the Dept. of Defense, re: Military Interrogation of Alien Unlawful Combatants Held Outside the United States* (14 Mar. 2003), 8 n. 10 ("[O]ur office recently concluded that the Fourth Amendment had no application to domestic military operations.").

7. Whitman v. American Trucking Associations, 531 U.S. 457 (2001); Chevron U.S.A. v. Natural Resources Defense Council, 467 U.S. 837 (1984).

8. Hannah Arendt, *The Origins of Totalitarianism,* new ed. (New York: Harcourt Brace Jovanovich, 1973), 463.

9. Norman Abrams, *Anti-terrorism and Criminal Enforcement,* 3rd ed. (St. Paul: Thomson-West, 2008), 9–10.

10. U.S. Department of Justice, Office of the Inspector General, *The September 11 Detainees: A Review of the Treatment of Aliens Held on Immigration Charges in Connection with the Investigation of the September 11 Attacks* (Apr. 2003), 11.

11. Id., 12 (quoting Ashcroft).

12. Id., 15, 21, 108; Stephen H. Legomsky, *Immigration and Refugee Law and Policy,* 4th ed. (New York: Foundation, 2005), 848; Migration Policy Institute, *America's Challenge: Domestic Security, Civil Liberties, and National Unity after September 11* (2003); Ricardo J. Bascuas, "The Unconstitutionality of Hold until Cleared," *Vanderbilt Law Review* 58 (2005): 680.

13. U.S. Department of Justice, Office of the Inspector General, *Supplemental Report on September 11 Detainees' Allegations of Abuse at the Metropolitan Detention Center in Brooklyn, New York* (Dec. 2003), 1.

14. Department of Justice, *September 11 Detainees,* 197.

15. Department of Justice, *Supplemental Report,* 28. See also Department of Justice, *September 11 Detainees,* 143–45.

16. Mayer, 49, 64.

17. Dana Priest, "CIA Holds Terror Suspects in Secret Prisons," *Washington Post,* 2 Nov. 2005, A1.

18. Dana Priest, "Covert CIA Program Withstands New Furor," *Washington Post,* 30 Dec. 2005, A1.

19. Dan Blaz, "Bush Warns of Casualties of War," *Washington Post,* 18 Sept. 2001, A1; "Bush's Remarks on U.S. Military Strikes in Afghanistan," *New York Times,* 8 Oct. 2001, B6; Mike Allen, "Bush Says Citizens Must Help in Fighting Terror," *Washington Post,* 9 Nov. 2001, A1. See Carol K. Winkler, *In the Name of Terrorism* (Albany: State Univ. of New York Press, 2006), 162.

20. Authorization for Use of Military Force, Pub. L. No. 107-40, § 2(a), 115 Stat. 224 (2001). See Mayer, 44–45.

21. John C. Yoo, Deputy Assistant Attorney General, *Memorandum Opinion for Timothy Flanigan, Deputy Counsel to the President, re: The President's Constitutional Authority to Conduct Military Operations against Terrorists and Nations Supporting Them* (25 Sept. 2001), in Karen J. Greenberg & Joshua L. Dratel eds., *The Torture Papers* (New York: Cambridge Univ. Press, 2005), 20–21.

22. "Transcript of President Bush's Address to a Joint Session of Congress on Thursday night, September 20, 2001."

23. Walter Pincus, "Silence of 4 Terror Probe Suspects Poses Dilemma for FBI, *Washington Post,* 21 Oct. 2001, A6; Jim Rutenberg, "Torture Seeps into Discussion by News Media," *New York Times,* 5 Nov. 2001, C1; Steven Lee Myers & Neil A Lewis, "Rumsfeld Offers Assurances about Use of Military Courts," *New York Times,* 16 Nov. 2001, B10.

24. Alan M. Dershowitz, "Is There a Torturous Road to Justice?" *Los Angeles Times,* 8 Nov. 2001, pt. 2, 19.

25. John C. Yoo & Robert J. Delahunty, *Memorandum for Alberto R. Gonzales, Counsel to the President, and William J. Haynes, General Counsel of the Department of Defense, re: Authority for Use of Military Force to Combat Terrorist Activities within the United States* (23 Oct. 2001), 17.

26. USA PATRIOT Act of 2001, Pub. L. No. 107-56, 115 Stat. 272 (2001).

27. Abrams, 11–12. See also USA PATRIOT Improvement and Reauthorization Act, Pub. L. No. 109-177, 120 Stat. 192 (2006).

28. Homeland Security Act, Pub. L. No. 107-296, 116 Stat. 2135 (2002); Intelligence Reform and Terrorism Prevention Act, Pub. L. No. 108-458, 118 Stat. 3638 (2004); REAL ID Act of 2005, Pub. L. No. 109-13, div. B, 119 Stat. 231 (2005). For discussion of the first two statutes, see Abrams, 39–47.

29. The Posse Comitatus Act prohibits use of the army or air force "as a posse comitatus or otherwise to execute the laws" except as "expressly authorized by the Constitution or Act of Congress" (18 U.S.C. § 1385). The Insurrection Act appears to fit that exception (see 10 U.S.C. § 333). The OLC also argued that the president has inherent power to use the military against terrorists wherever they may be. *See* Yoo & Delahunty, *Authority for Use of Military Force,* 4–14.

30. Michael Hardt & Antonio Negri, *Multitude* (New York: Penguin, 2004), 14.

31. *Detention, Treatment, and Trial of Certain Non-Citizens in the War against Terrorism,* 3 C.F.R. § 918 (2002), in Greenberg & Dratel, 26; id., 25. The order was buttressed by an OLC opinion; the opinion also concluded that trying suspected terrorists under the laws of war "does not mean that [they] will receive the protections of the Geneva Conventions or the rights that the laws of war accord to lawful combatants." See Patrick F.

Philbin, Deputy Assistant Attorney General, *Memorandum Opinion for the Counsel to the President re: Legality of the Use of Military Commissions to Try Terrorists* (6 Nov. 2001), 36.

32. Military Commission Order No. 1, § 6(D)(1) (21 Aug. 2005); Hamdan v. Rumsfeld, 548 U.S. 557, 613–15 (2006). The order originally issued on March 21, 2002, but was the subject of ongoing debate and amendment. See Tim Golden, "After Terror, a Secret Rewriting of Military Law," *New York Times,* 24 Oct. 2004, A1; Tim Golden, "Tough Justice: Administration Officials Split on Stalled Military Tribunals," *New York Times, 25* Oct. 2004, A1.

33. Golden, "Tough Justice"; Mayer, 183–87.

34. Golden, "Tough Justice."

35. Patrick F. Philbin & John C. Yoo, *Memorandum for William J. Haynes, II, General Counsel, Dept. of Defense, re: Possible Habeas Jurisdiction over Aliens Held in Guantánamo Bay, Cuba* (28 Dec. 2001), in Greenberg & Dratel, 29.

36. Id., 32–35.

37. Jay S. Bybee, Assistant Attorney General, *Memorandum for Alberto R. Gonzales, Counsel to the President, and William J. Haynes, General Counsel of the Dept. of Defense, re: Application of Treaties and Laws to al Qaeda and Taliban Detainees* (22 Jan. 2002), in Greenberg & Dratel, 81, 117. A draft of the OLC memorandum focused explicitly on Guantánamo; see John Yoo & Robert Delahunty, *Memorandum for William J. Haynes II, General Counsel, Dept. of Defense, re: Application of Treaties and Laws to al Qaeda and Taliban Detainees* (9 Jan. 2002), in Greenberg & Dratel, 79. For Bush's initial approval, see Armed Services Committee, *Inquiry into Treatment,* 1.

38. Colin L. Powell, *Memorandum to Counsel to the President and Assistant to the President for National Security Affairs re: Draft Decision Memorandum for the President on the Applicability of the Geneva Convention to the Conflict in Afghanistan* (n.d.), in Greenberg & Dratel, 122, 123.

39. Alberto R. Gonzales, *Memorandum for the President, Decision re: Application of the Geneva Convention on Prisoners of War to the Conflict with al Qaeda and the Taliban* (25 Jan. 2002), in Greenberg & Dratel, 118–20. See also Mayer, 124 (David Addington, legal counsel to Vice President Cheney, may have written the Gonzales memo). Ashcroft supported the OLC ("Letter from John Ashcroft to the President" (1 Feb. 2002), in Greenberg & Dratel, 126). The State Department's legal advisor provided additional arguments to support Powell; see William H. Taft, IV, *Memorandum to Counsel to the President re: Comments on Your Paper on the Geneva Conventions* (2 Feb. 2002), in Greenberg & Dratel, 129. The OLC prepared an additional memorandum that addressed some of the issues raised by the State Department; see Jay S. Bybee, Assistant Attorney General, *Memorandum Opinion for the Counsel to the President re: Status of Taliban Forces under Article 3 of the Third Geneva Convention of 1949* (7 Feb. 2002).

40. George Bush, *Memorandum for the Vice President et al. re: Humane Treatment of al Qaeda and Taliban Detainees* (7 Feb. 2002), in Greenberg & Dratel, 134. The January OLC memorandum argued that "in reaching a decision to suspend our treaty obligations . . . the President need not make any specific findings. Rather, he need only authorize or approve policies that would be consistent with the understanding that al Qaeda and Taliban prisoners are not POWs under Geneva III" (Bybee, *Memorandum for Alberto R. Gonzales,* in Greenberg & Dratel, 117). No statement of sovereign power could be clearer. Those who serve the sovereign must interpret and apply his decisions, but he need not explain those decisions, and the presumption is always—at least in the national security context—that he acts as the sovereign who suspends the law and maintains the state of exception.

41. Bush, *Memorandum for the Vice President et al.,* in Greenberg & Dratel, 134.

42. Id., 134–35. Sands (31) and Mayer (79) suggest that the decision not to follow the Geneva Conventions was made before the exchange of legal memos, as evidenced by statements made by Cheney before the memos. See note 37.

43. After the decision, the State Department legal advisor made an additional effort to ground the war on terror in traditional international humanitarian law. See *1949 Geneva Conventions: The President's Decisions under International Law,* attachment to William H. Taft, IV, "Note for Jim Haynes" (22 Mar. 2002), in Karen J. Greenberg ed., *The Torture Debate in America* (New York: Cambridge Univ. Press, 2006), 284–85.

44. Miranda v. Arizona, 384 U.S. 436 (1966).

45. Jay S. Bybee, Assistant Attorney General, *Memorandum for William J. Haynes II, General Counsel, Dept. of Defense, re: Potential Legal Constraints Applicable to Interrogations of Persons Captured by U.S. Armed Forces in Afghanistan* (26 Feb. 2002), in Greenberg & Dratel, 144, 148.

46. See "FBI Summary of Interview with Guantánamo Detainee" (6 Apr. 2002), in Jameel Jaffer & Amrit Singh, eds., *Administration of Torture* (New York: Columbia Univ. Press, 2007), A-228.

47. U.S. Department of the Army, *Field Manual 34-52: Intelligence Interrogation,* 1-7 to 1-9, 3-13 to 3-20 (28 Sept. 1992).

48. "Summarized Witness Statement of Former Interrogation Control Element Chief at Guantánamo" (22 Mar. 2005), in Jaffer & Singh, A-8. See Armed Services Committee, *Inquiry into Treatment,* 3–4, 8, 38, 43, 103–4; Mayer, 188, 197; Sands, 44, 47. Other military officials interrogated prisoners alongside FBI agents as part of a criminal investigative task force. See Mayer, 188–89, 215.

49. Darius Rejali, *Torture and Democracy* (Princeton: Princeton Univ. Press, 2007), 432. See Mayer, 157–62.

50. *Memo from Dept. of Defense Criminal Investigation Task Force Special Agent re: JTF GTMO "SERE" Interrogation SOP Dtd 10 Dec 02* (17 Dec. 2002), in Jaffer & Singh, A-18; Mayer, 189–90. For the SERE methods specifically approved for use at Guantánamo, see *JTF GTMO "SERE" Interrogation Standard Operating Procedure* (10 Dec. 2002).

51. Armed Services Committee, *Inquiry into Treatment,* 16, 21; "Sworn Statement of Lieutenant General Randall Schmidt" (2 Aug. 2005), in Jaffer & Singh, A-69; Mayer, 147.

52. Priest, "CIA Holds Terror Suspects." See also Dana Priest, "Foreign Network at Front of CIA's Terror Fight," *Washington Post,* 18 Nov. 2005, A1; Dana Priest, "Covert CIA Program." For approval of enhanced techniques and the Principals Committee, see Bruff, 235–37; Brian Ross & Richard Esposito, "CIA's Harsh Interrogation Techniques Described: Sources Say Agency's Tactics Lead to Questionable Confessions, Sometimes to Death," *ABC News,* 18 Nov. 2005; Jan Crawford Greenburg, Howard L. Rosenberg, & Ariane de Vogue, "Sources: Top Bush Advisors Approved 'Enhanced Interrogation,'" *ABC News,* 9 Apr. 2008; Lara Jakes, "Cheney, Others OK'd Harsh Interrogations," *ABC News,* 11 Apr. 2008; Mark Mazzetti, "Bush Aides Linked to Talks on Interrogations," *New York Times,* 9 Sept. 2008; Mayer, 143–44.

53. Jay S. Bybee, Assistant Attorney General, *Memorandum for Alberto R. Gonzales, Counsel to the President, re: Standards of Conduct for Interrogation under 18 U.S.C. §§ 2340–2340A* (1 Aug. 2002), in Greenberg & Dratel, 172.

54. Jack Goldsmith, *The Terror Presidency* (New York: W. W. Norton, 2007), 96. For discussion of the reasonable reliance defense, see John T. Parry, "Culpability, Mistake, and Official Interpretations of Law," *American Journal of Criminal Law* 25 (1997): 1.

55. Bybee, *Memorandum for Alberto R. Gonzales,* 176.

56. Id., 191.

57. Id., 203.

58. *E.g.,* José Alvarez, "Torturing the Law," *Case Western Reserve Journal of Int'l Law* 37 (2006): 175; Bruff, 337–52; Kathleen Clark, "Ethical Issues Raised by the OLC Torture Memorandum," *Journal of National Security Law & Policy* 1 (2005): 455; Goldsmith, 143–50; Harold Hongju Koh, "A World without Torture," *Columbia Journal of Transnational Law* 43 (2005): 661; Seth F. Kreimer, "'Torture Lite,' 'Full Bodied' Torture, and the Insulation of Legal Conscience," *Journal of National Security Law & Policy* 1 (2005): 187; David Luban, "Liberalism, Torture, and the Ticking Bomb," *Virginia Law Review* 91 (2005): 1425; Jeremy Waldron, "Torture and Positive Law," *Columbia Law Review* 105 (2005): 1726.

59. For claims that such rights are foundational or archetypal, see Lynn Hunt, *Inventing Human Rights* (New York: W. W. Norton, 2007); Waldron, "Torture."

60. Jay S. Bybee, Assistant Attorney General, *Memorandum for John Rizzo, Acting General Counsel of the Central Intelligence Agency, re: Interrogation of al Qaeda Operative* (1 Aug. 2002), 2.

61. Id., 11, 16–17.

62. See Greenburg et al., "Sources"; Jakes, "Cheney."

63. Ross & Esposito, "CIA's Harsh Interrogation Techniques"; Priest, "Covert CIA Program"; Scott Shane, David Johnston, & James Risen, "Secret U.S. Endorsement of Severe Interrogations," *New York Times,* 4 Oct. 2007, A1; Mayer, 248–55; White House, *President Discusses Creation of Military Commissions to Try Suspected Terrorists* (6 Sept. 2006). At least three were waterboarded. See "CIA Head IDs Waterboarding Subjects: Hayden Names 3 Suspected al-Qaida Operatives, Defends Practice," *MSNBC.com,* 5 Feb. 2007; Brian Ross & Richard Esposito, "Sources Tell ABC News Top al Qaeda Figures Held in Secret CIA Prisons," *ABC News,* 5 Dec. 2005. The CIA claims that no one has been waterboarded since 2003, and it may have ended the use of coercive methods in 2005, due to a combination of legal and political concerns and the waning of concerns about further attacks. See Mark Mazzetti, "Intelligence Chief Cites Qaeda Threat to U.S.," *New York Times,* 6 Feb. 2008; Mark Mozzetti & Scott Shane, "Interrogation Debate Sharply Divided Bush White House," *New York Times,* 4 May 2009, A13.

64. International Committee of the Red Cross, *Report on the Treatment of Fourteen "High Value Detainees" in CIA Custody* (Feb. 2007), 24.

65. "CIA Head IDs Waterboarding Subjects." See also Steven G. Bradbury, Principal Deputy Assistant Attorney General, *Memorandum for John Rizzo, Senior Deputy General Counsel, Central Intelligence Agency, re: Application of United States Obligations Under Article 16 of the Convention Against Torture to Certain Techniques that May Be Used in the Interrogation of High Value al Qaeda Detainees* (30 May 2005), 5 ("To date, the CIA has taken custody of 94 detainees"). For descriptions of the "black sites" and "ghost prisoners," see Human Rights Watch, *Ghost Prisoner* (Feb. 2007); Center for Human Rights & Global Justice at NYU School of Law, *Fate and Whereabouts Unknown: Detainees in the "War on Terror"* (17 Dec. 2005); Human Rights Watch, *The United States' "Disappeared"* (Oct. 2004).

66. Dana Priest, "Wrongful Imprisonment: Anatomy of a CIA Mistake," *Washington Post,* 4 Dec. 2005, A1.

67. Priest, "CIA Holds Terror Suspects"; Ross & Esposito, "Sources Tell"; Amnesty International, *United States of America/Yemen: Secret Detention in CIA "Black Sites,"* AMR 51/177/2005 (2005), 4; Amnesty International et al., *Off the Record* (2007). Funding came from "the classified annex of the first supplemental Afghanistan appropriation" (Priest, "CIA Holds Terror Suspects"), and that appropriation may also have exempted the program from extraterritorial application of federal criminal law.

68. Mayer, 251; Josh White, "Army Documents Shed Light on CIA 'Ghosting,'" *Washington Post*, 24 Mar. 2005, A15

69. Priest, "CIA Holds Terror Suspects." Egypt, Morocco, Syria, and Jordan were the "most common" destinations, but other countries also received suspects, and some people were returned to their own countries to be held in custody. See Mayer, 109–10; Ross & Esposito, "Sources Tell." See also Human Rights Watch, *Double Jeopardy* (Apr. 2008).

70. See Priest, "Wrongful Imprisonment," and the discussion of Maher Arar's allegations in chapter 5 in the present study. See also Margaret L. Satterthwaite, "Rendered Meaningless," *George Washington Law Review* 75 (2007): 1335–50; Michael Hirsh, Mark Hosenball, & John Barry, "Aboard Air CIA," *Newsweek*, 28 Feb. 2005; Scott Shane, Stephen Grey, & Margot Williams, "C.I.A. Expanding Terror Battle under Guise of Charter Flights," *New York Times*, 31 May 2005; Committee on International Human Rights of the Association of the Bar of the City of New York & Center for Human Rights and Global Justice at NYU School of Law, *Torture by Proxy: International and Domestic Law Applicable to "Extraordinary Renditions"* (2004). For overlap between black sites and third-party operations, see Craig Whitlock, "Jordan's Spy Agency: Holding Cell for the CIA," *Washington Post*, 1 Dec. 2007, A1.

71. See Ethan A. Nadelmann, "The Evolution of United States Involvement in the International Rendition of Fugitive Criminals," *New York Univ. Journal of Int'l Law & Policy* 25 (1993): 857.

72. See Mayer, 111–15, 118; Alfred W. McCoy, *A Question of Torture* (New York: Henry Holt, Owl Books, 2006), 109; Michael Scheuer, "A Fine Rendition," *New York Times*, 11 Mar. 2005, A23. OLC opinions upheld the legality of these renditions; see Goldsmith, 36–37, 106.

73. Priest, "CIA Holds Terror Suspects"; Mayer, 108–9; Amnesty International, *United States of America/Yemen;* Satterthwaite, 1343–44.

74. For a somewhat different analysis of these legal issues, see Satterthwaite, 1350–1418. See also Committee on International Human Rights & Center for Human Rights.

75. *Convention against Torture and Other Forms of Cruel, Inhuman, or Degrading Treatment or Punishment*, art. 3 (1984), 1465 U.N.T.S. 85.

76. U.S. Department of State, *United States' Written Response to Questions Asked by the Committee against Torture*, response to #13 (28 Apr. 2006); U.S. Department of State, *The United States' Response to the Questions Asked by the Committee against Torture* (8 May 2006) (citing materials from the drafting of the convention).

77. Foreign Affairs Reform and Restructuring Act, Pub. L. No. 105-277, § 2242, 112 Stat. 2681 (1998).

78. See also U.S. Department of State, *United States' Written Response*, response to #13.

79. Satterthwaite, 1379–94; U.S. Department of State, *List of Issues to be Taken Up in Connection with the Consideration of the Second and Third Periodic Reports of the United States of America*, response to #10 (17 July 2006). *Cf.* Khouzam v. Attorney General, 549 F.3d 235 (3rd Cir. 2008) (holding use of diplomatic assurances in the context of removal is subject to due process constraints).

80. *Convention against Torture*, art. 16(2).

81. U.N. Human Rights Committee, *General Comment 20*, ¶ 9 (10 Mar. 1992). See also J. Herman Burgers & Hans Danelius, *The United Nations Convention against Torture* (Dordrecht: Martinus Nijhoff, 1988), 150.

82. *Comments by the Government of the United States of America on the Concluding*

Observations of the Human Rights Committee, CCPR/C/USA/CO/3/Rev.1/Add.1, at 2–3 (12 Feb. 2008). See also U.S. Department of State, *Second and Third Periodic Report,* annex 1; Matthew Waxman, *Opening Statement on the Report concerning the International Covenant on Civil and Political Rights* (17 July 2006); U.N. Human Rights Committee, *Summary Record of the 1405th Meeting: United States of America,* ¶ 20, CCPR/C/SR.1405 (31 Mar. 1995).

83. People detained while seeking to enter the United States or while changing planes in a U.S. airport usually are not considered to be legally "inside" the United States. See Margaret Taylor, "Detained Aliens Challenging Conditions of Confinement and the Porous Border of the Plenary Power Doctrine," *Hastings Constitutional Law Quarterly* 22 (1992): 1128–33.

84. U.S. Department of State, *List of Issues,* response to #10; *Comments by the Government of the United States,* 8–9.

85. These views were rejected by the International Court of Justice and the Human Rights Committee. See chapter 1 in the present study; U.N. Human Rights Committee, *Concluding Observations of the Human Rights Committee: United States of America,* ¶ 284, CCPR/C/79/Add.50 (3 Oct. 1995). Compare Michael J. Dennis, "Non-Application of Civil and Political Rights Treaties Extraterritorially during Times of International Armed Conflict," *Israel Law Review* 40 (2007): 453.

86. U.S. Department of State, *United States Written Response,* response to #44.

87. William E. Moschella, Assistant Attorney General, "Letter to Senator Patrick Leahy" (4 Apr. 2005). For denial of intent to limit Article 16 in this way during ratification, see Abraham Sofaer, "No Exceptions," *Wall Street Journal,* 26 Nov. 2005, A11.

88. Moschella.

89. *Cf.* Chavez v. Martinez, 538 U.S. 760, 775 (2003) (opinion of Thomas, J.).

90. Alberto Mora, *Memorandum for Inspector General, Department of the Navy, re: Statement for the Record: Office of General Counsel Involvement in Interrogation Issues* (7 July 2004), 3. See also Mayer, 189–93; U.S. Department of Justice, Office of the Inspector General, *A Review of the FBI's Involvement in and Observations of Detainee Interrogations in Guantánamo Bay, Afghanistan, and Iraq* 84 (May 2008) (use of dogs in part from belief that Arabs fear dogs).

91. Mora, 193; Sands, 42–45.

92. Lt. Col. Jerald Phifer, *Memorandum for Commander, Joint Task Force 170, re: Request for Approval of Counter-Resistance Strategies* (11 Oct. 2002), in Greenberg & Dratel, 227–28. For the process of creating the list, including the possibility that Defense Department officials helped create it, see Sands, 45–48, 61–64; Joby Warrick, "Report Questions Pentagon Accounts," *Washington Post,* 17 June 2008, A1. For concerns about lack of authority, see Armed Services Committee, *Inquiry into Treament,* 50.

93. Lt. Col. Diane E. Beaver, *Memorandum for Commander, Joint Task Force 170, re: Legal Brief on Proposed Counter-Resistance Strategies* (11 Oct. 2002), in Greenberg & Dratel, 233–34. Beaver was not aware of the OLC memos. See Sands, 71.

94. Gen. James T. Hill, *Memorandum for Chairman of the Joint Chiefs of Staff re: Counter-Resistance Techniques* (25 Oct. 2002), in Greenberg & Dratel, 223; see also Armed Services Committee, *Inquiry into Treatment,* 67. For preliminary approval, see Department of Justice, *Review of the FBI's Involvement,* 87.

95. Armed Services Committee, *Inquiry into Treatment,* 71; see also Sands, 91–96, 228; Mark Benjamin, "Bush's Top General Quashed Torture Dissent," *Salon.com,* 30 June 2008. Note that Myers and his legal counsel were satisfied with the techniques ultimately recommended to Rumsfeld. See Armed Services Committee, *Inquiry into Treatment,* 95.

96. William J. Haynes II, General Counsel, *Action Memo for Secretary of Defense re:*

Counter-Resistance Techniques (27 Nov. 2002), in Greenberg & Dratel, 236–37; Sands, 103. Mayer (220) suggests that the memo initially contained a fourth category of techniques that was dropped before the final version.

97. Army General Counsel Steven Morello reportedly "tried to stop it" (Mora, 6). For the decision to bypass the typical process of legal review, including consultation with the top judge advocate general in each service branch, see Mayer, 221; Sands, 90–91, 175–76; see also Armed Services Committee, *Inquiry into Treatment,* 67–69.

98. See Bruff, 273 (Rumsfeld "showed signs of caution in what he was willing to approve").

99. U.S. Department of Justice, *Review of the FBI's Involvement,* 86, 88–91.

100. *Legal Analysis of Interrogation Techniques,* forwarded to Marion Bowman, Legal Counsel, FBI (27 Nov. 2002). See also Michael Isikoff, "Secret Memo—Send to Be Tortured," *Newsweek,* 8 Aug. 2005; Sand, 112–21.

101. U.S. Department of Justice, *Review of the FBI's Involvement,* 104–14.

102. Donald Rumsfeld, *Memorandum for Commander USSOUTHCOM, re: Counter-Resistance Techniques* (15 Jan. 2003), in Greenberg & Dratel, 239. See also Mora, 7–15; *Final Report of the Independent Panel to Review DoD Detention Operations* (Aug. 2004), in Greenberg & Dratel, 911 (hereinafter cited as Schlesinger Report); Mayer, 221–28; Sands, 132–43.

103. U.S. Department of Justice, *Review of the FBI's Involvement,* 118; Armed Services Committee, *Inquiry into Treatment,* 108, 128–30.

104. *Working Group Report on Detainee Interrogations in the Global War on Terrorism: Assessment of Legal, Historical, Policy, and Operational Considerations* (4 Apr. 2003), in Greenberg & Dratel, 287.

105. Yoo, *Memorandum for William J. Haynes II.* The report initially contained a more critical analysis, but Haynes informed the group that the OLC memo was controlling. See Armed Services Committee, *Inquiry into Treatment,* 118–20.

106. *Working Group Report,* in Greenberg & Dratel, 288–90.

107. Id., 291–93, 307–13, 316–23. The report does not adopt the torture memo's definition of severe physical pain. See id., 293–94.

108. Id., 305, 307.

109. As with Rumsfeld's earlier approval of interrogation techniques for Guantánamo, the working group's report did not receive the ordinary full review in its final version. See Mayer, 229–33; Sands, 231–34. The judge advocate generals of the army and navy, the staff judge advocate of the marines, and the deputy judge advocate general of the air force took issue with aspects of the report's legal analysis, worried that the report could subject service members to prosecution domestically or to harsh treatment in other countries, and noted that disclosure of these tactics would lead to outrage. See K. Greenberg, 377–91; Josh White, "Military Lawyers Fought Policy on Interrogations," *Washington Post,* 15 July 2005, A1. Navy general counsel Alberto Mora also objected to the draft report (Mora, 18–20). See also Bruff, 274–77.

110. *Working Group Report,* in Greenberg & Dratel, 341–47. The report stated that hooding, mild physical contact, and threats of transfer to another country are not exceptional techniques, but it cautioned that interrogators should consider their cumulative effects. One draft included waterboarding, but several members of the group objected that it "constitutes torture under both domestic and international law" (Rear Adm. Michael F. Lohr, *Memorandum for the Air Force General Counsel, Subj: Comments on the 6 March 2003 Detainee Interrogation Working Group Report,* in K. Greenberg, 391; see Vice Adm. A. T. Church III, *Review of Department of Defense Detention Operations and Detainee Interrogation Techniques* (7 Mar. 2005), 5 (hereinafter cited as Church Re-

port)). Three other methods were also considered and rejected (Church Report, 5. See also Armed Services Committee, *Inquiry into Treatment,* 124).

111. Donald Rumsfeld, *Memorandum for the Commander, US Southern Command, re: Counter-Resistance Techniques in the War on Terrorism* (16 Apr. 2003), in Greenberg & Dratel, 360. The four methods that required necessity were the use of incentives, "pride and ego down," "mutt and jeff," and isolation.

112. Mayer, 234.

113. Headquarters, Joint Task Force—Guantánamo, *Camp Delta Standard Operating Procedures* 3.3, 4.2–4.3 (28 Mar. 2003).

114. Id., 4.3, 6.7–6.8, & chs. 8–9.

115. The document provides that "policies and procedures will be reviewed every 120 days" and that "minor revisions" will be made periodically (id., ii, 1.1). A revision appeared in March 2004.

116. Giorgio Agamben, *Homo Sacer* (1995), trans. Daniel Heller-Roazen (Stanford, Cal.: Stanford Univ. Press, 1998), 169.

117. Id., 171. For the centrality of the prison and military camp to ideas of biopolitics and governmentality, see Michel Foucault, *Discipline and Punish,* trans. Alan Sheridan (New York: Pantheon, 1978); Michel Foucault, *Security, Territory, Population,* trans. Graham Burchell (New York: Palgrave Macmillan, 2007).

118. Thus, the identity produced at Guantánamo is in some sense an active political life, as opposed to the bare life produced in the Nazi camps, which, according to Agamben, "are not merely the place of death and extermination" but "also, and above all, the site of the production of the *Muselmann,* the final biopolitical substance to be isolated in the biological continuum," beyond which "lies only the gas chamber" (Giorgio Agamben, *Remnants of Auschwitz* (1999), trans. Daniel Heller-Roazen (New York: Zone Books, 2002), 85). The testimony of the Guantánamo detainee is not that of the Muselmann, who bears witness to what cannot be said.

119. Headquarters, Joint Task Force—Guantánamo, 2003, 17.1 & chs. 5, 24, 25; "Secret Report Questions Guantánamo Tactics," *New York Times,* 2 Feb. 2005, A14.

120. Neil A. Lewis, "Fresh Details Emerge on Harsh Methods at Guantánamo," *New York Times,* 1 Jan. 2005, 11. See also Armed Services Committee, *Inquiry into Treatment,* 132–46; Neil A. Lewis, "Broad Use of Harsh Tactics Is Described at Cuba Base," *New York Times,* 17 Oct. 2004, sec. 1, 27.

121. Neil A. Lewis, "Red Cross Finds Detainee Abuse in Guantánamo," *New York Times,* 30 Nov. 2004, A6. See also Josh White & John Mintz, "Red Cross Cites 'Inhumane' Treatment at Guantánamo," *Washington Post,* 1 Dec. 2004, A10. For CITF and FBI concerns, see U.S. Department of Justice, *Review of the FBI's Involvement,* 88, 120–28, 152–54; Jaffer & Singh, A-127–A-145, A-154–A-176, A-228–A-230; Mayer, 202–4, 216–17.

122. Lt. Gen. Randall Schmidt & Brig. Gen. John Furlow, *Army Regulation 15-6: Final Report, Investigation into FBI Allegations of Detainee Abuse at Guantánamo Bay, Cuba Detention Facility* (1 Apr. 2005, amended 9 June 2005), in Jaffer & Singh, A-109, A-113, A-116–A-118. See also U.S. Department of Justice, *Review of the FBI's Involvement,* 172–203 (detailing tactics observed by or reported to FBI agents at Guantánamo). Pouring water over the prisoner could be a form of waterboarding or an aspect of the extreme temperature method.

123. Thom Shanker, "6 G.I.'s in Iraq Are Charged with Abuse Of Prisoners," *New York Times,* 21 Mar. 2004, 9; Thom Shanker & Jacques Steinberg, "Bush Voices 'Disgust' at Abuse of Iraqi Prisoners," *New York Times,* 1 May 2004, A1; U.S. Department of the Army, Inspector General, *Report on Detainee Operations* (21 July 2004), in Greenberg & Dratel, 632–33, 637 (hereinafter cited as Mikolashek Report).

124. Schlesinger Report, 911, 925. See also Church Report, 196–201; U.S. Department of Justice, *Review of the FBI's Involvement*, 68–69; Mayer, 94, 126; Armed Services Committee, *Inquiry into Treatment*, 149–50, 153–54.

125. Chris Mackey & Greg Miller, *The Interrogators* (New York: Little, Brown, 2004), 195, 350, 354–63, 476.

126. Armed Services Committee, *Inquiry into Treatment*, 153.

127. Schlesinger Report, 911, 925, 941. See U.S. Department of Justice, *Review of the FBI's Involvement*, 213–31 (detailing tactics observed by or reported to FBI agents in Afghanistan); Suzanne Goldenberg & James Meek, "Papers Reveal Bagram Abuse," *Guardian*, 18 Feb. 2005, 1; Lara Jakes, "Pentagon Records Detail Prisoner Abuse by U.S. Military," *Associated Press*, 17 Apr. 2008; Tom Lasseter, "U.S. Abuse of Detainees was Routine at Afghanistan Bases," *McClatchy Newspapers*, 16 June 2008.

128. Armed Services Committee, *Inquiry into Treatments*, 158–61.

129. Schlesinger Report, 911, 925.

130. Schlesinger Report, 911, 925; Armed Services Committee, *Inquiry into Treatment*, 165–67, 169. See also U.S. Department of Justice, *Review of the FBI's Involvement*, 236–61 (reporting tactics observed by or reported to FBI agents in Iraq); "Sworn Statement of Capt. Carolyn Wood" (21 May 2004), in Jaffer & Singh, A-196–A-197; Mayer, 245 (reporting that some army commandos received SERE training for interrogation purposes). By April 2004, army officials had investigated 25 deaths in custody in Afghanistan and Iraq and a large number of abuse allegations. See *Information Paper re: Allegations of Detainee Abuse in Iraq and Afghanistan* (2 Apr. 2004), in Jaffer & Singh, A-260; *USMC Alleged Detainee Abuse Cases since 11 Sep 01* (16 June 2004), in Jaffer & Singh, A-271. See also Human Rights Watch, *"No Blood, No Foul"* (July 2006).

131. "Sworn Statement of Capt. Carolyn Wood," in Jaffer & Singh, A-192. For pressure placed on interrogators, see Schlesinger Report, 924, 940; Seymour M. Hersh, *Chain of Command* (New York: HarperCollins, 2004), 57–58.

132. *Investigation of Intelligence Activities at Abu Ghraib* (23 Aug. 2004), in Greenberg & Dratel, 1062–65 (Fay) (hereinafter cited as Fay-Jones Report). No standard operating procedures were in effect at that time for Abu Ghraib. See "Sworn Statement of Capt. Carolyn Wood," in Jaffer & Singh, A-193; Maj. Gen. Antonio M. Taguba, *Article 15-6 Investigation of the 800th Military Police Brigade* (Mar. 2004), in Greenberg & Dratel, 429 (hereinafter cited as Taguba Report). See also Sands, 151 (conditions of "near lawlessness" at Abu Ghraib when Miller visited).

133. Fay-Jones Report, 1045–46.

134. Id., 1047.

135. Maj. Gen. Geoffrey Miller, *Assessment of DoD Counterterrorism Interrogation and Detention Operations in Iraq*, in Greenberg & Dratel, 455 (annex 20 to the Taguba Report). See Schlesinger Report, 912, 925, 944, 946; Hersh, 31. The Schlesinger Report (946) concluded that while Miller intended dogs to be used in a manner similar to that provided in the standard operating procedures for Guantánamo, interrogators at Abu Ghraib misinterpreted him. The use of military dogs during interrogations at Guantánamo suggests a more complicated message.

136. Jaffer & Singh, A-220, A-223.

137. http://www.pbs.org/wgbh/pages/frontline/torture/paper/ponce.html; Josh White, "Soldiers' 'Wish Lists' of Detainee Tactics Cited," *Washington Post*, 19 Apr. 2005, A16.

138. Lt. Gen. Ricardo S. Sanchez, *Memorandum re: CJTF-7 Interrogation and Counter-Realisation Policy* (14 Sept. 2003), in Jaffer & Singh, A-232. See also Fay-Jones Report, 1035–36 (Fay), 1063 (Jones); Sands, 151. Sleep management and stress positions

are akin to the working group's prolonged standing and prolonged interrogation or sleep deprivation approaches, and use of military dogs is a subset of "increasing anxiety by use of aversions" (*Working Group Report,* in Greenberg & Dratel, 359). Deception seems a variation on the field manual's "file and dossier" tactic. *See* U.S. Department of the Army, *Field Manual 34–52,* at 3–19.

139. Mayer, 242.

140. Schlesinger Report, 925.

141. Lt. Gen. Ricardo S. Sanchez, *Memorandum re: CJTF-7 Interrogation and Counter-Resistance Policy* (12 Oct. 2003), in Jaffer & Singh, A-238–A-239.

142. Fay-Jones Report, 1004 (Jones). See also id., 1030, 1036 (Fay); Schlesinger Report, 925.

143. "Sworn Statement of Capt. Carolyn Wood," in Jaffer & Singh, A-197–A-198.

144. Fay-Jones Report, 1037 (Fay).

145. See also Sands, 151.

146. Church Report, 1.

147. J. White, "Soldiers' 'Wish Lists' "; Fay-Jones Report, 989 (executive summary), 1037 (Fay); Schlesinger Report, 925–26.

148. Fay-Jones Report, 995 (Jones), 1024, 1049, 1056–58 (Fay).

149. Taguba Report, 418. See also Fay-Jones Report, 1002, 1009 (Jones).

150. Fay-Jones Report, 1072, 1024 (Fay). Similarly, Miller suggested that dogs could be used for certain purposes, and Fay found that they were used for abuse as soon as they began to arrive in November 2003 (id., 1024–25). See also Hersh, 36.

151. Fay-Jones Report, 1072 (Fay).

152. Schlesinger Report, 911–12, 924.

153. Taguba Report, 416–17. See also Fay-Jones Report, 1070–71 (Fay).

154. Rejali, *Torture and Democracy,* 333.

155. Fay-Jones Report, 1007 (Jones), 1024 (Fay); Mikolashek Report, 633; Schlesinger Report, 914.

156. Schlesinger Report, 912–14, 928–33.

157. Susan T. Fiske, Lasana T. Harris & Amy J. C. Cuddy, "Why Ordinary People Torture Enemy Prisoners," *Science* 306 (26 Nov. 2004): 1483. See also Herbert C. Kelman, "The Social Context of Torture," in R. D. Crelinsten & A. P. Schmid, eds., *The Politics of Pain* (Boulder: Westview, 1995), 19.

158. Philip Zimbardo, *The Lucifer Effect* (New York: Random House, 2007), 211. See also Dianne Marie Amann, "Abu Ghraib," *Univ. of Pennsylvania Law Review* 153 (2005): 2132–36; Mark A. Drumbl, *Atrocity, Punishment, and International Law* (New York: Cambridge Univ. Press, 2007), 8, 30–31.

159. Zimbardo, 221–22.

160. Agamben, *Homo Sacer,* 125, 170.

161. Goldsmith, 152–55; Daniel Levin, Acting Assistant Attorney General, "Letter to DoD General Counsel William J. Haynes II re: Memorandum for William J. Haynes II, General Counsel of the Department of Defense, from John Yoo, Deputy Assistant Attorney General, Office of Legal Counsel, re: Military Interrogation of Alien Unlawful Combatants Held Outside the United States (Mar. 14, 2003)" (4 Feb. 2005).

162. Brig. Gen. Richard P. Formica, *Article 15-6 Investigation of CJSOTF-AP and 5th SF Group Detention Operations* (8 Nov. 2004), 7 n. 3. See also Church Report, 232 (new policy applied to Afghanistan in June 2004). General Miller was transferred to Iraq in spring 2004 to end abuse and restore order to detention and interrogation operations there (Sewell Chan & Jackie Spinner, "Guantánamo Official to Monitor Prison," *Boston*

Globe, 30 Apr. 2004). While this move allowed the transfer of Guantánamo abuses to Iraq, the goal was to professionalize operations in Iraq, and Guantánamo was still portrayed as a place that operated correctly and professionally.

163. Goldsmith, 158–60.

164. 542 U.S. 507, 521 (2004) (plurality opinion).

165. Id. at 520–21, 536–37; id. at 552 (Souter, J., concurring).

166. 542 U.S. 466, 483–84 (2004). See also id. at 498 (Scalia, J., dissenting) (decision "extends the scope of the habeas statute to the four corners of the earth").

167. The *Hamdi* plurality required "notice of the factual basis for . . . classification, and a fair opportunity to rebut the Government's factual assertions before a neutral decisionmaker," but it admitted that "proceedings may be tailored to alleviate their uncommon potential to burden the Executive" during military conflict (542 U.S. at 533).

168. Paul Wolfowitz, *Memorandum to the Secretary of the Navy* (7 July 2004); Gordon England, *Memorandum to the Secretary of State et al.* (14 Sept. 2004).

169. U.S. Department of Defense, *Combatant Status Review Tribunal Summary* (Mar. 2005).

170. Detainee Treatment Act of 2005, Pub. L. No. 109-148, § 1005(e)(2), 119 Stat. 2680, 2742 (2006).

171. Id., §§ 1002(a), 1003(a),(d).

172. Id., §§ 1004, 1005(b).

173. White House, *President's Statement on Signing of H.R. 2863, the "Department of Defense, Emergency Supplemental Appropriations to Address Hurricanes in the Gulf of Mexico, and Pandemic Influenza Act, 2006"* (30 Dec. 2005). See Bruff, 257–58.

174. Daniel Levin, *Memorandum for James B. Comey, Deputy Attorney General, re: Legal Standards Applicable Under 18 U.S.C. §§ 2340–2340A* (30 Dec. 2004), in K. Greenberg, 368.

175. Shane, Johnston, & Risen; Levin, *Memorandum for James B. Comey,* in K. Greenberg, 362 n. 8. See Bruff, 252–54; Mayer, 306–7.

176. Shane, Johnston, & Risen. See Stephen G. Bradbury, Principal Deputy Assistant Attorney General, *Memorandum for John A. Rizzo, Senior Deputy General Counsel, Central Intelligence Agency, re: Application of 18 U.S.C. §§ 2340-2340A to Certain Techniques That May Be Used in the Interrogation of a High Value al Qaeda Detainee* (10 May 2005); Stephen G. Bradbury, Principal Deputy Assistant Attorney General, *Memorandum for John A. Rizzo, Senior Deputy General Counsel, Central Intelligence Agency, re: Application of 18 U.S.C. §§ 2340-2340A to the Combined Use of Certain Techniques in the Interrogation of High Value al Qaeda Detainees* (10 May 2005); Bradbury, *Memorandum for John A. Rizzo, re: Application of United States Obligations.* For the suggestion that Daniel Levin, the author of the December 2004 memo, was pushed out at least in part because that memo displeased his superiors, see Jan Crawford & Ariane de Vogue, "Former AG Accused of Playing Politics with Justice," *ABC News,* 19 June 2008.

177. See Bradbury, *Memorandum for John A. Rizzo, re: Application of United States Obligations,* 28–31.

178. U.S. Department of State, "Press Availability with Ukrainian President Viktor Yushchenko" (7 Dec. 2005). See also Glenn Kessler & Josh White, "Rice Seeks to Clarify Policy on Prisoners," *Washington Post,* 8 Dec. 2005, A1.

179. Compare, *e.g.,* U.N. Commission on Human Rights, *Situation of Detainees at Guantánamo Bay,* E/CN.4/2006/120 (15 Feb. 2006), with *Reply to the Report of the Five UNCHR Special Rapporteurs on Detainees in Guantánamo Bay, Cuba* (10 Mar. 2006), 16, 17, 25–30, 34. See also John Bellinger & William Haynes, "Letter to Jakob Kellenberger on Customary International Law Study," in *Int'l Legal Materials* 46 (2007): 514.

180. J. White, "Military Lawyers"; *Reply to the Report of the Five UNCHR Special Rapporteurs*, 31.

181. Gordon England, *Memorandum for Secretaries of the Military Departments et al. re: Interrogation and Treatment of Detainee by the Department of Defense* (30 Dec. 2005); *Reply to the Report of the Five UNCHR Special Rapporteurs*, 46.

182. *Hamdan*, 548 U.S. at 625–35.

183. Id. at 2749. The Court avoided deciding whether the president may convene military commissions "in cases of 'controlling necessity' " (id. at 2774). Compare Madsen v. Kinsella, 343 U.S. 341, 348 (1952).

184. Guy Dinmore, "CIA Agents 'Refused to Operate' at Secret Jails," *Financial Times*, 20 Sept. 2006, 1.

185. White House, *President Discusses Creation of Military Commissions.* For Defense Department acceptance that Common Article 3 applied, see Gordon England, *Memorandum to the Secretaries of the Military Departments et al.* (7 July 2006).

186. U.S. Department of the Army, *Field Manual No. 2.22-3, Human Intelligence Collector Operations* (6 Sept. 2006), 5–6, 5-13–5-14, 5-17–5-18, 5-20.

187. Id., 5-19.

188. Id., 5-14–5-15.

189. Id., 5-15–5-16. See also id., 8-1.

190. Id., 5-21.

191. Id., 8-6–8-18, app. M.

192. Military Commissions Act, Pub. L. No. 109-366, §§3, 4, 7(a), 9, 10, 120 Stat. 2600, 2600–2631, 2636–37 (2006).

193. 128 S. Ct. 2229 (2008).

194. Military Commissions Act, § 6; White House, press release, *The Military Commissions Act of 2006* (17 Oct. 2006).

195. Military Commissions Act, § 6(a)(2).

196. Id., § 6(d)(1)(B), (2)(A),(D)&(E).

197. Id., §§ 5, 6(a)(2)&(3). Michael Matheson concludes that the new War Crimes Act "contains more ambiguities than the original version" ("The Amendments of the War Crimes Act," *American Journal of Int'l Law* 101 (2007): 51), but this conclusion may reflect less the content of the statute and more the author's unwillingness to admit the breadth of the MCA's redefinition and restriction of Common Article 3.

198. White House, *Executive Order: Trial of Alien Unlawful Enemy Combatants by Military Commission* (14 Feb. 2007). For notifications of sworn charges and other materials from military commission cases, see http://www.defenselink.mil/news/commissions.html.

199. White House, *Executive Order: Interpretation of the Geneva Conventions Common Article 3 as Applied to a Program of Detention and Interrogation Operated by the Central Intelligence Agency* (20 July 2007), § 3(b). See Bruff, 259–60.

200. For doctors, see Jonathan H. Marks, "Doctors as Pawns?" *Seton Hall Law Review* 37 (2007): 711; Physicians for Human Rights, *Broken Laws, Broken Lives* (June 2008), 21, 48, 57–58, 85–87. For Iraqi forces, see Human Rights Watch, *The New Iraq?* (Jan. 2005). For contractors, see Fay-Jones Report.

201. *Comments by the Government of the United States*, 3; Matt Spetalnick, "Bush Approved CIA Disclosure on Waterboarding," *washingtonpost.com* (6 Feb. 2008). See also Office of the Director of National Intelligence, *Summary of the High Value Terrorist Detainee Program* (2006), 3–5; Evan Thomas & Michael Hirsh, "The Debate over Torture," *Newsweek*, 21 Nov. 2005.

202. See John T. Parry, "Torture Warrants and the Rule of Law," *Albany Law Review* 71 (2008): 885–906.

203. See David Johnston & Charlie Savage, "Obama Reluctant to Look into Bush Programs," *New York Times,* 12 Jan. 2009, A1; William Glaberson & Helene Cooper, "Obama's Plan to Close Prison at Guantánamo May Take a Year," *New York Times,* 13 Jan. 2009, A1.

204. Slavoj Žižek, *Welcome to the Desert of the Real* (London: Verso, 2002), 104.

CONCLUSION

1. *Convention against Torture and Other Forms of Cruel, Inhuman, or Degrading Treatment or Punishment,* art. 1 ¶ 1, art. 16 ¶ 1 (1984), 1465 U.N.T.S. 85. The phrase "for such purposes as" suggests that the list is not exclusive, but the examples in the text of the convention provide an important reference point for international law's regulation of torture. Compare Darius Rejali, *Torture and Democracy* (Princeton: Princeton Univ. Press, 2007), 35 ("Torture is the systematic infliction of physical torment on detained individuals by state officials for police purposes, for confession, information, or intimidation."); Darius Rejali, "Modern Torture as Civic Marker," *Journal of Human Rights* 2 (2003): 153 (torture consists of "physical and often sanguinary violence on individuals sanctioned by state authorities for state purposes" and "is characterized by standard technology and procedures reproduced over time").

2. Kate Millet, *The Politics of Cruelty* (New York: W. W. Norton, 1994), 101, 108–9; Barrington Moore Jr., *Moral Purity and Persecution in History* (Princeton: Princeton Univ. Press, 2000).

3. Robert Cover, "Violence and the Word," *Yale Law Journal* 95 (1986): 1603. For a similar discussion, see Mordechai Kremnitzer, "The Landau Commission Report", *Israel Law Review* 23 (1989): 250. See also Henry Shue, "Torture," *Philosophy & Public Affairs* 7 (1978): 131–32 (torture solely for obtaining information is extremely rare).

4. Elaine Scarry, *The Body in Pain* (New York: Oxford Univ. Press, 1985), 41–42. See also Michel Foucault, *Discipline and Punish,* trans. Alan Sheridan (New York: Pantheon, 1978), 42.

5. Kremnitzer, 251.

6. Id., 250 n. 67; Cover, 1603; Millet, 108–10; Scarry, 35–37. Compare Shue, "Torture," 135 ("[B]etrayal is no escape for a dedicated member of either a government or its opposition, who cannot collaborate without denying his or her highest values.").

7. See Shue, "Torture," 130–31, 133–37 (assessing this logic).

8. For a roughly similar point, see Millet, 300.

9. E.g., Giorgio Agamben, *State of Exception,* trans. Kevin Attell (Chicago: Univ. of Chicago Press, 2005); Oren Gross, "The Normless and Exceptionless Exception," *Cardozo Law Review* 21 (2000): 1854, 1857 (2000); Sanford Levinson, "Torture in Iraq and the Rule of Law in America," *Dædalus* (Aug. 2004): 5.

10. Compare Sanford Levinson, "In Quest of a 'Common Conscience,'" *Journal of National Security Law & Policy* 1 (2005): 238 (broad definitions risk "trivializ[ing] the concept of torture and diminish[ing] the special horror attached to that term"). See also Rejali, *Torture and Democracy,* 38–39. Treating torture as a "special horror" too easily allows people to ignore the harder task of sorting out what it means to live under pervasive and sometimes violent authority derived from a variety of practices. Collapsing the definitions of torture and cruel, inhuman, or degrading treatment might prevent officials from arguing that no matter what they did, at least it was not torture. The only

issues would be whether they deliberately caused suffering and perhaps whether they could justify their actions. See also Malcolm D. Evans, "Getting to Grips with Torture," *Int'l & Comparative Law Quarterly* 51 (2002): 382.

11. In a causal sense, one can still hold the torturer legally or morally responsible for the mental suffering that the victim inflicts on himself or herself. But sorting out the causes and degree of mental anguish in these circumstances is a project of enormous complexity. Further, although perhaps perversely, the self-inflicted nature of the anguish adds elements of agency and control back into the equation on the victim's side.

12. *KUBARK Counterintelligence Interrogation* (July 1963), 90, 91, 94 (redacted version).

13. David Sussman, "What's Wrong with Torture?" *Philosophy & Public Affairs* 33 (2005): 19, 21. See also Scarry, 46–47.

14. Rejali, *Torture and Democracy,* 35.

15. Kremnitzer, 250; Scarry, 35, 38.

16. Cover, 1603; Rejali, *Torture and Democracy,* 35; Ñacuñán Sáez, "Torture: A Discourse on Practice," in Frances E. Mascia-Lees & Patricia Sharpe, eds., *Tattoo, Torture, Mutilation, and Adornment* (Albany: State Univ. of New York Press, 1992), 138. See also Paul Kahn, *Sacred Violence* (Ann Arbor: Univ. of Michigan Press, 2008), 31. For Scarry, torture involves "an almost obscene conflation of private and public," and she stresses destruction—"all the solitude of absolute privacy with none of its safety, all the self-exposure of the utterly public with none of its possibility for camaraderie or shared experience" (53). But this conflation of public and private also creates a new relationship with power.

17. Welat Zeydanlıoğlu, "Torture and Turkification in the Diyarbakır Military Prison," in John T. Parry & Welat Zeydanlıoğlu, eds., *Rights, Citizenship, and Torture: Perspectives on Evil, Law and the State* (Oxford: Inter-Disciplinary Press, 2009), 76, 84–85.

18. Stephen Holmes, *The Anatomy of Antiliberalism* (Cambridge, Mass.: Harvard Univ. Press, 1993), 230.

19. Joseph Raz, *The Morality of Freedom* (Oxford: Clarendon, 1986), 412, 423.

20. Foucault, *Discipline,* 193.

21. *KUBARK,* 83.

22. Id., 84.

23. Id., 83.

24. Michel Foucault, *Psychiatric Power,* trans. Graham Burchell (New York: Palgrave Macmillan, 2006), 184–85. Foucault also describes a therapeutic technique called "the shower." As the patient struggles, the doctor "directs the shower on him violently, deep in his throat." Sometimes, too, the patient would have cold water poured over his head (id., 149, 157).

25. Id., 234.

26. Id., 165.

27. See also Foucault, *Discipline,* 128–29 (discussing the shaping of an obedient subject through punishment).

28. This commonality helps explain why other writers have described aspects of modern torture in terms of Foucauldian discipline. *E.g.,* Talal Asad, "On Torture, or Cruel, Inhuman, and Degrading Treatment," in Arthur Kleinman et al., eds., *Social Suffering* (Berkeley: Univ. of California Press, 1997), 288–89.

29. Foucault, *Psychiatric Power,* 57. See also Foucault, *Discipline,* 194, 222.

30. *Cf.* Foucault, *Discipline,* 89–90 (noting the idea that an individual consents to punishment through social contract). See also id., 237–39 (discussing "self-regulation of the penalty"), 303 (discussing the role of the disciplines in counterpoint to the ideas of choice and contract).

31. For discussion of torture's failure to produce useful information, see Rejali, *Torture and Democracy*, chs. 21, 22.

32. Foucault, *Psychiatric Power*, 265–69, 317–18.

33. James Polk, "Testimony: Abu Ghraib Photos 'Just for Fun,'" *CNN.com*, 3 Aug. 2004.

34. Writing about photography of women's bodies in the nineteenth century, Abigail Solomon-Godeau describes an "economy of the spectacle," of which "a major part . . . is populated by more or less eroticized images of women" that support "fantasies of imaginary possession." In this economy, "any potential threat is neutralized by the debased situation of the woman thus portrayed and the miniaturization and immobilization inherent in photographic representation" ("The Legs of the Countess," in Emily S. Apter & William Pietz, eds., *Fetishism as Cultural Discourse* (Ithaca, N.Y.: Cornell Univ. Press, 1993), 294–95, 304). These passages can apply to Abu Ghraib with little alteration.

35. Mikhail Bakhtin, *Rabelais and his World* (1965), trans. Hélène Iswolsky (Bloomington: Indiana Univ. Press, 1984), 6, 10–11.

36. Private England had a baby in mid-October 2004, and the father was one of the other guards ("Soldier in Iraq Abuse Photos Has Baby," *Associated Press*, Oct. 13, 2004). The baby likely was conceived at roughly the same time the two were abusing prisoners.

37. Karen Halttunen argues that the creation of the concept "sadism" is linked to the rise of a humanitarian sensibility and a corresponding desire for reform, which, in turn, is an episode in the rise of the modern liberal state ("Humanitarianism and the Pornography of Pain in Anglo-American Culture," *American Historical Review* 100 (1995): 303). See also Michel Foucault, *Madness and Civilization,* trans. Richard Howard (New York: Vintage, 1988), 210; Thomas W. Laqueur, "Bodies, Details, and the Humanitarian Narrative," in Lynn Hunt ed., *The New Cultural History* (Berkeley: Univ. of California Press, 1989), 176.

38. Foucault, *Psychiatric Power,* 318.

39. Lisa Hajjar, "Sovereign Bodies, Sovereign States, and the Problem of Torture," *Studies in Law, Politics, & Society* 21 (2000): 110.

40. John T. Parry, "Terrorism and the New Criminal Process," *William & Mary Bill of Rights Journal* 15 (2007): 828–29.

41. Scarry insists that the body is always political, that "the political identity of the body is usually learned unconsciously, effortlessly, and very early," and that this identity is "not easily changed" (108–10). She emphasizes that the state's presence is more intense in times of war, with correspondingly greater impact on the body (112). I am interested less in the political identity "of the body"—although, plainly, torture functions on the body, and part of the political identity it creates is physical—than in how torture shapes a person's thoughts and beliefs. In this sense, the difference between Scarry's approach and my own is again her emphasis on torture's destructive quality and my stress on the ways in which this destruction also seeks an affirmative, creative result.

42. E.g., Foucault, *Psychiatric Power,* 164.

43. Rod Morgan, "The Utilitarian Justification of Torture," *Punishment & Society* 2, no. 2 (2000): 193. See also Jean Maria Arrigo, "A Utilitarian Argument against Torture Interrogation of Terrorists," *Science & Engineering Ethics* 10, no. 3 (2004): 1.

44. Hajjar, "Sovereign Bodies," 113 (citing Allen Feldman, *Formations of Violence* (Chicago: Univ. of Chicago Press, 1991)).

45. Michael Taussig, "Culture of Terror—Space of Death," *Comparative Studies in Society & History* 26, no. 3 (1984): 470.

46. Id., 496–97.

Works Cited

CASES

A v. State of Israel, CrimA 6659/06 (11 June 2008).

A. v. United Kingdom, ECHR, No. 100/1997/884/1096 (23 Sept. 1998).

A and Others v. Secretary of State, 2004 UKHL 56.

A and Others v. Secretary of State, 2005 UKHL 71.

A and Others v. United Kingdom, ECHR, No. 3455/05 (19 Feb. 2009).

Ahmed v. Keisler, 504 F.3d 1183 (9th Cir. 2007).

Akkoç v. Turkey, ECHR, Nos. 22947/93 & 22948/93 (10 Oct. 2000).

Aksoy v. Turkey, 23 EHRR 553 (1996).

Al-Adsani v. United Kingdom, 34 EHRR 273 (2001).

Aldana v. Del Monte Fresh Produce, N.A., Inc., 416 F.3d 1242 (11th Cir. 2005).

Aldana v. Del Monte Fresh Produce, N.A., Inc., 452 F.3d 1284 (11th Cir. 2006).

Al-Saher v. INS, 268 F.3d 1143 (9th Cir. 2001).

Al-Skeini v. Secretary of State, 2007 UKHL 26.

Anderson v. Creighton, 483 U.S. 635 (1987).

Arar v. Ashcroft, 414 F. Supp. 2d 250 (E.D.N.Y. 2006), *aff'd,* 532 F.3d 157 (2nd Cir. 2008), *rehearing en banc granted,* 12 Aug. 2008.

Ashcraft v. Tennessee, 322 U.S. 143 (1944).

Atwater v. City of Lago Vista, 532 U.S. 318 (2001).

Auguste v. Ridge, 395 F.3d 123 (3rd Cir. 2005).

Bati et al. v. Turkey, 2004 ECHR 246 (2004).

Bivens v. Six Unknown Named Agents of Federal Bureau of Narcotics, 403 U.S. 388 (1971).

Boicenco v. Moldova, ECHR, No. 41088/05 (11 July 2006).

Boumediene v. Bush, 128 S. Ct. 2229 (2008).

Boyd v. United States, 116 U.S. 616 (1886).

Brown v. Mississippi, 297 U.S. 278 (1936).

Canada v. Khadr, 2008 SCC 28.

Chahal v. United Kingdom, ECHR, No. 22414/93 (15 Nov. 1996).

Chambers v. Florida, 309 U.S. 227 (1940).

Charkaoui v. Minister of Citizenship and Immigration, 2007 SCC 9.

Chavez v. Martinez, 538 U.S. 760 (2003).

Chevron U.S.A. v. Natural Resources Defense Council, 467 U.S. 837 (1984).

Ciorap v. Moldova, ECHR, No. 12066/02 (19 June 2007).

City of Los Angeles v. Lyons, 461 U.S. 95 (1983).

Clark v. Martinez, 543 U.S. 371 (2005).

Colorado v. Connelly, 479 U.S. 157 (1986).

Cornejo-Barreto v. Siefert, 218 F.3d 1004 (9th Cir. 2000).

Cornejo-Barreto v. Seifert, 379 F.3d 1075 (9th Cir. 2004), *vacated as moot,* 389 F.3d 1307 (9th Cir. 2004) (en banc).

County of Sacramento v. Lewis, 523 U.S. 833 (1998).

Cuban American Bar Association v. Christopher, 43 F.3d 1412 (11th Cir. 1995).

Demore v. Kim, 538 U.S. 510 (2003).

DeShaney v. Winnebago County Dept. of Health and Human Services, 489 U.S. 189 (1989).

Dickerson v. United States, 530 U.S. 428 (2000).

Dıkme v. Turkey, ECHR, No. 20869/92 (11 July 2000).

Dorr v. United States, 195 U.S. 138 (1904).

Downes v. Bidwell, 182 U.S. 244 (1901).

El-Masri v. United States, 479 F.3d 296 (4th Cir. 2007).

EM v. Secretary of State, 2008 UKHL 64.

Eren v. Turkey, ECHR, No. 32347/02 (14 Oct. 2008).

Estelle v. Gamble, 429 U.S. 97 (1976).

Ex parte Endo, 323 U.S. 283 (1944).

Farmer v. Brennan, 511 U.S. 825 (1994).

Fernandez v. Phillips, 268 U.S. 311 (1925).

Filartiga v. Pena-Irala, 630 F.2d 876 (2nd Cir. 1980).

First Nat'l Bank of N.Y. v. Aristeguita, 287 F.2d 219 (2d Cir. 1960), *vacated as moot,* 375 U.S. 49 (1963).

Florida v. Bostick, 501 U.S. 429 (1991).

Florida v. J.L., 529 U.S. 266 (2000).

Gäfgen v. Germany, ECHR, No. 22978/05 (30 June 2008).

Georgiev v. Bulgaria, ECHR, No. 61275/00 (16 Oct. 2008).

Gillis v. Litscher, 468 F.3d 488 (7th Cir. 2006).

Graham v. Connor, 490 U.S. 386 (1989).

Greek Case, *Yearbook of the European Convention on Human Rights* 12 (1969): 186.

Haitian Centers Council v. McNary, 969 F.2d 1326 (2nd Cir. 1992).

Hamdan v. Rumsfeld, 548 U.S. 557 (2006).

Hamdi v. Rumsfeld, 542 U.S. 507 (2004).

Hape v. The Queen, 2007 SCC 26.

Harbury v. Deutch, 233 F.3d 596 (D.C. Cir. 2000), *rev'd on other grounds,* 536 U.S. 403 (2002).

Hirabayashi v. United States, 320 U.S. 81 (1943).

Hooker v. Klein, 573 F.2d 1360 (9th Cir. 1978).

Hope v. Pelzer, 536 U.S. 730 (2002).

Hudson v. McMillian, 503 U.S. 1 (1992).

Hudson v. Michigan, 547 U.S. 586 (2006).

İlhan v. Turkey, ECHR, No. 22277/93 (27 June 2000).

Illinois v. McArthur, 531 U.S. 326 (2001).

Idaho v. Horiuchi, 253 F.3d 359 (9th Cir.) (en banc), *vacated as moot,* 266 F.3d 979 (2001).

Ingraham v. Wright, 430 U.S. 651 (1977).

In re Debs, 158 U.S. 564 (1895).

In re Neagle, 135 U.S. 1 (1890).

Ireland v. United Kingdom, *Yearbook of the European Convention on Human Rights* 19 (1976): 512.

Ireland v. United Kingdom, 2 EHRR 25 (1978).

Jalloh v. Germany, ECHR, No. 54810/00 (11 July 2006).

Jhirad v. Ferrandina, 536 F.2d 478 (2nd Cir. 1976).

Jones v. Ministry of Interior al-Mamlaka al-Arabiya AS Saudiya, 2006 UKHL 26.

Kadic v. Karadžić, 70 F.3d 232 (2nd Cir. 1995).

Kay v. Ashcroft, 387 F.3d 664 (7th Cir. 2004).

Khouzam v. Ashcroft, 361 F.3d 161 (2nd Cir. 2004).

Khouzam v. Attorney General, 549 F.3d 235 (3rd Cir. 2008).

Korematsu v. United States, 323 U.S. 214 (1944).

Kwong Hai Chew v. Colding, 344 U.S. 590 (1953).

Legal Consequences of the Construction of a Wall in the Occupied Palestinian Territory, ICJ, No. 131 (2004).

Li v. Attorney General, 400 F.3d 157 (3rd Cir. 2005).

Los Angeles County v. Rettele, 550 U.S. 609 (2007).

Madrid v. Gomez, 889 F. Supp. 1146 (N.D. Cal. 1995).

Madsen v. Kinsella, 343 U.S. 341 (1952).

Mahjoub v. Minister of Citizenship and Immigration, 2006 FC 1503.

Mamatkulov & Askarov v. Turkey, ECHR, Nos. 46827/99 & 46951/99 (4 Feb. 2005).

Mathews v. Eldridge, 424 U.S. 319 (1976).

McCann v. United Kingdom, 21 EHRR 97 (1995).

McGill v. Duckworth, 944 F.2d 344 (7th Cir. 1991).

McKune v. Lile, 536 U.S. 24 (2002).

Medellin v. Texas, 128 S. Ct. 1346 (2008).

Michigan v. Summers, 452 U.S. 692 (1981).

Mikhayez v. Russia, ECHR, No. 77617/01 (26 Apr. 2006).

Miller v. Fenton, 796 F.2d 598 (3rd Cir. 1986).

Miranda v. Arizona, 384 U.S. 436 (1966).

Mironescu v. Costner, 480 F.3d 664 (4th Cir. 2007).

Missouri v. Seibert, 542 U.S. 600 (2004).

Mohamed v. Jeppesen Dataplan, Inc., 563 F.3d 992 (9th Cir. 2009), en banc review granted 27 Oct. 2009.

Mouwad v. Gonzales, 485 F.3d 405 (8th Cir. 2007).

Muehler v. Mena, 544 U.S. 93 (2005).

N. v. United Kingdom, ECHR, No. 26565/05 (27 May 2008).

NA. v. United Kingdom, ECHR, No. 25904/07 (17 July 2008).

Nevmerzhitsky v. Ukraine, ECHR, No. 54825/00 (5 Apr. 2005).

New York v. Quarles, 467 U.S. 649 (1984).

Nicaragua v. United States of America, ICJ, No. 70 (1986).

Nnyanzi v. United Kingdom, ECHR, No. 21878/06 (8 Apr. 2008).

Pierce v. Attorney General, 528 F.3d 180 (3rd Cir. 2008) (en banc).

Prasoprat v. Benov, 421 F.3d 1009 (9th Cir. 2005).

Prosecutor v. Brđanin, ICTY, No. IT-99-36-A (2 Apr. 2007).

Prosecutor v. Delalić, ICTY, No. IT-96-21-T (trial) (16 Nov. 1998).

Prosecutor v. Delalić, ICTY, No. IT-96-21-A (appeal) (20 Feb. 2001).

Prosecutor v. Furundžija, ICTY, No. IT-95-17/1-T (10 Dec. 1998).

Prosecutor v. Kunarac, ICTY, Nos. IT-96-23-T & IT-96-23/1-T (trial) (22 Feb. 2001).

Prosecutor v. Kunarec, ICTY, Nos. IT-96-23 & IT-96-23/1-A (appeal) (12 June 2002).

Prosecutor v. Tadić, ICTY, No. IT-94-1 (2 Oct. 1995).

Public Committee against Torture in Israel v. Israel, HCJ 769/02 (11 Dec. 2005).

Public Committee against Torture in Israel v. State of Israel, H.C. 5100/94, 53(4) P.D. 817 (1999).

Rasul v. Bush, 542 U.S. 466 (2004).

RB and Another v. Secretary of State, 2009 UKHL 10.

Refah Partisi v. Turkey, ECHR, Nos. 41340/98, 41342/98, 41343/98, & 41344/98 (31 July 2001).

Refah Partisi v. Turkey, ECHR, Nos. 41340/98, 41342/98, 41343/98, & 41344/98 (13 Feb. 2003) (Grand Chamber).

Reid v. Covert, 354 U.S. 1 (1957).

Reno v. Flores, 507 U.S. 292 (1993).

Rhodes v. Chapman, 452 U.S. 337 (1981).

Ruiz v. Johnson, 37 F. Supp. 2d 855 (S.D. Tex. 1999), *rev'd,* 243 F.3d 941 (5th Cir. 2001), *remanded,* 154 F. Supp. 2d 975 (S.D. Tex. 2001), *appeal dismissed,* 273 F.3d 1101 (2001).

Saadi v. Italy, ECHR, No. 37201/06 (28 Feb. 2008).

Sale v. Haitian Centers Council, 509 U.S. 155 (1993).

Samson v. California, 547 U.S. 843 (2006).

Sanchez-Llamas v. Oregon, 548 U.S. 331 (2006).

Saucier v. Katz, 533 U.S. 194 (2001).

Scarver v. Litscher, 434 F.3d 972 (7th Cir. 2006).

Schmerber v. California, 384 U.S. 757 (1966).

Scott v. Harris, 550 U.S. 372 (2007).

Selmouni v. France, 29 EHRR 25 (1999).

Shaughnessy v. United States *ex rel.* Mezei, 345 U.S. 206 (1953).

Soering v. United Kingdom, 11 EHHR 439 (1989).

Sosa v. Alvarez-Machain, 542 U.S. 692 (2004).

Stump v. Sparkman, 435 U.S. 349 (1978).

Suresh v. Canada, 2002 SCC 1.

Tennessee v. Garner, 471 U.S. 1 (1985).

Terry v. Ohio, 392 U.S. 1 (1968).

Tryer v. United Kingdom, ECHR, No. 5856/72 (25 Apr. 1978).

United States v. Aguilar, 883 F.2d 662 (9th Cir. 1989).

United States v. Alvarez-Machain, 504 U.S. 655 (1992).

United States v. Ankeny, 490 F.3d 744 (9th Cir. 2007).

United States v. Bailey, 444 U.S. 394 (1980).

United States v. Barker, 546 F.2d 940 (D.C. Cir. 1976).

United States v. Calley, 48 C.M.R. 19 (1973).

United States v. Corey, 232 F.3d 1166 (9th Cir. 2000).

United States v. Doherty, 786 F.2d 491 (2d Cir. 1986).

United States v. Drayton, 536 U.S. 194 (2002).

United States v. Knights, 534 U.S. 112 (2001).

United States v. Laub, 385 U.S. 475 (1967).

United States v. Oakland Cannabis Buyers' Coop., 532 U.S. 483 (2001).

United States v. Passaro, No. 5:04-CR-211-1, U.S. District Court for the Eastern District of North Carolina (17 June 2004) (indictment).

United States v. Pennsylvania Indus. Chemical Corp., 411 U.S. 655 (1973).

United States v. Schoon, 971 F.2d 193 (9th Cir. 1991).

United States v. Verdugo-Urquidez, 494 U.S. 259 (1990).

United States *ex rel.* Knauff v. Shaughnessy, 338 U.S. 537 (1950).

Washington v. Glucksberg, 521 U.S. 702 (1997).

Whitley v. Albers, 475 U.S. 312 (1986).

Whitman v. American Trucking Associations, 531 U.S. 457 (2001).

Wilkinson v. Austin, 545 U.S. 209 (2005).

Wilson v. Layne, 526 U.S. 603 (1999).

Wong Wing v. United States, 163 U.S. 228 (1896).

Woodford v. Ngo, 548 U.S. 81 (2006).

Youngstown Sheet & Tube v. Sawyer, 343 U.S. 579 (1952).

Z & Others v. United Kingdom, ECHR, No. 29392/95 (10 May 2001).

Zadvydas v. Davis, 533 U.S. 678 (2001).

U.S. GOVERNMENT DOCUMENTS NOT IN COLLECTIONS

Bellinger, John, & William Haynes. "Letter to Jakob Kellenberger on Customary International Law Study." *Int'l Legal Materials* 46 (2007): 514.

Bradbury, Stephen G., Principal Deputy Assistant Attorney General. *Memorandum for John A. Rizzo, Senior Deputy General Counsel, Central Intelligence Agency, re: Application of 18 U.S.C. §§ 2340-2340A to Certain Techniques That May Be Used in the Interrogation of a High Value al Qaeda Detainee* (10 May 2005).

Bradbury, Stephen G., Principal Deputy Assistant Attorney General. *Memorandum for John A. Rizzo, Senior Deputy General Counsel, Central Intelligence Agency, re: Application of 18 U.S.C. §§ 2340-2340A to the Combined Use of Certain Techniques in the Interrogation of High Value al Qaeda Detainees* (10 May 2005).

Bradbury, Steven G., Principal Deputy Assistant Attorney General. *Memorandum for John Rizzo, Senior Deputy General Counsel, Central Intelligence Agency, re: Application of United States Obligations Under Article 16 of the Convention Against Torture to Certain Techniques that May Be Used in the Interrogation of High Value al Qaeda Detainees* (30 May 2005).

Bybee, Jay S., Assistant Attorney General. *Memorandum for John Rizzo, Acting General Counsel of the Central Intelligence Agency, re: Interrogation of al Qaeda Operative* (1 Aug. 2002).

Charges of Cruelty, etc., to the Natives of the Philippines. S. Doc. 205, 57th Cong., 1st Sess. (19 Feb. 1902).

Church, Vice Adm. A. T. *Review of Department of Defense Detention Operations and Detainee Interrogation Techniques* (7 Mar. 2005).

Central Intelligence Agency, Inspector General. *Report of Investigation: Selected Issues Relating to CIA Activities in Honduras in the 1980s.* Doc. 96-0125-IG (27 Aug. 1997).

Congressional Research Service. *Treaties and Other International Agreements: The Role of the United States Senate.* S. Rpt. 71, 106th Cong., 2nd Sess. 39 (2001).

Convention against Torture. Hearing before the Senate Committee on Foreign Relations, 101st Cong., 2nd Sess. (30 Jan. 1990).

Convention against Torture and Other Cruel, Inhuman, or Degrading Treatment or Punishment, S. Exec. Rpt. 101-30, 101st Cong., 2nd Sess. (1990).

Declaration of Honolulu (8 Feb. 1966).

Department of Defense. *Combatant Status Review Tribunal Summary* (Mar. 2005).

Department of Homeland Security, Office of the Inspector General. *The Removal of a Canadian Citizen to Syria.* OIG-08-18 (Mar. 2008).

Department of Justice. *Legal Authorities Supporting the Activities of the National Security Agency Described by the President* (19 Jan. 2006).

Department of Justice. Press release, "Department of Justice Sends 25 Advisors to Iraq in Support of Provisional Authority Effort to Reconstruct Criminal System" (20 May 2003).

Department of Justice, Executive Office for Immigration Review. *FY 2006 Statistical Year Book* (Feb. 2007).

Department of Justice, Office of the Inspector General. *A Review of the FBI's Involvement in and Observations of Detainee Interrogations in Guantánamo Bay, Afghanistan, and Iraq* (May 2008).

Department of Justice, Office of the Inspector General. *The September 11 Detainees: A Review of the Treatment of Aliens Held on Immigration Charges in Connection with the Investigation of the September 11 Attacks* (Apr. 2003).

Department of Justice, Office of the Inspector General. *Supplemental Report on September 11 Detainees' Allegations of Abuse at the Metropolitan Detention Center in Brooklyn, New York* (Dec. 2003).

Department of State. *List of Issues to be Taken Up in Connection with the Consideration of the Second and Third Periodic Reports of the United States of America* (17 July 2006).

Department of State. "Press Availability with Ukrainian President Viktor Yushchenko" (7 Dec. 2005). http://www.state.gov/secretary/rm/2005/57723.htm.

Department of State. *Second and Third Periodic Report of the United States of America to the UN Committee on Human Rights concerning the International Covenant on Civil and Political Rights* (21 Oct. 2005).

Department of State. *The United States' Response to the Questions Asked by the Committee against Torture* (8 May 2006).

Department of State. *United States' Written Response to Questions Asked by the Committee against Torture* (28 Apr. 2006).

Department of the Army. *Field Manual No. 2.22-3, Human Intelligence Collector Operations* (6 Sept. 2006).

Department of the Army. *Field Manual 34-52: Intelligence Interrogation* (28 Sept. 1992).

England, Gordon. *Memorandum for Secretaries of the Military Departments et al. re: Interrogation and Treatment of Detainee by the Department of Defense* (30 Dec. 2005).

England, Gordon. *Memorandum to the Secretaries of the Military Departments et al.* (7 July 2006).

England, Gordon. *Memorandum to the Secretary of State et al.* (14 Sept. 2004).

Formica, Brig. Gen. Richard P. *Article 15-6 Investigation of CJSOTF-AP and 5th SF Group Detention Operations* (8 Nov. 2004).

Headquarters, Joint Task Force—Guantánamo. *Camp Delta Standard Operating Procedures* (28 Mar. 2003).

Headquarters, Joint Task Force—Guantánamo. *Camp Delta Standard Operating Procedures* (1 Mar. 2004).

Human Resource Exploitation Training Manual—1983. http://www.gwu.edu/~nsarchiv/NSAEBB/NSAEBB122/index.htm#hre.

Instructions for the Government of Armies of the United States in the Field. Prepared by Francis Lieber, LL.D. (Washington, D.C.: Government Printing Office, 1898). Originally issued as General Orders No. 100, Adjutant General's Office, 24 Apr. 1863.

International Covenant on Civil and Political Rights. Hearing before the Senate Committee on Foreign Relations, S. Hearing 478, 102nd Cong., 1st Sess. (21 Nov. 1991).

International Covenant on Civil and Political Rights. S. Exec. Rpt. 23, 102nd Cong., 2nd Sess. (1992).

International Human Rights Treaties. Hearings before the Senate Committee on Foreign Relations, 96th Cong., 1st Sess. (14, 15, 16, & 19 Nov. 1979).

"Investigation of the My Lai Incident." Report of the Armed Services Investigating Subcommittee of the Committee on Armed Services, 91st Cong., 2nd Sess. (15 July 1970).

JTF GTMO "SERE" Interrogation Standard Operating Procedure (10 Dec. 2002). http://www.torturingdemocracy.org/documents/20021210.pdf.

KUBARK Counterintelligence Interrogation (July 1963). Redacted version at http://www.gwu.edu/~nsarchiv/NSAEBB/NSAEBB122/index.htm#kubark.

Legal Analysis of Interrogation Techniques. Forwarded to Marion Bowman, Legal Counsel, FBI (27 Nov. 2002).

Levin, Daniel, Acting Assistant Attorney General. "Letter to DoD General Counsel

William J. Haynes II re: Memorandum for William J. Haynes II, General Counsel of the Department of Defense, from John Yoo, Deputy Assistant Attorney General, Office of Legal Counsel, re: Military Interrogation of Alien Unlawful Combatants Held Outside the United States (Mar. 14, 2003)" (4 Feb. 2005).

Message from the President of the United States Transmitting the Convention against Torture and Other Cruel, Inhuman, or Degrading Treatment or Punishment. S. Treaty Doc. 100-20, 100th Cong., 2nd Sess. (1988).

Message from the President Transmitting Four Treaties Pertaining to Human Rights. Sen. Exec. Doc. C, D, E, & F, 95th Cong., 2nd Sess. (1978).

Michel, Werner E., Assistant to the Secretary of Defense (Intelligence Oversight). *Memorandum for the Secretary of Defense re: Improper Material in Spanish-Language Intelligence Training Manuals* (10 Mar. 1992).

Mora, Alberto. *Memorandum for Inspector General, Department of the Navy, re: Statement for the Record: Office of General Counsel Involvement in Interrogation Issues* (7 July 2004).

Moschella, William E., Assistant Attorney General. "Letter to Senator Patrick Leahy" (4 Apr. 2005).

"Observations by the United States on General Comment 24." *Int'l Human Rights Reports* 3 (1996): 265.

Office of the Assistant Secretary of Defense/Public Affairs Office. *Fact Sheet concerning Training Manuals Containing Materials Inconsistent with U.S. Policy* (1992).

Office of the Director of National Intelligence. *Summary of the High Value Terrorist Detainee Program* (2006).

Philbin, Patrick F., Deputy Assistant Attorney General. *Memorandum Opinion for the Counsel to the President, re: Legality of the Use of Military Commissions to Try Terrorists* (6 Oct. 2001).

Reply to the Report of the Five UNCHR Special Rapporteurs on Detainees in Guantánamo Bay, Cuba (10 Mar. 2006).

Resolution of Advice and Consent to Ratification of the Convention against Torture and Other Forms of Cruel, Inhuman, or Degrading Treatment or Punishment. 136 Cong. Rec. S17491 (27 Oct. 1990).

Roosevelt, Theodore. "Fourth Annual Message to Congress" (6 Dec. 2004). http://www.presidency.ucsb.edu/ws/index.php?pid=29545.

"Transcript of President Bush's Address to a Joint Session of Congress on Thursday Night, September 20, 2001." http://archives.cnn.com/2001/US/09/20/gen.bush.transcript/.

Waxman, Matthew. *Opening Statement on the Report concerning the International Covenant on Civil and Political Rights* (17 July 2006).

White House. *Executive Order: Interpretation of the Geneva Conventions Common Article 3 as Applied to a Program of Detention and Interrogation Operated by the Central Intelligence Agency* (20 July 2007).

White House. *Executive Order: Trial of Alien Unlawful Enemy Combatants by Military Commission* (14 Feb. 2007).

White House. *President Discusses Creation of Military Commissions to Try Suspected Terrorists* (6 Sept. 2006).

White House. *President's Statement on Signing of H.R. 2863, the "Department of Defense, Emergency Supplemental Appropriations to Address Hurricanes in the Gulf of Mexico, and Pandemic Influenza Act, 2006"* (30 Dec. 2005).

White House. Press release, *The Military Commissions Act of 2006* (17 Oct. 2006).

White House. *Statement by the President on Death of Abu Musab al-Zarqawi* (8 June 2006).

Wolfowitz, Paul. *Memorandum to the Secretary of the Navy* (7 July 2004).

Yoo, John C., Deputy Assistant Attorney General. *Memorandum for William J. Haynes II, General Counsel of the Department of Defense, re: Military Interrogation of Alien Unlawful Combatants Held Outside the United States* (14 Mar. 2003).

Yoo, John C., & Robert J. Delahunty. *Memorandum for Alberto R. Gonzales, Counsel to the President, and William J. Haynes, General Counsel of the Department of Defense, re: Authority for Use of Military Force to Combat Terrorist Activities within the United States* (23 Oct. 2001).

OTHER GOVERNMENT AND INTERNATIONAL DOCUMENTS

The Aitken Report: An Investigation into Cases of Deliberate Abuse and Unlawful Killing in Iraq in 2003 and 2004 (25 Jan. 2008).

Commission of Inquiry into the Actions of Canadian Officials in Relation to Maher Arar. *Report of Professor Stephen J. Toope, Fact Finder* (14 Oct. 2005).

Commission of Inquiry into the Actions of Canadian Officials in Relation to Maher Arar. *Report of the Events Relating to Maher Arar: Analysis and Recommendations* (2006).

Convention (No. I) for the Amelioration of the Condition of the Wounded and Sick in Armed Forces in the Field (1949). 75 U.N.T.S. 31.

Convention (No. II) for the Amelioration of the Condition of the Wounded, Sick, and Shipwrecked Members of Armed Forces at Sea (1949). 75 U.N.T.S. 85.

Convention (No. III) Relative to the Treatment of Prisoners of War (1949). 75 U.N.T.S. 135.

Convention (No. IV) Relative to the Protection of Civilian Persons in Time of War (1949). 75 U.N.T.S. 287.

Convention Relative to the Treatment of Prisoners of War (27 July 1929).

Council of Europe. *Convention for the Protection of Human Rights and Fundamental Freedoms* (1950). 213 U.N.T.S. 222.

Council of Europe. *European Convention for the Prevention of Torture and Inhuman or Degrading Treatment or Punishment* (1989). 27 ILM 1152.

Council of Europe. *Guidelines of the Committee of Ministers of the Council of Europe on Human Rights and the Fight against Terrorism*, No. 4. Doc. 804/4.3 (app. 3) (11 July 2002).

Council of Europe. *Report on Alleged Secret Detentions and Unlawful Inter-State Transfers of Detainees Involving Council of Europe Member States*. Doc. 10957 (12 June 2006).

European Parliament. *Report on the Alleged Use of European Countries by the CIA for the Transportation and Illegal Detention of Prisoners*. Final A6-0020/2007 (30 Jan. 2007).

Iacobucci, Frank. *Internal Inquiry into the Actions of Canadian Officials in Relation to Abdullah Almalki, Ahmad Abou-Elmaati, and Muayyed Nurreddin* (2008).

International Committee of the Red Cross, *Report on the Treatment of Fourteen "High Value Detainees" in CIA Custody* (Feb. 2007).

Official Journal of the International Criminal Court: Elements of Crimes (9 Sept. 2002).

Protocol Additional (No. I) to the Geneva Conventions of August 12, 1949, and Relating to the Protection of Victims of International Armed Conflicts (1977). 1125 U.N.T.S. 3.

Protocol Additional (No. II) to the Geneva Conventions of August 12, 1949, and Relating to the Protection of Victims of Non-International Armed Conflicts (1977). 1125 U.N.T.S. 609.

Report of the Commission of Inquiry into the Methods of Investigation of the General Security Service regarding Hostile Terrorist Activity (1987). *Israel Law Review* 23 (1989): 146.

Rome Statute of the International Criminal Court (1998). 2187 U.N.T.S. 90.

U.N. Commission on Human Rights. *Civil and Political Rights, Including the Question of Torture and Detention: Report of the Special Rapporteur on the Question of Torture—Addendum, Visit to Spain.* E/CN.4/2004/56/Add.2 (2004).

U.N. Commission on Human Rights. *Civil and Political Rights, Including the Questions of Torture and Detention: Torture and Other Cruel, Inhuman, or Degrading Treatment—Report of the Special Rapporteur.* E/CN.4/2006/6 (23 Dec. 2005).

U.N. Commission on Human Rights. *Question of the Human Rights of All Persons Subjected to Any Form of Detention or Imprisonment, in Particular: Torture and Other Cruel, Inhuman, or Degrading Treatment or Punishment—Report of the Special Rapporteur.* E/CN.4/1997/7 (10 Jan. 1997).

U.N. Commission on Human Rights. *Question of the Violation of Human Rights and Fundamental Freedoms . . . Transfer of Persons.* E/CN.4/Sub.2/2005/L.12 (4 Aug. 2005).

U.N. Commission on Human Rights. *Situation of Detainees at Guantánamo Bay.* E/CN.4/2006/120 (15 Feb. 2006).

U.N. Committee against Torture. *Communication No. 161/2000: Yugoslavia.* CAT/C/29/D/161/2000 (21 Nov. 2002).

U.N. Committee against Torture. *Communication No. 171/2000: Serbia and Montenegro.* CAT/C/34/D/171/2000 (23 May 2005).

U.N. Committee against Torture. *Communication No. 172/2000: Serbia and Montenegro.* CAT/C/35/D/172/2000 (29 Nov. 2005).

U.N. Committee against Torture. *Conclusions and Recommendations of the Committee against Torture: Canada.* CAT/C/CO/34/CAN (7 July 2005).

U.N. Committee against Torture. *Conclusions and Recommendations of the Committee against Torture: France.* A/53/44 (1998).

U.N. Committee against Torture. *Conclusions and Recommendations of the Committee against Torture: United States of America.* CAT/C/USA/CO/2 (25 July 2006).

U.N. Committee against Torture. *Conclusions and Recommendations: United Kingdom of Great Britain and Northern Ireland—Dependent Territories.* CAT/C/CR/33/3 (10 Dec. 2004).

U.N. Committee against Torture. *General Comment No. 1.* A/53/44, annex IX (1997).

U.N. Committee against Torture. *General Comment No. 2.* CAT/C/GC/2/CRP.1/Rev.4 (23 Nov. 2007).

U.N. Counter-Terrorism Committee. *Survey of the Implementation of Security Council Resolution 1373 (2001).* S/2008/379 (10 June 2008).

U.N. Human Rights Committee. *Concluding Observations: Israel.* CCPR/CO/78/ISR (21 Aug. 2003).

U.N. Human Rights Committee. *Concluding Observations: United States of America.* CCPR/C/79/Add.50 (3 Oct. 1995).

U.N. Human Rights Committee. *Concluding Observations: United States of America.* CCPR/C/USA/CO/3 (15 Sept. 2006).

U.N. Human Rights Committee. *General Comment No. 24.* CCPR/C/21/Rev.1/Add.6 (4 Nov. 1994).

U.N. Human Rights Committee. *General Comment No. 29.* CCPR/C/21/Rev.1/Add.11 (31 Aug. 2001).

U.N. Human Rights Committee. *General Comment 20* (10 Mar. 1992).

U.N. Human Rights Committee. *General Comment No. 31.* CCPR/C/21/Rev.1/Add.13 (26 May 2004).

U.N. Human Rights Committee. *Summary Record of the 1405th Meeting: United States of America.* CCPR/C/SR.1405 (31 Mar. 1995).

U.N. Human Rights Council. *Report of the Special Rapporteur on the Promotion and Protection of Human Rights and Fundamental Freedoms while Countering Terrorism: Mission to Israel, Including Visit to Occupied Palestinian Territory.* A/HRC/6/17/Add.6 (16 Nov. 2007).

U.N. International Law Commission. *Fragmentation of International Law: Difficulties Arising from the Diversification and Expansion of International Law.* A/CN.4/L.682 (13 Apr. 2006).

United Nations. *Declaration on the Protection of All Persons from Being Subjected to Torture and Other Cruel, Inhuman, or Degrading Treatment or Punishment* (1975). U.N. G.A. Res. 3452.

United Nations. *Convention against Torture and Other Forms of Cruel, Inhuman, or Degrading Treatment or Punishment* (1984). 1465 U.N.T.S. 85.

United Nations. *Final Report of the Ad Hoc Committee on a Comprehensive and Integral International Convention on the Protection and Promotion of the Rights and Dignity of Persons with Disabilities.* A/61/611, annex 1 (6 Dec. 2006).

United Nations. *International Covenant on Civil and Political Rights* (1966). 999 U.N.T.S. 171.

United Nations. *Optional Protocol to the Convention against Torture and Other Cruel, Inhuman, or Degrading Treatment* (2002). U.N. G.A. Res. 57/199.

United Nations. *Optional Protocol to the International Covenant on Civil and Political Rights* (1966). 999 U.N.T.S. 302.

United Nations. Press release, "UN Special Rapporteur on Human Rights and Counter Terrorism Concludes Mission to Israel, Including Visit to Occupied Palestinian Territory" (10 July 2007).

United Nations. *Proclamation of Teheran, Final Act of the International Conference on Human Rights* (13 May 1968). A/CONF. 32/41.

United Nations. *Universal Declaration of Human Rights.* U.N. G.A. Res. 217A(III) (1948).

United Nations. *Vienna Declaration and Programme of Action* (12 July 1993). A/CONF. 157/23.

Universal Declaration of Human Rights by the World's Religions (2000). http://www .worldsreligionsafter911.com/pdf/UDHRWR.pdf.

U.N. Security Council. *Resolution 1373.* S. Res. 1373 (28 Sept. 2001).

U.S. Department of State. *Second and Third Periodic Report of the United States of America to the UN Committee on Human Rights concerning the International Covenant on Civil and Political Rights* ¶ 130 (21 Oct. 2005).

U.S. Senate Armed Services Committee. *Inquiry into the Treatment of Detainees in U.S. Custody,* 110th Cong., 2nd sess., 20 Nov. 2008.

Vienna Convention on the Law of Treaties (1969). 1155 U.N.T.S. 331.

Wood, M. C., Legal Advisor. Memo to Linda Duffield re: Uzbekistan: Intelligence Possibly Obtained under Torture (13 Mar. 2003). http://www.craigmurray.co.uk/docu ments/Wood.pdf.

SECONDARY SOURCES

Abrams, Norman. *Anti-terrorism and Criminal Enforcement.* 3rd ed. St. Paul: Thomson-West, 2008.

Abu-Lughod, Lila. "Do Muslim Women Really Need Saving?" *American Anthropologist* 104 (2002): 783.

Agamben, Giorgio. *Homo Sacer.* 1995. Trans. Daniel Heller-Roazen. Stanford, Cal.: Stanford Univ. Press, 1998.

Agamben, Giorgio. *Means without Ends.* Trans. Vincenzo Binetti & Cesare Casarino. Minneapolis: Univ. of Minnesota Press, 2000.

Agamben, Giorgio. *Remnants of Auschwitz.* 1999. Trans. Daniel Heller-Roazen. New York: Zone Books, 2002.

Agamben, Giorgio. *State of Exception.* Trans. Kevin Attell. Chicago: Univ. of Chicago Press, 2005.

Aldrich, George H. "The Taliban, al Qaeda, and the Determination of Illegal Combatants." *American Journal of Int'l Law* 96 (2002): 891.

Aleinikoff, T. Alexander, David A. Martin, & Hiroshi Motomura. *Immigration and Citizenship.* 5th ed. St. Paul: West, 2003.

"Algeria: Chirac Rejects 'Torture Apology.'" *BBC News,* 15 Dec. 2000.

Alidio, Kimberly. "When I Get Home, I Want to Forget." *Social Text* 59 (Summer 1999): 105.

Allen, Mike. "Bush Says Citizens Must Help in Fighting Terror." *Washington Post,* 9 Nov. 2001, A1.

Alschuler, Albert W. "A Peculiar Privilege in Historical Perspective." *Michigan Law Review* 94 (1996): 2625.

Alvarez, José. "Torturing the Law." *Case Western Reserve Journal of Int'l Law* 37 (2006): 175.

Amann, Dianne Marie. "Abu Ghraib." *Univ. of Pennsylvania Law Review* 153 (2005): 2085.

Amann, Dianne Marie. "Punish or Surveil." *Transnational Law & Contemporary Problems* 16 (2007): 873.

American Law Institute. *Restatement (Third) of Foreign Relations Law of the United States.* St. Paul: ALI, 1987.

"Amnesty International Criticizes U.S. Handling of Terror Suspects" *CNN.com,* 5 Mar. 2003. www.edition.cnn.com/2003/US/03/05/terror.amnesty.internet/index.html.

Amnesty International. *Combating Torture* (2003).

Amnesty International. *Race, Rights, and Police Brutality* (1999).

Amnesty International. *Report 2004—Spain* (2004).

Amnesty International. *Report 2005: The State of the World's Human Rights—Spain* (2005).

Amnesty International. Press release, *Selective U.S. Prosecutions in Torture Scandal Underscore International Obligation to Investigate U.S. Officials* (25 May 2005).

Amnesty International. *Spain: A Briefing on Human Rights Concerns in Relation to the Basque Peace Process* (1999).

Amnesty International. *Stonewalled: Police Abuse and Misconduct against Lesbian, Gay, Bisexual, and Transgender People in the U.S.* (2005).

Amnesty International. *Take a Step to Stamp Out Torture* (2000).

Amnesty International. *Torture in Israel* (2000).

Amnesty International. *UK: CIA Rendition Flights Used UK Airfields* (2005).

Amnesty International. *United States of America/Yemen: Secret Detention in CIA "Black Sites."* (2005).

Amnesty International et al. *Off the Record: U.S. Responsibility for Enforced Disappearances in the "War on Terror"* (2007).

Anderson, David. *Histories of the Hanged.* New York: W. W. Norton, 2005.

Anghie, Antony. *Imperialism, Sovereignty, and the Making of International Law.* Cambridge: Cambridge Univ. Press, 2005.

Anti-Imperialist League. *Soldiers Letters: Being Materials for the History of a War of Criminal Aggression.* Boston: Rockwell & Churchill, 1899.

Appiah, Kwame Anthony. "Liberalism, Individuality, Identity." *Critical Inquiry* 27 (2001): 305.

Arendt, Hannah. *The Origins of Totalitarianism*. New ed. New York: Harcourt Brace Jovanovich, 1973.

Arrigo, Jean Maria. "A Utilitarian Argument against Torture Interrogation of Terrorists." *Science & Engineering Ethics* 10, no. 3 (2004): 1.

Asad, Talal. "On Torture, or Cruel, Inhuman, and Degrading Treatment." In Arthur Kleinman et al., eds., *Social Suffering*. Berkeley: Univ. of California Press, 1997.

Astrain, Luis Núñez. *The Basques*. Trans. Meic Stephens. Wales: Welsh Academic Press, 1997.

Aussaresses, Gen. Paul. *The Battle of the Casbah*. New York: Enigma Books, 2005.

Babington, Charles. "Senator Critical of Focus on Prisoner Abuse." *Washington Post*, 12 May 2004, A18.

Bailkin, Jordanna. "The Place of Liberalism." *Victorian Studies* 48, no. 1 (2005): 83.

Bakhtin, Mikhail. *Rabelais and His World*. 1965. Trans. Hélène Iswolsky. Bloomington: Indiana Univ. Press, 1984.

Barber, Sotiros A. "Fallacies of Negative Constitutionalism." *Fordham Law Review* 75 (2006): 655.

Barrett, Devlin. "Senator Criticizes Hiring of 4 Iraq Prison Officials." *Houston Chronicle*, 3 June 2004, A6.

Bascuas, Ricardo J. "The Unconstitutionality of Hold until Cleared." *Vanderbilt Law Review* 58 (2005): 677.

Baylis, Elena A. "General Comment 24." *Berkeley Journal of Int'l Law* 17 (1999): 277.

Bellinger, John. "Unlawful Enemy Combatants" (17 Jan. 2007). http://www.opinio juris.org/posts/1169000173.shtml.

Benjamin, Mark. "Bush's Top General Quashed Torture Dissent." *Salon.com*, 30 June 2008.

Berlin, Isaiah. *Four Essays on Liberty*. London: Oxford Univ. Press, 1969.

"Berlusconi to Testify in C.I.A. Case," *Associated Press*, 14 May 2008.

Birtle, Andrew J. "The U.S. Army's Pacification of Marinduque, Philippine Islands, April 1900–April 1901." *Journal of Military History* 61 (1997): 255.

Blaz, Dan. "Bush Warns of Casualties of War." *Washington Post*, 18 Sept. 2001, A1.

Borelli, Silvia. "Casting Light on the Legal Black Hole." *Int'l Review of the Red Cross* 857 (2005): 39.

Borgen, Christopher J. "Resolving Treaty Conflicts." *George Washington Int'l Law Review* 37 (2005): 573.

Bosco, David. "Moral Principle vs. Military Necessity." *American Scholar*, Winter 2008.

Boulesbaa, Ahcene. *The U.N. Convention on Torture and the Prospects for Enforcement*. The Hague: Martinus Nijhoff, 1999.

Bowden, Mark. "The Dark Art of Interrogation." *Atlantic Monthly*, Oct. 2003.

Bowden, Mark. "The Lessons of Abu Ghraib." *Atlantic Monthly*, July/Aug. 2004.

Bradley, Curtis A., & Jack L. Goldsmith. "Treaties, Human Rights, and Conditional Consent." *Univ. of Pennsylvania Law Review* 149 (2000): 399.

Bravin, Jess, & Gary Fields. "How Do U.S. Interrogators Make a Captured Terrorist Talk?" *Wall Street Journal*, 4 Mar. 2003, B1.

"Britain Accused over Ulster Investigations: European Ruling Sidesteps Issue of Unlawful Killing but Questions Deaths after Long-Term Surveillance: Case Two." *Guardian*, 4 May 2001, 9.

"Britain Makes Glorifying Terrorism a Crime." *Gulf Daily News*, 14 Apr. 2006.

Brooke, James. "Cheney Praises Japan's Stand against Abductors in Iraq." *New York Times*, 13 Apr. 2004, A15.

Brooks, Rosa Ehrenreich. "War Everywhere." *Univ. of Pennsylvania Law Review* 153 (2004): 675.

Brown, Colin. "Straw Faces MPs over Claims MI6 Delivered Suspect for Torture." *Independent*, 12 Dec. 2005, 9.

Brown, Colin. "U.S. Planes Carrying Prisoners Were Allowed to Land in Britain." *Independent*, 13 Dec. 2005, 16.

Brown, Michelle. "'Setting the Conditions' for Abu Ghraib." *American Quarterly* 57 (2005): 973.

Bruff, Harold H. *Bad Advice: Bush's Lawyers in the War on Terror*. Lawrence: Univ. Press of Kansas, 2009.

B'Tselem & HaMoked. *Absolute Prohibition* (May 2007).

Burgers, J. Herman, & Hans Danelius. *The United Nations Convention against Torture*. Dordrecht: Martinus Nijhoff, 1988.

Burns, Robert. "U.S. Confirms Gitmo Soldier Kicked Quran." *Associated Press*, 3 June 2005.

"Bush's Remarks on U.S. Military Strikes in Afghanistan." *New York Times*, 8 Oct. 2001, B6.

"The Cages of Con San Island." *Time*, 20 July 1970.

Campbell, Lt. Col. James D. "French Algeria and British Northern Ireland." *Military Review*, Mar./Apr. 2005, 1.

Campomanes, Oscar V. "Casualty Figures of the American Soldier and the Other." In Angel Velasco Shaw & Luis H. Francia, eds., *Vestiges of War*. New York: New York Univ. Press, 2002.

Cannon, Lou. "One Bad Cop." *New York Times Magazine*, 1 Oct. 2000, 62.

Carrell, Severin. "Army Colonel Facing Trial for War Crimes." *Independent*, 22 May 2005.

Carrell, Severin. "Behind Three Lines in a Secret Army Log Lies Real Story of an Alleged War Crime." *Independent*, 22 May 2005.

Center for Human Rights & Global Justice at NYU School of Law. *Fate and Whereabouts Unknown: Detainees in the "War on Terror"* (2005).

Chan, Sewell, & Jackie Spinner. "Guantánamo Official to Monitor Prison." *Boston Globe*, 30 Apr. 2004.

Cheah, Pheng. *Inhuman Conditions*. Cambridge, Mass.: Harvard Univ. Press, 2006.

Chesney, Robert M. "Leaving Guantánamo." *Univ. of Richmond Law Review* 40 (2006): 657.

Chirot, Daniel. Review of *Torture and Modernity*, by Darius M. Rejali. *Contemporary Sociology* 23 (1994): 680.

"CIA Head IDs Waterboarding Subjects: Hayden Names 3 Suspected al-Qaida Operatives, Defends Practice." *MSNBC.com*, 5 Feb. 2007.

"Civilian Sentenced in Afghan Beating." *Associated Press*, 14 Feb. 2007.

Clark, Kathleen. "Ethical Issues Raised by the OLC Torture Memorandum." *Journal of National Security Law & Policy* 1 (2005): 455.

"Cleared Terror Suspect Seeks Amends." *Oregonian*, 30 Sept. 2006, A6.

Cloud, Morgan. "A Liberal House Divided." *Ohio State Journal of Criminal Law* 3 (2005): 33.

"Coast Police Chief Accused of Racism." *New York Times*, 13 May 1983, A24.

Cobain, Ian. "Revealed: UK Wartime Torture Camp." *Guardian*, 12 Nov. 2005, 1.

Cobain, Ian. "Revealed: Victims of UK's Cold War Torture Camp." *Guardian*, 3 Apr. 2006, 1.

Cobain, Ian. "Torture: MPs Call for Inquiry into MI5 Role." *Guardian*, 15 July 2008, 1.

Cobain, Ian. "The Truth about Torture: Britain's Catalogue of Shame." *Guardian*. 8 July 2009, 7.

Cobb, Kim. "Ex-head of TDCJ Set Up Iraq Jail." *Houston Chronicle*, 16 May 2004, A1.

Cogan, Jacob Katz. "Noncompliance and the International Rule of Law." *Yale Journal of Int'l Law* 31 (2006): 189.

Cohn, Gary, Ginger Thompson, & Mark Matthews. "Torture Was Taught by CIA: Declassified Manual Details the Methods Used in Honduras; Agency Denials Refuted." *Baltimore Sun,* 27 Jan. 1997, 1A.

Committee on International Human Rights of the Association of the Bar of the City of New York & Center for Human Rights and Global Justice at NYU School of Law. *Torture by Proxy: International and Domestic Law Applicable to "Extraordinary Renditions"* (2004).

Conroy, John. *Unspeakable Acts, Ordinary People.* New York: Alfred A. Knopf, 2000.

"Court to Try a Filipino: A Military Commission Will Sit in Judgment on a Bandit at Calambra To-day." *New York Times,* 21 Feb. 1900, 4.

Cover, Robert. "Violence and the Word." *Yale Law Journal* 95 (1986): 1601.

Crawford, Jan, & Ariane de Vogue. "Former AG Accused of Playing Politics with Justice." *ABC News,* 19 June 2008.

Crewdson, John. "CIA Chiefs Reportedly Split over Cleric Plot." *Chicago Tribune,* 8 Jan. 2007, 1.

Crowder, George. "Two Concepts of Liberal Pluralism." *Political Theory* 35 (2007): 121.

Curran, Vivian Grosswald. "Politicizing the Crime against Humanity." *Notre Dame Law Review* 78 (2003): 677.

D'Amato, Anthony. "International Law." In Kermit L. Hall et al., eds., *The Oxford Companion to American Law.* New York: Oxford Univ. Press, 2002.

Damrosch, Lori F., et al. *International Law.* 4th ed. St. Paul: West, 2001.

Danner, Allison Marston. "When Courts Make Law." *Vanderbilt Law Review* 59 (2006): 1.

Dawes, James. *The Language of War.* Cambridge, Mass.: Harvard Univ. Press, 2002.

Dayan, Joan. "Held in the Body of the State." In Austin Sarat & Thomas R. Kearns, eds., *History, Memory, and the Law.* Ann Arbor: Univ. of Michigan Press, 1999.

Dean, Mitchell. "Four Theses on the Powers of Life and Death." *Contretemps* 5 (Dec. 2004): 16.

Dean, Mitchell. "Powers of Life and Death beyond Governmentality." *Cultural Values* 6 (2002): 119.

"Death for Filipino Bandits." *New York Times,* 4 Sept. 1901, 6.

"Death for Luzon Bandits: Guerillas Caught by Col. Smith Will Be Shot or Hanged." *New York Times,* 13 Dec. 1899, 1.

Dembour, Marie-Bénédict. *Who Believes in Human Rights? Reflections on the European Convention.* Cambridge: Cambridge Univ. Press, 2006.

Dennis, Michael J. "Application of Human Rights Treaties Extraterritorially in Times of Armed Conflict and Military Occupation." *American Journal of Int'l Law* 99 (2005): 119.

Dennis, Michael J. "Non-Application of Civil and Political Rights Treaties Extraterritorially during Times of International Armed Conflict." *Israel Law Review* 40 (2007): 453.

Dershowitz, Alan M. "Is There a Torturous Road to Justice?" *Los Angeles Times,* 8 Nov. 2001, pt. 2, 19.

Devji, Faisal. *Landscapes of the Jihad.* Ithaca, N.Y.: Cornell Univ. Press, 2005.

Dinmore, Guy. "CIA Forced Bush Hand on Secret Prisons." *Financial Times,* 21 Sept. 2006, 1.

Dodds, Paisley. "Gitmo Soldier Details Sexual Tactics." *Associated Press,* 28 Jan. 2005.

Dow, Mark. *American Gulag.* Berkeley: Univ. of California Press, 2004.

Doward, Jamie. "UK Link to Torture Jail's Rules." *Observer,* 20 Feb. 2005, 2.

Drumbl, Mark A. *Atrocity, Punishment, and International Law.* New York: Cambridge Univ. Press, 2007.

DuBois, Page. *Torture and Truth*. New York: Routledge, 1991.

Duffy, Helen. *The "War on Terror" and the Framework of International Law*. Cambridge: Cambridge Univ. Press, 2005.

Dvorak, Petula. "A Covert Chapter Opens for Fort Hunt Veterans." *Washington Post*, 20 Aug. 2006, A1.

Dworkin, Ronald. *Is Democracy Possible Here?* Princeton: Princeton Univ. Press, 2006.

Dworkin, Ronald. *Taking Rights Seriously*. Cambridge, Mass.: Harvard Univ. Press, 1977.

Dyer, Clare. "Ministers Seek to Overturn Torture Rule in Deportations." *Guardian*, 3 Oct. 2005, 11.

Dyer, Clare. "UK Treatment of Terror Suspects 'Inhuman.'" *Guardian*, 10 June 2005, 5.

Eddy, Frederick W. "Obstacles to Order in the Philippines: Natives Abandon Open Warfare and Resort to Guerilla Methods." *New York Times*, 7 Oct. 1900.

Elkins, Caroline. *Imperial Reckoning*. New York: Henry Holt, 2005.

Evans, Malcolm D. "Getting to Grips with Torture." *Int'l & Comparative Law Quarterly* 51 (2002): 365.

Farrell, Amy, & Patrice McDermott. "Claiming Afghan Women." In Wendy S. Hesford & Wendy Kozol, eds., *Just Advocacy?* New Brunswick, N.J.: Rutgers Univ. Press, 2005.

Fathi, David C. "The Common Law of Supermax Litigation." *Pace Law Review* 24 (2004): 675.

Feldman, Noah. "Cosmopolitan Law?" *Yale Law Journal* 116 (2007): 1022.

Fellner, Jamie. "Torture in U.S. Prisons." In Kenneth Roth & Minky Worden, eds., *Torture: Does It Make Us Safer? Is It Ever OK?* New York: New Press, 2005.

Fernandes, Leela. "The Boundaries of Terror." In Wendy S. Hesford & Wendy Kozol, eds., *Just Advocacy?* New Brunswick, N.J.: Rutgers Univ. Press, 2005.

"Filipino Bandits' Methods: Gen. MacArthur's Remarks on Their Inhuman Ways—Several to be Hanged." *New York Times*, 14 Jan. 1901, 1.

Fiske, Susan T., Lasana T. Harris, & Amy J. C. Cuddy. "Why Ordinary People Torture Enemy Prisoners." *Science* 306 (26 Nov. 2004): 1482.

Foucault, Michel. *The Birth of Biopolitics*. Trans. Graham Burchell. New York: Palgrave Macmillan, 2008.

Foucault, Michel. *Discipline and Punish*. Trans. Alan Sheridan. New York: Pantheon, 1978.

Foucault, Michel. *Madness and Civilization*. Trans. Richard Howard. New York: Vintage, 1988.

Foucault, Michel. *Psychiatric Power*. Trans. Graham Burchell. New York: Palgrave Macmillan, 2006.

Foucault, Michel. *Security, Territory, Population*. Trans. Graham Burchell. New York: Palgrave Macmillan, 2007.

Foucault, Michel. *"Society Must Be Defended": Lectures at the Collège de France, 1975–1976*. Trans. David Macey. New York: Picador, 2003.

"Francais de Guantánamo: Affaire Renvoyée en 05/07." *Nouvel Observateur*, 27 Sept. 2006.

Fraser, Nancy. *Unruly Practices*. Minneapolis: Univ. of Minnesota Press, 1989.

Freitag, Sandria B. "Crime in the Social Order of Colonial North India." *Modern Asian Studies* 25, no. 2 (1991): 227.

Friedman, Lawrence M. *American Law in the 20th Century*. New Haven, Conn.: Yale Univ. Press, 2002.

Friedman, Lawrence M. *Crime and Punishment in American History*. New York: Basic Books, 1993.

Friedman, Leon. *The Law of War*. 2 vols. New York: Random House, 1972.

Garland, David. *The Culture of Control*. Chicago: Univ. of Chicago Press, 2001.

Gerecht, Reuel Marc. "Against Rendition." *Weekly Standard,* 16 May 2005.

Gillan, Audrey. "British Soldiers Found Guilty of Abuse." *Guardian,* 24 Feb. 2005, 1.

Glaberson, William, & Helene Cooper. "Obama's Plan to Close Prison at Guantánamo May Take a Year." *New York Times,* 13 Jan. 2009, A1.

Golden, Tim. "After Terror, a Secret Rewriting of Military Law." *New York Times,* 24 Oct. 2004, A1.

Golden, Tim. "Tough Justice: Administration Officials Split on Stalled Military Tribunals." *New York Times,* 25 Oct. 2004, A1.

Goldenberg, Suzanne, & James Meek. "Papers Reveal Bagram Abuse." *Guardian,* 18 Feb. 2005, 1.

Goldsmith, Jack. *The Terror Presidency.* New York: W. W. Norton, 2007.

Goldsmith, Jack L., & Eric A. Posner. *The Limits of International Law.* New York: Oxford Univ. Press, 2005.

Graff, Peter. "British Judge Says Headquarters Okayed Iraq Abuse." *Reuters,* 12 Mar. 2007.

Greenberg, Jason S. "Torture of Terrorists in Israel." *ILSA Journal of Int'l & Comparative Law* 7 (2001): 539.

Greenberg, Karen J., ed. *The Torture Debate in America.* New York: Cambridge Univ. Press, 2006.

Greenberg, Karen J., & Joshua L. Dratel, eds. *The Torture Papers.* New York: Cambridge Univ. Press, 2005.

Greenburg, Jan Crawford, Howard L. Rosenberg, & Ariane de Vogue. "Sources: Top Bush Advisors Approved 'Enhanced Interrogation.'" *ABC News,* 9 Apr. 2008.

Greer, Steven. *The European Convention on Human Rights: Achievements, Problems, and Prospects.* Cambridge: Cambridge Univ. Press, 2006.

Grewal, Inderpal. Foreword to Wendy S. Hesford & Wendy Kozol eds., *Just Advocacy?* New Brunswick, N.J.: Rutgers Univ. Press, 2005.

Grewal, Inderpal. *Transnational America.* Durham, N.C.: Duke Univ. Press, 2005.

Gross, Oren. "The Normless and Exceptionless Exception." *Cardozo Law Review* 21 (2000): 1825.

Gross, Oren, & Fionnuala Ní Aoláin. *Law in Times of Crisis.* Cambridge: Cambridge Univ. Press, 2006.

Gupta, Anandswarup. *The Police in British India, 1861–1947.* New Delhi: Concept, 1979.

Gur-Arye, Miriam. "Can the War against Terror Justify the Use of Force in Interrogations?" In Sanford Levinson, ed., *Torture: A Collection.* New York: Oxford Univ. Press, 2004.

Hajjar, Lisa. *Courting Conflict.* Berkeley: Univ. of California Press, 2005.

Hajjar, Lisa. "Sovereign Bodies, Sovereign States, and the Problem of Torture." *Studies in Law, Politics, & Society* 21 (2000): 101.

Halttunen, Karen. "Humanitarianism and the Pornography of Pain in Anglo-American Culture." *American Historical Review* 100 (1995): 303.

Haney, Craig. "Mental Health Issues in Long-Term Solitary and 'Supermax' Confinement." *Crime & Delinquency* 49 (2003): 124.

Harbury, Jennifer K. *Truth, Torture, and the American Way.* Boston, Mass.: Beacon, 2005.

Hardt, Michael, & Antonio Negri. *Empire.* Cambridge, Mass.: Harvard Univ. Press, 2000.

Hardt, Michael, & Antonio Negri. *Multitude.* New York: Penguin, 2004.

Harris, John F. "Bush Gets More International Support for U.S. 'Crusade' against Terrorism." *Washington Post,* 17 Sept. 2001, A1.

Hathaway, Oona. "The Promise and Limits of the International Law of Torture." In Sanford Levinson, ed., *Torture: A Collection.* New York: Oxford Univ. Press, 2004.

Haugard, Lisa. "Declassified Army and CIA Manuals Used in Latin America: An Analysis of Their Content" (18 Feb. 1997). http://www.lawg.org/misc/Publications-manu als.htm.

"Have Talking Cell, Will Travel." *Time,* 25 Feb. 1966.

Hazard, Geoffrey C., et al. *The Law and Ethics of Lawyering.* 3rd ed. New York: Foundation, 1999.

Heins, Volker. "Giorgio Agamben and the Current State of Affairs in Humanitarian Law and Human Rights Policy." *German Law Journal* 6 (2005): 845.

Henckaerts, Jean-Marie. "Study on Customary International Humanitarian Law." *Int'l Review of the Red Cross* 857 (2005): 175.

Henckaerts, Jean-Marie, & Louise Doswald-Becj. *Customary International Humanitarian Law.* Vol. 1. Cambridge: Cambridge Univ. Press, 2005.

Henkin, Louis. *The Age of Rights.* New York: Columbia Univ. Press, 1990.

Hersh, Seymour M. *Chain of Command.* New York: HarperCollins, 2004.

Hess, Pamela. "Cause and Effect—Another Look at *Newsweek.*" *United Press,* 16 May 2005.

Hiatt, Fred. "Why Hawks Should Be Angry." *Washington Post,* 31 May 2004, A23.

Hing, Bill Ong. *Making and Remaking Asian America through Immigration Policy, 1850–1990.* Stanford, Cal.: Stanford Univ. Press, 1993.

Hirsh, Michael, Mark Hosenball, & John Barry. "Aboard Air CIA." *Newsweek,* 28 Feb. 2005.

"The History of International Law at Columbia." http://www.law.columbia.edu/center_program/intl_progs/History (accessed 6 Sept. 2007).

Hollis, Duncan B. "A Comparative Approach to Treaty Law and Practice." In Duncan B. Hollis, Merritt R. Blakeslee, & L. Benjamin Ederington, eds., *National Treaty Law and Practice.* Leiden: Martinus Nijhoff, 2005.

Hollis, Duncan B. "Why State Consent Still Matters." *Berkeley Journal of Int'l Law* 23 (2005): 137.

Holmes, Stephen. *The Anatomy of Antiliberalism.* Cambridge, Mass.: Harvard Univ. Press, 1993.

Holmes, Stephen. *Passions and Constraint.* Chicago: Univ. of Chicago Press, 1995.

Hope, David. "Torture." *Int'l & Comparative Law Quarterly* 53 (2004): 807.

Human Rights Watch. *Double Jeopardy* (Apr. 2008).

Human Rights Watch. *Ghost Prisoner* (Feb. 2007).

Human Rights Watch. *The New Iraq?* (Jan. 2005).

Human Rights Watch. *"No Blood, No Foul"* (July 2006).

Human Rights Watch. *Reports of Torture of Al-Qaeda Suspects* (Dec. 2002).

Human Rights Watch. *The United States' "Disappeared"* (Oct. 2004).

Hunt, Lynn. *Inventing Human Rights.* New York: W. W. Norton, 2007.

Hunt, Terence. "Bush Calls Human Rights Report 'Absurd,'" *Associated Press,* 31 May 2005.

Ignatieff, Michael. *Human Rights as Politics and Idolatry.* Ed. Amy Gutman. Princeton: Princeton Univ. Press, 2001.

Ingelse, Chris. *The UN Committee against Torture.* The Hague: Kluwer, 2001.

"Interrogation." *Washington Post,* 21 Jan. 1968, A1.

Isikoff, Michael. "Secret Memo—Send to Be Tortured." *Newsweek,* 8 Aug. 2005.

Isikoff, Michael, & Mark Hosenball. "Canada Tosses Terror Testimony Obtained through Waterboarding." *Newsweek,* 5 Mar. 2008.

Isikoff, Michael, & Mark Hosenball. "Don't Ask, Don't Tell." *Newsweek,* 8 Dec. 2005.

"Italian Questions Prosecutor's Motives." *Associated Press,* 22 Nov. 2005.

Jaffer, Jameel, & Amrit Singh, eds. *Administration of Torture.* New York: Columbia Univ. Press, 2007.

Jakes, Lara. "Cheney, Others OK'd Harsh Interrogations." *ABC News*, 11 Apr. 2008.

Jakes, Lara. "Pentagon Records Detail Prisoner Abuse by U.S. Military." *Associated Press*, 17 Apr. 2008.

Jehl, Douglas. "C.I.A. Says Berg's Killer Was Very Probably Zarqawi." *New York Times*, 14 May 2004, A12.

Jinks, Derek. "The Declining Significance of POW Status." *Harvard Int'l Law Journal* 45 (2004): 367.

Jinks, Derek. "Protective Parity and the Laws of War." *Notre Dame Law Review* 79 (2004): 1493.

Johnston, David, & Charlie Savage. "Obama Reluctant to Look into Bush Programs." *New York Times*, 12 Jan. 2009, A1.

Kahn, Paul. *The Cultural Study of Law*. Chicago: Univ. of Chicago Press, 1999.

Kahn, Paul. *Sacred Violence*. Ann Arbor: Univ. of Michigan Press, 2008.

Kaiser, David. "A Letter on Rape in Prisons." *New York Review of Books*, 10 May 2007, 22.

Kalhan, Anil, et al. "Colonial Continuities." *Columbia Journal of Asian Law* 20 (2006): 93.

Kanstroom, Daniel. *Deportation Nation*. Cambridge, Mass.: Harvard Univ. Press, 2007.

Kelman, Herbert C. "The Social Context of Torture." In R. D. Crelinsten & A. P. Schmid, eds., *The Politics of Pain*. Boulder: Westview, 1995.

Kennedy, David. *The Dark Sides of Virtue*. Princeton: Princeton Univ. Press, 2004.

Kennedy, David. *Of War and Law*. Princeton: Princeton Univ. Press, 2006.

Kepner, Timothy J. "Torture 101." *Dickinson Journal of Int'l Law* 19 (2001): 475.

Kessler, Glenn, & Josh White. "Rice Seeks to Clarify Policy on Prisoners." *Washington Post*, 8 Dec. 2005, A1.

Kester, John G. "Some Myths of United States Extradition Law." *Georgetown Law Journal* 76 (1988): 1441.

Kochi, Tarik. "Terror in the Name of Human Rights." *Melbourne Journal of Int'l Law* 7 (2006): 127.

Koh, Harold Hongju. "America's Offshore Refugee Camps." *Univ. of Richmond Law Review* 29 (1995): 139.

Koh, Harold Hongju. "Why Do Nations Obey International Law." *Yale Law Journal* 106 (1997): 2599.

Koh, Harold Hongju. "A World without Torture." *Columbia Journal of Transnational Law* 43 (2005): 641.

Kramer, Paul A. *The Blood of Government*. Chapel Hill: Univ. of North Carolina Press, 2006.

Kreimer, Seth F. "Exploring the Dark Matter of Judicial Review." *William & Mary Bill of Rights Journal* 5 (1997): 427.

Kreimer, Seth F. "Too Close to the Rack and the Screw." *Univ. of Pennsylvania Journal of Constitutional Law* 6 (2003): 300.

Kreimer, Seth F. "'Torture Lite,' 'Full Bodied' Torture, and the Insulation of Legal Conscience." *Journal of National Security Law & Policy* 1 (2005): 187.

Kremnitzer, Mordechai. "The Landau Commission Report." *Israel Law Review* 23 (1989): 216.

Kristoff, Nicholas D. "Martyrs, Virgins, and Grapes." *New York Times*, 4 Aug. 2004, A17.

Ku, Julian. "The Third Wave." *Emory Int'l Law Review* 19 (2005): 105.

LaFave, Wayne R., et al. *Criminal Procedure*. 4th ed. St. Paul: West, 2004.

Langbein, John. *Torture and the Law of Proof*. Chicago: Univ. of Chicago Press, 1977.

Laqueur, Thomas W. "Bodies, Details, and the Humanitarian Narrative." In Lynn Hunt, ed., *The New Cultural History*. Berkeley: Univ. of California Press, 1989.

Lasseter, Tom. "U.S. Abuse of Detainees Was Routine at Afghanistan Bases." *McClatchy*

Newspapers, 16 June 2008. http://www.mcclatchydc.com/homepage/story/38775.html.

LeBlanc, Daniel. "Calls Grow for Torture Inquiry." *Globe & Mail,* 8 Sept. 2005.

Lebovics, Herman. "The Uses of America in Locke's Second Treatise of Government." *Journal of the History of Ideas* 47, no. 4 (1986): 567.

Lee, Erika. *At America's Gates.* Chapel Hill: Univ. of North Carolina Press, 2003.

Legomsky, Stephen H. *Immigration and Refugee Law and Policy.* 4th ed. New York: Foundation, 2005.

LeMoyne, James. "Testifying to Torture." *New York Times,* 5 June 1988, sec. 6.

Leo, Richard A. "The Impact of Miranda Revisited." *Journal of Criminal Law & Criminology* 86 (1996): 621.

Leo, Richard A., & Richard J. Ofshe. "The Consequences of False Confessions." *Journal of Criminal Law & Criminology* 88 (1998): 429.

Leonnig, Carol D., & Dana Priest. "Detainees Accuse Female Interrogators." *Washington Post,* 10 Feb. 2005, A1.

Letsas, George. *A Theory of Interpretation of the European Convention on Human Rights.* Oxford: Oxford Univ. Press, 2007.

Levinson, Daryl J. "Rights Essentialism and Remedial Equilibration." *Columbia Law Review* 99 (1999): 857.

Levinson, Sanford. "Constitutional Norms in a State of Permanent Emergency." *Georgia Law Review* 40 (2006): 1.

Levinson, Sanford. "In Quest of a 'Common Conscience.'" *Journal of National Security Law & Policy* 1 (2005): 231.

Levinson, Sanford. "Torture in Iraq and the Rule of Law in America." *Daedalus,* Aug. 2004, 5.

Lewis, George G., & John Mehwa. *History of Prisoner of War Utilization by the United States Army, 1776–1945.* Washington, D.C.: Department of the Army, 1955.

Lewis, Harold S., Jr., & Elizabeth J. Norman. *Civil Rights Law and Practice.* 2nd ed. St. Paul: Thomson-West, 2004.

Lewis, Neil A. "Broad Use of Harsh Tactics Is Described at Cuba Base." *New York Times,* 17 Oct. 2004, A1.

Lewis, Neil A. "F.B.I. Saw Inmates Treated Harshly at Abu Ghraib." *New York Times,* 26 Oct. 2004, A6.

Lewis, Neil A. "Fresh Details Emerge on Harsh Methods at Guantánamo." *New York Times,* 1 Jan. 2005, 11.

Lewis, Neil A. "Red Cross Finds Detainee Abuse in Guantánamo." *New York Times,* 30 Nov. 2004, A6.

Lewis, Neil A. "Red Cross Found Abuses at Abu Ghraib Last Year." *New York Times,* 11 May 2004, A13.

Linn, Brian McAllister. *The Philippine War, 1899–1902.* Lawrence: Univ. Press of Kansas, 2000.

Linn, Brian McAllister. *The U.S. Army and Counterinsurgency in the Philippine War, 1899–1902.* Chapel Hill: Univ. of North Carolina Press, 1989.

Lobel, Jules. "Emergency Power and the Decline of Liberalism." *Yale Law Journal* 98 (1989): 1385.

Luban, David. "Liberalism, Torture, and the Ticking Bomb." *Virginia Law Review* 91 (2005): 1425.

Luce, Don. "The Tiger Cages of Viet Nam." In *Torture, American Style.* Historians against War Pamphlet 3. http://www.historiansagainstwar.org/resources/torture/luce.html.

MacDonogh, Giles. *After the Reich.* New York: Basic Books, 2007.

Mackey, Chris, & Greg Miller. *The Interrogators.* New York: Little, Brown, 2004.

Malanczuk, Peter. *Akehurst's Modern Introduction to International Law.* 7th ed. London: Routledge, 1997.

Mamdani, Mahmood. "Good Muslim, Bad Muslim." *American Anthropologist* 104 (2002): 766.

Mandel, Michael. "Democracy and the New Constitutionalism in Israel." *Israel Law Review* 33 (1999): 259.

Maran, Rita. *Torture: The Role of Ideology in the French-Algerian War.* New York: Praeger, 1989.

Marks, Jonathan H. "Doctors as Pawns?" *Seton Hall Law Review* 37 (2007): 711.

Mashaw, Jerry L. "The Supreme Court's Due Process Calculus for Administrative Adjudication in *Mathews v. Eldridge.*" *Univ. of Chicago Law Review* 44 (1976): 28.

Massing, Michael. "Trial and Error." *New York Times Book Review,* 17 Oct. 2004.

Matheson, Michael J. "The Amendments of the War Crimes Act." *American Journal of Int'l Law* 101 (2007): 48.

Matheson, Michael J. "The United States Position on the Relation of Customary International Law to the 1977 Protocols Additional to the 1949 Geneva Conventions." *American Univ. Journal of Int'l Law & Policy* 2 (1987): 419.

Mayer, Jane. *The Dark Side.* New York: Doubleday, 2008.

Mazzetti, Mark. "Bush Aides Linked to Talks on Interrogations." *New York Times,* 9 Sept. 2008.

Mazzetti, Mark. "Intelligence Chief Says al Qaeda Improves Ability to Strike in U.S." *New York Times,* 6 Feb. 2008, A1.

Mazzetti, Mark, & Scott Shane. "Interrogation Debate Sharply Divided Bush White House." *New York Times,* 4 May 2009, A13.

McCoy, Alfred W. *A Question of Torture.* New York: Henry Holt, Owl Books, 2006.

McGoldrick, Dominic. "Extraterritorial Application of the International Covenant on Civil and Political Rights." In Fons Coomans & Menno T. Kamminga, eds., *Extraterritorial Application of Human Rights Treaties.* Antwerp: Intersentia, 2003.

Meehan, Patricia. *A Strange Enemy People.* London: Peter Owen, 2001.

Mehta, Uday Singh. *Liberalism and Empire.* Chicago: Univ. of Chicago Press, 1999.

Meron, Theodor. "Revival of Customary International Law." *American Journal of Int'l Law* 99 (2005): 817.

"MI5 'Given Secret Prisons Data.'" *BBC News,* 23 Nov. 2005.

Michaelson, Scott, & Scott Cutler Shershow. "The Guantánamo 'Black Hole': The Law of War and the Sovereign Exception" (12 Jan. 2004). http://world.mediamonitors.net/content/view/full/3849.

Miga, Andrew. "War on Terror; 'Stain on Our Honor'; Prez Backs Rumsfeld, Apologizes." *Boston Herald,* 7 May 2004, 4.

Migration Policy Institute. *America's Challenge: Domestic Security, Civil Liberties, and National Unity after September 11* (2003).

Mill, John Stuart. *Considerations on Representative Government.* 1861. New York: Henry Holt, 1873.

Mill, John Stuart. *On Liberty.* 1859. Indianapolis: Bobbs-Merrill, 1956.

Miller, Ruth A. *The Erotics of Corruption.* Albany: State Univ. of New York Press, 2008.

Miller, Ruth A. *The Limits of Bodily Integrity.* Aldershot: Ashgate, 2007.

Miller, Stuart Creighton. *Benevolent Assimilation.* New Haven, Conn.: Yale Univ. Press, 1982.

Millet, Kate. *The Politics of Cruelty.* New York: W. W. Norton, 1994.

Monaghan, Henry P. "Constitutional Common Law." *Harvard Law Review* 89 (1975): 1.

Monaghan, Henry P. "The Protective Power of the Presidency." *Columbia Law Review* 93 (1993): 1.

Moore, Barrington, Jr. *Moral Purity and Persecution in History*. Princeton: Princeton Univ. Press, 2000.

Moore, Michael S. "Torture and the Balance of Evils." *Israel Law Review* 23 (1989): 280.

Morgan, Rod. "The Utilitarian Justification of Torture." *Punishment & Society* 2, no. 2 (2000): 181.

Morrow, James D. "When Do States Follow the Laws of War?" *American Political Science Review* 101 (2007): 559.

Mowbray, A. R. *The Development of Positive Obligations under the European Convention on Human Rights by the European Court of Human Rights*. Oxford: Hart, 2004.

Moyar, Mark. *Phoenix and the Birds of Prey*. Annapolis, Md.: Naval Institute Press, 1997.

"Mr. Hull on the Filipinos: Iowa Congressman Says They Are Not Fit for Self Government—Spooner Bill a Mistake." *New York Times*, 29 Aug. 1901, 2.

Mula, Shosh. "Changed Position." *Yedioth Ahronoth*, "*Shi'vah Yamin*" *Weekend Magazine Supplement*, 4 Apr. 2005. Translated for the Public Committee against Torture.

Murphy, Jeffrie G. "Moral Death." *Ethics* 82, no. 4 (1972): 284.

Myers, Steven Lee, & Neal A. Lewis. "Rumsfeld Offers Assurances about Use of Military Courts." *New York Times*, 16 Nov. 2001, B10.

Myre, Greg, & Mona El-Naggar. "Death Toll Rises in Egyptian Bombings." *New York Times*, 24 July 2005, 1.

Nadelmann, Ethan A. "The Evolution of United States Involvement in the International Rendition of Fugitive Criminals." *New York Univ. Journal of Int'l Law & Policy* 25 (1993): 813.

Nagel, Thomas. "Progressive but Not Liberal." *New York Review of Books*, 25 May 2006, 45.

Navarro, Mireya. "For Guantánamo Refugees, Hope Fades as Time Passes." *New York Times*, 10 Dec. 1994, 1.

Navarro, Mireya. "Guatemalan Army Waged 'Genocide,' New Report Finds." *New York Times*, 26 Feb. 1999, A1.

Navarro, Mireya. "Resources Strained at Guantánamo Bay." *New York Times*, 4 Sept. 1994, 12.

Nelson, Deborah, & Nick Turse. "A Tortured Past." *Los Angeles Times*, 20 Aug. 2006, A1.

Neuman, Gerald L. "Counter-Terrorist Operations and the Rule of Law." *European Journal of Int'l Law* 15 (2004): 1019.

Neuman, Gerald L. "Extraterritorial Rights and Constitutional Methodology after *Rasul v. Bush*." *Univ. of Pennsylvania Law Review* 153 (2005): 2073.

Ní Aoláin, Fionnuala. "The European Convention on Human Rights and Its Prohibition on Torture." In Sanford Levinson, ed., *Torture: A Collection*. New York: Oxford Univ. Press, 2004.

Ní Aoláin, Fionnuala, & Colm Campbell. "The Paradox of Transition in Conflicted Democracies." *Human Rights Quarterly* 27 (2005): 203.

Noronha, Charmaine. "Canada to Revise Manual, Terror At-Risk List." *MiamiHerald .com*, 19 Jan. 2008.

Nussbaum, Martha C. *Frontiers of Justice*. Cambridge, Mass.: Harvard Univ. Press, 2006.

"Obstacles to Order in the Philippines: Natives Abandon Open Warfare and Resort to Guerrilla Methods." *New York Times*, 7 Oct. 1900, 19.

O'Connell, Mary Ellen. "Affirming the Ban on Harsh Interrogation." *Ohio State Law Journal* 66 (2005): 1231.

"Official: Abu Ghraib Like 'Animal House.'" *Rush Limbaugh Show*, 30 Aug. 2004. http://www.rushlimbaugh.com/home/daily/site_083004/content/see_i_told_you_ so.guest.html.

Ofshe, Richard J., & Richard A. Leo. "The Decision to Confess Falsely." *Denver Univ. Law Review* 74 (1997): 979.

Oliver, Wesley McNeil. "The Rise and Fall of Material Witness Detention in Nineteenth Century New York." *NYU Journal of Law & Liberty* 1 (2005): 727.

Olson, Elizabeth. "Israel Denies Groups' Charge that It Is Torturing Detainees." *New York Times,* 21 Nov. 2001, A10.

Ortiz, Dianna. *The Blindfold's Eyes.* Maryknoll, N.Y.: Orbis Books, 2002.

"The Other Prisoners." *Time,* 19 Mar. 1973.

Otterman, Michael. *American Torture.* London: Pluto, 2007.

Ovey, Claire, & Robin White. *Jacobs & White: The European Convention on Human Rights.* 4th ed. Oxford: Oxford Univ. Press, 2006.

Pahuja, Sundhya. "This Is the World: Have Faith." *European Journal of Int'l Law* 15 (2004): 381.

Pakenham, Thomas. *The Boer War.* London: Weidenfeld & Nicolson, 1979.

Pape, Robert A. *Bombing to Win.* Ithaca, N.Y.: Cornell Univ. Press, 1996.

Parry, John T. "Constitutional Interpretation, Coercive Interrogation, and Civil Rights Litigation after *Chavez v. Martinez.*" *Georgia Law Review* 39 (2005): 733.

Parry, John T. "Culpability, Mistake, and Official Interpretations of Law." *American Journal of Criminal Law* 25 (1997): 1.

Parry, John T. "Judicial Restraints on Illegal State Violence." *Vanderbilt Journal of Transnational Law* 35 (2002): 73.

Parry, John T. "The Lost History of International Extradition Litigation." *Virginia Journal of Int'l Law* 43 (2002): 93.

Parry, John T. "The Shape of Modern Torture." *Melbourne Journal of Int'l Law* 6 (2005): 516.

Parry, John T. "Terrorism and the New Criminal Process." *William & Mary Bill of Rights Journal* 15 (2007): 765.

Parry, John T. "Torture Nation, Torture Law." *Georgetown Law Journal* 97 (2009): 1001.

Parry, John T. "Torture Warrants and the Rule of Law." *Albany Law Review* 71 (2008): 885.

Parry, John T. "The Virtue of Necessity." *Houston Law Review* 36 (1999): 397.

Parry, John T., & Welsh S. White. "Interrogating Suspected Terrorists." *Univ. of Pittsburgh Law Review* 63 (2002): 743.

Paulsen, Michael Stokes. "The Constitution of Necessity." *Notre Dame Law Review* 79 (2004): 1257.

Paust, Jordan. "Executive Plans and Authorizations to Violate International Law concerning Treatment and Interrogation of Detainees." *Columbia Journal of Transnational Law* 43 (2005): 811.

Paust, Jordan. "Post-9/11 Overreaction and Fallacies regarding War and Defense, Guantánamo, the Status of Persons, Treatment, Judicial Review of Detention, and Due Process in Military Commissions." *Notre Dame Law Review* 79 (2004): 1335.

Peters, Edward. *Torture.* Expanded ed. Philadelphia: Univ. of Pennsylvania Press, 1996.

Physicians for Human Rights. *Broken Laws, Broken Lives* (June 2008).

Pictet, Jean S., ed. *The Geneva Conventions of 12 August 1949: Commentary.* 4 vols. Geneva: International Committee of the Red Cross, 1952–60.

Pincus, Walter. "Silence of 4 Terror Probe Suspects Poses Dilemma for FBI." *Washington Post,* 21 Oct. 2001, A6.

Pitts, Jennifer. *A Turn to Empire.* Princeton: Princeton Univ. Press, 2005.

Podhoretz, Norman. "World War IV." *Commentary,* Sept. 2004.

Polk, James. "Testimony: Abu Ghraib Photos 'Just for Fun.'" *CNN.com,* 3 Aug. 2004.

Porch, Douglas. *The French Secret Services.* New York: Farrar, Straus & Giroux, 1995.

Porter, Roy. *The Greatest Benefit to Mankind.* New York: W. W. Norton, 1997.

Powell, Bill. "Struggle for the Soul of Islam." *Time,* 13 Sept. 2004.

Priest, Dana. "CIA Holds Terror Suspects in Secret Prisons." *Washington Post,* 2 Nov. 2005, A1.

Priest, Dana. "Covert CIA Program Withstands New Furor." *Washington Post,* 30 Dec. 2005, A1.

Priest, Dana. "Foreign Network at Front of CIA's Terror Fight." *Washington Post,* 18 Nov. 2005, A1.

Priest, Dana. "Italy Knew about Plan to Grab Suspect." *Washington Post,* 30 June 2005, A1.

Priest, Dana. "Help from France Key in Covert Operations." *Washington Post,* 3 July 2005, A1.

Priest, Dana. "U.S. Instructed Latins on Executions, Torture." *Washington Post,* 21 Sept. 1996, A1.

Priest, Dana. "Wrongful Imprisonment: Anatomy of a CIA Mistake." *Washington Post,* 4 Dec. 2005, A1.

Priest, Dana, & Barton Gellman. "U.S. Decries Abuse but Defends Interrogations." *Washington Post,* 26 Dec. 2002, A1.

Public Committee against Torture. *Back to a Routine of Torture* (n.d.).

Public Committee against Torture. *Ticking Bombs* (May 2007).

Public Committee against Torture. *Shackling as a Form of Torture and Abuse* (June 2009).

Quigley, John. "The Rule of Non-Inquiry and Human Rights Treaties." *Catholic Univ. Law Review* 45 (1996): 1213.

Ragavan, Chita. "The Letter of the Law: The White House Says Spying on Terror Suspects without Court Approval Is OK; What about Physical Searches?" *U.S. News & World Report,* 27 Mar. 2006.

Rajan, Rajeswari Sunder. *The Scandal of the State.* Durham, N.C.: Duke Univ. Press, 2003.

Ramsey, Carolyn B. "In the Sweat Box: A Historical Perspective on the Detention of Material Witnesses." *Ohio State Journal of Criminal Law* 6 (2009): 681.

Ranelagh, John. *The Agency.* New York: Simon & Schuster, 1986.

Rao, Anupama. "Problems of Violence, States of Terror." *Interventions* 3, no. 2 (2001): 186.

Rao, Anupama. "Torture, the Public Secret." *Economic & Political Weekly,* 5 June 2004.

Raustiala, Kal. "The Geography of Justice." *Fordham Law Review* 73 (2005): 2501.

Rawls, John. *Political Liberalism.* Expanded ed. New York: Columbia Univ. Press, 2005.

Rawls, John. *A Theory of Justice.* Cambridge, Mass.: Harvard Univ. Press, 1971.

Raymond, Margaret L. "The Right to Refuse and the Obligation to Comply." *Buffalo Law Review* 54 (2007): 1483.

Raz, Joseph. *The Morality of Freedom.* Oxford: Clarendon, 1986.

Redman, Renee C. "Defining 'Torture.'" *NYU Annual Survey of American Law* 62 (2007): 465.

Rejali, Darius. "Modern Torture as Civic Marker." *Journal of Human Rights* 2 (2003): 153.

Rejali, Darius. *Torture and Democracy.* Princeton: Princeton Univ. Press, 2007.

Riley, Patrick. *Will and Political Legitimacy.* Cambridge, Mass.: Harvard Univ. Press, 1982.

Risen, James, David Johnston, & Neil Lewis. "Harsh Methods Cited in Top Qaeda Interrogations." *New York Times,* 13 May 2004, A10.

Ristroph, Alice. "Professors Strangelove." *Green Bag 2d* 11 (2008): 243.

Ristroph, Alice. "Sexual Punishments." *Columbia Journal of Gender & Law* 15 (2006): 139.

Robertson, James E. "Houses of the Dead." *Houston Law Review* 34 (1997): 1003.

Robin, Marie-Monique. "Counterinsurgency and Torture." In Kenneth Roth & Minky Worden eds., *Torture: Does It Make Us Safer? Is It Ever OK?* New York: New Press, 2005.

Rodenbeck, Max. "Islam Confronts Its Demons." *New York Review of Books,* 29 Apr. 2004.

Rodley, Nigel S. "The Definition(s) of Torture in International Law." *Current Legal Problems* 55 (2002): 467.

Rodley, Nigel S. *The Treatment of Prisoners under International Law.* 2nd ed. Oxford: Oxford Univ. Press, 1999.

Roosevelt, Kermit, III. "Guantánamo and the Conflict of Laws." *Univ. of Pennsylvania Law Review* 153 (2005): 2017.

"Roosevelt Speaks to Republican Clubs." *New York Times,* 18 July 1900, 7.

Ross, Brian, & Richard Esposito. "CIA's Harsh Interrogation Techniques Described: Sources Say Agency's Tactics Lead to Questionable Confessions, Sometimes to Death." *ABC News,* 18 Nov. 2005.

Ross, Brian, & Richard Esposito. "Sources Tell ABC News Top al Qaeda Figures Held in Secret CIA Prisons." *ABC News,* 5 Dec. 2005.

Ross, James. "Bush, Torture, and Lincoln's Legacy." *America: The National Catholic Weekly* (15 Aug. 2005).

Rousseau, Jean-Jacques. *On the Social Contract.* 1762. Trans. Judith R. Masters. New York: St. Martin's Press, 1978.

Ruger, Jennifer Prah. "Toward a Theory of a Right to Health." *Yale Journal of Law & the Humanities* 18 (2006): 273.

Rutenberg, Jim. "Torture Seeps into Discussion by News Media." *New York Times,* 5 Nov. 2001, C1.

Sáez, Ñacuñán. "Torture: A Discourse on Practice." In Frances E. Mascia-Lees & Patricia Sharpe, eds., *Tattoo, Torture, Mutilation, and Adornment.* Albany: State Univ. of New York Press, 1992.

Sager, Lawrence Gene. "Fair Measure." *Harvard Law Review* 91 (1978): 1212.

Said, Edward W. *Orientalism.* New York: Pantheon, 1978.

Sallot, Jeff. "For the First Time, Abdullah Almalki Tells His Story." *Globe & Mail,* 27 Aug. 2005, A1.

Sallot, Jeff. "Once a Muhajed Who Took Flying Lessons, Ahmad El Maati Seemed to Fit the Profile of a Terrorist." *Globe & Mail,* 29 Aug. 2005, A1.

Salyer, Lucy E. *Laws Harsh as Tigers.* Chapel Hill: Univ. of North Carolina Press, 1995.

Sanders, Mark. "Extraordinary Violence." *Interventions* 3, no. 2 (2001): 242.

Sandoz, Yves, et al., eds. *Commentary on the Additional Protocols of 8 June 1977 to the Geneva Conventions of 12 August 1949.* Geneva: Martinus Nijhoff, 1987.

Sands, Phillippe. *Torture Team.* New York: Palgrave Macmillan, 2008.

Satterthwaite, Margaret L. "Rendered Meaningless." *George Washington Law Review* 75 (2007): 1333.

Sayre, Joan. Review of *The Breaking of Bodies and Minds,* by Eric Stover & Elena O. Nightingale. *Contemporary Sociology* 16 (1987): 543.

Scarry, Elaine. *The Body in Pain.* New York: Oxford Univ. Press, 1985.

Schabas, William A. "The Crime of Torture and the International Criminal Tribunals." *Case Western Reserve Journal of Int'l Law* 37 (2006): 349.

Scheppele, Kim Lane. "Hypothetical Torture in the 'War on Terrorism.'" *Journal of National Security Law & Policy* 1 (2005): 285.

Scheuer, Michael. "A Fine Rendition." *New York Times,* 11 Mar. 2005, A23.

Schlanger, Margo. "Inmate Litigation." *Harvard Law Review* 116 (2003): 1557.

Schmemann, Serge. "Israel Allows Use of Physical Force in Arab's Interrogation." *New York Times,* 16 Nov. 1996, 8.

Schmid, Alex P. "The Response Problem as a Definition Problem." In Alex P. Schmid & Ronald D. Crelinstein, eds., *Western Responses to Terrorism.* London: F. Cass, 1993.

Schmitt, Carl. *The Concept of the Political.* 1932. Trans. George Schwab. Chicago: Univ. of Chicago Press, 1996.

Schmitt, Carl. *The Crisis of Parliamentary Democracy.* 1926. Trans. Ellen Kennedy. 2nd ed. Cambridge, Mass.: MIT Press, 1988.

Schmitt, Carl. *Legality and Legitimacy.* 1932. Ed. & trans. Jeffrey Seitzer. Durham, N.C.: Duke Univ. Press, 2004.

Schmitt, Carl. *Political Theology.* 2nd ed., 1934. Trans. George Schwab. Chicago: Univ. of Chicago Press, 2005.

Schoultz, Lars. *Beneath the United States.* Cambridge, Mass.: Harvard Univ. Press, 1998.

Schwartz, Stephen S. "Is There a Common Law Necessity Defense in Federal Criminal Law." *Univ. of Chicago L. Rev.* 75 (2008): 1259.

"Secret Report Questions Guantánamo Tactics." *New York Times,* 2 Feb. 2005, A14.

Shane, Scott. "The Costs of Outsourcing Interrogation: A Canadian Muslim's Long Ordeal in Syria." *New York Times,* 29 May 2005, 10.

Shane, Scott, Stephen Grey, & Margot Williams. "C.I.A. Expanding Terror Battle under Guise of Charter Flights." *New York Times,* 31 May 2005, A1.

Shane, Scott, David Johnston, & James Risen. "Secret U.S. Endorsement of Severe Interrogations." *New York Times,* 4 Oct. 2007, A1.

Shanker, Thom. "6 G.I.'s in Iraq Are Charged with Abuse of Prisoners." *New York Times,* 21 Mar. 2004, 9.

Shanker, Thom, & Jacques Steinberg. "Bush Voices 'Disgust' at Abuse of Iraqi Prisoners." *New York Times,* 1 May 2004, A1.

Shapiro, Jeremy, & Bénédicte Suzan. "The French Experience of Counter-Terrorism." *Survival* 45, no. 1 (2003): 67.

Shue, Henry. *Basic Rights: Subsistence, Affluence, and U.S. Foreign Policy.* 2nd ed. Princeton: Princeton Univ. Press, 1996.

Shue, Henry. "Torture." *Philosophy & Public Affairs* 7 (1978): 124.

Shue, Henry. "Torture in Dreamland." *Case Western Reserve Journal of Int'l Law* 37 (2006): 231.

Siemon-Netto, Uwe. "Analysis: Horror over Women Torturers." *United Press,* 6 May 2004.

Sifton, John. "United States Military and Central Intelligence Personnel Abroad." *Harvard Journal on Legislation* 43 (2006): 487.

Sigler, Mary. "By the Light of Virtue." *Iowa Law Review* 91 (2006): 561.

Silverman, Lisa. *Tortured Subjects.* Chicago: Univ. of Chicago Press, 2001.

Simmons, Ric. "Private Criminal Justice." *Wake Forest Law Review* 42 (2007): 911.

Simons, Marlise. "Spanish Court Weighs Inquiry on Torture for 6 Bush-Era Officials." *New York Times,* 29 Mar. 2009, A6.

Simpson, A. W. Brian. *Human Rights and the End of Empire.* Oxford: Oxford Univ. Press, 2001.

Singha, Radhika. *A Despotism of Law.* Delhi: Oxford Univ. Press, 1998.

Sklansky, David A. "The Private Police." *UCLA Law Review* 46 (1999): 1165.

"A Small Something for Hanoi." *Time,* 10 Sept. 1965.

Smith, George P., II. "Human Rights and Bioethics." *Vanderbilt Journal of Transnational Law* 38 (2005): 1295.

Smith, Peter H. *Talons of the Eagle.* 2nd ed. New York: Oxford Univ. Press, 2000.

Sofaer, Abraham D. "No Exceptions." *Wall Street Journal,* 26 Nov. 2005, A11.

"Soldier in Iraq Abuse Photos Has Baby." *Associated Press,* 13 Oct. 2004.

Solis, Gary D. "Military Justice, Civilian Clemency." *Transnational Law & Contemporary Problems* 10 (2000): 59.

Solis, Gary D. *Son Thang: An American War Crime.* Annapolis, Md.: Naval Institute Press, 1997.

Solomon-Godeau, Abigail. "The Legs of the Countess." In Emily S. Apter & William Pietz, eds., *Fetishism as Cultural Discourse.* Ithaca, N.Y.: Cornell Univ. Press, 1993.

Spector, Ronald. Review of *Schoolbooks and Krags,* by John M. Gates. *Military Affairs* 37, no. 4 (Dec. 1973): 159.

Spetalnick, Matt. "Bush Approved CIA Disclosure on Waterboarding." *washingtonpost .com* (6 Feb. 2008).

Stalker, John. "Guarded with the Truth." *Times* (London), 23 Feb. 1997, features section.

Stalker, John. *The Stalker Affair.* New York: Viking, 1988.

Sterngold, James. "Los Angeles Police Officials Admit Widespread Lapses." *New York Times,* 17 Feb. 2000, A16.

Sterngold, James. "Police Corruption Inquiry Expands in Los Angeles." *New York Times,* 11 Feb. 2000, A16.

Stevenson, Richard W. "Bush, on Arab TV, Denounces Abuse of Iraqi Captives." *New York Times,* 6 May 2004, A1.

Stewart, David P. "The Torture Convention and the Reception of International Criminal Law within the United States." *Nova Law Review* 15 (1991): 449.

Stoler, Ann Laura. *Carnal Knowledge and Imperial Power.* Berkeley: Univ. of California Press, 2002.

Storey, Moorfield, & Julian Codman. *Secretary Root's Record.* Boston: Geo. H. Ellis, 1902.

Strassfield, Robert N. "American Innocence." *Case Western Reserve Journal of Int'l Law* 37 (2006): 277.

Strauss, Marcy. "Torture." *New York Law School Law Review* 48 (2003): 201.

Struck, Doug. "Canadian's Lawyers Blame U.S.: Agents Accused of Sending Man to Syria for Torture in '02." *Washington Post,* 1 July 2005, A14.

Struck, Doug. "Fallout from Abduction Continues for Mounties." *Oregonian,* 15 Dec. 2006, A5.

Stumpf, Juliet. "The Crimmigration Crisis." *American Univ. Law Review* 56 (2006): 367.

Sussman, David. "What's Wrong with Torture?" *Philosophy & Public Affairs* 33 (2005): 1.

Svensson-McCarthy, Anna-Lena. *The International Law of Human Rights and States of Exception.* The Hague: Martinus Nijhoff, 1998.

Talbot, Margaret. "The Lost Children." *New Yorker,* 3 Mar. 2008, 58.

Tamanaha, Brian Z. *On the Rule of Law.* Cambridge: Cambridge Univ. Press, 2004.

Taussig, Michael. "Culture of Terror—Space of Death." *Comparative Studies in Society & History* 26, no. 3 (1984): 467.

Taylor, Margaret. "Detained Aliens Challenging Conditions of Confinement and the Porous Border of the Plenary Power Doctrine." *Hastings Constitutional Law Quarterly* 22 (1992): 1087.

"Tell of 'Water Cure' Cases: Witnesses Give Further Testimony before the Senate Committee on the Philippines regarding Filipino's Treatment." *New York Times,* 13 June 1902, 3.

"Testified on 'Water Cure.'" *New York Times,* 22 Apr. 1902, 2.

Thomas, Evan, & Michael Hirsh. "The Debate over Torture." *Newsweek,* 21 Nov. 2005.

"Torture Policy." *Washington Post,* 16 June 2004, A26.

"Torture Victim to Get Millions." *Oregonian,* 27 Jan. 2007, A8.

Travis, Alan. "Clarke Confronts Judges on Terror Law." *Guardian,* 7 Sept. 2005, 2.

Tremlett, Giles. "Spanish Court Opens Investigation of Guantánamo Torture Allegations." *Guardian.co.uk,* 29 Apr. 2009.

Turse, Nick, & Deborah Nelson. "Vietnam Horrors: Darker Yet." *Los Angeles Times,* 6 Aug. 2006, A1.

United against ~~Torture.~~ *Getting Around the International Prohibition of Torture* (Dec. 2006).

Van Bergen, Jennifer, & Douglas Valentine. "The Dangerous World of Indefinite Detentions." *Case Western Reserve Journal of Int'l Law* 37 (2007): 449.

van den Herik, L. J. *The Contribution of the Rwanda Tribunal to the Development of International Law.* Leiden: Martinus Nijhoff, 2005.

Van Natta, Dale, Jr. "Questioning Terror Suspects in a Dark and Surreal World." *New York Times,* 9 Mar. 2003, sec. 1, 14.

Vázquez, Carlos Manuel. "The Four Doctrines of Self-Executing Treaties." *American Journal of Int'l Law* 89 (1995): 695.

Vázquez, Carlos Manuel. "Treaties as Law of the Land." *Harvard Law Review* 122 (2008): 599.

Venator-Santiago, Charles R. "From the Insular Cases to Camp X-Ray." *Studies in Law, Politics, & Society* 39 (2006): 15.

Vercher, Antonio. *Terrorism in Europe.* Oxford: Clarendon, 1992.

Verkaik, Robert. "UK in the Dock on Human Rights after Judges Accuse Ministers of Ducking Responsibilities." *Independent,* 3 Oct. 2005, 6.

Volpp, Leti. "The Citizen and the Terrorist." *UCLA Law Review* 49 (2002): 1575.

Waldron, Jeremy. *Liberal Rights.* Cambridge: Cambridge Univ. Press, 1993.

Waldron, Jeremy. "Torture and Positive Law." *Columbia Law Review* 105 (2005): 1681.

Wallach, Evan. "Drop by Drop." *Columbia Journal of Transnational Law* 45 (2007): 468.

Walzer, Michael. *Spheres of Justice.* New York: Basic Books, 1983.

"A War for Civilization." *Washington Post,* 15 Mar. 1906, 6.

Warbrick, Colin. "The European Response to Terrorism in an Age of Human Rights." *European Journal of Int'l Law* 15 (2004): 989.

Warrick, Joby. "Report Questions Pentagon Accounts." *Washington Post,* 17 June 2008, A1.

Wasserstrom, Silas J. "The Court's Turn Toward a General Reasonableness Interpretation of the Fourth Amendment." *American Criminal Law Review* 27 (1989): 119.

"The Water Cure Described: Discharged Soldier Tells Senate Committee How and Why the Torture Was Inflicted." *New York Times,* 4 May 1902, 13.

Weiner, Allen S. "*Hamdan,* Terror, War." *Lewis & Clark Law Review* 11 (2007): 997.

Weiner, Tim. "C.I.A. Taught, Then Dropped, Mental Torture in Latin America." *New York Times,* 29 Jan. 1997, A11.

Weisburd, A. Mark. "Al-Qaeda and the Laws of War." *Lewis & Clark Law Review* 11 (2007): 1063.

Weisburd, A. Mark. "Customary International Law and Torture." *Chicago Journal of Int'l Law* 2 (2001): 81.

Weissman, Deborah M. "The Human Rights Dilemma." *Columbia Human Rights Law Review* 35 (2004): 259.

White, Josh. "Army Documents Shed Light on CIA 'Ghosting.'" *Washington Post,* 24 Mar. 2005, A15.

White, Josh. "Military Lawyers Fought Policy on Interrogations," *Washington Post,* 15 July 2005, A1.

White, Josh. "Soldiers' 'Wish Lists' of Detainee Tactics Cited." *Washington Post,* 19 Apr. 2005, A16.

White, Josh, & John Mintz. "Red Cross Cites 'Inhumane' Treatment at Guantánamo." *Washington Post,* 1 Dec. 2004, A10.

White, Martin N. "Charging War Crimes: A Primer for the Practitioner." *Army Lawyer,* Feb. 2006, 1.

White, Welsh S. *Miranda's Waning Protections.* Ann Arbor: Univ. of Michigan Press, 2001.

Whitlock, Craig. "Europeans Investigate CIA Role in Abductions: Suspects Possibly Taken to Nations that Torture." *Washington Post,* 13 Mar. 2005, A1.

Whitlock, Craig. "French Push Limits in Fight on Terrorism: Wide Prosecutorial Powers Draw Scant Public Dissent." *Washington Post,* 2 Nov. 2004, A1.

Whitlock, Craig. "Jordan's Spy Agency: Holding Cell for the CIA." *Washington Post,* 1 Dec. 2007, A1.

Whitlock, Craig. "New Swedish Documents Illuminate CIA Action." *Washington Post,* 21 May 2005, A1.

Wildhaber, Luzius. "A Constitutional Future for the European Court of Human Rights?" *Human Rights Law Journal* 23 (2002): 161.

Wildhaber, Luzius. "The Role of the European Court of Human Rights: An Evaluation." *Mediterranean Journal of Human Rights* 8 (2004): 9.

Williams, Patricia. *The Alchemy of Race and Rights.* Cambridge, Mass.: Harvard Univ. Press, 1991.

Winkler, Carol K. *In the Name of Terrorism.* Albany: State Univ. of New York Press, 2006.

Winter Soldier Investigation (31 Jan. & 1–2 Feb. 1971). http://www2.iath.virginia.edu/six ties/HTML_docs/Resources/Primary/Winter_Soldier/WS_entry.html.

Wintour, Patrick. "After Eight Years in Power Tony Blair Hears a New Word: Defeat." *Guardian,* 10 Nov. 2005, 1.

Wolfowitz, Paul. "The First Draft of Freedom." *New York Times,* 16 Sept. 2004, A27.

Wolin, Sheldon S. *The Presence of the Past.* Baltimore, Md.: Johns Hopkins Univ. Press, 1989.

Woodworth, Paddy. *Dirty War, Clean Hands.* New Haven, Conn.: Yale Univ. Press, 2002.

Woolls, Daniel. "Spanish Lawmakers Vote to Limit Cross-Border Justice Law Used to Indict Pinochet, bin Laden." *Associated Press,* 25 June 2009.

Wynn, Jennifer R., & Alisa Szatrowski. "Hidden Prisons." *Pace Law Review* 24 (2004): 497.

Zagorin, Adam. "Source: British Territory Used for U.S. Terror Interrogation." *Time,* 31 July 2008.

Zeydanlıoğlu, Welat. "Torture and Turkification in the Diyarbakır Military Prison." In John T. Parry & Welat Zeydanlıoğlu, eds., *Rights, Citizenship, and Torture: Perspectives on Evil, Law, and the State.* Oxford: Inter-Disciplinary Press, 2009.

Zimbardo, Philip. *The Lucifer Effect.* New York: Random House, 2007.

Žižek, Slavoj. *Welcome to the Desert of the Real.* London: Verso, 2002.

Zulaika, Joseba, & William A. Douglass. *Terror and Taboo.* New York: Routledge, 1996.

Index

Prison Rape Elimination Act of 2003,
    U.S., 156–57
prison violence in United States, 153–59
Prisoners Convention (Third Geneva
    Convention), 21, 22, 141, 250n36
private and public spheres, 79–80, 239n7
psychiatric practice and torture, 209–11,
    213, 273n24
psychopaths, rights of, 86–88, 89–90, 95
public and private spheres, 79–80, 239n7
*Public Committee against Torture in Israel
    v. State of Israel* (Israeli Supreme
    Court), 123–24, 125
public safety exception to Miranda rights,
    68

racism. *See* colonialism and racism
Rampart scandal, Los Angeles, 153
Rao, Anupama, 105, 106
Rasul v. Bush (U.S.), 196
Rawls, John, 86, 88, 94, 240n32
Raz, Joseph, 85, 95
Reagan administration, 55, 57, 58, 148
reasonableness in U.S. law
    behavior of rights-bearers, 63–65
    Fourth Amendment test case, 75–77
    practical limitations on rights, 66–70
    rights, reasonableness doctrine applied
        to, 62–63
Red Cross, 24, 138, 178, 187
Rejali, Darius, 1, 98, 100, 114, 175, 193, 207,
    254n64
religious beliefs, Islamist. *See* Islam
religious desecration as coercive tactic in
    war on terror, 8, 12, 175, 210
remedies for rights violations in United
    States, 70–71
rendition/deportation/extradition, 126–33
    black sites, use of, 1, 63, 65, 175–76,
        178–79, 181, 182, 198
    by Canada, 127, 129–32
    colonialist and racist aspects of, 132–33
    customary international law and, 17
    diplomatic assurances, 180
    European Convention of Human
        Rights on, 48–49, 50
    extraordinary rendition, defined,
        126–27, 179
    by France, 104
    Human Rights Committee on, 34

ICCPR and, 131, 180–81
    by Italy, 127–28
    by Sweden, 127, 128–29
    timelessness and placelessness pro-
        duced by, 53
    U.N. Convention on, 17, 131, 163, 179,
        180–81
    by United Kingdom, 115
    U.S. use of, 126–30, 132
        immigration law, 56, 160–61, 163
        in war on terror, 175, 177–82
reservations, understandings, or declara-
    tions (RUDs), 20, 55–59, 105
Rice, Condoleeza, 198
rights, torture in context of, 78–96
    archetypes, rights as, 80–83
    biopolitics, 88–91, 95
    concept of rights, 78–80
    European law (*see under* European law
        on torture)
    ICCPR (*see* International Covenant on
        Civil and Political Rights)
    international law, 18–19, 91–93
    legal definitions of torture, 3
    liberal government, consistency of use
        of torture with, 13–14
    liberal rights and state power, 82, 83,
        84–91, 93–96
    modern democracies' use of torture,
        contribution of rights ideology to,
        93–96
    moral reasoning and, 86–87, 89–90, 95
    positive rights, 88–90
    state authority, derivation of rights
        from, 79–80
    U.N. Convention (*see* U.N. Convention
        against Torture and Other Cruel,
        Inhuman, or Degrading Treat-
        ment or Punishment)
    in United States
        behavior of rights-bearers, 63–65
        extraterritoriality, 65–66
        narrow versus liberal reading of,
            62–63, 66
        positive rights, 89
        practical limitations on protected
            rights, 66–70
        reasonableness and rights, 62–63
        remedies/damages for rights viola-
            tions, 70–71